——————————— ANDEAN COSMOPOLITANS ———————————

ANDEAN COSMOPOLITANS

*Seeking Justice and Reward
at the Spanish Royal Court*

JOSÉ CARLOS DE LA PUENTE LUNA

UNIVERSITY OF TEXAS PRESS
Austin

Requests for permission to reproduce material from this work should be sent to:
Permissions
University of Texas Press
P.O. Box 7819
Austin, TX 78713-7819
utpress.utexas.edu/rp-form
♾ The paper used in this book meets the minimum requirements of ANSI/NISO
Z39.48-1992 (R1997) (Permanence of Paper).

Library of Congress Cataloging-in-Publication Data

Names: Puente Luna, José Carlos de la, author.
Title: Andean cosmopolitans : seeking justice and reward at the Spanish royal court /
    José Carlos de la Puente Luna.
Description: First edition. | Austin : University of Texas Press, 2018. | Includes
    bibliographical references and index.
Identifiers: LCCN 2017009444 | ISBN 978-1-4773-1443-2 (cloth : alk. paper) |
    ISBN 978-1-4773-1486-9 (pbk. : alk. paper) | ISBN 978-1-4773-1487-6
    (library e-book) | ISBN 978-1-4773-1488-3 (non-library e-book)
Subjects: LCSH: Indians of South America—Peru—Government relations—16th
    century. | Indians of South America—Peru—Government relations—17th century. |
    Indians of South America—Peru—Ethnic identity. | Peru—History—1548-1820. |
    Peru (Viceroyalty) | Habsburg, House of.
Classification: LCC F3444 .P795 2017 | DDC 985/.02—dc23
LC record available at https://lccn.loc.gov/2017009444

doi:10.7560/314432

To Lynda and Matías

CONTENTS

ILLUSTRATIONS

ACKNOWLEDGMENTS

As I am about to finish this book, I can think of few academic pursuits that would prove more challenging than writing a scholarly monograph in a language other than one's own. For this reason, I first wish to thank the many who, during the ten years that it took to create this volume, helped me grapple with my English prose and finally make peace with it: in a now distant Lima, Elizabeth Silva and Marcos Cueto; at Texas Christian University, Susan E. Ramirez, Peter Szok, Robert Little, and the late Mark Gilderhus; at Texas State University, my colleagues Paul Hart, John Mckiernan-González, Margaret Menninger, Anadelia Romo, and especially Jesús F. de la Teja, as well as the participants in the Swinney Faculty Writing Group organized by Shannon Duffy. I also wish to thank Marsha Ostroff for her valuable editorial work and help in translating difficult passages as I finished the first draft of the manuscript, as well as Jon Howard for his superb editorial work, careful advice, and patience throughout. At the University of Texas Press, my gratitude goes to Kerry E. Webb, Angelica Lopez-Torres, Amanda Frost, and their extraordinarily supportive editorial team.

Several institutions provided funds and support to make research and writing possible. A full-year faculty grant from the National Endowment for the Humanities afforded me the time to complete the first full draft. Other fellowships, grants, and invitations from Harvard's International Seminar on the History of the Atlantic World, the Escuela de Estudios Hispano-Americanos, the Universidad Pablo de Olavide, the Royal Danish Library, the Newberry Library, Duke University, Northern Arizona University, Texas Christian University, and the Pontificia Universidad Católica del Perú (still my alma mater) allowed me to visit different libraries and archives, discuss my ideas, learn from others, and find the peace of mind to write this book. The ongoing generosity of Texas State University and my history colleagues has materialized in more ways than I can name here, but I do wish to gratefully acknowledge the support of the Office of the Provost and Vice President for

Academic Affairs, the College of Liberal Arts, the History Department, and the Center for the Study of the Southwest.

Many people turned travel, research, and writing into a very pleasant experience. I wish to express my special gratitude to Carmen Rosa Guzmán, Alonso Espinoza, Nancy Huamán, Donato Amado, and Amelia Almorza for their invaluable research assistance in Cuzco, Lima, and Seville. In Huancayo and at the Archivo Regional de Junín, I owe a debt of gratitude to Víctor Solier, Manuel Perales, and Mariela Contreras Ruiz. I am thankful to Ana Luisa Izquierdo for her help at the Archivo General de la Nación in Mexico, to Marta Chanduví at the Archivo Regional de La Libertad, to Laura Gutiérrez at the Archivo Arzobispal de Lima, and to Yolanda Auqui and Celia Soto at the Archivo General de la Nación, also in Lima.

I presented earlier versions of this book in different academic venues, where I benefited greatly from the comments and criticisms of many colleagues and friends: Rolena Adorno, Norah Andrews, Ivan Boserup, Galen Brokaw, Kathryn Burns, Vera Candiani, Paul Charney, Ananda Cohen-Aponte, Caroline Cunill, Marco Curatola Petrocchi, Alcira Dueñas, Alan Durston, Marcela Echeverri, Martha Few, Luis Miguel Glave, Pablo Gómez, Alex Hidalgo, Renzo Honores, Christine Hünefeldt, Susan Kellogg, Víctor Maqque, Laura Matthews, Kelly McDonough, Jeremy Mumford, Rachel O'Toole, Liliana Pérez, Caterina Pizzigoni, Gabriela Ramos, Joanne Rappaport, Karen Spalding, Sara Vicuña Guengerich, Juliet Wiersema, and Yanna Yannakakis. Earlier versions of chapters 2 and 5 appeared, respectively, in *The Americas* (72, no. 1 [2015]: 19–54) and *Allpanchis* (39, no. 72 [2012]: 11–60). Jorge Cañizares-Esguerra, John D. Charles, Karen Graubart, Paul Hart, Jane Mangan, Susan E. Ramirez, and Frank Salomon read previous drafts of this work. To them and all the others, my heartfelt gratitude at the end of this journey.

—José Carlos de la Puente Luna
  Austin, Texas
  April 2017

──────────── ANDEAN COSMOPOLITANS ────────────

ONE

DON MELCHOR IS DEAD

On May 23, 1610, the indigenous inhabitants of Cuzco rejoiced in the beatification of Ignatius of Loyola, founder of the Jesuit order. To represent their *República* or Republic, the participants carried eleven gentlemen of royal Inca descent in litters through the former imperial capital up to the imposing Jesuit church of La Compañía in the main square, known in Inca times as Aucaypata—the great plaza. Led by the captain Don Alonso Topa Atauchi and dressed in full Incaic regalia, each nobleman embodied one of eleven former emperors and royal houses that these emperors were said to have established for the luster and pride of their descendants. The anonymous chronicler, perhaps a Jesuit, identified Don Alonso as "the uncle of Melchor Inca, now at the royal court." Thus he revealed the relevance and immediacy that events transpiring in distant kingdoms of the Spanish monarchy had for a local *cuzqueño* audience keen to determine what kind of genealogical legitimacy permitted Topa Atauchi to claim, on behalf of Don Melchor, the leading position among the parading Inca royals. As the narrator and his immediate audience knew well, Don Melchor Carlos Inca, Don Alonso's nephew, was the one who should have been anointed captain. The great-grandson of Huayna Capac, the last undisputed Inca emperor (and, according to many in Peru and Spain, his only remaining descendant through the direct male line), Don Melchor outranked his uncle Don Alonso and the ten others, at least according to Spanish notions of primogeniture and legitimate descent. But he was unable to attend. He was in Spain, having left eight years earlier partly because of the political risks that, to some, the continued presence of this Inca prince in Peru presented. The viceroy had persuaded him to seek favor and recompense at the king's court in person. Don Melchor had remained there since.[1]

Five years after the celebrations, the indigenous chronicler Felipe Guaman Poma de Ayala departed his native Huamanga, another heavily indigenous region in the southern highlands of Peru, immediately north of Cuzco.

Claiming to be too old and tired to make the journey to the king's court, he settled for a shorter trip down to coastal Lima to place his illustrated treatise, *El primer nueva corónica y buen gobierno,* in the hands of Viceroy Juan de Mendoza y Luna, the Marquis of Montesclaros. As he trekked across the central Andes and approached Huancavelica, home of the famous mercury mines, Guaman Poma met three grieving indigenous women. During the previous weeks, an overzealous priest and anti-idolatry investigator had disrupted ordinary life in their village of Atunjauja, one of several along the main road linking Cuzco and Huamanga with Huancavelica and Lima. While pretending to be discovering the shrines and burial sites still worshiped by the Indians, the ecclesiastic inspector kept demanding goods and services from local parishioners, causing the three women to flee southward into the mining region. The women complained to Guaman Poma. They said they were living in troubled times, with nobody to defend them or weep alongside them, "not even our *Inga* who is the king, and Don Melchor is dead." In October 1610, only four months after the celebrations honoring Ignatius, Don Melchor Carlos Inca died unexpectedly in a monastery near Madrid. Through channels unknown to us, news of his death among his private retinue traveled some six thousand miles from the Spanish city of Alcalá de Henares, where Melchor died, to the south-central Andes where the paths of Guaman Poma and the women of Atunjauja were to cross in 1615.[2] In fact, the memories of Don Melchor did not fade. Forty years later, invocations to this "last Inca king" resurfaced in the chants and spells of certain women accused of witchcraft in Lima.[3]

What specific colonial actors, networks, and interactions carried this type of information across the Atlantic Ocean by way of the Pacific seaboard, into the coastal cities, and deep into the Andes? How did Guaman Poma and his fellow Andean travelers learn about Don Melchor's affairs at court and his subsequent demise in Alcalá? How did they envision that place, the distant Iberian lands, and the royal court, where the Inca prince had sought the king's favor? More important, why did the news matter to them, the Inca royals of Cuzco, and many other Andean subjects of the time? One may be tempted to discard the entire story of this fortuitous encounter as another of Guaman Poma's complex rhetorical devices: through the voice of three anonymous Andean women, the indigenous writer was engaging in political commentary. He sought to emphasize that the desperate situation of the natives would find relief only if they were to be ruled by a just and merciful king, a title that Don Melchor Carlos Inca could have inherited. Even in that scenario, however, elucidating the peoples, channels, and mechanisms through which a man like

FIGURE 1.1
The Indies of Peru and the kingdom of Castile. From Felipe Guaman Poma de Ayala, El primer nueva corónica y buen gobierno, *42[42]. Royal Danish Library, GKS 2232 quarto.*

Guaman Poma, who had never left Peru, learned the news of Melchor's death is a pressing historical task. And Guaman Poma's keen interest in "the things of Spain" was by no means unique.[4] To the contrary, attention to the world beyond the kingdoms of the Indies, as well as awareness that the lands and people contained therein, along with Castile and other royal possessions, belonged to a larger entity and were subject to a powerful ruler, destined to preside over a universal monarchy, were characteristic of other men and women of his class (Figure 1.1).[5]

Far from Peru in Mexico and only a few days after the festivities honoring Ignatius, Don Domingo de San Antón Muñón Chimalpahin, an indigenous historian and a cosmopolitan like Guaman Poma, registered the same beatification in an entry of his *Annals*. After moving to Mexico City in 1593, and over a period of two decades, Chimalpahin, a literate Nahua originally from

FIGURE 1.2

Don Melchor Carlos Inca, Prince, Auqui Ynga. *From* Felipe Guaman Poma de Ayala, El primer nueva corónica y buen gobierno, *739[753]. Royal Danish Library, GKS 2232 quarto.*

the Chalco-Amecameca region, meticulously recorded important events in New Spain and the metropole, including the death in Valladolid of Don Diego Luis de Moctezuma, grandson of the last Mexica emperor and Melchor's Mexica counterpart. A comparable interest in the transatlantic affairs of indigenous peoples of illustrious descent inspired Guaman Poma to list a number of royal Inca scions and lineages that, thanks to a series of successful legal campaigns dating back to the 1540s, were now enjoying honors, pensions, and other royal favors in such disparate parts of the empire as Cuzco, Lima, Quito, and Madrid. Guaman Poma even drew a fine portrait of Don Melchor Carlos Inca, depicting him in Spanish clothes and seemingly at the royal court. In the accompanying description, he informed his local audience that "it is with such princes that our lord the king and emperor speaks" (Figure 1.2).[6] Guaman Poma was right: the king did "speak" with Melchor, who was granted a knighthood and the post of *gentilhombre de boca* at the king's table, thereby joining the ranks of Philip III's honored courtiers.[7]

Melchor's voyage and dozens of similar overseas ventures inspired this book. It centers on the journeys of indigenous subjects from the jurisdiction of the *Real Audiencia de Lima* (the Royal High Court of Appeals)—in one of the most important and largest cities within the viceroyalty of Peru—to the royal court of the Spanish Habsburgs and back to the Andes. It covers the period from the first expeditions of conquest into the Inca realm in the 1530s to the Habsburg Dynasty's twilight in the late 1690s. With some minor variations, the district of the *Audiencia de Lima*, the area under study in this work, included some fifty *corregimientos* (judicial and administrative subdivisions) at this time. These subdivisions fell under the jurisdiction of various Spanish-founded cities such as Trujillo, Lima, Huamanga, Arequipa, and the former imperial center of Cuzco (founded again in 1534 for the Spanish king). To the north, the *Audiencia de Lima* shared borders with the *audiencias* of Quito and Santa Fe; to the southeast lay the *audiencia* of La Plata or Charcas, and to the west the Pacific Ocean. To the east lay the unexplored provinces of the Peruvian Amazon. Most indigenous travelers to Spain came from Spanish cities and ports along the Pacific coast and from the Indian villages of the central and south-central highlands to the east of Lima, seat of the royal high court.[8]

The intertwined stories of Don Melchor Carlos, Felipe Guaman Poma, Chimalpahin, and the three indigenous women from Jauja are but pieces of this much wider and intricate dynamic. Despite their fragmentary nature, these records offer a window into some of the defining experiences of native Andeans living under Spanish rule. An unprecedented movement of peoples, goods, and ideas across the Atlantic marked the beginnings of the modern era. Overseas voyagers, in particular, *wove* the webs of early modern European empires.[9] Andeans, notably indigenous travelers to the Habsburg court, belonged to this world in flux. After conquest, enslaved Indians and noble sojourners at the royal court, as well as indigenous petitions, *pleitos* (court cases), *escudos* (coats of arms), *probanzas* (proofs of merit and services), and the ideas contained in them, started to circulate by means of intricate webs of exchange, patronage, and obligation, as well as within communities of law, interest, and knowledge. We are only starting to uncover their specific relationship to Amerindian peoples, both free and enslaved.[10] Andean transatlantic litigants, private letters, proofs of merit, powers of attorney, and other legal instruments—along with oral accounts and testimonies of all sorts—helped spread news and rumors such as that of Don Melchor Carlos Inca's sojourn and death in Iberia, as well as similar stories of legal success or failure for other pilgrims of native and Spanish-indigenous descent in Habsburg Spain. This movement of people and information made their affairs at the royal court and the repeated encounters with the king known in colonial Peru, charging their journeys with social and political significance.

The rhetorical formulas of letters and petitions make it impossible to state with certainty whether some of these travelers made at least a brief acquaintance with the monarch.[11] Even so, the image of the "royal encounter" between king and indigenous subject, in part rooted in the accumulated experience of these Andean Atlantic journeys, provided Indians who voyaged and those who didn't with a model and a language to reenact the rights and obligations of monarchs and vassals. These interdependencies could serve, in turn, as inspiration for action. As María Elena Díaz has argued, the image of the king was an "ideological vessel" with multiple, even contradictory meanings. This image rested on a symbolic figure "onto which all manner of benevolent and protective policies could be projected."[12] In a poignant criticism of the limits of the Atlantic paradigm, Paul Cohen has noted "the all too modest place Amerindians currently occupy within Atlantic history."[13] This book seeks to correct this omission. It is the native peoples' engagement with this larger setting, and their simultaneous participation in local and global affairs, that reveals them as modern imperial subjects, allowing for a reinscription of their histories in the larger narratives about the formation of the Atlantic world.[14] Cohen and other scholars have urged us to reconstruct the histories of the Amerindians who traversed the Atlantic in order to recover "their social experiences [and] highlight the roles they played within European strategies to exploit the Americas."[15] My own inscription recovers indigenous travelers' social experiences and their participation in the making of the Spanish Atlantic, while inserting Andean history into a wider transatlantic narrative and exploring the voyagers' role in the construction and continuation of the Andean colonial world.

After the Spanish victories over the Inca claimed Tawantinsuyu for Charles V in the 1530s, native Andeans began to undertake a series of perilous trips from Peru to the Habsburg royal court in Spain in a search for privilege, justice, and reward. In the spring of 1561, Madrid became the permanent residence of King Philip II and the fixed seat of his court and government.[16] Philip's *casa y corte* (household and court) centered on the *alcázar*—the royal palace and its adjacent buildings. Comprising more than two thousand individuals, the bustling court incorporated members of the king's extended family and household, as well as the governing councils of the monarchy. The secretarial offices and audience-chambers of these royal councils, including those of the *Real y Supremo Consejo de Indias* (the Royal and Supreme Council of the Indies), founded around 1520 to oversee the king's American possessions, occupied the ground floor of the royal residence. The *Consejo*, which dealt with matters of *justicia* (justice), *gracia* (privilege, grace), and *gobernación* (governance), was the supreme tribunal for American affairs in the Spanish Empire. It held administrative and judicial authority over royal subjects in the American kingdoms, also playing a key role in the allocation of royal favor. Its rooms, located in the northeast corner of the *alcázar*, had a separate entrance that led through the patio to the suites of the monarch himself. (Philip II was said to supervise the weekly affairs of his councilors from a hidden vantage point.) Within an expanding political formation under a Catholic monarch with universal aspirations, countless visitors, litigants, and favor-seekers crossed the gates, circled around the courtyards, and walked in and out of the hallways of the palace, waiting to be called. They appeared before the royal ministers to share their stories of sacrifice and bravery, failure and success. For these subjects, and for the many Andean natives and *mestizos* (people of Spanish and indigenous ancestry) who joined their ranks, the royal court, distant but still within reach, became the focus of their aspirations and sometimes the graveyard of their hopes.[17]

Andean visitors petitioned for what they thought they deserved based on prevailing notions of kingship, subjecthood, and justice, negotiating a place within the interlocking legal and political communities that the monarchy comprised. It was the "unequal but reciprocal and mutually understood" relationship between colonial indigenous subjects and the king that allowed the former to seek the justice of the latter.[18] Just rule required that the monarch recognized the pleas, introduced any legal correctives, and rewarded the services of these loyal vassals and their descendants. Royal justice, they wanted to believe, was to be given to each supplicant according to his or her merit and quality. In that sense, and on a symbolic plane, petitioning for grace or requesting a reward did not essentially differ from winning a court case or obtaining administrative redress; both were part of the duties of a just and merciful king.[19]

Impossible to capture in a single vignette, the transatlantic experiences, motives, and aspirations of Andean visitors were shared by other travelers and reflected the complexity of colonial societies born after the conquest of the Inca Empire. While in Spain, prominent travelers like Don Melchor and his distant relatives requested *encomiendas* (royal grants conferring one the right to demand tribute and forced labor from native peoples), coats of arms, patents of nobility, knighthoods, and official recognition of their elite, nontributary status. But these aristocratic travelers were not the majority.

Humbler visitors of plebeian and tributary status, often overlooked in previous treatments of transatlantic travel and emigration, also "spoke" with the king and petitioned for what they thought was their due, not as hypothetical members of an undistinguishable class of "Indians" but as individual subjects with their own merits, status, and circumstances.[20] They sometimes demanded that the highest representatives of the Crown in America—the viceroy and the ministers of the *audiencia*—be forced to deliver justice and relief to one or more aggrieved parties. Some petitioned for release from tribute, forced labor, and other duties. Others beseeched the king for privileges for themselves, relatives, and social equals, their local peasant communities, or other indigenous corporations with urban roots. A few denounced the excesses of private citizens, religious orders, Crown agents, and Indian subjects. Still others, taken to Spain against their will, begged the *Consejo* for a few coins to survive at the expensive court or perhaps an official license to return to Peru. Ranging from almost total coercion to relatively free will, from a native commoner entrusted with delivering birds of prey for courtly entertainment to the Inca prince who spent the rest of his days amid titles, pensions, and other royal favors, no journey or traveler was fully exceptional or paradigmatic. Andean sojourns at court unraveled somewhere between individual concerns and collective aspirations.

Carefully pieced together, these fragmentary lives and stories constitute the bulk of this study. *Andean Cosmopolitans* weaves the journeys of indigenous peoples into the larger movements of fellow travelers who made Peru, the Spanish domains, and the Habsburg court their destination. The narrative unfolds simultaneously in distant but related settings of the early modern Spanish Empire. The focus is less on fixed ethnic and legal identifications, or places and regions, and more on situational identities, exchanges, interconnections, and the interplay between local histories and global forces.

In her landmark study of Spanish emigration from Extremadura to Peru, Ida Altman advocated writing a history that could bring the histories of Spanish America and early modern Spain into direct contact, arguing that sixteenth-century Spanish and Spanish American societies were variants within an expanding early modern world. Careful consideration of the ties between individuals in these two societies, she posited, would reveal that they were more closely intertwined and interdependent than previously thought. Spain and America also met in Europe, or as she eloquently put it, "Trujillo [of Extremadura] was as closely tied to Peru as it was to Seville or the court."[21] This book takes up Altman's view from the opposite shore. The different trajectories of Andean travelers recaptured in these pages reveal that "Spain" and "Peru" functioned as parts of a larger unit in various previously unchartered ways. Altman's "variants" require a Spanish norm, something that did not necessarily exist. *Andean Cosmopolitans* recovers indigenous travelers' experiences, simultaneously highlighting their profound influences on the making and remaking of the colonial world. While Spain's American possessions became Spanish in many ways, Andean travelers (in their cosmopolitan lives and journeys), and those who imagined and experienced Iberia through their voyages, also helped to shape Spain in the image and likeness of Peru. As far as one can tell, Don Carlos Visa and Don Juan Bautista Vilca Apaza, *caciques* (native lords) of the Lupaca people near Lake Titicaca (on the border of modern Bolivia and Peru) never journeyed to the Iberian Peninsula. Yet, in a letter penned in Potosí in 1604, the Lupaca lords told their attorney in Spain that the Andean mining center was teeming with so many people that "it resembled another Seville." Iberia was simultaneously imagined from, and through the lenses of, the Indies.[22]

The exact number of native Andeans who voluntarily crossed the Atlantic between the 1530s and 1690s is, at the moment, unknowable. Indigenous travelers, overwhelmingly males, move in and out of the historical record.[23] Like their Spanish counterparts—migrants, sailors, merchants, but also stowaways who made their way on the ships between the Indies and Spain—Andean voyagers mastered the intricacies of imperial law and bureaucracy, only to follow or dismiss orders and dispositions depending on degree of agency and favorable circumstances. Such strategies often render them invisible in official documentation.[24] Moreover, it is likely that many Andeans visited Spain and returned without ever interacting directly with the *Consejo* in Madrid or the *Casa de la Contratación* (the House of Trade) in Seville. Local and imperial archives contain but a handful of formal licenses for native Andeans to travel to Spain.[25] In explaining the difficulties of quantifying these movements, one must also consider that some travelers who requested authorization from local and metropolitan authorities probably never left Peru. Of those who did make the journey, some probably lived anonymous lives in the Iberian Peninsula, leaving little to no documentary trace within the documents presented or generated at court, so one would have to painstakingly follow them into local and provincial Spanish archives.[26] A few stayed in the peninsula for long periods; others, it seems, made it their permanent home. Complicating matters, those who did engage with the *Consejo* or the *Casa* in preparation for their journey appear in the record at the initial stages of their trip, while conducting their legal affairs at the court, or after receiving a license to return to the New World. Many do not state reason or motive. Sometimes a traveler's brief passenger record, which bears little more than a name and the *Indio* label applied to the individual, is the only remaining proof of her or his voyage to, and stay in, Spain.

Travelers shaped the terms that identify and categorize them in the documents in multiple and complex ways. Early modern Atlantic and colonial identities were dynamic, situational, and evolving, born of multidirectional agency and change.[27] When deployed, negotiated, and finally registered in specific bureaucratic settings, categories such as *indio* (Indian), *cacique* (lord of vassals), *indio del común* (commoner; tribute payer), and other early modern categories of governance, status, and difference fall within a continuum of social experiences and classificatory practices. Such categories range from "practical accomplishments", by the travelers, of plausible legal identities— that is, acceptable in the eyes of the royal officials who helped produce them— to external or imposed categorizations of "Indianness," usually in the form of the *indio* label that royal officials placed on them.[28] For that reason, ethnonyms and individual identifications included in the sources do not necessarily constitute rigid assertions of the travelers' allegedly *true* or *essential* self-image.

Unlike the so-called passing that characterized classic colonial scenarios marked by an attempt to escape fiscal obligations or consolidate upward social mobility, however, there was little incentive for travelers facing the *Consejo de Indias* or the *Casa de la Contratación not* to identify themselves as *indios*, unless they claimed to be *caciques*, in which case their Indian ancestry was more or less implied but (unlike their nobility) rarely openly stated.[29] Nor were there any real procedural enticements for Andean visitors to contest the classificatory schemes of royal ministers, clerks, and witnesses, who labeled them as *indios* (Indians), *naturales de las Indias* (natives of the Indies; members of a distinct political community or Republic), or *Indios de nación* (Indians by means of their birth and origin), all based on a handful of fairly stable conventions including ancestry, upbringing, physical appearance, legal status, and public fame and reputation. Though not always applied systematically to classify "Indians," comparable categories had served to identify other peoples throughout the Mediterranean for centuries. Early in the sixteenth century, bureaucrats and indigenous travelers adapted—and in the process transformed and strategically redefined—the handful of categories initially devised to identify the *indios* of the New World and their particular *República* or political community.[30]

At the *Consejo* or the *Casa*, imperial ministers and indigenous travelers engaged with each other through classificatory procedures that ultimately distilled social constructs, juridical categories, individual perceptions, and claims of nobility into "legal assertions" of indigeneity and *cacique* status.[31]

As a result, the *indio* identifications and categorizations that mark countless petitions, licenses, certificates, legal opinions, and other documents produced at the royal court must be understood, first and foremost, as the recorded result of often hidden — and, until recently, overlooked — transactions between the travelers' strategic self-presentation and the understandings, expectations, and eventual interpolations of officials they encountered in the hallways and chambers of the House, the Council, and the royal palace.[32] At court or in Seville, both sides engaged in increasingly institutionalized modes of classification, but they did so within a framework of reference that — especially in the case of self-proclaimed *caciques* and *procuradores* (advocates or procurators) — time, distance, and the travelers' agency and strategic self-fashioning had made especially elastic and negotiable. In some instances, which this book seeks to illuminate, certain travelers successfully reinscribed themselves in the imperial archive as something more than an *indio*. Thus, this work employs *indio* (often translated as "Indian," "native," or "indigenous"), *cacique*, *noble* (noble), and similar categories in their early modern context, but without losing sight of the fact that their social and historical construction was as much an act of imperial power as the result of indigenous legal agency.[33]

Indeed, this power to name, identify, and characterize did not flow unilaterally: it involved negotiation. As free vassals of His Majesty who nevertheless fell within the general characterization of dependents and legal minors or neophytes, many travelers made strategic use of the protections and procedural advantages afforded them by law and custom, whether as *Incas*, *indios*, *caciques*, *vecinos* (permanent residents of a Spanish or Spanish American city or town), or even *encomenderos* (holders of *encomiendas*), sometimes all at once or sequentially.[34] They thereby tested the limits of these categories, interpelating them and shaping the contours on their own terms. Thus they pushed for the reenvision and reembodiment of themselves and their identity at every encounter.[35] *Indio* and other identifications used at court were part of this larger matrix of plausible legal identities, providing Crown-endorsed but not fully controlled "legal locations" or "positions" from which to *speak*, however modestly, in pursuit of individual and collective interests and to petition the king to act upon them.[36] Through legal rhetoric and judicial agency, litigants and favor-seekers wove these interests into the state-making process during the Habsburg era. Petitioning and litigating became paramount forms of indigenous political action and state building.

Andean Cosmopolitans lies at the crossroads of several lines of scholarship that enhance our comprehension of the overall significance of indigenous participation in these transoceanic circuits and their importance for the formation of the Atlantic world. New studies devoted to Indians in the colonial urban world reveal the multiple ways that indigenous women and men experienced, performed, and redefined indigeneity.[37] A related historiographical development has brought Indians—almost invariably males, as women could not hold public or ecclesiastic office, but not always urban denizens—back into the privileged sphere of the colonial *letrados*: the polemicists, advisers, lawyers, and civil and ecclesiastic magistrates who constitued what Ángel Rama once called "The Lettered City."[38] These studies have opened the world of this hitherto understudied segment of native intermediaries, producers of knowledge, and experts of the law by showing the multiple roles played by indigenous intellectuals, notaries, parish assistants, interpreters, and transatlantic advocates in the construction of the *lettered* order and the maintenance of the fundamental mechanisms of political power.[39]

Reinforcing these trends, other works have revealed imperial legal systems as dynamic forces that, because of the circulation of people and information inherent to them, instilled local experiences into global designs and systems.[40] The strong dual-identification—of monarchy with justice and of king with judge—developed in the Iberian late Middle Ages and continued to be strong into the early modern period. Between the fifteenth and seventeenth centuries, the kingdom of Castile experienced an extraordinary proliferation of judicial institutions and a rise in the number of litigants and *letrados* (university-trained and formally appointed judges, lawyers, and procurators). After 1492, renewed social relations constructed via these interactions between subjects and legal experts were transferred to the New World, where they took on a life of their own. Henceforth, the state-building process acquired a markedly dialogical and even "polyphonic" character, infused with constant negotiations between center and peripheries, monarch and subjects, advocate and clients.[41] The subjects of the Castilian monarch shared a general conviction that the sovereign's "absolute" authority would guarantee that justice would be done and that devoted service to God and Crown would receive its due reward within the expanding realm. This expectation of royal justice contributed to the forging of political identities and loyalties that bound together "the disparate and globally dispersed domains" of the Spanish monarchy for three centuries. That same expectation also created the appropriate conditions for subjects to become involved in the state-building process at different levels.[42]

This perspective is not the only way to look at indigenous subjects, empire, and law, but it is an illuminating one. For native Andean subjects, participation in the imperial network of courts and magistrates—the web of interrelated agents, facilitators, and jurisdictions so central to the Habsburg monarchy—became one of the main ways to join a larger flow. As they negotiated their claims with imperial institutions and officials, and through the language and requirements of law and "justice," Amerindian peoples helped forge an emerging literate sphere that sustained the expanding Habsburg realm's political imaginary, as well as the connections that gave the first century of the global age its defining character. By contributing to the construction of one of the master fictions sustaining the colonial order—the contractual, voluntary, and unmediated relationship between the king and his indigenous subjects— these journeys reinforced the hegemony of the Crown, as did any other form of reliance on royal justice and patrimonial power, whether "Indian" or otherwise. In the process, however, native legal activism shaped the empire's legal order, turning indigenous subjects into state-builders of a special kind.[43]

The twentieth century saw a resurgent interest in the making of indigenous legal and political cultures through the natives' constant, pragmatic, and generally strategic uses of local and metropolitan courts of law.[44] This interest in legal cultures and strategies extended to other social actors, for negotiation and constant "dialogue" between the king and the different social bodies of the kingdom through the courts lay at the heart of the emerging monarchical order. Scholars have shown that legal systems provided a set of interrelated forums and plural normative orders that facilitated establishment of colonial categories of rule, definition of social and jurisdictional boundaries, resolution of intra- and intercommunal conflicts, and creative exchange of indigenous and Spanish ideas of law, justice, and customary practices (*usos y costumbres*).[45] Above all, judicial forums became a privileged space where indigenous litigants, witnesses, procurators, interpreters, and petitioners of grace and favor—despite undeniable asymmetries of power—constantly negotiated and coproduced the colonial order.[46]

Indigenous recourse to the law did not eliminate exploitation. On the contrary, by profoundly challenging its terms and setting its limits, local and imperial law built from the ground up turned state-regulated exploitation into a permanent, sustainable element of colonial social relations. Natives shaped the empire as it shaped them. Incorporation of customary rights into juridical frameworks; proclamation of new laws or application of existing ones to novel circumstances; preparation of royal decrees based, sometimes verbatim, on individual and collective petitions; and implementation of legal procedures and institutions for dealing specifically with native litigants turned Spanish empire building and state making into a protracted compromise among negotiated interests.[47]

Andean Cosmopolitans explores the complex and layered nature of Habsburg monarchical rule from the Indians' perspective. Native Andean travelers to the royal court participated in the construction, maintenance, and eventual transformation of transoceanic judicial networks. This book shows how they became key to the production and transmission of legal knowledge—theoretical and pragmatic—in the early modern Atlantic world.[48] Spanning rural and urban contexts, the legal specialists, intermediaries, and indigenous petitioners of all kinds described here created legal networks that soon reinforced individual and collective relationships between native subjects and the king, as well as among indigenous towns, viceregal centers, and the royal court. Such networks helped spread the news of what transpired there.[49]

Through these networks, Indians negotiated interests and countered those of rival actors, both indigenous and nonindigenous. These networks also reveal the political agency of different actors enmeshed in various social groups across the realm. This game was partially played within the local arena of colonial—and particularly indigenous—politics, with its concrete interactions and contexts for the articulation of interests and the exercise of influence. Recent contributions by Atlanticists and colonial ethnohistorians with keen eyes for larger Atlantic processes point to the need for reconstructing these legal networks while accounting for the unequal relationships of power and other constraining forces within which imperial and Atlantic legal identities and judicial activism emerged and evolved.[50] The *República de Indios* (literally, "Republic of the Indians") was, as historian Luis Miguel Glave once noted, "crosscut by de facto differentiations of class, race, and access to power."[51] It has now become necessary to bring power back into the analysis. Although modern scholars, in reconstructing imperial networks, have rightly emphasized the critical role played by mediation and the intermediaries who made it possible, this focus should not obscure the equally important fact that the exercise of power was a key ingredient in how networks were built, functioned, and changed through time.

At the viceregal level, the main indigenous architects of Lima's *Nación Índica* (literally, "Nation of the Indies" or "of the Indians"), a separate political entity—or, as Juan Carlos Estenssoro characterized it, "a society within society, defined by land and blood, with its own kings, festivals, and dances"—endeavored to fill the void left by the Inca leadership's weakening and retreat after the conquest and the overall declining significance of traditional rural indigenous elites in the political life of their communities.[52] Numbering some 1,500 individuals in the eighteenth century, the colonial Inca nobility in and around the city of Cuzco was no doubt "the largest and most cohesive group of Indian nobles in colonial Peru."[53] Nevertheless, as the Great Insurrection led by José Gabriel Tupac Amaru and the Cataris would make painfully evident in 1780–1781, the power and prestige of this ruling caste of Inca *caciques*, urban merchants, and prosperous artisans remained restricted to the area of about twenty or thirty miles surrounding the southern Andean city. And, even there, their largely self-attributed symbolic preemince was sometimes contested.[54] By the mid-seventeenth century, the colonial Indian elite was not composed solely of Inca nobles and prominent *caciques*. Well-off and well-connected urban denizens who advocated for a locally governed *Nación* of original inhabitants of the Indies, based on a symbolically constructed common origin and a single, all-encompassing, Christian, and noble "Indian" identity, had come to the fore. In cities like Trujillo or Lima where, unlike Cuzco, the permanent Indian populations were never a majority, the elite and commoner sectors that coalesced behind the idea of a *Nación Índica* were composed of individuals who came from geographically and culturally diverse regions of the Peruvian viceroyalty.[55]

When seen in this light, the natives' generalized and undeniable engagement with the judicial system on an imperial scale becomes an important avenue for reexamining power relations and reallocations, not only between the two so-called *Repúblicas* (of Indians and Spaniards) or between them and the Crown but also within the *República de Indios*—a partially autonomous, self-governing commonwealth under customary Indian laws and subject to the authority of king and church. The study of these interactions and reallocations allows for a reinterpretation of Andean indigenous societies during the first two centuries of Spanish rule.

This story reconstructs the worlds of Andean travelers to the Habsburg court from the inside out. It begins with a case study of the social and historical conditions behind the transatlantic journey of one ethnic lord, then it expands outward by reconstructing the mechanisms used by Andean polities of the Peruvian central highlands and others in conversation with the greater viceregal and metropolitan courts of justice. This book follows these subjects from Peru to Spain and back to the Andes. Its organization is at once chronological and thematic, starting with the early litigant lords of the mid-sixteenth century, then finishing with the great attorneys-general for the Indians of the late seventeenth century.

Chapter 2 draws from recent studies on "paper" and ethnographic knotted strings (*khipus*) as well as on current discussions of indigenous participation in the colonial justice system to reclaim the *pueblo* (village or town), in its political expression as a governing council, as one of the main scenarios for indigenous collective legal activism in the rural Andes during the early Habsburg era. It shows that traditional mechanisms for allocating labor tasks and apportioning tribute quotas among different *ayllus* (Andean kinship groups) underscored communitywide litigation and the search for favor and redress at local and metropolitan courts. These processes conferred a moderate degree of control over legal strategies and decisions to midranking *ayllu* and *cabildo* (municipal council) authorities and, ultimately, to the Andean commoners directly involved in the reproduction of the political economy needed to gain access to the justice of the king.

Chapter 3 is the first full-scale examination of the system of courts linking Peru and Spain from the perspective of indigenous peoples. It follows the Atlantic community of native litigants, petitioners, and favor-seekers converging on the court from distant parts of the Andes. Because of the very nature of its movements and connections, this community defied and partially subverted the grander schemes of local and imperial rule. This community's most visible members were the indigenous voyagers traveling within the viceroyalty, first to the *Audiencia de Lima* and eventually to the Habsburg royal court. By engaging with court officials placed at the different levels of appeal of the imperial judiciary, either in person or by proxy, or by simply traveling unauthorized to Castile to seek royal favor, Andean cosmopolitans brought to life a three-tiered judicial system that, with only slight modifications, endured until the end of the colonial period.

Chapter 4 reframes native urban ethnogenesis, increasing class stratification, and deep cultural transformations within pan-hemispheric and pan-Atlantic processes linking indigenous cosmopolitan trajectories to similar experiences of hybridization among Africans, Europeans, and their descendants. The chapter studies indigenous travelers and legal intermediaries who gathered around the viceregal palace and were able to arrive at the Habsburg court largely because of their participation in the networks of patronage and service that sustained civil and religious state bureaucracies. Taking the capital of Lima as the main setting, the analysis shows the exceptional capacity of these individuals to re-create a discourse about the privileges and obligations of their *Nación* within the monarchy. The *Nación Índica* or *Nación Indiana* ("Nation of the Indies" or "Nation of the Indians") rested on notions of cultural distinctiveness, political autonomy, and indigenous elite rule. As such, it was as much based on ethnicity as it was on one's ancestors' place of origin and noble or plebeian birth. The Atlantic journeys explored in this book serve as an allegory for a deeper historical process: the gradual emergence of new forms of indigenous leadership in colonial Peru.

Chapter 5 explores the specific constellations of power within which native Andeans' visits to the Habsburg court unfolded. Early decrees issued in the 1560s forbade indigenous lords and commoners from seeking favor and redress in Madrid in person. Nevertheless, royal responses to specific petitions by Andean visitors and to the *Consejo de Indias*'s formal inquires and dissenting opinions about these travelers were more ambivalent. Such responses often centered around reminding ministers and their counterparts in the *Casa de la Contratación* that, once these Andean visitors had set foot in the royal court and called on the monarch for support and protection, they were to be heard and, hopefully, enticed to return to the New World. By setting foot in the court, indigenous travelers created a relatively safe space for negotiation. The seemingly subtle distinction between guiding or helping versus forcing or coercing was central to the nature of the king's claim to authority over his Indian vassals. Requests for royal support became a sophisticated example of how the seemingly powerless, when able to place themselves within the web of social obligations and expectations that held the Habsburg court in place, could profit from the relationship of interdependence that existed among king, councilors, and, in this case, indigenous vassals.

Chapter 6 explores the politics of identity and indigeneity in this metropolitan setting. It focuses on the travelers' engagement with the construction of basic categories of rule such as *indio, cacique,* and *miserable* (poor, wretched, deserving legal protection). At the royal court, Andean visitors, magistrates, and other agents negotiated their "Indianness" in several ways. But distinguishing nobles from commoners in Spain became increasingly difficult as the seventeenth century progressed. The ambiguity of such categories, especially that of *cacique*, opened new avenues to power and prestige for certain travelers. Their claims to *cacique* status did not constitute a mere exercise at self-promotion but were charged with juridical meanings. This catch all term had become insufficient to capture newly emerging cosmopolitan leaders. However, the recognition of *cacique* status that some sought at court was a requisite for speaking to the king on behalf of the commons. Successful forms of representation before the monarch and his ministers, and thus of access to royal justice and favor, depended on the proper and effective deployment of such categories of legitimization. Thus, the same social conditions that made this style of leadership appealing, appropriate, or even necessary in the seventeenth century made these Andean cosmopolitans' claims to

FIGURE 1.3

Delegates of the community of Huasicancha, Huancayo, at the train station in Lima (1937).
Courtesy: Archivo Regional de Junín (Huancayo, Junín, Peru).

authority and legitimacy ever partial, incomplete, and contested. Midcolonial Andean leaders operating under the umbrella of *cacique* status benefited from this tension, but they never fully resolved it.

In 1937, more than three centuries after the Spanish Conquest of Peru, fourteen delegates from the peasant community of Huasicancha, near Huancayo (in what was known in colonial times as the Jauja Valley, the region studied in chapter 2), carried and delivered their demands for full citizenship to the capital in Lima. Addressing president Óscar Benavides in writing, these *comuneros* denounced neighboring landowners for encroaching on communal lands, as well as local authorities for unjustly imprisoning the community's elected representatives. They reminded the president of their rights as "citizens of a free and democratic republic" and as "members of an officially recognized indigenous community." Their own *república* was in fact older than the Peruvian Republic, they argued, providing evidence of recorded property deeds going back to 1607 (when they were still labeled "Indians"). Moreover, according to their filing petition, the community had fulfilled its dues and contributions to the state government since "time immemorial," thereby honoring the fundamental ideals of the old monarchical-republican compacts.[56]

This photograph of the delegates was taken at Lima's train station to assure President Benavides that they had made the long journey (Figure 1.3). It was neither their first nor last venture into the center of state power at Lima. As the title of this book suggests, Andean cosmopolitans such as the *comuneros* of Huasicancha were tapping into a deep current of native politics full of historical meaning. They modeled themselves on a profound tradition of local polities and community leaders seeking redress, favor, and self-government in an increasingly centralized political system. By 1937 (when the photo was taken) this tradition, though weakened and reduced in its scope after centuries of colonialism and liberal attacks on communal forms of organization, echoed centuries past (the early modern era and the aftermath of the conquest), when indigenous leaders, commoners, and their appointed representatives started to embark on similar journeys over hundreds and sometimes thousands of miles, not only to the viceregal court in Lima but also to the Habsburg royal court in Spain. It is through their journeys that we can learn how colonial and postcolonial politics connected—and sometimes collided—in the Andes and across the Atlantic.

TWO

KHIPUS, COMMUNITY, AND THE PURSUIT OF JUSTICE IN SIXTEENTH-CENTURY PERU

In the early 1540s, few participants in the conquest of the Inca empire would have described it as a fait accompli. The initial cycle of instability that began with encounter (at Cajamarca in 1532) only intensified with armed Inca resistance (from Vilcabamba, led by Manco Inca Yupanqui) and murder (of conquistador Francisco Pizarro by a rival faction in 1541). Even though a long period of conflict and unruliness still lay ahead, the redrawing of the Andean judicial landscape was already under way. Constant war, desolation, and side-switching by natives and Spaniards alike during these first decades of Indian-Spanish interactions did not prevent Pizarro and his brothers from building a wide network of relatives, followers, dependents, and legal professionals—up to four hundred individuals according to one estimate. The Pizarros—Francisco; Hernando, while imprisoned in Spain; and Gonzalo, while raising the banner against the king in Peru—entrusted some of these individuals with protecting their social aspirations, political claims, and economic interests in multiple courts of law, thus opening alternative battlegrounds—this time legal ones—within the larger struggle for control of the lands and peoples of the disintegrating Inca kingdom.[1]

Procurators and solicitors, called *procuradores de causas, solicitadores*, and *agentes de negocios*, came to occupy a central position in the *Pizarrista* legal web. They represented the Pizarro clan and its allies before a still-itinerant royal court, the *Consejo de Indias*, the *Casa de la Contratación* in Seville, the other *audiencias* (superior courts of appeal) of Lima and La Plata, and the older chancelleries of Valladolid and Granada. Kinship, patronage, locality, common interest, and contractual obligations tightened the powerful network at multiple levels. Moreover, it was the scope and versatility of the power of attorney, inherited from the Roman legal system and codified in the medieval and early modern laws of Iberia, that granted these agents the necessary authority to function as a transoceanic community of interest. Legal mediation through *procuradores* and powers of attorney—key ingredients for requesting the king's favor in royal courts—allowed the Pizarros to appear as claimants in multiple parts of the expanding Spanish Empire simultaneously.[2]

In April 1540, while the Pizarros were still fighting on battlefields and in law courts to maintain control over the Andes, Paullu Tupac Inca, son of the deceased Inca emperor Huayna Capac and a crucial ally of the anti-*Pizarrista* faction, began to supervise the elaboration of his proof of merits and services (*probanza de méritos y servicios*) in his native Cuzco. Paullu had just returned from the first two Indian-Spanish expeditions to Chile and the Collao region, present-day southern Peru and Bolivia. Appearing before Licentiate Antonio de la Gama, one of Francisco Pizarro's lieutenants, and most likely with the aid of an unnamed procurator (*procurador de causas*), Paullu legally articulated his intention to live as a Christian and inform the king of his services in the conquest "so that he will reward me as I deserve." As was customary, Paullu's *probanza* included the responses of ten Spanish witnesses to a twenty-item questionnaire, likely prepared by his *procurador*. It was in all likelihood the earliest such document drafted on behalf of a native Andean—commoner or noble—to request royal favor while reminding the king of the contractual nature of his authority over the empire that Paullu's ancestors once ruled. After reaching the royal court in Spain through an intermediary, this legal instrument became the cornerstone of Paullu's multiple claims. The king confirmed his *encomienda* in Cuzco, also conferring a coat of arms and other privileges and possessions that the Inca prince passed on to his numerous descendants[3]

Thus, only a handful of years after the pivotal encounter of Pizarro and Atahualpa at Cajamarca in 1532, indigenous claimants, petitioners, and legal facilitators began the long process of making their own the legal cultures that Iberian immigrants, bureaucrats, and experts at law were planting in the recently annexed kingdom of New Castile. After Paullu, other noble Inca descendants began to engage with local, intercolonial, and metropolitan courts, preparing letters, reports, petitions, and *probanzas* aimed at securing their status within the new order.[4] In the 1550s, the Uchu Inca lineage, whose branches, claims to nobility, and search for royal privilege spanned two continents and two and a half centuries, began to compile decrees, titles, nobility patents, proofs of merit, and other family treasures that, carefully bequeathed onto each succeeding generation, were to uphold their rank and privilege in Peru and Mexico until the early 1800s. The portrait that the Uchu Incas commissioned of their illustrious ancestor, king Tupac Inca Yupanqui, adorns the cover of this book (Figure 2.1).[5]

FIGURE 2.1

Arms granted to the descendants of Gonzalo Uchu Hualpa and Felipe Tupa Inga Yupanqui. Ministerio de Educaión, Cultura y Deporte. Archivo General de Indias MP-ESCUDOS, 78.

Non-Inca native lords (*caciques*) and communities entered the scene almost concurrently. They joined the Incas as active claimants in the late 1540s, hiring advocates and solicitors and sending their own delegations to tend to their legal affairs in Lima—the City of Kings—seat of a royal court of appeal. During the two decades that followed promulgation of the New Laws in 1542, which granted this and soon to be established *audiencias* the right to assess and revise Indian tributary quotas, the viceregal court experienced an explosion of litigation. Native polities began to request a reduction of fiscal burdens, while *caciques* sought confirmation of their chiefly ranks. Lawsuits pertaining to lands and pastures, town boundaries, and *cacicazgo* (lordship) rights emerged. In early 1562, the first high-ranking Andean *cacique* from the central highlands crossed the Atlantic on behalf of his community and reached the still-mobile Habsburg court. Indigenous groups quickly became expert litigators in secular and ecclesiastical courts, and their legal activism continued unabated throughout the Habsburg era and beyond.[6]

NATIVE ANDEANS GO TO THE COURTS

This chapter examines the political economy that made it possible for indigenous communities to petition the king and litigate in royal courts, especially those in the Old World. Given the previous scenario of increasing engagements with the king's justice from the mid-sixteenth century onward, a key question is: Which norms, practices, and strategies formed the social basis for the collective legal actions that lured these travelers to Peruvian and Spanish courts? In line with Castilian judicial procedure, bringing petitions and filing lawsuits before the *audiencia* in Lima or the *Consejo de Indias* in Madrid was done mostly in writing, sometimes by indigenous petitioners and litigants themselves, acting on behalf of their communities. Moreover, Spanish advocates, defenders, and attorneys who handled these cases often took over once the initial complaint or petition had been filed. As a result, surviving dossiers seem like discrete and self-contained worlds of ink and paper wherein the opening demand or petition signals the *beginning* of concerted legal action.[7] Nevertheless, as Bianca Premo has observed, tracing the "pre-histories" of petitions and complaints—that is, the "genealogy of prior actions" that led to them—offers an important avenue for unraveling colonial subjects' legal culture and agency.[8] Petitioning and litigating were difficult and expensive affairs. Submitting written pleas to the magistrates of the king, in early colonial Peru but especially in Spain, was oftentimes the culmination of communal mechanisms of coordination, negotiation, and decision-making that Andean groups had set in motion before filing the initial petition. Internal and collective processes that guaranteed a regular stream of resources, some of which were reinvested in securing legal counsel and royal favor at different levels, also escape the record.[9]

This chapter counters the tendency of judicial archives to efface the contributions made by midranking native officials—municipal councilmen, legal intermediaries, commoners—to perceived native Andean litigiousness. Such a perspective seeks to return "politics" to the interpretation of colonial litigation and its processes.[10] Judicial advocacy opened multiple paths to power within litigating communities. But these paths were not necessarily restricted to the native elite and their descendants or to the different factions within this privileged *cacique* class. Power did not always flow from top to bottom: in fact, large-scale and protracted litigation, were it to succeed, demanded that some of that power be built and maintained from the ground up.

In part because of built-in distortions in judicial records and procedural rules as well as the matters most commonly litigated (tribute and compulsory labor), traditional Andean elites (generally, the *caciques*) appear as the primary parties in most lawsuits and administrative procedures. Their Crown-sanctioned legal position at the top of the *República de Indios* demanded as much.[11] In addition, they stood at the front of the legal offensive that commenced in earnest in the 1550s. Many Andean lords, by adapting to roles as administrators of communal labor and wealth as well as advocates of the weak and destitute, reinvented themselves as the "legal benefactors" of their subjects.[12] Yet, the legal advocacy of the *cacique* class was ambivalent. As records show, *caciques* frequently dragged their own subjects into court and sued other Andean nobles and neighboring communities, non-Indian actors, and representatives of the Crown. And some, because of their wealth, power, literacy, and access to the justice system, were at an advantage to seize land, labor, and other resources by judicial means, passing on gains to descendants—as Paullu Tupac Inca did—and protecting assets from communal control. Among certain indigenous communities, these and other strategies must have unfolded simultaneously and over a long period of time.[13]

Using the Quechua-speaking communities of Jauja in the central highlands of Peru as the main case under study, this chapter takes a novel direction, reframing *cacique* legal activism of the sixteenth century within wider social norms, constraints, and expectations to which it belonged: the ritual and fiduciary responsibilities of internal management and defense of communal assets—the so-called *bienes del común* or *bienes de comunidad*. Some contemporary testimonies identify these assets with the concept of *sapci*, a Quechua term that colonial and modern dictionaries translate as "what belongs to everyone," or "that which is common to all."[14] Sources characterize these shared and politically controlled endowments as common resources that ideally "belonged" to the collectivity: a reserve to be used for the exclusive benefit of the commons, especially its most vulnerable members. The study of colonial Jauja shows that these communal funds, obtained through the labor of able-bodied members, provided one of the most important resources for making large-scale, communitywide litigation possible. As Crown bureaucrats gradually replaced labor-based tribute with demands for money and goods during the second half of the sixteenth century, the colonial courts became especially useful to indigenous communities engaged in preserving or increasing communal assets as a way to guarantee their own existence and autonomy within the Spanish Empire.[15] By amassing and properly managing these resources through local and internal mechanisms for attaining consensus and collective decision-making, some native groups funded and undertook litigation at regional and imperial courts.[16] Thus, among certain Andean polities, litigation—irrespective of the outcomes—became one of the driving forces behind communal survival and reproduction inasmuch as it encour-

24

aged these corporate groups to generate and preserve the *sapci* funds needed to seek justice and favor from the Crown. These funds became a mechanism to protect their interests and communal resources vis-à-vis other colonial actors, *caciques* included. *Sapci* practices were, at the turn of the seventeenth century, as much a continuation of former use as a colonial innovation.[17]

The analysis of *sapci* funds places *cacique* legal activism at the center of a wider reality. Nevertheless, an intracommunal perspective of the different *ayllus* and *pueblos* of the Jauja Valley allows for a reconceptualization of native litigation that includes additional segments of indigenous rural society, in particular tribute-paying commoners who, though generally relegated to the background in the documentation, provided the surplus that allowed the authorities to seek legal redress. Because Andean polities of the Habsburg era were indeed "litigant villages" (*pueblos litigantes*), the discussion should also include officials of the Indian municipal councils (*cabildos*) and the men entrusted with managing collective endowments.[18] In this view, the stewards of communal funds (*administradores* or *mayordomos*), along with the indigenous accountants (*contadores*), cord-keepers (*khipucamayuq*), and municipal attorneys (*procuradores*), emerge as key legal brokers and imperial intermediaries facilitating the articulation of native polities and royal courts. In this retelling of a well-known story, Andean commoners and municipal authorities, more so than traditional elites, become essential actors in the process of appropriation of Iberian legal culture from the ground up.

LORDS AND COMMUNITIES:
TOLEDO'S 1570 INVESTIGATION

In November 1570, at the beginning of his administration (1569–1581), Viceroy Francisco de Toledo summoned native leaders of Jauja to provide testimony for an *información* (a detailed account) of expenses that these communities had incurred after two decades of litigation before the *audiencia* and the *Consejo de Indias*. Traditionally hostile to the Incas, the Huanca ethnic group was a set of interrelated *ayllus* (agro-pastoral kinship groups) living about 120 miles east of Lima in the narrow but fertile Jauja Valley and its neighboring high pastures. The Huancas totaled around 45,000 individuals some forty years after conquest. Because of their geographical proximity to the *Audiencia de Lima*, the shrewdness and commitment of some of their legal agents, and the infrastructure they developed for managing communal assets, the Huancas enjoyed ready access to the high court of appeal and eventually to the *Consejo de Indias*, generating dozens of *pleitos* at local and metropolitan tribunals and inspiring imperial policies on how to deal with indigenous litigiousness. They were, in many respects, legal pioneers.

The pre-Hispanic social order was still discernible in Jauja at the time of Toledo's investigation. Upon taking control of the valley and its surrounding highlands sometime in the fifteenth century, the Incas had reorganized the population into three units of 10,000 tributary households each, elevating three local chiefs to the highest rank of lord of ten thousand households (*hunu curaca*) or great lord (*hatun curaca*) of their respective units. This decimal division, along with its subdivisions (rounded-off units of thousands and hundreds known as *huarangas* and *pachacas*) survived for several decades after the Spanish Conquest.[19] The Incas' reorganization served as the fundamental basis for the allocation of the first *encomiendas* and thus the formation of three main *repartimientos de indios*: Atunjauja, Luringuanca, and Ananguanca.[20] Each was ruled by a paramount lord or *cacique principal* (the colonial heir of the *hatun curaca*) and his subordinate *caciques* and *principales*, forming the units that came to include a series of *pueblos*, Spanish-style native villages, founded along the Jauja River in the late 1560s and the early 1570s. Throughout the rest of the colonial period, native authorities and royal bureaucrats assigned fiscal and administrative duties in the valley, which included paying tribute and fulfilling rotational labor drafts (*mita*), for the three main jurisdictions.[21]

The structure of the *información* reflects native hierarchies of power, Andean notions of wealth and tribute-as-labor, and kinship-based principles of social organization. The leading *caciques* of the three *repartimientos* rendered their testimony first, aggregating the total legal expenses of their polities. A second round of testimonies by lesser-ranking authorities followed. These subordinate lords—generally *caciques* or *indios principales* but sometimes *cobradores* (tribute collectors)—were in charge of organizing labor services and levying tribute from smaller units: corporate, self-governing kinship groups the natives called *ayllus* and the Spaniards generally termed *parcialidades* (sectors, or segments). As in the rest of the Andes, these kin-based, landholding, ritual groups, organized for the fulfillment of communal labor, constituted, along with the individual household, the basic cell of native social life in the Jauja Valley, giving *caciques* their raison d'être.[22]

But there is more in Toledo's November 1570 *Información*, especially about what it meant to live under the mantle of royal justice. The native lords of Jauja organized their testimony around the following "expenses": The number of native messengers, retainers, and porters of commoner origin that each of the *parcialidades* had contributed to aid *caciques* engaged in litigation, including those who had never returned from the warmer climate of the coastal plains (thus becoming "lost" to the group); the cost in pesos of these legal initiatives before the *Audiencia de Lima* and the *Consejo de Indias*; and the communal assets they had to sell in local and regional markets to generate enough funds to litigate. In the two decades prior to Toledo's inspection, the centuries-old model of the vertical archipelago, which had served indigenous communities to gain access to discrete ecological niches situated at different altitudes, probably facilitated the Huancas' relatively quick adaptation to the dynamics of visiting distant colonial courts.[23]

The most striking feature of the *Información*, however, was the use of *khipus* (knotted cords, an ancient form of communication among the Inca and other prehispanic groups) to record events for the impending litigation. In fact, Jauja's Andean lords based their accounting and recounting of the group's legal endeavors almost solely on the information that heads of *ayllus* and tribute-collectors had recorded through *khipus*. Using this time-honored accounting method tells us a great deal about the importance that collective litigation had come to occupy among these Andean communities only twenty years after the Spanish Conquest.

Scholars have located multiple alphabetic "transcriptions" of the famous Andean knotted strings. As several testimonies attest, information contained in *khipus* was "recited," often through the mediation of an interpreter, in courtrooms across the Andes from the mid-sixteenth to at least the mid-seventeenth century. Huanca *ayllus* were among the first groups to adapt this practice to litigation. In 1549, Huanca lords displayed before the chronicler Pedro de Cieza an earlier set of *khipus*, which registered their contributions to the Spaniards since arrival. These and other knotted strings were the basis for the elaboration of several detailed lists (*memorias*) that morphed into more complex *probanzas* presented before the *audiencia* and the Council of the Indies between 1558 and 1562. The *memorias* contained the numbers of warriors, porters, and servants, as well as the amounts of clothes, foodstuffs, and other goods, that the Huancas contributed between 1532 and 1554.[24]

The *khipus* became part of the record, and oftentimes held as much probative heft (if not more), as any document or other testimony presented to the court. Spanish judges and inspectors generally admitted the cords and the transactions they memorialized, as evidence in civil and administrative procedures, relying on the authority and expertise of the lords and cord masters who "read out" the multicolored strings before them.[25] As in some of the best-known cases of *khipu* transcriptions, the cords of Jauja contained information about the management of collective labor and corporately owned resources, a matter of constant contention in the many lawsuits that relied on the knotted strings as substantiating evidence. Late pre-Hispanic and early colonial *khipus* also recorded census data, agricultural production and heads of cattle, tribute assessments (usually measured in the number of workers and days owed by the *ayllus* to the larger group or the state), and the amounts and types of produce stored in communal and state-controlled storehouses.[26]

Given these precedents, *khipus* constituted an ad hoc medium for an accurate recording of the legal expenses of the Huanca *ayllus*. However, the cords displayed and interpreted before the authorities in 1570 also contained the "context" of the communities' *pleitos* (the generic term for a lawsuit or court case during the colonial period). The Huanca *khipus* included information about what was spent on court affairs in connection with how, by whom, and from which funds the expenses were paid, thus presenting a type of privileged metadata about the act of litigating itself. *Khipus* documented how the Jauja *ayllus* and authorities adapted to the demands of the Spanish judicial system, realigning internal mechanisms of governance and collective resource management with the challenge of gaining access to different legal niches, demanding justice, and obtaining the king's reward.

These *khipu*-based alphabetic records allow modern scholars to reembed *cacique* legal activism within the social and political contexts in which the indigenous communities initiated litigation during the sixteenth century. To begin, Viceroy Toledo's 1570 inquest draws a fundamental distinction between two categories of *pleitos*: *private* versus *communal*. Such a classification rested on the nature of the court case and the aims of the litigants, as well as the origins of the resources that sustained the case at hand. The division is already documented in the 1566 ordinances of *oidor* (supreme justice of the *Audiencia*) Gregorio González de Cuenca for the government of native villages on the northern coast, but it is likely older.[27] In 1570, the native lords of Jauja similarly recalled having engaged in *pleitos particulares* (private lawsuits), filed in local and viceregal courts of justice by certain lords (or by their subjects against them), usually with the aid of Spanish advocates and attorneys. Any *caciques* who were acting as individual plaintiffs or defendants in these private or individual lawsuits had been expected to fund the litigation from their own *hacienda privada* (personal or private estate).[28] *Pleitos del común* (communal lawsuits), by contrast, were handled differently: Andean lords pursued justice on behalf of their subjects, sometimes litigating against paramount lords or neighboring *ayllus* in Jauja and beyond. The sale of communal holdings—including cattle, cloth, and baskets of coca—had financed these legal actions. *Ayllu* members kept this legal fund as secret as possible, that is, it was undeclared and outside the control of local Spanish magistrates, at least until the arrival of Viceroy Toledo.[29]

Since the early 1560s, Don Carlos Apoalaya, chief lord of Ananguanca, had filed a series of court cases in Lima, to the great hardship of his family: the arduous physical effort required, including dramatic changes in altitude and climate, had perhaps led to the deaths of his father and fourteen close relatives. The litigation also cost the Apoalaya clan much more: more than 21,000 pesos from the family estate, including gold, silver, fine clothes, horses, cattle, and slaves. But the stakes were high. The Apoalayas had invested *their* resources seeking confirmation of their noble status and exemption from tribute and labor drafts. They had also sought to defend their *cacicazgo* rights from aspiring nobles and relatives and to secure the allotment of goods and retainers that went along with the title of *cacique principal*. Despite his evident frustration with the elevated costs of seeking justice and defending his noble rank, Don Carlos was careful to distinguish his *private* court cases—those involving him, his father, and his paternal uncles—from the communal lawsuits in which the *ayllus* of his *repartimiento* were the plaintiffs. On some of these occasions, lesser-ranking lords had litigated or petitioned in the name of the kinship groups of Ananguanca and *against* the labor and tribute demands of the Apoalayas, questioning the legitimacy of their claims to collective energy. These litigants had covered the expenses with the sale of communal assets, carefully inscribing these transactions on their colored strings. Don Carlos ultimately prevailed in maintaining his chiefly status and passing on the office to his direct descendants—the Apoalayas would rule Ananguanca for another 150 years. Interestingly enough, unlike the *caciques* of lower rank, who were subordinates, the *cacique principal* did not rely on the string devices to keep track of his family legal expenses, revealing perhaps their impracticality for such a task and the *cacique*'s degree of acculturation.[30]

The legal initiatives among neighboring Luringuancas between the early 1550s and the late 1560s further illustrate this basic distinction between *pleitos* that concerned certain lords and *pleitos* that, although brought before the courts by *caciques*, called for the involvement of the *ayllus* as a whole. The paramount lord Don Carlos Limaylla had to defend himself against the legal attacks of subordinate *caciques*. Nonetheless, he also spent a considerable number of pesos, registered on *khipus*, in lawsuits in which he stood for his group against other *repartimientos* and Spanish miners and *encomenderos*. Don Carlos also led other legal actions to lower the fiscal and labor demands of the Crown.[31] Don Carlos's records listed one *pleito* to lower the tribute quota owed to the Spanish *encomendero*. He had filed another two asking to have native tributaries declared exempt from working in nearby silver mines and to prevent them from serving in the Lima and Huamanga labor markets and way stations along those commercial routes. Don Carlos had also brought a fourth lawsuit to counter accusations of sedition against the Luringuancas. When he fell sick as a result of his constant trips to and from Lima, three *ayllus* covered his medical expenses. The Luringuanca *parcialidades* even contributed a number of Indian porters, messengers, and retainers to the service of Don Carlos and other legal representatives making the perilous journey to the *audiencia*.[32]

The *paper khipus* of Jauja also offer interesting clues as to how households and *ayllus* parceled out their contributions to the *repartimientos'* legal funds. Such customary principles offer another insight into the material bases of the *pleitos del común*.[33] The 1570 testimony shows that indigenous stewards and cord masters did not divide the in-kind and labor contributions equally among the different descent groups and leaders who participated in the intertwined processes of planning, collecting, and accounting. Instead, they assigned each quota on the basis of fractions or percentages that mirrored the *ayllus'* wealth and, especially, their size—both reflections of their precedence within an internal ranked order. As a royal magistrate explained in 1571, in assigning these duties, the Indians "still followed the old ways, keeping in mind the possibilities of the people and the wealth of the province in question."[34] Thus, in apportioning contributions, the nature and scope of the legal issue at hand—that is, whether the matter pertained to a specific segment, such as an *ayllu* or group of *ayllus*, or to the ethnic polity as a whole—certainly played a role.

Khipus, in combination with corn seeds and pebbles of different sizes and colors, were especially suited to the task of dividing obligations proportionately and adding them up later for accounting and auditing purposes. *Khipu* masters moved grains and stones around, sometimes on boards and sometimes on the ground, in order to calculate how much each *ayllu* had to give or pay. Through the manipulation of these tokens and relatively simple arithmetic, *caciques*, stewards, and cord-keepers joined efforts to "balance" their accounts, proportionally allocating each *ayllu's* share and accounting for that contribution later. As a result, tasks and tributes, both paid and due, were recorded on knotted strings.[35]

In line with these practices, the Huanca lords asked the five *ayllus* of Mataguasi and Marivilca to supply a total of thirty pesos in gold to fund the pioneering journey of one of the paramount *caciques*, Don Felipe Guacrapaucar, to the Spanish court in 1562. The lords and cord masters operating at the *ayllu* level employed the procedures described above and came up with proportional shares. One *ayllu* contributed ten gold pesos, while the others gave smaller quantities, ranging from four to six pesos each, as their *khipus* were to reveal to Toledo a few years later.[36] The 1570 inquest shows that analogous principles were at play at the higher *repartimiento* level. Each *ayllu*'s contribution to the legal fund, whether cattle, baskets of coca, pieces of cloth, or cash, was assessed and assigned proportionately, according to customary notions of wealth, value, and, ultimately, fairness.[37]

Thus, by the mid-sixteenth century, the Huancas of Jauja—and, very likely, other Andean groups—had adapted internal mechanisms previously employed for the control of labor and the fulfillment of tributary and labor-service obligations to meet the new requirements and the challenges of prosecuting communitywide *pleitos* and pursuing justice before local and metropolitan courts. By 1570, Huanca authorities were handling them as they had handled tributary dues at least since Inca times. They allocated responsibilities to support litigation and built the temporary legal funds required, as they apportioned quotas of labor and kind among the different corporate descent groups—proportionately, with the aid of *khipus* and tokens, stewards, and cord masters.

PLANNING, PERFORMANCE, AND ACCOUNTABILITY

This use of *khipus* to record legal expenditures among the *ayllus* of Jauja hints at other principles associated with large-scale communal litigation, particularly collective planning and performance as well as elite accountability. Native lords and commoners engaged in concerted legal action according to their own expectations as to how leaders should use funds and seek justice, or otherwise be held accountable. Up to the early 1570s, the performance of native authorities involved in these court cases was still subject to internal auditing and, sometimes, even open opposition. The legal initiatives in which the lords of Jauja took part were subject to public assessment and discussion as part of the overall process of litigating. The evidence available for other Andean polities speaks of a series of widespread practices associated with *cacique* accountability and town hall–style meetings called *juntas* or *cabildos*.[38]

Until the very recent past, the knotted strings of Tupicocha, an Andean village west of the Jauja Valley, similarly articulated kinship organization at the *ayllu* level with the larger, multi-*ayllu* sphere of the town (the *parcialidad*) and the ethnic group. As part of their centuries-old shared endowment, the Tupicochan *ayllus* controlled community fields, pastures, and herds, along with related infrastructure—canals, terrace walls, and reservoirs. As important, control and accounting of the collective labor that generated these re-sources was, according to Frank Salomon, the "single most important ingre-dient" of *khipu* content in Tupicocha. The fulfillment of coordinated duties is still a matter of high intra- and inter-*ayllu* politics because it calls for meticu-lous planning and recordkeeping by the different *parcialidades*. Although au-thorities have kept records of community herds, tribute quotas, work obli-gations levied on *ayllu* members, and the disposition of goods made with communal resources in village record books since the late nineteenth or early twentieth century, they once registered them only on knotted cords not un-like the ones the ethnic authorities of Jauja displayed before Toledo in 1570.[39]

Furthermore, the Tupicochan *khipus* were versatile devices capable of both simulating *and* documenting collective action, allowing communities to con-trast previous planning against actual performance. These *khipus* were thus "an assembly of movable parts" that specialists operated in order to weigh these two important aspects. For that reason, *khipus* mimicked and encoded social and economic domains, such as inventorying, accounting, taking atten-dance, scheduling, and assigning quotas and confirming fulfillment. In all these spheres, the coordination and reconciliation of planning versus perfor-mance through public auditing was the ultimate goal.[40]

These findings about the "modern life" of the Tupicochan *khipus* shed im-portant light on the early colonial legal actions of the Huancas, particularly the expectations that nobles and commoners placed upon those charged with undertaking them. Tupicocha was part of the colonial province of Huarochirí, immediately west of the Jauja province. In part because of Inca and Spanish policies—including the management of communal endowments, as will be discussed below—Andean communities in Huarochirí exhibited a certain homogeneity of social structures with Jauja and other central Andean poli-ties located in the provinces of Tarma, Chinchaycocha, and Yauyos. Their intertwined historical experiences, in the courtroom and elsewhere, under-score that, for the people of Huarochirí as well as for those of Jauja, local and metropolitan litigation constituted one of the collective "problems" to which Salomon refers in his ethnography of Tupicocha. The lords and cord-keepers of Jauja registered *pleitos* on khipus because litigating and favor-seeking in royal tribunals embodied analogous processes of planning and performance on the part of the native lords, midranking authorities, and their tribute-paying subjects.[41]

In 1570 Don Carlos Limaylla explained that the *ayllus* under his rule had contributed 7,070 gold pesos for the 1562 journey to Spain of his brother Don Felipe Guacrapaucar. Don Felipe had been actively involved in the prepara-tion of a famous set of *probanzas*, intended for the eyes of His Majesty, which documented the contributions of the Luringuanca *ayllus* during the conquest and pacification of the Andes. Through unknown channels, Guacrapaucar reached Spain and started following the itinerant court in 1562. For several months prior to his return to Jauja in 1564, Don Felipe campaigned to secure royal decrees instructing the *audiencia* to hear the natives' complaints on several issues, some related to the protection of communal land and cattle and the defense of political autonomy vis-à-vis Spanish magistrates, *encomenderos*, and municipal council officials. To raise the money needed, and following the system of proportional allocations, the different *ayllus* of Luringuanca sold livestock, coca, maize, and other communal assets before and after Don Felipe's voyage, meticulously recording transactions on *khipus*.[42]

Don Felipe's journey to the royal court in Castile highlights the link between indigenous litigation and self-auditing mechanisms. Some authorities in the communities of Luringuanca held Don Felipe partially accountable after his return for the legal and administrative expenses that he incurred during his long journey. In 1566, some *caciques* and cord-keepers complained to a Spanish magistrate that, after evaluating the tangible outcomes of this transatlantic affair, they had concluded that Don Felipe had received money in excess. The *cacique* had promised to obtain a royal decree excusing the natives of his *repartimiento* from tribute obligations, but he failed to secure the coveted royal concession. Therefore, the *caciques* argued that a fair portion of the original contribution should be returned to their *ayllus*. Some also questioned Don Felipe's securing of a coat of arms, a perpetual pension, and a plot of land while in Spain—all royal favors perceived to benefit the *cacique* and his immediate kin directly, as opposed to enhancing the welfare of the Luringuanca peoples that Don Felipe had been sent to promote.[43]

Moreover, the aggrieved party pointed out that Don Felipe had spent some of the money, around a thousand gold pesos, to purchase merchandise to be sold in Peru, allegedly for private gain, a charge that Guacrapaucar denied.[44] To substantiate their claim, the Indian officials displayed their *khipus* and declared the amount of money contributed by each *ayllu*. Native authorities at the *parcialidad* level were careful to note that the money they had given to Don Felipe was not the property of any particular *cacique* or individual— not even themselves—but "belongs to our communities and has not been returned to us," thus pointing toward another central aspect of sixteenth-century indigenous legal activism and social mediation.[45]

LITIGATION AS *SAPCI*

The voices of Huanca lords come to us through the words of an interpreter assigned to Toledo's 1570 inquest.[46] This level of mediation hinders our understanding of the original concepts introduced by the *caciques* in their native language.[47] Nonetheless, the sworn statement of Don Pedro Yaldama, chief accountant and *khipu* master of the town of Mataguasi in Luringuanca, offers an important clue about the categories and principles that Toledo's staff were translating. In 1566, Yaldama testified against Don Felipe Guacrapaucar, the lord who had resided at the Habsburg court between 1562 and 1564. Yaldama declared, through the words of a Spanish-Quechua interpreter, that the money given to Guacrapaucar to fund his journey derived from the sale of coca, cattle, and cloth that belonged to "the poor and the community" (*los pobres y comunidad*).[48] One should not understand *los pobres*—literally, the poor or destitute—in a narrow sense. Acute observers at the time also linked the phrase to those who could not rely on themselves or next of kin to aid in fulfilling agricultural and other tasks; they depended on support from the larger *ayllu* and community for survival.[49] Although the inquest does not elaborate on the original expression used by Yaldama, the chronicler Felipe Guaman Poma de Ayala, writing at the beginning of the seventeenth century, helps us identify the ideas presented by the accountant and other native leaders.

As to the rhetorical question posed by King Philip III himself on how the Indians of the kingdom would enrich themselves and prosper, Guaman Poma replied, "I should let Your Majesty know that they must hold some property in common (*hacienda de comunidad*), which they call *sapci*" (Figure 2.2).[50] In this imaginary dialogue with Philip and throughout his work, Guaman Poma applied the "law" and practice of *sapci* to three strategic resources: foodstuffs, herds, and textiles.[51] Moreover, as Frank Salomon observes, Guaman Poma's *sapci* was a "half-ancient, half-innovative" institution that, in the chronicler's estimation, provided a legitimate continuity to the Andean pre-Inca, Inca, and Toledan eras under the concept of good government.[52] By the early seventeenth century, native Andeans were also applying the term *sapci* to community welfare deposits (*collcas*), which Guaman Poma accurately defines as "community storehouses and *sapci*."[53] Upon the implementation of the model of the nucleated village in the Andes in the late 1560s and 1570s, storehouses came to be part of the architectural complex that native authorities devoted to the administration and protection of intracommunal holdings. The notion of *sapci*, symbolized by the colonial *collca*, came to encompass a productive base, specifically an agricultural field or herd; the amount of col-

FIGURE 2.2

Felipe Guaman Poma presents his Corónica *to Philip III. From* Felipe Guaman
Poma de Ayala, El primer nueva corónica y buen gobierno, *961[975].*
Royal Danish Library, GKS 2232 quarto.

lective labor applied to it; and the infrastructure and technologies needed to
count, store, use, and defend these resources under the new Spanish regime
(Figure 2.3).[54]

By 1615, then, Felipe Guaman Poma was clearly describing a widespread
regime of production, consumption, and accumulation under the category
of *sapci*, a social and economic system that operated above and beyond the
household and *ayllu* subsistence levels. Its main purpose was to generate a
"contingency" or "welfare" surplus fund that Andean leaders could use in
multiple scenarios and with different degrees of autonomy. Guaman Poma
offered examples of this category, which he frequently glossed as "communal
assets" (*hacienda de comunidad*), applying it to the affairs of everyday life in
the Andes.

FIGURE 2.3

Steward of communal deposits and sapci. *From* Felipe Guaman Poma de Ayala, El primer
nueva corónica y buen gobierno, *808[822]. Royal Danish Library, GKS 2232 quarto.*

Like the Huanca accountant Don Pedro Yaldama before him, Guaman
Poma linked *sapci* to the poor and destitute of the communities. He also explained that May was the period in which native authorities inspected *sapci*
foodstuffs and the common herds, reprimanding the stewards of communal
assets if they had not kept good and straightforward accountings.[55] July, in
turn, was associated with storage of harvested produce in communal ware-
houses, counting of common herd animals, and redistribution of agricultural
plots. Native authorities set aside a portion of fruits and vegetables not destined for immediate consumption, depositing them in special facilities, which
Guaman Poma identified as belonging "to the poor Indians [*yndios pobres*]
and to the communities."[56] During the same month, *caciques* inspected fields,
just as the *ayllus* were about to begin a new agricultural cycle. They redistributed land and water rights among active households and *ayllus*, assigning un-

used lands (*tierras ualdias*) and water to "the poor." The *caciques* made sure that even if these people could not work the plots themselves, others farmed them "for the community and sapci," thereby fulfilling a basic social obligation. Collective fields were called *sapci chacara*, with produce redistributed during times of low agricultural yields.[57] Ideally, then, *sapci* funds were the output of the able-bodied members of the different *ayllus*, and as such, that which was common to all. In this case, "the poor" stood for the community as a whole and, potentially, for each of its members. Anyone could fall on hard times.[58]

Thus "the poor" constituted a broad social category that incorporated different classes and their immediate circumstances: orphans and widows who could not rely on close kin, men and women who had already served their community (*biejos pasados*), and members who were "impeded" from serving (*impedidos*), such as the sick and handicapped. According to the chronicler, it was only fair that these individuals be exempted (*reservados*) from tributary duties, instead covered by funds drawn from the "community and *sapci*" (*comonidad y sapci*).[59] A seventeenth-century census of Jauja shows the vitality of these social categories and their close relationship to *sapci* and community. Each *ayllu*, irrespective of the town to which its members had been relocated, classified its tributary population as active (*efectivos*), retired or no longer tributary (*pasados de tasa*), deceased (*muertos*), or absent (*ausentes*).[60] In sum, *sapci* funds and endowments could be enjoyed by inactive or disabled community members. Because of age or some other permanent or temporary circumstance, they could not be expected to participate full time in the production process. Even they, however, were expected to contribute to the reproduction of *sapci* resources, or to other productive and ritual activities according to age and ability. In a way, even the dead who were listed in official rolls had access to these funds.[61]

The planning and funding of communitywide litigation in early colonial Peru fell under the category of *comunidad y sapci* and was governed by the same social norms. In his admonitions to King Philip, Guaman Poma listed mills, vineyards, textile workshops, tanneries, and even liens (*censos*) on real estate as examples of communal endowments administered according to this regime.[62] The use of these assets for the reproduction of *sapci* norms and endowments circa 1615, when the *Nueva corónica* was completed, shows that some native communities and their legal intermediaries had successfully adapted and expanded this traditional law to deal with the judicial system and the impositions of colonialism. Just as important, litigating *caciques* were expected to reciprocate by giving back to the *ayllu* by obtaining rulings, royal decrees, and other grants and exemptions for the group—a skill that was to

37

become the mark of a good Andean leader, regardless of blood. Indian leaders were expected to return to the community welfare fund any money remaining after litigation expenses were paid, either in cash or through institutionalized generosity and hospitality.[63] To criticize his own brother before the commoners of Luringuanca, Don Felipe Guacrapaucar often said, "What kind of *cacique* is this Don Carlos that he does not seek justice in Lima?" Successful litigation was, from this perspective, the *caciques'* expected contribution to the protection and reproduction of *sapci*.[64]

In describing their communities' *pleitos* of the 1550s and 1560s, the lords of Jauja pointed toward *sapci* funds and the stream of revenue they generated as essential resources for financing costly and lengthy legal cases. In 1570, the official interpreter glossed the original expression as *bienes del común* or *hacienda de los pobres y comunidad*. However, it is very likely that the original Quechua term *sapci* was used in this context. It remained in use at least until the mid-seventeenth century, when it resurfaces in other local documents from Jauja and elsewhere.[65] Behind this broad term, *ayllus* and their leaders operated as the main keepers of this endowment. Though almost always hidden in the documents of the era, these social segments, supported by *sapci* regimes, were also some of the main litigants in the king's courts.[66]

THE PRICE OF JUSTICE

The *repartimientos* of Jauja still held significant *sapci* endowments in the mid-seventeenth century. Back in the 1560s, the Ananguancas received a donation of 8,000 pesos as restitution from Antonio de Ribera, their guilt-ridden *encomendero*. The native leaders invested a portion of these funds, which were probably initially held in the first *cajas de comunidad* (community chests), in liens against real estate in Lima, either directly or through the Caja General de Censos in Lima.[67] Around the same time, the *ayllus* of Luringuanca added similar restitutions and donations of cattle, vineyards, and houses in Huamanga to their already substantial collective assets. Archbishop Toribio de Mogrovejo's inspection of the Lima diocese lists 50,000 llamas as part of their endowment at the end of the sixteenth century. The Luringuanca *ayllus* later secured other resources, especially land through titles granted by the Crown. The revenues from these lands, along with those obtained from the sale of communal cattle, were placed into a series of similar investments in Lima and Huamanga. Throughout the sixteenth and seventeenth centuries, the *caciques* and indigenous officials of the *cabildo* rented out communal property and lent hundreds of pesos to individuals and institutions. In the city of Huamanga and its hinterland alone, in the mid-seventeenth century, these communal assets were valued at 10,000 pesos.[68]

Part of this revenue supplemented the payment of the *repartimiento*'s annual tribute, some 9,000 pesos at the turn of the seventeenth century.[69] Another portion, however, was designated for financing the community's legal affairs in Peru and Spain. Royal justice was seldom free, despite the series of decrees exempting Indian commoners and communities from legal fees. Court cases could cost significant amounts of money. According to Toledo's estimates, the Luringuancas had spent more than 17,800 pesos in the 1560s alone on different court cases taken before the *audiencia* and the *Consejo de Indias*. Overall, the valley communities had disbursed more than 30,000 pesos of communal funds for traveling to the *audiencia* and hiring advocates, attorneys, interpreters, and solicitors. To this figure, the communities had to add the human cost: the many natives, more than six hundred according to one estimate, who had perished as a result of the ten-day journey across the Andes.[70] In *pleitos* pitting *caciques* against *ayllus* and their *principales*, the communities of Luringuanca had spent 6,800 pesos, roughly eight and a half times the combined yearly salaries of all the *caciques* of the *repartimiento* around this time. To put these amounts in perspective, travelers passing through the valley paid a fraction of a peso for three pounds of bread, a peso for a sheep, and a peso and a half for one and a half bushels of maize.[71] In light of other documented cases, these legal expenses do not seem excessive or fictitious.[72]

Thus, Toledo's 1570 investigation revealed what the Huanca people knew very well: litigating and soliciting in colonial Peru was expensive. In order to absorb the high costs, local authorities and *ayllus* planning to engage with the court system tried to supplement *sapci* funds with regular and extraordinary levies of collective labor and goods, the last of which the documents often call *derramas*.[73] There was clearly a political economy of the *pleito* at play. For the Huancas and other Andean groups, litigating meant assessing the immediate or long-term value of the resource or exemption being litigated against the cost of local, regional, and transoceanic litigation. Like other polities, the communities of Jauja continued to fight in the courts of Lima and Castile for a reduction of both their tribute and *mita* population quotas over the next 150 years, probably at a very elevated cost. Given what was at stake, however, it was worth the investment.[74] The evidence suggests that other indigenous communities simply could not afford these initiatives, especially if they entailed journeying to Lima or Madrid.[75]

The amply documented legal activism of certain groups is hard to explain without taking into account the inner workings of *sapci* resources. After the formal implementation of the system of public legal assistance in 1574–1575, discussed later, Crown-appointed legal aides, mainly public defenders and attorneys for the Indians, were supposed to charge reduced fees or no fees at all to native claimants. This meant that many of the informal and extralegal costs simply never made it into the historical record. Scattered evidence for the first two centuries of colonial rule shows that fees and other costs of gaining access to the justice system did not disappear but were simply not recorded. In fact, it can be argued that the payment of legal and extralegal fees for indigenous plaintiffs and petitioners appearing before the *audiencia* continued throughout the colonial period. Let us take a closer look at these expenses.[76]

The communities of Jauja, perhaps like many other communities throughout the Andes, spent a significant portion of their *sapci* funds on *sacar provisiones*, securing favorable rulings from the *Audiencia de Lima* and taking notarized copies back to the community. The fees of private attorneys and solicitors, scribes, interpreters, and even witnesses, some apparently paid in kind directly from *sapci* funds, labor, and lands, only added to expenses.[77] At the turn of the seventeenth century, native plaintiffs appearing before the *audiencia* could spend sixty pesos to hire a private attorney and half that amount to secure a solicitor for a single court case.[78] Having a petition drafted in Lima could cost between eight and ten pesos in 1585. In 1620, however, one community paid six times that amount to have theirs delivered in secret all the way to the *Consejo de Indias*. Having the secretariat of government dispatch a copy of a decree could add another thirty pesos. Some notaries also demanded payment to look up past lawsuits and other papers in their records. Litigation in local courts continued to be a heavy burden to many indigenous litigants during the rest of the Habsburg period.[79]

In addition to these expenses, native claimants participated fully in the economy of favor and engaged in the networks of patronage and dependence that held viceregal and royal courts together. As in Castile, litigants offered bribes, gifts, and bonuses to influence judicial decisions or curry favor with court officials.[80] Don Carlos Apoalaya, *cacique* of Ananguanca, became famous in mid-seventeenth-century Peru for the "copious gifts of gold and silver" that he made to different viceroys, including a pair of "large scissors made of gold" that he dispatched to the viceroy to strengthen a previous "generous gift."[81] Such "gracious" or "voluntary" donations (*donativos graciosos*) were especially useful for winning the king's favor. During the last three decades of the sixteenth century alone, the communities of Jauja donated the staggering sum of 200,000 pesos from their common funds to the Crown with the hope that, as a royal representative had promised, His Majesty would perpetually exempt them from *mita* labor at the mercury mines. The offer never materialized.[82]

INDIGENOUS STEWARDS: MANAGING THE COMMONS

Aside from money, gaining access to the justice system rested on building wider structures and appointing community agents for administering *sapci* holdings. It also depended on securing effective legal representation through communal attorneys. Control over community treasuries and endowments was highly contested. Although cross-complaints of corruption and mis-appropriation among priests, *corregidores* (local magistrates), *caciques*, and *cabildo* officials were indeed chronic, Andean communities relied on inter-nal management mechanisms, based on consensus-building and internal decision-making processes, whenever possible. Though very difficult to trace in the sources, these mechanisms seem to have gone beyond the particular interests, alliances, and actions of the traditional aristocracy to involve other indigenous intermediaries and even commoners. The strategic investment of *sapci* funds and the periodic election of indigenous stewards and *procuradores* to maintain direct control over these funds must have become an important vehicle for wider communal participation.[83]

In a series of decrees and ordinances issued between 1569 and 1575, in part inspired by his experience in Jauja, Viceroy Toledo outlined the ways he expected native authorities to organize, register, and manage community endowments. Particularly relevant were his "General Ordinances for Com-munal Life in Indian Towns."[84] Toledo's reorganizations were a response to local conditions but also an attempt to reshape such conditions according to the communitarian traditions of agro-pastoral municipalities in early mod-ern Castile. As stated by Thomas Abercrombie, "Nearly all the institutions that Toledo instructed his visitors to establish had precedents in Castilian villas."[85] Thus, the infrastructures and spaces that Indians were to develop in the 1570s and 1580s for the administration of *bienes de comunidad* stemmed from natives' creative adaptation of traditional *sapci* regimes to deeply rooted traditions imported from Spain. Colonial *sapci* practice was much more than a continuation of a former use.[86]

Toledo initially entrusted colonial bureaucrats such as the *corregidor* and *administrador de bienes de comunidad* (steward of communal assets), almost invariably Spaniards, with overseeing *sapci* funds at local and provincial levels. Nevertheless, the viceroy, guided by his now proverbial animosity toward *caciques*, left the everyday management to officials of indigenous town councils. Moreover, he ordered the appointment of communal administrators or stewards to be directly in charge of accounting, storage, and circulation of *sapci* funds and resources within the *pueblo* or *repartimiento*.[87] According to the plan for *pueblo* design that spread throughout the Andes, the community houses (*casas de comunidad*) were to comprise communal storehouses, to hold cloth, maize, potatoes, and other goods, and community treasuries (*cajas de comunidad*). Storehouses, built adjacent to the town hall in the main square, guaranteed the safeguarding and reproduction of *sapci* goods. Toledo's idea was to guarantee that *sapci* funds would be under the purview of elected authorities in the town council.[88]

As they implemented this infrastructure, native communities adapted Toledo's ordinances to their own interests and practices.[89] In a way, the search for freedom to invest and administer collective assets, whether alienable lands, herds, or funds from market activities, makes the development of colonial *sapci* regimes a response to the initial control held by Spanish authorities such as the *corregidor*. Taking a significant step, the *ayllus* of Jauja campaigned in the 1580s to remove the Spanish administrator and entrust management of *sapci* holdings to *caciques* and local stewards.[90] Thanks to these negotiations, by the early 1590s *repartimientos* were keeping tribute and *sapci* funds in two separate strongboxes to meet normal expenses and as a contingency fund outside supervision by Spanish authorities. In an effort to preserve resources, unspent funds periodically passed from the "tribute" to the "community" lockbox in the sixteenth century, speaking to the relative agency and freedom to use such resources.[91] Although the Spanish magistrate kept one of the keys to the *cajas*, he held no direct control over its contents, relinquishing it to the local steward, usually a *cacique* or a *principal* who had been selected at a general council meeting or assembly. The Jauja strongbox contained the silver generated through the *sapci* regime, which the *ayllus* tried to spend as they saw fit.[92]

The case of the Huancas, as well as that of the neighboring province of Lucanas, reveals that community lockboxes doubled as archives—another important resource for success in courtrooms.[93] Stored records, available to *cabildo* and *repartimiento* procurators, contained, often in separate books, inventories of communal rents and holdings as well as partial or full transcriptions of titles, deeds, donations, and other original documents guaranteeing the rights of the *ayllus* to their endowment.[94] Felipe Guacrapaucar brought from Spain so many decrees that the papers barely fit in the chest where the Luringuancas stored them. Don Carlos Apoalaya, another local *cacique*, claimed to have had another chest filled with legal documents in his possession until Toledo ordered them burned during his visit to Jauja. By the time of Toledo's 1570 inquiry, the natives had managed to put together their own "strongbox and archive" (*caxa y archibo*).[95]

Town stewards combined alphabetic writing with knotted cords, working alongside indigenous accountants and town scribes or sometimes occupying these posts themselves.[96] In Jauja during the 1580s, these *mayordomos* kept a "community book" (*libro de comunidad*), which Guaman Poma significantly calls "account book of the property of the poor Indians, both male and female." This book helped organize accounts and present them to the *corregidor* and local priests. Native tax collectors registered the payments in kind from commoners using knotted strings, then delivered the goods to *caciques* and stewards for registration in the community book and sale at public auction. *Khipus* and alphabetic records became indispensable whenever initiating a complaint against a priest or magistrate. Like officials on the indigenous municipal council, some stewards were subject to internal audits during the annual or biannual meeting (*cabildo* or *asamblea*), often held at the beginning of the year. On such occasions, indigenous accountants and stewards balanced their books and *khipus* and, if being replaced in their posts, turned over communal holdings to incoming officials.[97]

Given the centrality of managing *sapci* resources and keeping written records as a means to pursue cases in the legal system, native groups in Jauja kept affairs as internal as possible. As prescribed in the Toledan legislation inspired by the Castilian precedent, native Andeans were to gather in town meetings periodically to discuss communal affairs and coordinate the different *parcialidades*, especially if collective endowments were to be invested in legal matters.[98] If the still mysterious and poorly understood workings of the Andean *cabildos* resembled those in Mesoamerican ones, elections and town meetings granted commoners a "voice" in some decisions.[99]

The use of collective funds to link the communities of Jauja with the larger framework of the Habsburg state is further evidence of the importance of periodic meetings. Certain communal investments, especially real estate, point to the creation, through the law of *sapci*, of a more permanent infrastructure associated with seeking justice and favor at the viceregal court. The ownership of real estate in colonial centers such as Lima and Huamanga is a case in point. In the 1550s the Luringuancas acquired houses in Lima, the seat of the *audiencia* and an important locus of legal activities. In the 1560s and 1570s, royal officials assigned the earliest lots (*solares*) in El Cercado, the Indian ward gradually taking shape on the eastern side of Lima.[100] Distribution was based on ethnic affiliation and geographic origin, and lots were intended for lodging the *repartimiento*'s temporary workers (*mitayos*) fulfilling *mita* duties in the city. After appraising each lot, officials prorated its value among the tribute payers of Luringuanca, turning it into a communal asset, paid for according to the law of *sapci*.[101] Such urban dwellings soon expanded their original function to include lodging for indigenous authorities sojourning in Lima to collect debts and communal revenues or to litigate before the *audiencia* or archbishopric.[102] As Viceroy Toledo's 1570 investigation and other independent testimony attest, native lords journeying to Lima were accompanied by an entourage of messengers and retainers (eight to ten in the case of the polities of Jauja). Because litigation could extend for months or even years, owning houses in Lima must have shielded visitors from some of the costs of living and litigating.[103]

Moreover, some *casas y tiendas* (houses and stores) collectively owned by Jauja *ayllus* were outside El Cercado, on the west side of Lima's main square. Some were built below the portals occupied by scribal offices, only a few steps from the viceroy's palace and the *audiencia*. Native authorities rented out these houses, purchased and maintained with communal funds, to notaries and others, generating a secure source of income.[104] Just as important, the specific locations, along with the professional identities of some occupants, hints at the relevance that such assets had for community businesses where the written word was the fundamental interface. Some indigenous scribes, interpreters, and procurators probably received informal training at communal houses.[105]

INDIGENOUS ATTORNEYS:
REPRESENTING THE COMMONS

Who were these communal legal agents? Accessing the justice system required Andean communities to develop their own legal specialists. Native *procuradores* came to play a strategic role in weaving Indian communities into the fabric of the Habsburg imperial state. Town attorneys often became conduits for transmitting legal knowledge and expertise from village to village, *repartimiento* to *repartimiento*, and beyond. They also mastered different legal registers and discourses. Local attorneys were instrumental to the networks of communication through which laws, legal concepts, and news developed, circulated, and took root in different regions.[106] Being called *licenciados* by other community members is an indicator that some of these communal attorneys were clearly very knowledgeable in the laws and judicial procedures of the kingdom. Their election by colonial authorities as "defenders" of other Indians in local court cases is another one.[107] Communal procurators could pen petitions in Spanish and handle legal documents, but one of their most significant tasks was that of legal representation: to embody the corporate identity of their community, to impart upon it its juridical personhood. Along with the traditional *cacique* class, with which it overlapped, communal attorneys became an emblem of their *república* or *comunidad* as a distinct political body whose interests would be heard in the king's courts.

The annual or biannual election of Indian procurators coincided with that of other *oficiales de república*: municipal magistrates, aldermen, bailiffs, and stewards of communal assets. Toledo's 1575 ordinances gave the task of electing new officials to the incumbents. On New Year's Eve, with the Indian scribe writing down the proceedings, the currently serving officials were to gather in the town hall and cast a vote for their candidates. Those with the most votes would then be registered by the same scribe on the final list and later invested by the local *corregidor*. The ceremony consisted of bestowing the *vara* (royal staff). The new officers were to serve for one or two years.[108] Although not much about indigenous electoral customs during the Habsburg period is known, late seventeenth-century data from the Peruvian northern coast indicates that some town attorneys were selected by "popular acclamation," by the candidate of the incumbent officials, or according to the wishes of the *caciques* or the Spanish magistrate—even if this use of customary law meant going against the Toledan ordinances. In these cases, the assembled electors sought consensus rather than the more potentially divisive casting of votes.[109]

Future studies of Andean municipal councils' internal elections may reveal a significant degree of local variation. Almost certainly, distance from Spanish oversight—particularly the *corregidor's*—along with customary practices and politicking, helped shape distinct local experiences across the Andean region. Per the ordinances of the kingdom, reelection was forbidden and procurators were to be replaced periodically. Yet, as in the case of communal stewards, the communal attorneys' activities relied on specialized knowledge and skills and required some familiarity with procedural rules. Because of their qualifications, some village or *repartimiento* attorneys probably held their positions repeatedly for many years. Although their salary was to be paid by the community, some attorneys used their own resources to partially cover litigation costs. Serving as procurator, then, could become someone's self-funded "duty" to the community. The *procuraduría* was probably one rung in the ladder of civil-ecclesiastic offices that was beginning to crystallize in the seventeenth century.[110]

Toledo envisioned one attorney for each Indian town, but in some regions there was a procurator-general for a *repartimiento*.[111] It was probably an attempt, on the part of the communities, to share costs. This broadening of the procurators' jurisdiction could also imply a concession from the supreme government to communities seeking to replace Spanish procurators with native ones. This might explain why some seventeenth- and eighteenth-century procurators-general claimed to have received their title directly from the viceroy.[112] Furthermore, following Toledo's ordinances, some communities institutionalized the practice of empowering their own procurators during the town council meeting, in anticipation of the next year's legal activities.[113] Toledo's regulations had also prescribed the celebration of weekly *asambleas*, often in the municipal hall of the main town of the province or *repartimiento*. During *asambleas*, indigenous leaders were to discuss "everything related to their community goods and other affairs pertaining to their Republic."[114] Natives quickly appropriated this space, re-creating some previous meanings (and perhaps prolonging the *caciques'* traditional roles) and redefining some main functions.[115] Though primarily intended for electing new officials and assessing the performance of outgoing ones, *asambleas* became an ideal venue for deposing illegitimate authorities and resolving local disputes, orally or in writing, especially the mismanagement or appropriation of collective assets. Thus, gathering for a town hall meeting (*hacer cabildo*) also meant to hold court.

Asambleas were the also place for lodging formal complaints, often prepared with the aid of *corregidores* and parish priests (and sometimes even against them). Indigenous communities could also file complaints against stewards of church and confraternity funds. Church stewards were supposed to settle accounts periodically, especially when being replaced by new officials. Their performance in office was subject to review by municipal authorities, administrators of communal funds, priests, and perhaps even *corregidores*, thus configuring a typical scenario for competing jurisdictions to wear each other out.[116]

Casting lots, voting, or deliberating in favor of or against initiating or continuing legal action, at least by the *caciques* and other authorities, was probably on the agenda.[117] The decision was made to reach out to defenders for the Indians and ecclesiastic judges, depending on the available resources and the jurisdiction that seemed most appropriate. Guaman Poma offers a composite picture of steps followed by countless native plaintiffs when filing court cases and petitions. Leaders and commoners gathered in a *cabildo* or *audiencia* to discuss individual and collective grievances, demanding the presence of municipal judges, *caciques*, and stewards. After determining the appropriate jurisdiction in which to sue, natives formalized complaints by having *caciques*, municipal scribes, *repartimiento* attorneys, or other literate agents draft and sign petitions, presenting them to the defender, ecclesiastic judge, or civil magistrate. Some petitions were written in Quechua, suggesting they were generated internally.[118]

An appeal to Lima's royal and ecclesiastical courts or the *Consejo de Indias* in Spain was probably also decided.[119] *Cabildos* also became the locus for indigenous municipal and church authorities to decide upon legal strategies, draft initial petitions and accusations, and select and empower town and *repartimiento* procurators to act on their behalf. Just as important, assemblies and legal facilitators became the vital nexus between Andean rural communities and the middle echelons of the imperial judicial system, an intermediate space where monarchical rule was constantly negotiated. A series of powers of attorney granted by the Luringuanca communities to delegates between the 1640s and 1660s reveals how administrators of *sapci* funds took an active part in planning legal action. Furthermore, indigenous delegates, usually *caciques*, procurators, or accountants, journeyed to Lima, Huamanga, or the mining center of Huancavelica; collected debts and interest owed to the community; rented or sold vacant properties; reinvested capital gains; and summoned tributaries who had run away to avoid making payment. Any money collected was to be brought to the community treasuries of the province. On certain occasions, native authorities authorized delegates to carry out tasks or present demands to the *audiencia*, such as seeking a reduction in tribute dues or the commutation of certain tribute items for money. In other cases, they were to meet and empower Spanish advocates and laymen to represent the interests of their communities in legal forums. This scene repeated itself over the years. In Huamanga alone the delegates of Luringuanca collected several thousand pesos—an average of six or seven hundred annually—as goods that belonged to *sapci*, which they used in part to undertake the very legal actions that so infuriated Viceroy Francisco de Toledo in the 1570s.[120]

Unlike appointed *caciques* and governors, who were subject to the burdensome duties of their posts, procurators enjoyed a greater freedom of movement. Their activities help us understand how indigenous-Spanish justice actually functioned in colonial Peru. Through procurators and delegates, indigenous people were able to interact with the web of local, provincial, and viceregal defenders of the Indians who, while guaranteeing the natives' "protection," also guarded the gates of law and justice. As much as these defenders, communal attorneys helped to articulate local, regional, and imperial spheres of justice. Native procurators from all over the Andes converged on provincial cities or the viceregal capital for legal business, where they gained from other litigants and attorneys valuable information that they would share upon returning to their towns and villages. Well-known *procuradores* for the so-called

"Indian Nation" (*Nación Índica*) or the "Indians of Peru," active at the royal court especially in the eighteenth century, stemmed from a local tradition deeply connected to the proper management of *sapci* funds.

TOWARD RECENTERING THE PUEBLO

This reconstruction of Huanca interactions with the court system over a century has revealed the centrality of collective endowments and *cabildo* officials for understanding Andean efforts at attaining justice. What larger implications can be drawn from this microhistory of *sapci* endowments, village attorneys, and *cabildo* structures? This chapter has sought to recenter the *pueblo* as a governing council of indigenous collective legal activism. Traditional mechanisms for allocating labor and, after the Spanish Conquest, apportioning tribute quotas among *ayllus* underscored communitywide litigation and the search for favor at local and metropolitan courts, thus subjecting this type of legal initiative to the social rules, practices, and expectations governing *sapci* endowments and funds. The chance to evaluate the performance of *pueblo* and multi-*pueblo* authorities in charge of collective resources and to hold leaders accountable for mismanagement or misappropriation of *sapci* legal funds was embedded in the planning and assessment of collective action that *khipus* facilitated and *cabildos* made possible. These interwoven processes conferred a moderate, yet previously overlooked, degree of control over legal strategies and decisions to midranking *ayllu* and *cabildo* authorities and, ultimately, to Andean commoners.

There is much to gain from this recentering of indigenous collective legal experiences. By moving away from the still-dominant world of traditional elites, the litigation-as-*sapci* model highlights the contributions of other local legal facilitators and literate agents, some of whom were also versed in the art of the *khipu*. *Cabildo* scribes, town procurators, and stewards of communal endowments also became actively engaged in litigation. This privileged constellation of *cabildo* and *repartimiento* intermediaries and the traditional segment of native *caciques* and *gobernadores* only partially overlapped, thus making possible identifications between these two groups a matter for further research. The deployment of strategies was an expression of creative mediation that infused colonial legal practices with multiple Andean meanings. These strategies not only reveal certain principles of communal consciousness and basic considerations of social balance; they were also essential to allowing intermediaries to exercise and remain in their positions as such. After all, constant access to the justice system constituted a significant effort on the part of Andean groups and intermediaries to uphold basic social norms constantly being transgressed, sometimes from within, by agents of the new colonial order, *caciques* included.

Continual efforts at compromise and consensus-building likely developed inside native governing councils and regular assemblies whenever there was a need to set *sapci* funds aside for litigation, to adopt a specific course of legal action, to prosecute or drop a lawsuit, or to appoint and dispatch native procurators to the viceregal capital. A further exploration of these internal mechanisms and the main actors involved in them might help us refine our understanding of broad categories such as "*cacique*" or "Andean elite." Especially in rural settings, the interlocking of *cacique* and *cabildo* power, at least in community lockboxes and *sapci* litigation funds, seems to have been more significant than previously thought. Among the Huancas, commoners generated the surplus needed by authorities to seek legal redress. In some instances, tribute-payers themselves seem to have been at least partially and indirectly involved in initiating legal efforts that depended on ad hoc funds and collective endowments, likely bringing problems and complaints to the attention of their leaders during periodic meetings and demanding that they engage with royal authorities at local, regional, and metropolitan levels. In other cases, native leaders must have acted on their own initiative, identifying problems and then requisitioning additional funds and communal backing to resolve them in the courts.

The *ayllus* of the Jauja Valley were likely not unique in communal strategies for gaining access to the justice system by effectively managing collective holdings. New research will help to refine the litigation-as-*sapci* model, particularly for Andean polities and communities less prosperous or cohesive and more isolated. Their remote geographic locations and the relative absence of collective endowments due to mismanagement and privatization, permanent migration, land dispossession, and excessive fiscal burdens must have meant that many communities did not enjoy ready access to Lima's superior court. In that sense, the peaks and downturns in indigenous engagements with the justice system throughout the colonial period could be also linked to the increases and declines in the collective holdings' proximity to courts, as well as the particular actions of those in charge of defending and expanding them—and not only to the venality and corruption of colonial judges, the varying policies of the Crown, or greater access to the legal system after the 1570s judicial reforms.

Throughout the Habsburg period, the Huancas and other native groups encountered a stable and predictable system of courts, magistrates, and legal practitioners. Despite its cumbersome nature and the constant complaints of colonial users, this apparatus quickly became a multifaceted interface connecting Spain with its New World empire. But, far from being a structure imposed by the Crown or its ministers from above, it became an organic social reality also built from the bottom up. Native officials, litigants, and petitioners helped to construct it, infusing it with a life of its own and shaping it through countless interactions at the local and regional levels. As a result, the justice system helped bring local experiences and concrete cases into imperial debates and policies at the time. This constant appeal to viceregal and imperial courts promoted a legal consciousness sensitive to the basic written genres, archival practices, and bureaucratic vectors through which litigants and seekers of office, grace, and favor moved from the Andes to the metropolis and back. In the imagination of native plaintiffs and defendants, this Crown-endorsed interface—a vast transoceanic judicial arena—encouraged training of communal delegates and their dispatch to Lima and eventually Castile, as well as the later reliance on more ambitious attorneys for the Indians to reach out to the distant king and his body of close advisers. To these Andean cosmopolitans the rest of this book is devoted.

THREE

THE EXPANDING WEB

Indigenous Claimants Join the Early Modern Atlantic

After licentiate Pedro de la Gasca's "pacification" campaign of the late 1540s, Crown officials and Spanish settlers had barely finished redistributing the wealthiest Andean *encomiendas* when colonial reformers faced the increasing need to keep natives within clear geographic and juridical boundaries. In an influential 1567 treatise, Juan de Matienzo, supreme justice of the *audiencia* established in Charcas in 1559, reflected on his experiences of governance during the two preceding decades, a period of generalized experimentation in imperial statecraft. It had also been a time of expanding indigenous litigation, which Matienzo and his fellow justices in the three *audiencia* seats of Charcas, Quito, and Lima had witnessed firsthand and criticized. An outspoken critic of "litigiousness" and a prominent advocate for resettling natives in permanent Iberian-style villages (*pueblos* or *reducciones*), Matienzo argued that established custom in Spain had been for the king's subjects to live "anywhere they wished." Nevertheless, His Majesty could not allow the same unrestricted liberty among *naturales* of the New World. Their freedom, Matienzo contended, was bound by considerations of a higher order. "Nature" had created Indians to obey and serve. Though free vassals of the king, and therefore not subject to servitude, they had to be compelled to do "that which is good for them [like] a tutor does with a minor under his care," even if (or perhaps precisely because) their natural inclinations constantly drove them to err.[1]

For Matienzo, therefore, the king no doubt had the legitimate supreme authority to coerce his native subjects into relocating to the villages soon to be designed and founded en masse across the vast Andean landscape and to remain there, thus revoking Iberian freedom of movement. (In fact, Matienzo was providing the legal framework for extending previous isolated *reducción* experiments to a grand practice.) The same royal imperative, Matienzo argued, allowed the sovereign to also command or force his Indian vassals to work *outside* their towns whenever he understood that the resulting displacements—temporary, regulated, and supervised—would contribute to the greater good and the preservation and prosperity of the kingdom. Even at the risk of death, Indian laborers would sometimes have to abandon their homes, lands, and families and journey from the lowlands to the highlands and vice-versa. While upholding the idea that "Indians" and their lords ought to remain in their "natural" or native homelands and the settlements specially devised for them, colonial policies also legitimized the massive displacement of a relevant segment of the native communal labor pool for two and a half centuries. Throughout the Andes, mandatory work in silver and mercury mines as well as rural and urban labor drafts (*mitas*) on behalf of this elusive *common good* became the foremost example of how Matienzo and other like-minded officials of his time, most prominently Viceroy Francisco de Toledo, tried to put this dual political project, based on fixity *and* displacement, into effect.[2]

Thus, the colonial project surely depended on immovable and strong communities reshaped after the Iberian model, but Indian town-dwellers could not enjoy the same liberties as their peninsular counterparts. As Brian Owensby observes, policy makers of the mid-colonial period came to understand native tributaries' "liberty" to be and live where they would in terms of a more restricted "freedom from being forced to live in places outside their home towns."[3] Pure-blooded natives of the kingdoms of Spain would be allowed to emigrate to the Americas, but the opposite, in the case of the Indians, would not be true.[4] They were to remain in their *naturalezas*—the ancestral homelands—as members of a distinct political community, now bound by a common juridical status as *indios* (Indians) or *naturales de las Indias* (natives of the Indies) and under the tutelage and guidance of ecclesiastical and civil authorities. The kingdom of Peru was to become their common *patria*.[5]

To make this theory a reality on a grand scale, the king had to place his justice within the Indians' reach. Antilitigation reforms, in particular, would become an important part of the *reducción* policy. Within the imperial arena where royal ministers exchanged information, debated ideas, and generated political knowledge, other theorists and policy makers concerned with the broader issues of a world empire in the making emphasized fixity, permanence, and integration—but also access to the courts. These, rather than fluidity and movement, were the perfect means for preserving the social structure and political allegiance of *others* circulating within and among the realms of the monarchy.[6]

THERE BUT NOT HERE

This chapter follows one such community and its experience: local, regional, and transatlantic Andean litigants. Because of the very nature of its movements and connections within the Andean world and across the Atlantic, it defied and partially subverted the grander schemes of local and imperial rule devised by Matienzo, Toledo, and others. Its most visible members were the indigenous voyagers, some of them plaintiffs, favor-seekers, and legal agents, traveling within the viceroyalty, especially to Lima's *audiencia*, and eventually to the Habsburg court. Matienzo and other equally influential reformers who followed posited that placing the administration of swift and effective justice in the hands of local actors was a necessary condition — albeit not the only one — if the twin goals of converting the natives to Catholicism and compelling fixed and self-sustaining communities to work for the *greater good* were to be met. In this chapter, I highlight the belief of colonial architects of the second half of the sixteenth century that, for the purpose of keeping native Andeans in their own locales, a wholesale reform of the judicial system — one that would place increasing local and transatlantic indigenous legal activism firmly under the Crown's grasp — was an important component for establishing towns and parishes where the *naturales* could live politically, in civic order and peace, that is, *en policía*.

Despite what royal and viceregal norms dictated, however, so-called ethnic groups, indigenous communities, and their delegates never became insular realities. Nor were they always tied to specific Andean locales. On the contrary, legal reform had, in important respects, the opposite effect than what Matienzo and others intended. In certain ways, social webs of pre-Hispanic origin shrank, but in other, equally important ways, these webs expanded, sometimes considerably.[7] From the mid-sixteenth century onward, Andean cosmopolitans wrote letters of attorney, engaged with court officials at different levels of the imperial judiciary (either in person or by proxy), and traveled to Castile to seek royal favor. By doing so, they helped infuse a discernible three-tiered judicial system — local, regional, and imperial — with a life of its own. Provincial and viceregal *protectores de los naturales*, Crown-appointed protectors for the Indians, charged with advocating for the natives in the court system, also played a significant part in expanding the web of legal representation, long-distance communication, and transatlantic movement available to Andean claimants. From the vantage point of indigenous polities and *pueblos* such as the Huancas of Jauja discussed in chapter 2, this system opened outward into a web of regional, viceregal, and metropolitan forums where judicial redress and royal favor were actively sought and royal justice was sometimes achieved, often with the aid of a multitude of official and informal legal facilitators. In building the colonial legal edifice, these indefatigable pilgrims, real "users" of civil and ecclesiastic courts, were as important as Juan de Matienzo and other prominent men of the law.

Links of patronage, positions of power and influence, legal representation, and long-distance communication knit this early modern community together, allowing its members to play a key function in the movement of people and the production and transmission of legal experience within the emerging Atlantic world. Creole patriotism, a shared sense of grievance, and common religious beliefs, intellectual concerns, and political projects, along with ties of kinship, reciprocal relations, a common provenance, and commercial relationships, generally patterned Andean as well as other Atlantic communities.[8] The activities of local, regional, and transatlantic Andean travelers and petitioners that this chapter follows were particularly influenced by the imperial system of justice that Andeans coconstructed in the second half of the sixteenth century. This legal interface was a multicentered hub-and-spokes structure composed of royal tribunals, appellate courts, and jurisdictions connecting the king's palace in Madrid with viceregal capitals, as well as provincial cities and towns, ultimately reaching into the Indian *repúblicas* that dotted the Andean countryside. The letter of attorney, one of the system's most flexible features, was one of the main lettered threads with which travelers, claimants, and favor-seekers wove a web of common experiences. Powers of attorney were central to the colonial legal experience and made long-distance legal representation viable, allowing many subjects of indigenous descent to experience the empire—even if they never left Peru—and to break free from the system devised in the 1560s and 1570s to confine Indians to their recently created *pueblos* and to channel complaints exclusively through Crown-appointed officials at all levels.

Litigants and favor-seekers, along with their legal documents and ideas of subjecthood, justice, and reward, moved within this larger legal framework. Without the judicial circuits shaping their spatial movements, social connections, forms of knowledge, and legal strategies would have left virtually no documentary trace. Strong interpersonal links—ties of kinship, clientage, and authority, along with traditional habits of deference—were as important for them in their efforts to cross the Atlantic as they were for other early modern individuals and communities. Moreover, these travelers and the people they represented were bound by the shared experience of the journey and, more specifically, by the strategies displayed in voyaging into the heart of empire to negotiate, sometimes in person but most times by proxy, with the king and his ministers. These movements rested on delegated agency, common legal experience, and judicial knowledge, developed gradually as a result of countless interactions with the courts and magistrates of the Habsburg era. The most significant historical development was the production, accumulation, and transmission of the legal capital that came to sustain a series of eighteenth-century campaigns orchestrated by the Indian elite of Lima and their rural allies.

The focus of this chapter on the Atlantic community's "Indian" core is more a heuristic and methodological device than an expression of historical reality, for the permeable boundaries of this group of travelers and claimants stands as one of its central features.[9] Although in many ways Lima, the viceregal seat, was the door to the legal Atlantic, the networks in which this community rested were ultimately polycentric: they relied on other "nodes" or "decentralized centers" articulating smaller legal spaces. Their members moved in and out of a network of litigant villages, high courts of appeal, royal magistrates, licensed and unlicensed legal specialists, and influential patrons at all levels of the civil and ecclesiastic hierarchies. Nonetheless, beyond basic community and *repartimiento* spheres, the viceregal and imperial networks had little that was inherently "Indian" about them, at least in the established sense.[10] On the ground, trans-Andean and transoceanic litigation, negotiation, and favor-seeking were often interethnic, as native authorities and legal agents joined efforts with nonnative (predominantly Spanish and *mestizo*) travelers and specialists in the law. These colonial voyagers and litigants generally relied on similar circuits, strategies, and practices, forging alliances out of the need for mutual support and shared interests, before, during, and after their journeys.[11] Indigenous travelers moved through webs of communication and advancement that, to a significant degree, were "known and predictable" to the people who traveled extensively within the early Spanish Atlantic world.[12]

OUR TRICKS AND WICKED WAYS

Viceroy Francisco de Toledo's ordinances for the city of Cuzco, issued on October 18, 1572, commanded the appointment of two arbitrators—one layman and one man of the cloth—to mediate legal disputes. In Toledo's view, avoiding the proliferation of lawsuits was a way to preserve peace among the Spanish residents of the burgeoning Andean center and the integrity of the (Spanish) *república* at large. Toledo justified the urgency of this innovation by arguing that, in these lands, the Spaniards "have become used to engaging in *pleitos*, more than in any other place."[13]

This was a rare admission on the part of the famed viceroy who was to govern Peru during the next nine years. Like Matienzo, royal officials of the pre-Toledan and Toledan eras were quick to condemn the "litigious" nature of indigenous peoples and their lords, blaming a series of (purportedly generalized) social maladies on the legal agency of the Huancas and other ethnic groups. Letters, court mandates, and opening statements included in legal dossiers between the 1550s and the 1570s often reproduced the corresponding stereotypes. Viceroys, justices, and nonindigenous litigants and their attorneys regularly complained that natives were "liars" (*mentirosos*) and "overly fond of going to court" (*amigos de pleitos*).

Even so, colonial commentators were rarely as open in criticizing the engagement of Spaniards with the courts and its perceived excesses. Spanish litigiousness was as widespread and, in the eyes of many, as potentially threatening to the fabric of the *República de Españoles* as it was to its indigenous counterpart. Nor were these officials especially inclined to state the obvious: since the reopening of Lima's *audiencia* in 1549, it was mainly Spaniards, particularly members of the *encomendero* class and associates, whom native litigants had brought to court over excessive tribute demands, land dispossessions, and other abuses. And if Andean cases seemed endless, it was probably because judges and court officials dragged them out unnecessarily for months or years to profit from their client-litigants.[14]

Therein lay one of the fundamental paradoxes of colonial rule: litigation was a by-product of colonialism, but it also created a delicate counterbalance between the two. Policy makers in mid-sixteenth-century Peru regularly blamed the natives' "natural" inclination and love for papers and lawsuits, even while sometimes admitting that Andeans had quickly learned "our" tricks and wicked ways—the Spaniards' own *trampas y maldades*.[15] Indigenous litigants, this argument went, offended God and king by hiring false witnesses or by bearing fake testimony themselves, thus undermining due process and hampering the exercise of justice.[16] Furthermore, royal ministers argued, Indian complainants easily fell prey to private lawyers, greedy solicitors and scribes, informal interpreters, and even evil *caciques*—all of whom deceived and manipulated indigenous commoners due to the latter's disingenuous characters. Since the reopening of the *audiencia*, colonial officials claimed, frivolous lawsuits and exorbitant fees had robbed commoners of their meager *haciendas* while depleting communal treasuries.[17] To make matters worse, litigants had to travel through dramatically different climate zones to seek justice before the high court in Lima, experiencing abrupt changes in altitude and temperature, which many claimed were harmful to their health. In sum, the lengthy, expensive, and ultimately petty court cases that Indian parties filed were taking natives away from their lands, distracting them from fiscal and religious obligations, and diminishing their wealth and numbers.[18]

Toledo's ideas were hardly novel. The viceroy's predecessors—Viceroy Diego López de Zúñiga, the Count of Nieva (1561–1564), and Lope García de Castro (1564–1569), governor and president of the *audiencia*—had already justified a series of fundamental legal reforms in light of this ideological construct.[19] Theirs was a deliberate attempt to contain the natives' excessive reliance on and, in their eyes, abuse of the law courts installed to "protect" them. At least on paper, these officials promoted the idea that precluding natives from pointless litigation was necessary not only for the natives' own good but also as an act of loyalty and Christian piety. These arguments helped them rationalize efforts to rein in indigenous legal initiatives. They proposed these policies as vehicles to unburden His Majesty's conscience and contribute to his salvation. Rarely stated as overtly was the fact that preserving the different *repúblicas de indios* by offering their members some degree of redress and protection was the only way to safeguard a kingdom that a group of unruly and dissatisfied *encomenderos* had already put in peril during the uprisings of the 1540s and 1550s.[20]

The 1560s opened in an atmosphere of increased fiscal pressure and royal expenditure, which shifted not only the Crown's priorities regarding its American realms but also the political alliances that had characterized the previous decade. While commanding its ministers to shield native Andeans from the unjust demands of *encomenderos* and priests and to defend them from the most extreme forms of exploitation, the Crown—seemingly on the brink of bankruptcy—called for senior officials to establish royal authority among Indians and Spaniards more firmly. Officials were also to secure a steady labor pool for the mines and other ventures, all in an effort to maximize the profitability of the conquered territories and increase the revenue being dispatched to the Iberian Peninsula. Guaranteeing that protective laws be enforced and that Indians have access to a revamped system of public legal assistance became these ministers' pragmatic response to the royal mandate commanding them to reconcile these conflicting impulses.[21] Without partial reconciliation, which allowed indigenous communities to reproduce and maintain moderate control over resources under increased fiscal pressure, the colonial project in the Andes would not have been viable.

Early reformist projects targeted at native Andean societies are rarely associated with imperial efforts to rechannel the perceived high volume of litigation and to limit its implications.[22] However, Toledo's famous judicial innovations of the 1570s (such as the final establishment of a web of public advocates and defenders for the Indians in 1574–1575 and his better-known reorganization of indigenous hierarchies of authority along with his resettlement of agro-pastoral *ayllus* in Spanish-style towns during his 1570 General Inspection) were closely linked to this wider intercolonial, and ultimately transoceanic, debate. In retelling the story, I wish to shed light on this particular incentive for the larger Toledan reforms. Within this area of colonial governance, and notwithstanding other concerns and important precedents, the crux of the matter was how to rein in and redirect Indian litigiousness, thereby limiting the unsanctioned displacements of Andean individuals and families. A key idea was that maintaining the natives in their locales and finally stopping their legal pilgrimages to *audiencia* seats or Iberian courts would require that ministers place royal justice within the Indians' reach.

As in Mexico, the specific interests behind proponents and opponents of Andean judicial reform quickly surfaced. Although not much is known about behind-the-scenes negotiations, it is likely that two interrelated groups weighed in to influence royal policy. First, the *encomendero* class, with its desire to maximize revenue from Indian labor and minimize Crown oversight, was interested in decreasing the natives' previous successes at having tribute quotas revised by the courts. Second, fee-levying officials and private practitioners of law, who profited from the first three decades of indigenous recourse to the courts within the free market of legal services, were also likely interested in shaping the new status quo.[23]

Thus, while maintaining open dialogue with members of the *Consejo de Indias* and trying to keep abreast of local pressures, viceroys and *audiencia* ministers (some of whom were to become members of the Council) initiated discussions about the difficulties that notaries, solicitors, procurators, advocates, secretaries, and other professionals posed to their plan for bringing royal justice to natives. For officials, channels other than private and largely independent intermediaries had to be opened and placed under the purview of the Crown. In Mexico, this eventually led to the implementation of a specialized tribunal and a separate jurisdiction for indigenous legal affairs: the famous General Indian Court. No such court came to exist in the Andes, and thus some of the outcomes of this dialogical process were ultimately different. Nonetheless, similar attitudes had crystallized in both viceroyalties in the early 1560s. Common to both scenarios was the perceived need to reorient indigenous litigation toward royally approved judicial conduits and more specialized, Crown-approved bureaucratic bodies. By the early 1560s, this project had become the new colonial consensus.[24]

PLACING JUSTICE WITHIN THE INDIANS' REACH

Indian *pueblos* fit within an older and wider Iberian tradition of respect of customary laws (*fueros*), local jurisdictions, and *repúblicas* within the monarchy.[25] Based on this legacy, and against the backdrop of earlier royal decrees reminding American magistrates that the best way to guarantee the "good treatment" of the Indians was to facilitate access to courts, two main ideas inspired the first general efforts at legal reform. First, the king's justice had to reach native vassals in their homelands, not the other way around. Second, the Crown had to devise and generalize a special, partially autonomous and supracommunal jurisdiction for Indian cases, entrusted to a combination of *audiencia* magistrates, provincial governors, magistrates, and other court officials. This apparatus included indigenous peoples almost from its inception, in various capacities as interpreters, interim defenders, and assistants. As royal magistrates with restricted jurisdiction, moreover, natives were not only granted judicial authority but also were able to adjudicate small claims at the local level and, as explained in chapter 2, eventually represent communities before regional and metropolitan tribunals.[26] Early experiments at indigenous administration of local justice, which date back to as early as 1549, were tried in specific parts of the viceroyalty. The *repartimientos* that were directly entrusted to the Crown (as opposed to particular *encomenderos*) acted as laboratories before royal officials applied them to the vast jurisdiction of Lima's appellate court.[27]

In April 1563, Supreme Justice Gregorio González de Cuenca wrote to the king offering advice to prevent native delegations from undertaking perilous trips to the *audiencia*, a concern that fellow *oidor* Juan de Matienzo was to express in writing a few years later. Echoing the king's general orders to simplify procedures and reduce legal costs for *naturales* in the New World, Cuenca emphasized the need to select native municipal magistrates (*alcaldes*) and aldermen (*regidores*)—a plan modeled after the Spanish precedent of local government—and to place them in charge of handling small claims within their communities.[28] Such limitations on the *alcaldes* were not particularly new; as Karen Graubart demonstrates, their restricted jurisdiction was largely inherited from the Iberian late-medieval tradition.[29] Cuenca also suggested that *audiencia* magistrates should tour the land regularly and adjudicate certain court cases that, because of their magnitude or importance, would lie outside the scope of municipal officials' limited jurisdiction. In the same letter to the king, Cuenca summarized a proposal that, in fact, he was to partially implement the following year during his own inspection tour of the native settlements of the northern coastal region surrounding the city of Trujillo. Royal justice, Cuenca wrote, "should pass by the Indians' own doorstep."[30]

This evolving policy resonated with similar experiments concerning magistrates of higher rank than the officials of the indigenous *cabildos*. In April 1563, Viceroy Count of Nieva ordered the election of one Spanish alderman as judge for the Indians (*juez de naturales*) of Cuzco, where Cuenca had served as *corregidor* in 1562. The viceroy granted these *jueces de naturales* authority in the first instance over indigenous civil and criminal cases concerning fifty pesos or less. Moreover, many native residents were only recently being reorganized into different urban parishes, each with its own indigenous municipal magistrate (*alcalde*). These magistrates were also granted authority to hear cases involving minor offenses and intercommunal conflicts.[31] The viceroy-count's wish for native urban residents was not unlike Cuenca's for the northern coast: Indians of Cuzco need not journey to Lima in search for justice. Nieva had told the Council, in a letter penned right after Christmas 1562, that "it would be for the Indians' own sake if they ignored the meaning of the word *pleito* and the path to this *Audiencia*."[32] The Spanish *juez de naturales*, to be selected by Cuzco's municipal council every year, in combination with *alcaldes* in Indian urban parishes, was to provide summary justice to litigants, locally and (allegedly) at no cost.[33]

Two years later, Governor Lope García de Castro—Nieva's successor in office, councilor of the Indies, and interim president of the *audiencia*—took similar steps. Moving from reinforcing judicial administration to modifying established legal culture, Castro restated a prohibition on *caciques* and *principales* traveling to the *audiencia* to litigate. Influential and experienced ministers who supported Castro claimed to have seen entire highland delegations perish after their descent onto the warmer coastal plains where the *audiencia* was located. (One wonders if this is how the fourteen members of the Apoalaya lineage mentioned in chapter 2 met their fate while litigating in Lima.) Castro claimed to have corroborated that Andean leaders were accompanied by servants and retainers during legal pilgrimages. But as their lords sojourned in Lima, these dependents went "back and forth," bringing "provisions and supplies" into the city. Some *caciques*, Castro said, had taken this practice as a means of personal gain (*granjeria*), filing frivolous court cases in order to continue enjoying personal services and tribute. Castro limited the number of indigenous delegates to two individuals. Traveling litigants should not be *caciques* but rather "the most capable [i.e., knowledgeable and savvy] Indians."[34]

Between April and May 1565, moreover, Castro selected the first commissioners or magistrates to serve within the Indian *repartimientos*—the unpopular *corregidores de indios*—amid loud protests from indigenous leaders, clergy, and *encomenderos*. Through procurators in Lima and Madrid, these three major political forces lobbied the Crown to revert or modify its decision.[35] The provincial administrative judges were to oversee local elections of *alcaldes* and *alguaciles* (bailiffs), who were to aid in the dispensation of summary justice, with only the final ruling committed to writing. In Castro's view, this combination of Spanish local magistrates, modeled after the Iberian experience of the late medieval and early modern eras, with the officials of the still incipient Indian municipal councils proposed by Cuenca, Matienzo, and others, was to administer swift justice to natives in their new villages. Castro outlined how the first *corregidores* and *alcaldes* would resolve Indian lawsuits in their jurisdictions. By implementing these policies, Castro, a *letrado* (formally trained lawyer and counselor; holder of the highest law degrees), was aligning himself with the emerging consensus about the need to regulate, and in fact limit, natives' direct access to viceregal and metropolitan courts of law as much as possible.[36]

Like the supreme justices of the *audiencia*, Spanish provincial magistrates and Andean municipal officers were to carry an ornamental staff (*vara de justicia*), which signaled their competence to mete out justice in the name of the king. A proxy for the royal scepter, the *vara* symbolized the office: it was to become a powerful emblem of these officers' governmental prerogatives, judicial attributes, and special jurisdiction among native subjects and within the *República de Indios*. The Indian magistrates' authority derived from the king's power: they were *alcaldes* and justices "by His Majesty's will" and "by His Majesty's authority" (*por Su Majestad*). The *varas* and what they stood for laid out the ideological foundations for dismissing illegitimate Spanish authorities and abusive officials, or even to rebel against them if needed, as an act of royal justice.[37] Castro and others saw this as a way to guarantee that the officers' decisions, especially if they were commoners, would be obeyed and the sentences carried out. Several decades later, Felipe Guaman Poma de Ayala praised the appointment of indigenous staff-holding magistrates and assistants. For him, whenever an Indian *alcalde* took up the staff, "the lord king himself is there in person." The Spanish *corregidores* and the native *alcaldes* were, in his view, "justices of God and His Majesty." According to this famous Andean polemicist, "One does not take precedence over the other."[38]

In September 1565, García de Castro shared with the *Consejo de Indias* what he considered the most tangible outcome of these reforms. "This *audiencia* used to be filled with Indian litigants who spent all of their worldly possessions to bring lawsuits, even losing their lives because they were natives of different climates. . . . We should praise Our Lord that there are so few of them doing that now." Six years later, in an effort to capitalize on established American practices and shared American experiences, the *Consejo* authorized the incoming viceroy, Francisco de Toledo (1569–1581), to finish carving out a special jurisdiction for native litigants of the imperial system of justice now linking Castile and its overseas domains.[39]

TRANSOCEANIC CONVERSATIONS

These reorganizations, foundational in the Andes, were part of a larger conversation, sometimes whispered into His Majesty's ear. General policies implemented at the royal court and events unfolding in other New World domains shaped the debate in multiple ways. Exchanges across the Atlantic generally took the form of letters, reports, consultations, learned opinions, and royal provisions and should be seen as ways through which competing factions within the court and in other centers of power, including native lords and commoners themselves, constructed the empire in the sixteenth and seventeenth centuries. Evidently, the early Habsburg monarchs and their close secretaries, advisers, and courtiers also took an active part in this process.

Back in 1552, the Franciscan friar Pedro de Gante had already warned his nephew Charles V that, as Viceroy Antonio de Mendoza had put it into practice in Mexico, the plan for legal reform through summary proceedings rather than protracted cases, and recognizing indigenous customary law, was failing. Father Pedro, like Charles before him, blamed procurators, notaries, and lawyers for the Indians' wasteful legal expenditures.[40] Philip II took a similar personal interest in restructuring indigenous access to royal justice, assuming an active role in the general suspension of the post of *protector* (defender) of the Indians. This temporary suspension came in 1582 as a result of written exchanges between the *Consejo de Indias* and the viceregal authorities in Mexico and Peru. A "tripartite relationship" arose between the drafting of reports by officials in the Indies, their assessment by members of the Council, and decisions implemented by the king.[41] The natives followed these exchanges closely and, as their opposition to Castro's *corregidores* shows, participated in them. Imperial debates and colonial anxieties bear the imprint of this open-ended participation.

The legal opinions of local actors seeking to keep indigenous litigants and petitioners in their place, along with official rules and regulations they established with that end in mind, resonate in a series of metropolitan laws issued in the 1560s aimed at preventing native Andeans from voyaging overseas. A 1551 royal decree reveals that the Crown seriously entertained the possibility of authorizing New Spain's Indian provinces, cities, and corporations to dispatch two or three indigenous procurators to the royal court for a period of three years, provided they held signed letters of attorney and were not representing Spanish interests.[42] The same year, the king also decided to charge the *Consejo de Indias's* prosecuting attorneys (*fiscales*) with the task of representing indigenous subjects directly before the councilors, thus transferring jurisdiction from previous religious defenders of the Indians to secular ones. This order, restated in 1563, likely carried an intention similar to the one pertaining to indigenous procurators from New Spain. Until then, these Crown prosecutors (*fiscales de Su Majestad*) had been entrusted with upholding the laws intended to protect native vassals even if enforcing them meant going against the actions of the ruler. Following the advice of the Council, however, the Crown ultimately shifted its approach to natives visiting the royal court. The 1563 decision to transfer the title and attributions of the Council's prosecutors-turned-defenders to the prosecuting attorneys of the American *audiencias*, with the corresponding empowerment of these local tribunals, signaled the reversal of earlier policies.[43] The orders given to the Marquis of Cañete (1556–1560) upon his appointment as viceroy of Peru, instructing him to select *alcaldes* from among native Andeans to adjudicate "things among the Indians themselves that are of minor importance," were cast in a similar vein.[44]

These changes partially originated in reports sent by ministers in America, often in response to inquiries by the Council. In altering earlier policies, however, the flow of people was as significant as the flow of information. A decree addressed in December 1566 to the *Audiencia de Lima* explained some motivations behind the royal decision to restrict Indian visits to the court. First, the fruitful stay of the Huanca lord Felipe Guacrapaucar in Spain, as he followed the itinerant king between 1562 and 1564, set a powerful precedent at a time when other indigenous vassals of illustrious descent were journeying to Iberia from other parts of the empire, such as Quito and New Spain. Second, papers reaching the court from the *audiencia* informed Philip II that some native lords were planning to replicate these experiences, in part to oppose Lope García de Castro's appointment of provincial governors in the Andes. Other indigenous authorities were considering sending their own delegates to Spain in order to plead their causes directly to the king.[45]

The 1566 royal decree highlighted the profound differences in climate that separated the Peninsula from the Andean region. It had been proven, the 1566 royal order stated, that the effects of this climate contrast were detrimental to the natives' health and well-being. There was undeniable evidence that "those who have come here have perished." Thus, the king's will was that viceroys and *audiencia* magistrates serving in Peru impede native travelers from undertaking the journey. They were to make sure that indigenous leaders and commoners understood very well that, were it not for the risk of their demise that a visit to the Peninsula involved, the just but distant king would have been pleased with their visit.[46]

The Council issued similar orders throughout the rest of the colonial era, motivated by the regular appearance of indigenous travelers at the royal court.[47] A *memorial* drafted around 1579 warned the king and the Council that, in spite of the general prohibition, Spanish ship masters and captains of the fleet kept bringing "many yndios and yndias" every year. Officials alleged "they were meztizos, children of Spaniards" in order to successfully circumvent royal regulations. The anonymous author recommended enforcing the ban, allowing *mestizos* to travel only after an investigation conducted before governors and *audiencias* had established their Spanish ancestry.[48] Backed by these prohibitions, royal officials sometimes used their power and connections to pursue and seize unlicensed travelers in intermediate ports such as Panama and Havana. Such was the predicament of Don Andrés de Ortega Lluncon in 1647. That year, Don Andrés, an *indio principal* from the northern coast, denounced Viceroy Marquis of Mancera and one of the supreme justices of Lima's *audiencia* for obstructing his journey to Spain to expose a series of land appropriations. They ordered authorities in Havana to imprison him. Declared an unauthorized traveler, Don Andrés remained in jail for five months. Although he eventually made it to court, where he appeared before the Council, the reforms of the 1560s had charged royal ministers with preventing unsanctioned movements by all possible legitimate means.[49]

TOLEDO'S JUDICIAL UTOPIA

Licentiate Lope García de Castro did not return to Spain until 1572, but the winds of reform were already in the air when successor Francisco de Toledo received his appointment in 1569. Influential men of the colonial lettered establishment such as Gregorio González de Cuenca, Polo Ondegardo, and Juan de Matienzo, all instrumental in the reforms of previous decades, remained in Peru and quickly resumed their roles as advisers upon the arrival of the new royal official. Their influence guaranteed a certain degree of continuity for earlier initiatives. In now familiar terms, the *Consejo de Indias* tasked Toledo with devising a way so that "as much as possible, the natives be prevented from bringing lawsuits against each other."[50]

Initially, the viceroy proved to be less optimistic about the role of the new *corregidores de indios* than Governor Castro had been only four years earlier. In February 1570, Toledo wrote to the Council from Peru stating that Castro's *corregidores* had been somewhat effective in the initial stages of local lawsuits, such as gathering witness testimonies and filing initial complaints. Yet, because of either incompetence or laziness (or a combination of both), *corregidores* often sent cases to the *audiencia* for resolution, swelling its caseload and defeating the main purpose of Castro's innovations. As a result, Toledo claimed, "these days there is no room for all of the Indians who arrive here from many places to bring lawsuits, many of whom die along the way." Toledo also denounced that private advocates and even royal officials were still charging native litigants, albeit secretly, "a higher salary than what the lawsuit is worth," worsening the problem.[51] The diligent viceroy had come to the same conclusion—which also happened to justify his own reformist plans—as the justices Matienzo and Cuenca had in preceding years. Toledo told the Council in 1570, "The greatest good that can be done [for the Indians] is to order them not to leave their homes in search of justice but for them to seek it in their own provinces." For Toledo, the basic framework of local judicial forums subject to viceregal and metropolitan appellate courts had to become a reality if indigenous vassals were to receive the benefits of the king's justice.[52] Soon after the start of his General Inspection tour (*Visita general*) in November 1570, Toledo issued several ordinances and decrees seeking to drastically limit the human and material costs of Andean access to the courts, in the process redefining the ways natives were to seek royal justice for the next three hundred years.[53]

In line with prevailing efforts to reinforce the king's authority in colonial Peru, and building upon previous ideological currents and experiments in Cuzco, Lima, and Trujillo, Toledo's ordinances for the organization of native towns confirmed the prerogative of the officers of the still fairly novel municipal councils to resolve minor civil and criminal disputes.[54] Toledo's reforms empowered the *corregidores* to supersede all other local officials in matters of justice, but they subordinated their authority to that of *audiencias*, the Council of the Indies, and ultimately the Crown. Indian *cabildos*, for their part, were to be preferably composed of commoners and not traditional members of the elite. Such policies reflected Toledo's will to finally strip native lords, parish priests, and *encomenderos* of their judicial attributions and unsanctioned powers, relocating jurisdiction over indigenous legal affairs to elected or appointed representatives of the king.[55] Under the new system, for instance, parish priests were neither to inflict corporal punishment nor to impose pecuniary fines upon parishioners, although clerical violence, especially in the form of whippings, remained a relatively common occurrence. While one of the long-term effects was the creation of a mixed system of elite-plebeian authority within indigenous villages, this transfer of power from patrician to plebeian Indians, especially in the case of traditional elites who initially protested the prerogatives awarded to upwardly mobile municipal authorities, was probably never complete.[56]

Building on Iberian precedent, the laws governing everyday life in indigenous villages limited the jurisdiction of native *alcaldes*, selected every one or two years, to criminal and civil disputes of modest import. Intercommunal quarrels over labor or resources and complaints against native lords were to be handed over to the *corregidor* for adjudication. Similarly, civil cases involving more than a few dozen pesos and criminal suits requiring the death penalty or severe corporal punishment were to be delegated to the Spanish magistrate—not to *caciques*—for resolution.[57] Depending on the complaints, native communities and commoners were given the right to appeal adverse rulings to judges of the *audiencia*, the second level of the three-layered system of appeal. For their part, the indigenous hereditary aristocracy, especially lords of vassals and officially appointed governors, were to enjoy certain privileges and exemptions. Municipal officials and provincial magistrates were not permitted to remove *caciques*, imprison them for minor faults, or settle lawsuits over their right to succeed in the *cacicazgos* (lordships, entailed estates) of their fathers and ancestors. Such prerogatives fell under the exclusive jurisdiction of *audiencias*.[58]

Thus, Toledo's new judicial order was to be a corrective to two decades of Indian "litigiousness." The heyday of private lawyers and informal solicitors, as well as the journeys of multitudinous Indian delegations to Lima that this free legal market encouraged, was soon to be over—or so Toledo thought. The viceroy built this legal edifice on the now widely accepted notion that natives ought to be classified as legal minors. As such, Andean litigants deserved special assistance from public defenders and enjoy certain procedural privileges.[59] These included lower standards of proof, lighter punishments and penalties, and the right to rely on customary norms that did not contradict reason and religion—a fundamental premise that the Crown had been pushing since the 1540s. Whenever possible, natives were to have summary hearings with swift decisions. There would be no direct cost to complainants, unless the litigants were *caciques* suing on their own behalf, not in the name of their communities.[60]

Aimed at providing Indian vassals with real justice at no direct cost, Toledo's reforms also sought to keep Indian litigants and favor-seekers in their place. Appeal and accountability were part of the peaceful and orderly exercise of justice. And even though no free vassal of the king should ever be denied the right to reach out to His Majesty, when it came to Indians the viceroy knew better. In his legal utopia, natives seeking justice and recompense would be obliged to remain in their homeland (*patria*) and to maintain their nature (*naturaleza*). Indigenous litigants would need to put their trust in this imperial framework flowing downward and outward from the king, but they were not to reach out to the sovereign directly.

Rather than leaving to petition and litigate, indigenous corporations and their leaders were to air their complaints before their own local magistrates. Only under extreme circumstances, whose definition was vague in Toledo's massive legislation, and only with authorization from higher ministers at the *audiencia*, were indigenous subjects to have recourse to the *Consejo de Indias*, the supreme tribunal for American affairs in the Spanish Empire.[61] This kind of appeal would be reserved for high-stakes cases, such as *pleitos* over *encomiendas*, and individual aspirations, such as a coat of arms or a lifetime pension. Indigenous lords seeking recompense or redress were to prepare proofs of merit before viceroys, governors, and *audiencias*—that is, in the Andes and not in Castile. These judges would then render a secret opinion (*parecer*) about the merits of the candidates and the soundness of their legal arguments and then seal and dispatch it to the Iberian Peninsula, along with the proper documentary evidence, for the Council to make the final decision.[62]

When seen in this light, Toledo's famous policies for general native resettlement and judicial reforms were based on a common core of experiences, legal theories, and ideological constructs. They pursued similar objectives: in particular, keeping natives contained within a political community rooted in ancestral (or newly assigned) lands. As argued by Brian Owensby, native municipalities "could be distinguished from other political communities by the fact that its inhabitants were not free to abandon it."[63] Toledo had little sympathy for Andeans who "simply chose to live away from their homes," unless of course they were serving mandatory labor terms in cities, mines, and textile workshops.[64] Litigants were, actually and symbolically, a key component of this group of indigenous vassals who *chose* to move away from home and who were the target of Toledo's bitter criticisms. The viceroy's assumption was that, when shown the benefits of living *en policía*, natives would remain in the new villages. Easy access to the justice of the king was a central part of Andean civilized life as Toledo envisioned it. Justice would come to the towns—but at a steep price.

In terms of overt motivations—to reduce native litigation and to do away with private and informal facilitators—the system of public legal assistance did not really meet with great success. In fact, it might have had the opposite effect, opening other avenues for *caciques* and commoners to go to court. After Toledo's term in office was over, royal ministers used the same pessimistic and alarmist tone that the viceroy had used when pondering his immediate predecessors' reforms and justifying his own, longing for a past that had never existed and a future that would never be. Upon arriving in Peru in 1581, Viceroy Martín Enríquez compared the situation with that of Mexico, where he had served in the same capacity. "What I see ... now is that more Indians are bringing lawsuits here than in New Spain." For Enríquez, Toledo's secular protectors of the Indians were partially to blame: "I suspect that these protectors, whose job it is to look after the good of the Indians, do not do justice to their titles."[65] A decade later, Cristóbal Ramírez de Cartagena, justice of the *Audiencia de Lima* and a magistrate with many years of experience in Indian court cases, held the same somber outlook. Disenchanted with Toledo's protectors and procurators, Ramírez de Cartagena closed his assessment of the first fifty years of justice in Peru by lamenting that the natives "are involved in more meaningless and baseless disputes than ever."[66]

Just as important, the great reformer could not foresee that indigenous subjects quickly incorporated royal and viceregal "privileges" (*privilegios*) and "favors" (*gracias*) into their legal strategies. By making constant use of procedural advantages, especially when litigating against Spaniards and powerful ethnic lords, Indians throughout the Andes secured them as the foundational *fueros* (privileges; customary laws) of their colonial *repúblicas*. Furthermore, neither legislation nor direct viceregal action prevented the journeys of native Andeans to Lima and Spain, though they probably decreased them somewhat. Even though earlier mandates gave viceroys and *audiencias* the authority to grant exceptional licenses to native lords "who must come to these kingdoms," ministers holding office in Peru during the Habsburg period proved very reluctant to issue them.[67] In theory, the judicial system established during the crucial decades of the 1560s and 1570s had left very little room for indigenous litigants and procurators to reach Iberia. The king would allow officially stamped proofs of merit and other legal dossiers, letters, and petitions on behalf of his indigenous subjects to circulate and eventually reach him and his *Consejo de Indias*, but none of the plaintiffs were to carry these papers across the ocean. Individuals like Don Juan Bustamante Carlos Inca, whose trip from Cuzco to the royal court via Cartagena, Caracas, and Cádiz took a mind-boggling total of eight years, were very aware of the perils of journeying to the royal court. Yet he and other travelers also knew well that the voyage could be worth the trouble.[68]

INDIANS AND THEIR DEFENDERS

In 1609, royal treasurers reported that the salaries of *corregidores* and *protectores* for Indians amounted to 26 percent of the total tribute of the natives of the kingdom.[69] Thirty-five years after the watershed reforms of Toledo's era, public defenders had become central to indigenous individual and collective legal experiences. A *protector general* or defender-general, whose appointment fell within the purview of the viceroy, joined the permanent staff of the *audiencia* in 1575.[70] Subordinate provincial defenders, at least eleven in the early seventeenth century, served as ad hoc procurators in different *corregimientos* of the court district where the potentially explosive combination of significant indigenous populations, Spanish residents, and nearby cities, mines, and *haciendas* made lawsuits and other complaints highly likely. By 1630, the number of *corregimientos* that include defenders of the Indians had increased to twenty-one.[71]

Public defenders intervened in indigenous or "mixed" petitions and lawsuits in which at least one of the parties was identified as "Indian." They represented individuals (elites and commoners) and communities (one or several) and undertook judicial action ex officio or ex parte (at the initiative of the court or the aggrieved party, respectively). They mediated between parties willing to reach an agreement outside the courts. With the aid of *escribanos* (notaries) and interpreters, protectors offered legal counsel at no direct cost to the parties, since a per-capita tax built into the indigenous subjects' biannual tribute payments funded their salaries. Protectors wrote, signed, and authorized "Indian" petitions, often with the aid of an official interpreter, although some *mestizo* defenders were probably speakers of the native languages. They advised and represented their clients before local *corregidores*, *audiencias*, and city judges as well as bishops, ecclesiastic judges, and inspectors. A few *protectores* outside Lima's close legal circle of defenders-general and magistrates of the *audiencia* seem to have been *letrados* (university-trained experts) in the law; most were probably *hidalgos* and nobles of the sword (*hombres de capa y espada*) with little formal preparation. Formally trained advocates (*abogados* or *letrados de naturales*) and the more empirically trained solicitors (*procuradores de causas*) completed this cast of characters.[72]

In line with the theory of the Indians' legal minority and "wretched" status, public protectors acted as guardians and guarantors of indigenous parties during the preparation of notarial documents and proofs of merit (*probanzas*).[73] Documented cases from the sixteenth to the eighteenth century mention protectors in civil and criminal actions; conflicts over the sale and rent of lands; the acquisition of land titles during official inspections; complaints about excessive fiscal impositions; labor conflicts in mines, *haciendas*, and textile workshops; charges against Spanish and indigenous authorities; lawsuits over *cacicazgos*, proofs of merit, and privileges of indigenous nobles; and an array of local cases that, in theory, involved fines of up to fifty pesos and ten days of jail time.[74]

Native groups often sent their own delegates to towns and cities to meet with protectors, present evidence, round up witnesses, discuss cases, and design legal strategy. In the 1640s, Viceroy Marquis of Mancera claimed that Lima's defender-general "went about the city surrounded by twenty, thirty, or fifty Indians."[75] Defender-general Diego de León Pinelo claimed to have in his possession almost 10,000 pages of complaints filed by Indians before the viceroy and the *audiencia* between 1655 and 1661. Francisco de Valenzuela, the previous defender-general, claimed in 1650 to have overseen more than 12,000 court cases resulting from the controversial Second General Land Inspection (*Composición General*) of the viceroyalty, which particularly affected native villages and their communal lands. Don Andrés de Ortega, the *principal* that royal authorities imprisoned in Havana, had journeyed to court to denounce the judges of the Second Inspection.[76]

For natives, the need to rely on provincial and *audiencia* defenders, given their multiple attributions and considerable outreach, seemed inescapable. They were, in many ways, gatekeepers of the law in colonial Peru. Native Andeans seemed to have used them heavily, but they also turned to alternative legal facilitators (often at a moderate to high cost). Crown procurators operated within a larger market of legal services, especially in cities such as Lima and Cuzco, where they competed with private advocates, unsanctioned solicitors, interpreters-cum-attorneys, and other informal practitioners to attract and retain Andean clientele.[77] These alternative legal channels remained open even after Viceroy Toledo enforced his exclusive system of "free" legal assistance.[78]

Native groups and individuals held variable degrees of control over the legal services they contracted, such as choosing agents and negotiating specific terms. In January 1596, Don Pedro de la Cruz, *cacique* principal of Huancho Huaylas and a transient in Lima, gave power of attorney to Pedro Ortiz de Valdelomar, another procurator of the *audiencia*, for legal services. Don Pedro was careful to add a key proviso to protect himself from any lawsuit: Ortiz was not to lodge any complaint without his consent, or their agreement would be null and void.[79]

The capacity of Spanish protectors and procurators to follow instructions and demonstrate results was important for building trust among actual and potential clients. This ability was probably the foundation of permanent partnerships between certain public defenders and native communities.[80] In 1626, five *caciques* and tax collectors from Cajamarca wrote two letters to their protector seeking legal defense. The *corregidor* had imprisoned them for failure to render tribute in full. From the local jail, they asked the defender to request immediate liberation so that they could collect the remainder. A comparison between the petitions filed by the defender and the original letters reveals that the attorney closely followed the legal narrative and argumentation sketched by the Andean lords in their written instructions, sometimes verbatim.[81]

Similar appeals to regional protectors were the outcome of a previous history of collaboration. In 1624, defender-general Mateo de Vivanco petitioned the *Consejo de Indias*, on behalf of the *repartimientos* of Vilcas and Lucanas, for a ten-year exemption from work at the Huancavelica mercury mines. Four years before, Vivanco had pleaded to Viceroy Prince of Esquilache for the same cause, informing him that his clients had filed a similar request eight or ten years earlier. Having served in that province as a royal official, Vivanco called upon himself as a first-hand witness to the natives' need for relief. (A sharp decrease in the tributary population made meeting these work obligations unfair.) Esquilache denied the petition but authorized Vivanco to seek redress from the Council. In 1621, the defender secured a royal decree ordering the viceroy to make amends to the Indians (*los desagrauieis*), so that they "may ... suffer no injustices nor have the need or occasion to send someone to complain." Three years later, Vivanco petitioned the Council again but was directed back to the new viceroy, the Marquis of Guadalcázar.[82]

Andean litigants and petitioners knew that the expertise and connections of the chosen notary, advocate, or procurator had a great bearing on the outcome of a petition or court case. Letters praising the activities of a handful of protectors-general, prepared by or on behalf of indigenous communities and signed by their leaders, reached the royal court in the seventeenth century. These testimonies suggest that the signatories saw these defenders as useful allies in lawsuits and other legal endeavors, especially if heard by the *audiencia* or the Council. Some of them likely supported the protectors' own petitions and ambitions in hopes that this backing would result in a successful outcome to their own aspirations and complaints. It had been, since the beginning, a relation of mutual benefit and occasional simultaneous success.[83]

There were, however, less harmonious scenarios. At the *audiencia* level, indigenous litigants found defenders-general hard to circumvent because the Toledan laws of the 1570s had granted protectors a virtual monopoly over official legal writing. After receiving a verbal account from their indigenous clients, defenders-general were to pen the corresponding petition in Spanish, relying on the interpreter-general if necessary (protectors collected an extra two hundred pesos of salary for writing the petitions). Protectors-general were expected to reject any petitions written by the natives or their legal agents (they were, in fact, to pursue those responsible for these infractions and denounce them before the authorities). Similar laws mandated *audiencia* secretaries, rapporteurs, and advocates to dismiss any indigenous petitions if they had not been signed by the defender-general or the subordinate provincial protectors.[84] The public attorneys' exclusive control over legal writing and petitioning before the *audiencia* might explain why complaints against corrupt and inefficient defenders-general and local protectors are not as common as one could expect. The scene of a defender crafting a self-incriminating petition is difficult to imagine.[85]

The point is not so much that colonial magistrates, court officials, and protectors always followed the Toledan ordinances to the letter. Nor is it that native petitioners and litigants were totally unable to circumvent protectors-general and attorneys-general and communicate directly with the *audiencia* or the Council. The power that protectors and related officials held as gatekeepers rested on the fact that they could *choose* to enforce the Toledan ordinances and follow their procedures strictly, *if and when* doing so suited their own interests or those of their patrons, clients, relatives, or associates. Enforcing the ordinances literally and claiming the privilege to speak on the natives' behalf could be an effective strategy for actually blocking indigenous access to the justice system, leaving claimants with no alternative but to write to the king or accept the injustice and carry on as best as possible. There were certainly many literate Andeans in Lima, including interpreters and communal and *repartimiento* attorneys sojourning at the viceregal capital, who dominated the basic legal genres, and thus were perfectly capable of writing directly to the magistrates of the civil and ecclesiastic courts.[86] This course of action, however, though always available, placed the plaintiffs at risk of having their voices fall on deaf ears or, perhaps more literally, into the wrong hands.[87]

In 1607, the *Consejo de Indias* received a letter signed by several indigenous authorities of Chucuito, a predominantly Aymara-speaking province bordering Lake Titicaca. The letter praised the government of the local *corregidor*, the Count de la Gomera. The *caciques'* purported wish was to thank His Majesty for having sent a "true protector," from whom they had received "all of the money and satisfaction that we are entitled to receive from our work" and "kind and gentle treatment and rule regarding to our needs and in the administration of justice." Strangely enough, the letter was placed within another letter signed by a *licenciado* named Salamanca, which painted a very different picture.

According to Salamanca, the count had "destroyed" the entire province, selling the lieutenantship to the highest bidder. He had also appointed one of his dependents to be a steward of native collective endowments to misappropriate the communal herds. The count had also handpicked an incompetent local defender. When the Chucuito leaders arrived in Lima to complain, their petition was sent back to the province for Gomera. Another complaint followed an equally frustrating trajectory: Gomera handed it over to the lieutenant about whom the Indians had complained in the first place. He apprehended the native leaders, whipping them publicly and shaming them by cutting their hair short, "so that the others would not get the idea to complain." For the author of this account, injustice reigned supreme in a remote province of the high Andean plateau.[88]

An equally dramatic case demonstrates the opposite scenario: by simply refusing to follow rightful procedure to the letter, defenders-general, *audiencia* magistrates, and even viceroys hampered Indian access to justice. In 1620, the native authorities of Lampas journeyed to Lima to oppose the creation of an *obraje* (textile mill) on their lands. Contradicting previous general orders, the king had granted the influential counts of Lemos authorization to establish several of these *obrajes* within Indian lands. The *caciques* journeyed to Lima and put Don Juan Chaupis Condor in charge of handling the lawsuit. Chaupis Condor was an embroiderer who served as the *repartimiento's* chief procurator. Following procedure, the *audiencia's* advocate for the Indians crafted the legal argument, while the procurator penned the resulting formal complaint on the *caciques'* behalf. But when Chaupis Condor took the document to defender Mateo de Vivanco to obtain his mandatory signature, he snatched the petition away and refused to sign it. (Vivanco was the protector-general who, in a previous example, advocated for the natives of Lucanas and Vilcas before the Council.)

In the following days, the protector-general eluded the leaders of Lampas with frivolous excuses, claiming to have lost the original petition, hiding behind doors at the viceregal palace, and even having Chaupis Condor arrested. A viceregal decree, no doubt influenced by Vivanco and the interests he really defended, further threatened the native leaders with imprisonment if they did not abandon the city immediately. This left them with no choice but to appeal to the Council of the Indies via informal channels. They drafted a long petition with the aid of a mysterious solicitor: an anonymous Spaniard who charged the *caciques* 60 pesos for adapting it to the appropriate legal genre and dispatching it to Spain. In their appeal, the aggrieved authorities exposed a network of corruption by denouncing the defender-general, other court officials, and the viceroy as accomplices of the counts. The *caciques* secured a decree ordering that they be granted a personal hearing at the *audiencia* and proper defense by the advocate-general. In spite of their efforts, however, they lost the legal battle and the counts prevailed.[89]

From the perspective of Andean leaders and communities, then, there were in all likelihood "good" and "bad" defenders. Moreover, one individual could embody multiple contradictory sides and an inherent conflict of interest. Given the available evidence, it is hard to deny that indigenous subjects perceived some protectors as diligent and effective advocates who fulfilled their roles appropriately, even under pressure from bureaucrats, colonists, and rival communities to do otherwise.[90] *Caciques* and communities on the northern coast, perhaps realizing how important it was to have these officials on their side, worked, rented, and purchased lands whose revenues funded the activities of their local protector and covered his salary.[91] In an effort to foster good relationships, some Andean leaders directly empowered protectors and procurators to serve as their legal agents in Lima, revealing how facilitators acted as both public defenders and private counselors within the larger legal service economy in Habsburg Peru.[92] The defenders' larger significance, however, lay outside specific court cases. Because of their position in the legal network, they articulated the Andes within the larger imperial scene.

CONDUITS FOR JUSTICE

Whether litigants liked them or not, defenders had become part of the Andean legal landscape. The number of cases entrusted to defenders is explained in part by their right of direct recourse to Lima's appellate court. It is also a rough indicator of the natives' cautious trust and tepid preference for public procurators. Preliminary estimates based on surviving *audiencia* cases are revealing, as they show that, of all the legal actions filed in the sixteenth century, "Indian" ones were about 25 percent of the total for 1570–1579 and 28 percent for 1590–1599. Interestingly, this percentage fell to only 6 percent in the intermediate period 1580–1589. This drop was due perhaps to the Crown's suspension of the *protectoría* (as a separate appointment) between 1582 and 1589, which transferred direct legal advocacy on behalf of natives to the *audiencia*'s already overworked prosecuting attorneys (*fiscales*).[93] Albeit temporary, this suspension might have hampered the use of a viable, low-cost, and relatively effective channel, forcing indigenous plaintiffs and petitioners to hold on to their lawsuits or rely almost exclusively on the web of semiprivate legal assistance from *letrados*, scribes, procurators, and secretaries charging high fees.[94]

The effects of the Crown's decision seem to have been felt almost immediately. In a 1591 *memorial, audiencia* magistrate Cristóbal Ramírez de Cartagena complained about the dismissal of public attorneys. He assured the king that, only a few days after their removal from office, private lawyers, procurators, and solicitors started to shepherd Indian cases throughout the system. As a result, the natives had spent "great sums of money made through contributions [*derramas*] and other means and from the community chest."[95] Indigenous litigants raised similar complaints.[96]

After the Crown reinstated its defenders and procurators in the next decade, the *audiencia* went back to business as usual. According to Viceroy García Hurtado de Mendoza (1590–1596), seventy-nine lawsuits involving indigenous plaintiffs, Spanish land inspectors, and individual and communal lands awaited resolution in this royal tribunal by the end of his term, all in the context of the First General Land Inspection (*Composición General*). Three decades later a full and perhaps self-serving list compiled by Lima's defender-general and procurator-general to convince the Council of the necessity of preserving the post and paying their salaries on time included thirty-five "Indian" court cases currently in the hands of the *audiencia*'s many rapporteurs. Indians were no doubt reaching out to these defenders.[97]

Given the almost complete lack of specific studies on the life and careers of Peru's provincial and viceregal defenders, perhaps it is safe to assume for now that, as a professional group, public defenders of the sixteenth and early seventeenth centuries were neither more nor less corrupt, venal, or inefficient than other colonial officials of similar status and function.[98] Nor were their interests more or less entrenched in local society—to the point of it being a serious detriment to native legal interests—than those of other bureaucrats of comparable rank, role, and importance.[99] Future case studies will qualify or correct these general assertions. Yet, the evidence suggests that protectors remained relevant for indigenous claimants as long as they offered a Crown-sanctioned channel to seek redress beyond the local venue, where entrenched powers were much harder to defeat and arbitrary power much harder to tolerate. In the case of Lampas, the *caciques'* legal strategy of appealing to the imperial authorities failed because their adversaries (the Counts of Lemos) held as much power within viceregal circles as they did at the *Consejo de Indias* and the royal court.[100]

The natives' intermittent trust in and support for some public advocates become evident in letters and proofs of merit prepared by advocates to bolster their professional ambitions at the court.[101] Appeals to *audiencia* ministers and protectors-general offered a certain guarantee against the excesses of local agents, including priests, *corregidores*, colonial residents, and even *caciques*. In some instances, moreover, protectors represented commoners against lords, opening legal avenues for redress otherwise rarely available.[102] Furthermore, reaching out to these protectors created an ideal opportunity for jurisdictional jockeying (venue-shopping), especially when indigenous complainants decided to exploit the secular-ecclesiastic conflicts of jurisdiction inherent to the colonial order.[103]

Besides partial but important legal victories, public defenders and procurators offered privileged access to judicial channels and circuits that, as part of the economy of patronage and favor, linked not only the Andean countryside with the viceregal capital but also the Peruvian viceroyalty with the royal court.[104] The lawsuit pitting the Indians of Lampas against the Counts of Lemos was not decided based on the legal arguments presented by the former but in terms of the influence exerted in Peru and Spain by the latter. Any decision by native authorities to appeal directly to the Council showed awareness of the need to play by the rules of the political game, even if the possibility of failing was high. The attitudes behind such a legal strategy, perhaps combined with the possibility for native commoners to receive legal counsel at no or reduced cost, offer alternative—but not mutually exclusive—explanations as to why *caciques* and communities were willing to undertake the long journey to provincial capitals and Lima to meet public defenders and procurators and secure a hearing with the viceroy and the *audiencia*.

At the local level, protectors could guarantee an audience with the *corregidor*, the aldermen of the Spanish *cabildo*, and other magistrates with whom native communities needed to interact regularly.[105] *Audiencia* defenders belonged to the viceroy's close circle; some of them were in all probability his *criados* (dependents). Defenders could secure royal decrees and viceregal orders, presenting them at the *real acuerdo* (high plenary session). At these regular meetings held behind closed doors, viceroys and *audiencia* magistrates reviewed the *memoriales* and complaints flowing into Lima from all parts of the kingdom, discussed legal disputes affecting the Indians, and rendered verdicts. Public defenders and procurators were expected to be present, lending some indigenous claimants a voice in an otherwise seemingly impenetrable space.[106]

Was there anything to gain for these Spanish procurators? Of course, salaries (when they could collect them) were important. The 1,200 assayed pesos of annual salary that defenders-general of the *audiencia* received in the early 1620s—later increased to about 1,700 or 1,800 pesos—was a significant sum (whereas procurators for the Indians received about half that amount).[107] Soft "loans" from the Caja General de Censos de Indios constituted another source of potential enrichment.[108] Such misappropriations, along with extra-legal fees, bribes, and other "gifts" received from Andean litigants, might have been tempting and likely complemented yearly incomes. Otherwise, it is hard to explain why, in 1640, after the Crown included the post on the list of saleable offices, an incumbent paid 9,000 pesos to purchase the title of defender-general at Lima's *audiencia*—an amount that hints at the lucrative and influential nature of the post.[109]

From their position within the judicial structure, defenders and procurators often used official channels to promote their own interests, arguing the necessity of keeping the post alive, recommending friends and relatives for office, and demanding individual and corporate *mercedes* (royal favors, graces). Yet doing so meant, at the very least, fulfilling a fundamental obligation: to inform the Crown of the pleas of the natives of the kingdom and denounce them through letters and reports, to which these advocates attached their own legal opinions and proposed solutions, thereby justifying their bureaucratic existence. In this sense, the information that protectors exchanged with the Crown—far from being neutral—had the defenders' own interests embedded in it.[110]

Defenders often wove their own personal demands and interests into the documents prepared in defense of clients. Thus, the interests of one party (such as men who staffed the *protectoría*) could be advanced by formally and simultaneously protecting—or claiming to protect—the interests of the other party (the natives of the kingdom), thereby creating an opportunity for the king to unburden his conscience.[111] The act of openly promoting the cause of native vassals and demanding their protection by denouncing colonial subjects and viceregal authorities for a series of wrongdoings (or at least giving the impression of doing so) constituted the main path for defenders and attorneys to simultaneously advance careers, promote self-interests, and improve social standing. It was the defenders' public advocacy for natives—cloaked in the language of "service" to God and king—that justified their existence before a patrimonial state not always eager or even capable of honoring the agreed salaries. Protectors stood, then, as conduits for the entrenched interests of their clients and themselves simultaneously.[112]

Though often penned as if the pleas of some were the pleas of all, letters and *memoriales* dispatched to the Council by the *audiencia's* chief defenders reveal injustices and past and pending lawsuits upon which protectors built their claims and arguments. Indigenous clients in the *audiencia* district no doubt contributed this information, orally or in writing, offering another clue to their relative trust in the system at this level.[113] The protectors' obligation to raise their voices in defense of native subjects before king and Council became a coveted opportunity to bypass local authorities by sending letters (which were in theory confidential) and other documents to the royal court with little interference.[114] Only occasionally were indigenous leaders and provincial defenders able to circumvent the protector-general of the *audiencia* to communicate directly with the Council, attesting to the importance of securing these channels for negotiating with the Crown.[115]

This precarious but partially successful working alliance between native litigants and their assigned defenders remained at least until the latter half of the seventeenth century. It began to crumble when informal indigenous and *mestizo* procurators-general entered the Atlantic setting, gradually taking over and offering an alternative set of actors, strategies, and possibilities for indigenous legal activism.[116] Perhaps a combination of factors prompted the appearance of the first indigenous procurators, who traveled to the royal court and began to operate on a viceregal and imperial scale: venality on the part of key royal officials, the increased desire for autonomy among certain indigenous subjects, and, toward the end of the seventeenth century, the king's decision to include the post of defender within the list of saleable offices (which likely increased the public perception of corruption). There was perhaps, also, a decline in the quality of judicial administration, associated elsewhere with the last decades of the Habsburg Dynasty.[117]

In some cases, the rhetoric, methods, and strategies of Spanish defenders-general were appropriated, strengthened, and expanded as indigenous actors entered into multiethnic and supracommunity alliances and as native procurators-general began to act on behalf of communities and others directly before the *Consejo de Indias*.[118] Yet, even after certain natives started to bypass public protectors and rely on a new caste of Andean Atlantic procurators, the vehicles for legal action forged in the previous century and the legal strategies remained largely the same. They were the Spanish defenders' contribution to the Indian reconquest of the Atlantic.

The trend among native legal specialists of the late Habsburg period, however, was toward autonomy from Spanish facilitators.[119] Limited independence, though, was not always attainable because of legal constraints. Even when Spanish officials were available, certain native groups chose to connect with metropolitan structures via informal notaries, solicitors, agents, and fellow transatlantic travelers, who lay partially outside the purview of the Crown. Relying on these agents might reflect previous disappointments with official attorneys and defenders, but they are further proof of the effective appropriation of Iberian legal culture.

THE POWER TO REPRESENT

Native Andeans got a taste of the versatility and effectiveness of the formal letter of attorney during the so-called perpetuity controversy. To oppose the perpetual sale of *repartimientos* to *encomenderos*, which would have also granted them civil and criminal jurisdiction over native vassals, almost two hundred *caciques* and *principales* from disparate regions of the viceroyalty gathered in a series of meetings (*juntas*) held between 1559 and 1562. Equally important, they empowered Fathers Jerónimo de Loaysa (archbishop of Lima) and Domingo de Santo Tomás—both Dominicans—as well as Father Francisco de Morales (the provincial of the Franciscans in Peru) to plead their case before the king. At the royal court, these proxies raised the impressive offer of 7.5 million pesos made by the *encomenderos*. Transatlantic negotiations, alliances, and travels involving *caciques*, friars, and Crown ministers unfolded to curb the king's desire to accept the *encomenderos*' offer. Countering their influence, wealth, and well-connected *procuradores*—not to mention convincing a still hesitant Philip to distrust the plausibility of the offer—would have been impossible without powers of attorney. The *Partido de los Indios* (roughly, the "Pro-Indian" Party) coordinated efforts in Peru and Spain. The letters of attorney endorsed by dozens of *caciques* became their tool for legitimizing a collective strategy and winning the battle against the *encomenderos* by making sure the matter was left undecided.[120]

The letter of attorney signed by these Andean *caciques* lay at the center of the imperial system of justice. Traditionally called a *carta de poder* (or simply a *poder*), this legal device had been widely used in the Iberian world in oral and written form since at least the thirteenth century.[121] As basic as the notion of the proxy may sound, the notarial formulas enshrined in this instrument explain the formation of a shared legal community across the Atlantic. Such formulas gave someone the *poderío* (power) to represent or appear in place of somebody else, creating invisible bonds of obligation, delegated agency, and common interest between two or more parties. The juridical theory behind this instrument even shaped the essence of royal power in the Indies, for monarchs themselves empowered their viceroys with letters of attorney, authorizing them to do and provide "all that of whatever nature and condition I might do and decide in said provinces if I myself was governing them."[122]

The authority of the written word legitimized the *poder* and validated future legal acts invoking this delegated agency in distant scenarios. The *poder* allowed individual and collective wills to journey in juridical form throughout the empire. The original document usually remained with the local notary, while legal agents received a copy. Other copies were often inserted in legal dossiers or presented directly at the Council of the Indies as proof of valid legal authority. Since the original addressees could transfer this authority to other delegates, the initial act of empowerment became the potential starting point of a chain of consecutive representations, which built and maintained legal networks linking actors and their proxies in far-off parts of the empire. Not all individuals granted *poderes* were entrusted with legal representation; some transported money, documents, and instructions and hired on-site advocates and procurators, especially in Lima and Madrid.

Colonial archives are filled with *poderes*. They could be drafted virtually anywhere a scribe was available and two or three witnesses could be summoned for the occasion. By the early 1550s, native Andeans were signing them for multiple reasons. In particular, *poderes* for court cases and other judicial affairs (*pleitos y negocios*) allowed indigenous leaders to overcome the significant obstacles of time and distance involved in reaching the royal court and its local counterparts: the American *audiencias* of Quito, Lima, and Charcas. Even if native delegates were able to travel to appellate courts, they sometimes signed letters to benefit from the legal expertise, influence, and connections of certain procurators and solicitors, some of whom boasted a large indigenous clientele.

A significant number of letters were open-ended (*poderes generales*), authorizing an attorney or local resident to request royal favor (*mercedes*), collect debts, bring petitions, and file lawsuits with *audiencias* and the *Consejo de Indias* for an indefinite period. Other letters revolved around a specific purpose or court case, at the conclusion of which the signatories could revoke the letter or grant it to someone else. Hiring advocates and procurators at different levels of the judiciary and then signing the necessary letters became one of the foundations of indigenous legal praxis, all within a larger colonial legal culture that relied extensively, and in fact thrived, on this type of document.[123]

This widespread legal practice became even more salient at key moments in the history of indigenous societies under Spanish rule. During the First General Land Inspection (1594–1596), royal inspectors toured the viceroyalty to regularize private and communal titles to land, forests, and pastures. They gave de facto landholders, many of them Spaniards, the chance to pay the Royal Exchequer a fee in exchange for a formal title. The dynamics of these inspections, including allegations of corruption and abuse, convinced native communities and private individuals of the need to protect landholdings by obtaining viceregal confirmation. Numerous Andean authorities in Cuzco, Huamanga, and Jauja gave *poderes* to lower-rank *caciques*, *principales*, and literate Andeans for this purpose. These legal agents were to take the titles to

Lima (or receive them there from other previously empowered agents), secure viceregal approvals, and obtain official confirmations. They were also to send the title back to their clients. To minimize legal costs and take full advantage of the opportunity presented by the long journey, some attorneys were also to file additional complaints, seek recompense for themselves or others, and conduct other business for the *caciques* and communities they represented. In such cases, and according to established legal praxis, the agents transferred the original *poderes* to solicitors, procurators, and other legal experts practicing their trade in Lima or Castile.[124]

TAKING THE NEW WORLD TO THE OLD WORLD

The use of *poderes* was not confined to local or regional spaces within the Andean region. Their portable, transferable, and flexible nature aided in the process of taking the New World to the Old World. Sixteenth-century Madrid, a common destination for these letters, offered a burgeoning market of legal services to which Andean litigants and favor-seekers could appeal. In the 1540s, indigenous subjects began to appear before the king and his itinerant court through the voices of public and private procurators. Especially prior to Toledo's legal reforms, the prosecuting attorneys of the Council—the recipients of some transatlantic *poderes*—were entitled to accept cases and file petitions on behalf of indigenous claimants as part of their duty of defending the king's own jurisdiction, patrimony, and most destitute vassals. These attorneys were not only to speak on behalf of Indians but also to inform the king if laws devised to protect them had been broken. At least on paper, they enjoyed the prerogative of demanding (*exigir*) that the king and his Council issue the appropriate laws and sanction transgressors. When representing Indian subjects, they were to work in tandem with the Council's advocates and attorneys for the poor (*abogados* and *procuradores de pobres*, respectively). In general, both posts had existed in different Iberian courts of law since at least the fifteenth century. However, they took on new meanings after the Spanish Conquest of the New World. The duties of prosecuting attorneys and advocates made them ideal transatlantic agents.[125]

Besides these ministers of the Council, a set number of licensed procurators (*procuradores de número*) also represented native subjects and corporations before this court of justice. The accompanying solicitors (*solicitadores*), of lesser legal and social standing, were in charge of the everyday vicissitudes of litigation: preparing documents, gathering witnesses, seeking the advice and signatures of professional lawyers, and developing legal strategies. The tribunals of Seville, home to the *Casa de la Contratación* that oversaw the movement of people and goods between Spain and the Indies, had dozens of licensed procurators and probably even more solicitors. The Royal Council in Madrid had thirty-one licensed attorneys in 1574, forty in 1584, and forty-eight in 1619. By the 1530s, a decade or so after its establishment, an increasingly busy *Consejo de Indias* had attracted a great number of legal facilitators; since they became almost indispensable for litigation before this superior court, native Andeans sought their services early on.[126]

Indigenous and *mestizo* visitors at the royal court hired solicitors and procurators directly, empowering them in preparation for legal engagements with the Council. Others sent *poderes* from the Andes via intermediary. The cost of hiring court procurators could be high, encouraging the proliferation of more informal practitioners who probably catered to less well-off clients. The duties of solicitors could go beyond legal representation. On the advice of Father Bartolomé de las Casas, Tlaxcalan delegates visiting the court in 1563 hired the licentiate Andrés de Cervera, a cleric. Cervera hired medical doctors, lawyers, and scribes for the Tlaxcalans; supervised the preparation of proofs of merit and other documents; ordered that royal decrees and coats of arms obtained at court be illuminated; accompanied the litigants to different Spanish cities; and secured clothes, food, and entertainment for them. Being proficient in Nahuatl, Cervera also interpreted before the king and the Council.[127]

As in the American realms, where there was not always a clear-cut distinction between private practice and public service, some professionals combined duties as legal agents (*agentes de negocios*) with posts inside the Council, including royal prosecutor, procurator, and advocate for the poor. In 1585, for example, the *caciques* of Yanqui Collaguas and Lari Collaguas, near the Andean city of Arequipa, signed a *poder* charging the Council's prosecutor and their own local Spanish magistrate (*corregidor*) with legal representation. This dual empowerment, as well as the fact that the local defender was not involved, suggest that (at least in this case) the prosecutor was acting as a private advocate and not as a public defender.[128]

Other cases of wealthy members of the Inca elite confirm the activities of ministers of the Council as transatlantic *agentes de negocios*. In April 1616, the nuns of Saint Catherine of Cuzco, among them Doña Melchora Clara Coya—illegitimate daughter of Don Melchor Carlos Inca—gave their *poder* to the Count of Lemos, president of the *Consejo de Indias*. The count was to bring the case before the Council in an effort to protect the assets and rents of Don Melchor, a portion of which belonged to Melchora Clara and, thus, to the nunnery. The count transferred the *poder* to two licensed attorneys and one solicitor, who represented the nuns in a first settlement, reached in

Madrid in 1619. In 1621, the nuns dispatched another *poder*, this time authorizing a *vecino* (urban citizen) of the town of Don Benito in Extremadura, and his two sons, one of them a trained advocate, to pursue their case further. The next year, this advocate gave powers of attorney to two licensed procurators and to his own brother, a knight of Santiago who, as a chaplain of the king, had close ties to the royal court. These agents brought the case to a close.[129]

The mechanisms of transatlantic empowerment were available to Andean claimants who had connections overseas and could afford the often undisclosed, but probably significant, fees charged by the couriers and the legal specialists looking after their cases. Indian petitioners and litigants with transoceanic aspirations realized that endorsing general and particular *poderes* to two or three individuals already in, or about to embark to, Spain increased the chances that these documents reached their final destination. Spanish *vecinos* of Iberian towns were favored for this reason, though they were not the only ones. In exchange for a fee, other individuals en route to Spain would then write petitions and letters, take the litigants' documents to Spain, speak on their behalf at court, or, more often, hire professional advocates and procurators to settle their cases.[130]

Thus, native groups and individuals, *caciques* and otherwise, gave powers of attorney to an array of people journeying to Spain or living in Iberia, from *encomenderos* and *vecinos* to clergymen, *caciques*, Indian commoners, and fellow native travelers. This practice, which offered an alternative to an expensive and perilous trip, continued well into the seventeenth century.[131] *Caciques* and individuals of noble Inca descent—especially when facing adverse rulings or official neglect in America—seem to have pioneered the legal strategy of empowering one or several individuals residing in Spain or staying there temporarily to represent them. However, this practice quickly became available to other segments of indigenous society.[132]

These chains of representation sometimes extended across noble families and lineages. After preparing his *probanza* in January 1562, Don Sancho Hacho de Velasco, *cacique* of Latacunga (in the *audiencia* of Quito), gave his *poder* to the Spaniard Esteban Pretel, then at the royal court with his brother-in-law, Don Francisco Atahualpa. Pretel and Atahualpa were to present Hacho's *probanza* and supporting documents before the Council. In September 1563, Pretel transferred the *poder* to Juan de Peña, licensed procurator of the Council. Pretel and Atahualpa also received a *poder* from Don Mateo Inga Yupanqui, *alguacil mayor* (chief bailiff) of the Indians of Quito. The professional bonds established among these travelers continued to prove fruitful after these exchanges. They illustrate the complexities of the transatlantic networks forged through the letter of attorney.[133]

A LEGAL CULTURE IN THE MAKING

Back in the Andes, litigants and petitioners regularly endorsed powers of attorney to transatlantic agents living or staying temporarily in Spain. These *poderes* show that, in some cases at least, the endorsers knew the whereabouts and specific circumstances of those being empowered to act for them.[134] News, messages, and practical information traveled through multiple conduits and points of contact, some of which speak to the formation of a common legal culture.[135] Letters, oral messages, royal decrees, and court rulings sent from Spain, along with tales told by travelers and claimants returning to America, conveyed images, both imagined and real, of life in Spain, the magnificence of the Habsburg court, and the workings of royal justice. If we are to trust the testimony of an anonymous Franciscan, several lords in Mexico gathered together in a *junta* in 1545 to question a *principal* whom they had sent "to see the things of Spain," inquiring about Charles's military might and the ways of the Spaniards "from Spain." Among other details, the traveler reported that "Your Majesty was a man like any other but had great power."[136]

Some litigants and petitioners communicated with their agents in Spain regularly, sending them written instructions (generically called *memorias* or *instrucciones*). Clients often attached such instructions to the letters of attorney: the first link in the chain of legal representation. The donors explained at great length what their aspirations and demands were, appending supporting evidence such as older decrees, official appointments, and proofs of merit. On certain occasions the instructions were notarized, which indicates they were part of formal agreements between claimants and attorneys. Given that relatively few of these instructions have been located in imperial archives, it seems that claimants and litigants intended them to be read only by the agent bringing their case to the attention of the authorities.

As early as 1555, Juan de Alvarado, an Indian conquistador and court interpreter for the *Audiencia de Lima*, sent one such set of instructions to Father Domingo de Santo Tomás. Alvarado, who knew how to read and write and probably wrote the instructions himself, explained the *merced* that he hoped to secure: a *repartimiento* in his native region of Chachapoyas.[137] Another example of this legal strategy takes us to the last Inca refuge of Vilcabamba, in the jungles of Cuzco, where in 1570 Inca Titu Cusi Yupanqui prepared his famous *Instruction to Licentiate Lope García de Castro* with the aid of a scribe and an interpreter. This *Instruction* is an early example of the legal strategy to secure the king's largesse among the Inca royals. Nevertheless, historians have overlooked key aspects of the *Instruction* that anchor this document in colonial legal culture.[138] The *Instruction*, along with a power of attorney and a historical account of the Spanish Conquest, was intended for the use of Governor Lope García de Castro, the Inca's legal agent at court. The *poder* gave meaning and purpose to the narrative of the conquest. García de Castro was supposed to use it as an aid to preparing a legal argument in favor of the Inca's aspirations at court: to see the recognition of his privileges so that he could be free to leave Vilcabamba.[139]

Private letters, though they took months to travel between the Andes and the Iberian Peninsula, fulfilled similar purposes. Letter-writing was a mature genre in the early modern Spanish world.[140] Multiple magistrates were constantly writing to higher authorities and the Crown, but so were individual subjects, corporations, and various interest groups.[141] Through these official letters and attached petitions, residents in America and Spain sometimes learned about the legal activities of litigants and petitioners.[142] Elizabeth Penry has noted that, throughout the colonial period, Andeans were generally responsible for delivering correspondence. Spanish officials complained that official letters and documents were sometimes opened and read prior to their reaching their formal recipient. Direct access to this type of information, Penry has suggested, "helps to explain how Andeans managed to stay well informed of many controversies" during the Great Rebellion of the eighteenth century.[143]

Official and extraofficial conduits allowed imperial subjects to write to the king and bring petitions and *memoriales* to his attention. At least one thousand such petitions passed Philip II's desk between 1583 and 1586 alone. A Venetian ambassador claimed in 1587 that His Majesty might sign as many as two thousand items in a single day.[144] Royal councilors were supposed to read letters and petitions from the Indies before attending to any other affairs, no matter how important, although it is difficult to know how much they abided by this royal order. Subjects were expected to inform local authorities and seek redress from them first, yet they were permitted to overlook this formal procedure, write directly to the Crown, and thereby sidestep officials in the Indies if they suspected them to be the source of the grievance or wrongdoing.[145] Throughout the colonial period, many native subjects, from paramount Inca nobles to leaders of small villages and remote towns, made use of this prerogative, even addressing their letters and petitions directly to the king "in" his Council. In one such letter, Doña Bárbara Atahualpa, a resident in Quito and a descendant of Inca king Atahualpa, reminded His

Majesty about the *mercedes* granted to Don Melchor Carlos Inca (Atahualpa's great nephew), also reminding the monarch of his responsibility to hear the claims of all of his vassals.[146]

These official lines of communication were a small part of a much larger web of transatlantic connections and interactions. Indians and *mestizos* of royal Inca blood wrote to relatives with regard to family affairs in Spain. Less prominent travelers also corresponded with kin and townsfolk, sometimes via literate intermediaries.[147] They wrote to communicate their wishes concerning their property in Spain and America, to describe the outcome of their legal affairs, to gather information about other travelers and their aspirations, or simply to awe their audience with tales of their journeys in Iberia and beyond.[148] Correspondence also flowed in the opposite direction.[149]

Private correspondence was also important for litigating and petitioning in the royal courts. Letters of attorney usually specified that legal agents were expected to send any royal decrees and other written rulings secured at court back to the Andes at the litigants' expense. This expectation indicates that paths of communication remained open after the initial act of empowerment. Claimants could use correspondence to inform other parties, relatives, and associates about incoming lawsuits; to try to dissuade potential rivals; or to request additional funds, witnesses or testimony, and documents for litigation.[150] Legal agents sometimes notarized legal expenses and sent them along with private letters to Andean (and Mesoamerican) clients.[151] Litigants and petitioners, for their part, inquired about the state of their cases, referred to previous correspondence, and acknowledged the receipt of royal decrees and other documents.[152] Thus, letters of attorney, private letters, and instructions had the power to connect native litigants and petitioners traversing the Atlantic, supplementing the news brought by returning travelers and keeping the image of the judge-king alive in the Andes.

Cosmopolitan and gateway cities like Lima, Madrid, or Seville played an important role in the foundation and maintenance of these transatlantic networks. In Seville, Andean travelers had to deal with officials of the *Casa de la Contratación* and prepare for the return voyage or the journey across the region of La Mancha to the king's court. All of these arrangements could prove confusing, dangerous, and expensive without the aid and support of fellow travelers, patrons, relatives, and compatriots (*paisanos*) living in the Peninsula. As in the case of Spanish and Portuguese emigrants and returnees, "these people from home probably served as important contacts [for the travelers], assisting them in making their arrangements, attending to their business as well as that of people at home."[153] Martín Fernández, a self-declared "Indian" from the town of Moquegua in southern Peru, journeyed to Spain in 1604 to "search for one of his kinsmen." *Paisanos* played different supporting roles, likely sharing information on how to obtain licenses to travel from the House of Trade or how to prepare for the challenges of the Atlantic crossing or the overland journey to the court. While waiting for the royal fleet to arrive in Seville in 1670, Don Pedro Chafo Çavana, an official interpreter of Lima's *audiencia*, requested authorization from the House of Trade to move temporarily with his family to Cádiz. There, Chafo declared, "I have friends and acquaintances from my homeland [*patria*] who will help me ... until the time comes for me to embark."[154]

Some of these travelers, moreover, shared the same residences in Spain. While at the royal court in 1607, Don Pedro Carrillo de Soto Inga, grandson of conquistador Hernando de Soto and great-grandson of Inca Emperor Huayna Capac, lived "at the rented home (*posada*) of Don Melchor Carlos Ynga" in Madrid. Garcilaso Inca de la Vega hosted the *mestizo* Don Juan Arias Maldonado at his house in Andalusia twice. The Crown had condemned Don Juan, the son of conquistador Diego Maldonado and Doña Luisa Palla, an alleged daughter of Emperor Huayna Capac, to exile in Spain in 1571. After the king granted him a permit to return to Cuzco for three years to sell his property, collect any debts, and return to Spain, he visited Garcilaso before his departure for Peru.[155]

As a result of these multiple connections, high-profile travelers frequently appointed other travelers as stewards of their patrimony or as legal guardians of their children.[156] Furthermore, visitors at the royal court acted as witnesses to each other's proofs of merit (*probanzas*).[157] As well, social bonds created or strengthened in Iberia could extend across the sea. In the mid-1650s, Don Bartolomé Aylas, a *principal* from Jauja, decided to support Jerónimo Limaylla with favorable testimony during a court case before the *audiencia* of Lima. When prompted to reveal why he was supporting Limaylla, Aylas declared that "we spent time with each other in Madrid; we are friends and so I should help him."[158]

Multiple links of legal advocacy and support among subjects in different parts of the empire reveal the existence of broad, complex networks of representation, patronage, and communication, reinforcing the idea that, within this legal arena, there was no such thing as an exclusively "Indian" sphere.[159] Because of the specific nature and purpose of these links, Andean litigants and favor-seekers were generally aware of one another's whereabouts in Peru and Spain. They were also familiar with some of the outcomes of each other's legal actions, which allowed for the gradual accumulation of a knowledge base of experiences during the first two colonial centuries. These experiences turned into legal precedents, which future Andean petitioners and litigants called upon during their own legal battles and requests of royal favor.[160] Letters of attorney, moreover, created chainlike connections and acts of legal ventriloquism in which legal agents spoke on behalf of individuals who could not reach the royal court in person. By the seventeenth century, networks of representation had broadened significantly. They had gone well beyond the more circumscribed spheres of influence of the official Indian procurators of the Toledan era, discussed in the previous chapter. Although these native specialists remained key to the facilitation of chains of representation reaching Spain from the Andes, many other legal actors had entered the Atlantic scene. Viceroy Toledo had been defeated.

Descripción bastante detallada
Tal vez muy, descriptivo - pero
posiblemente útil -
Pudo ser más corto -

FOUR

WHO SPEAKS FOR THE INDIANS?

Lima, Castile, and the Rise of the Nación Índica

They were called *aletos* in Castile and *huamanes* in Peru. Attendants at the Spanish royal court praised these Andean hunting falcons for their worth in sport and entertainment. Throughout the seventeenth century, viceregal authorities dispatched dozens of these birds to Iberia in an effort to please the king and his courtiers. In October 1676, the viceroy count of Castelar informed the *Consejo de Indias* of one such dispatch, "in quantity and quality [the] greatest ever made from these provinces." Castelar had entrusted a hundred falcons to Don Miguel de Chávarri, a member of his retinue who was to lead eight "young men well-versed" in the art of falconry. Per the king's own request, Chávarri and his crew would be following a set of detailed instructions, prepared by the royal cosmographer, on how to safely transport the birds. Chávarri, who received 7,400 pesos for travel expenses, finally delivered the birds in Seville a year later. To everyone's disappointment, however, only nineteen made it to Spain. Chávarri excused himself before the displeased councilors: despite all the attentions provided to the birds, a strange case of food poisoning had ruined the precious cargo. The Peruvian sheep (*carneros*) that Chávarri's assistants had been feeding to the falcons had themselves fallen sick after drinking too much seawater, infecting and killing the birds of prey in an ironic turn of events.[1]

Andrés Dávila and Álvaro Enríquez were among Chávarri's ill-fated crew. Castelar had personally put the birds under the care of Dávila in Lima, where the latter practiced his trade. A nineteen-year-old shoemaker, he was to manufacture the hoods to cover the birds' heads, and thus prevent them from getting frightened or distracted, as well as the straps (*pihuelas*) needed to hold the falcons on a fist or tie their feet to a perch. Originally from the indigenous village of San Jerónimo in the Jauja Valley, Dávila had moved to Lima in his youth. Peninsular authorities sometimes graced him with the honorary *Don* before his name, but they also labeled him with the seemingly puzzling *Indio mestiço*, perhaps an Indian of mixed descent or acculturated ways. Having been promised two hundred pesos in Lima, he arrived in Spain with the birds in November 1677, enduring a nine-month journey from the viceregal court to Panama and Portobello, then to Cartagena, Havana, the Azores Islands, and finally the port of San Lúcar in Andalusia. Álvaro Enríquez, for his part, served as the improvised cook for the expedition. He was a twenty-two-year-old tailor of similar plebeian status. Crown officials described him indistinctly as a *mestizo* (of indigenous and Spanish descent) and an *indio de nación*, someone of Indian ancestry or upbringing, an *indio* by birth and origin. Though a native of Lima, Enríquez had left his hometown several years prior to set up shop farther north in the city of Panama, where Chávarri recruited him to replace one of his sick men. Allegedly, Enríquez's "wish to see the things of Spain" was so strong as to make him volunteer in Chávarri's crew without recompense. He reached Cádiz at the beginning of 1678 aboard an English ship, after falling sick and being left behind in the Azores by a master desperate to deliver the remaining birds in Seville.[2]

FALCONS FOR THE KING

The eventful journeys of Dávila and Enríquez are illustrative of the urban worlds of many other Andean cosmopolitans. Yet, their life stories hardly fit into established narratives about the social origins and motivations of indigenous travelers to Spain. Their journeys remain caught up within a set of assumptions about native leadership, political culture, and ethnogenesis that center on certain images of the Andean *cacique*. Current views tend to overstate the role of these ethnic lords as the most visible agents of social change and the main travelers within distant regions of the empire. The larger sample of travelers, especially in reference to individuals occupying the upper echelons within the group, reveals a much more complex social hierarchy in the making. Dávila and Enríquez were not *caciques*—that is, recognized noble descendants of the pre-Hispanic lords of the land, exempt from tribute and personal service due to their high birth and right of lordship over indigenous vassals. Although motivation is often difficult to discern, travelers like them did not voyage to Spain to uphold their noble status, request a family crest, or defeat a rival to the post of *cacique* in the courtroom. (This did not, however, prevent them from using their failed commission and two-year sojourn at the court to further their own aspirations.) Nor did Dávila and Enríquez visit the court to reinforce their "ethnic legitimacy" by advocating for the interests of their indigenous subjects and their communities; they spoke for none but themselves.[3]

These two travelers were city Indians, a tailor and a shoemaker of comparable rank who had set up shop in important centers along the Pacific and Atlantic routes from Peru to Spain. Dávila, moreover, enjoyed the confidence of Viceroy Count of Castelar and his close circle, as the delicate task commissioned to this improvised falconer attests. These travelers' identities and their strategies for ascending the social ladder, their urban relations, and aspirations—to "see" the things of Spain or to obtain a coveted post in the viceroy's personal guard—were anchored in the world of the Indians who dwelled and prospered in multifaceted cities. Their ventures were indeed representative of the experiences of many other Andeans who moved within the Spanish Empire in the sixteenth and seventeenth centuries, much more so than were those of the relatively few *indios* and *mestizos* of royal Inca blood who petitioned the king in person or the indigenous lords of vassals who managed to set their governmental and communal obligations aside and cross the ocean.[4]

Different aspects of early colonial society, such as increased access to European goods and tastes, the development of cash and credit economies, and the establishment of the king's system of courts, opened meaningful avenues for wealth and power for Andeans who lived in urban spaces. Significantly, a considerable number of native voyagers to the court belonged to the fluid middle and upper sectors of urban denizens with rural backgrounds and social connections. The complex cultural and political transformations in which this meaningful phenomenon rests have sometimes been dubbed the "tragedy" or "contradiction" of "successful" Indians, their "Hispanism" being similarly characterized as the condition of being "suspended" between two social worlds—Indian and Spanish.[5] These dynamics and the imperial experiences of relocation and negotiation that indigenous transatlantic travels reveal are, instead, an indicator of the dynamism of colonial Andean cultures. Reconstituted and redistilled within new (yet not completely unfamiliar) cultural settings and a new sense of collective self, Indian urban identities within the empire were built by men and women through ordinary and extraordinary experiences—Atlantic journeys included.[6]

Native urban ethnogenesis and increasing class stratification must be framed within pan-hemispheric and pan-Atlantic processes also affecting Africans, Europeans, and their descendants. People within and around the Atlantic experienced similar processes of multidirectional cultural change, albeit within clear, sometimes abysmal asymmetries of power. Different groups tried to "re-create stable worlds" and "reliable communities" in which they could reembed themselves, often under very adverse circumstances.[7] Mapping native ethnogenesis, however, also calls for a deeper understanding of one of the most significant outcomes of the incorporation of the Andes into the larger Atlantic world. Native cultural transformation and reproduction, especially as they unfolded in Lima and its hinterland, were heavily dependent on internal processes of reallocation of power, prestige, and authority, not only among Indians, Africans, and Spaniards but also within the *República de Indios* in the seventeenth century.

"Posts" and "institutions" become a suitable framework for beginning to map these complex processes of acculturation and cultural transmission, making the distinction between Indian "society" and Indian "culture" relevant again.[8] As new institutional spaces and loci of power emerged to rule over the growing indigenous populations of colonial urban centers, novel institutional venues also took shape to express corporate identities and try to influence the direction of political and cultural change *from*—not only *within*—urban settings. These channels were largely independent, though not totally detached, from *cacicazgo* politics and rural Indian communities' internal mechanisms for legitimizing authority and distributing power. Although the larger processes triggering these transformations were of a pan-hemispheric and pan-Atlantic nature, they were "fundamentally driven by local variables" such as contingency, geography, demography, and other conditions.[9] Ethnogenesis in colonial Lima was as much linked to "place" and "fixity" as it was to fluid exchanges, interconnections, and the interplay between the global and the local.

Lima, seat of the viceregal court and the *audiencia*, was in important respects the main gateway into the legal Atlantic. It was the place where the high officialdom and the ecclesiastic hierarchy converged and the most visible site of Habsburg rule in the Southern Hemisphere. In part as a result of its political and economic centrality within the Andean realm, the city became a space from which elite indigenous inhabitants and its rural allies—sustained by the institutional vehicles and bureaucratic posts from which they gave voice to their corporate identity and political consciousness—imagined a place for themselves within the increasingly global *imaginaire* of the universal monarchy. An emerging segment of *indios ricos* or *prósperos*—prosperous or well-off Indians who received relatively high wages and profited from the commercial economy—came to develop in the city. This sector included Crown officials, schoolteachers, notaries, artisans, traders, and militia officers occupying positions of authority and prestige reserved for "Indians" within the urban milieu.[10] This prosperity created the conditions from which to promote their class interests and reinforce their position vis-à-vis other indigenous leaders by claiming to speak for the *República de Indios* in local and metropolitan forums.

Colonial rule was to simultaneously carve out other positions of leadership within rural communities. The parallel hierarchies of religious and civil government that took root in these native towns in the 1570s and 1580s granted *mita* (draft labor) and tribute exemptions to church and municipal officials in the countryside, significantly increasing their opportunities for upward social mobility and turning privileged Andeans from across the viceroyalty into potential migrants to the city. When seen in the long term, these were two partially overlapping groups. Urban artisans, retainers, and wage earners of all sorts, many of them first- and second-generation immigrants themselves or the children and grandchildren of native rural town dwellers, secured analogous (though de facto) privileges and exemptions in colonial cities, thanks in part to their own efforts but also to the economy of favor and patronage that held urban society together. These urban ties help us make sense of Dávila's and Enríquez's Pacific and Atlantic experiences.

Native demands for autonomy, justice, and reform for the so-called Indian Nation and the *República de Indios* must be framed within these transformations. By the end of the seventeenth century, the viceregal capital had harbored the social and political conditions for the articulation and circulation of discourses about the contours, privileges, and hierarchies of this "Indian Nation" (*Nación Índica*) in Peru and Spain.[11] A series of transatlantic campaigns, some of which influenced colonial policies, called for the protection of native subjects and communities while noting that the king's justice was too far removed and too tenuous to reach them. But such a legal defense was to be exercised by the native *letrados*, officials, and notables who came to spearhead Indian society in Lima. Their advocacy of the *Nación Índica* placed them in the position of power brokers but also reinforced their primacy within the *República de Indios*. This process of political mobilization and negotiation exhibited multiple connections with other Andean cities and their countryside. Yet, it was fundamentally sponsored by Lima's multifaceted Indian elite and was aimed at reinforcing their acquired, and in part self-attributed, prominent role within the *República de Indios*, supported in turn by the structures of indigenous governance that had crystallized in this urban space. As such, these political projects, which unfolded within a larger imperial scenario, expressed the contexts of asymmetrical power that distinguished European, African, and Indian Atlantic experiences almost as much as they illustrated the inner fissures and hierarchies of a reconstituted indigenous society in midcolonial Peru.

TO SEE THE THINGS OF SPAIN

How did travelers who were not part of an official contingent manage to go to Spain? Perhaps unsurprisingly, indigenous travelers, like other travelers in the early modern Spanish world, followed generally established routes in reaching Castile and the Habsburg court. Circuits of commerce and authority started to shape these routes since initial encounter. Familial ones did so too. The idea of "seeing [the things of] Spain," which Álvaro Enríquez identified as his main motivation for making the transatlantic voyage, appears in licenses and license requests by Spaniards and *mestizos* who wanted to seek out or reunite with members of their mixed families on both shores of the ocean. Starting in the 1540s, bringing wives and other relatives to the New World as well as "moving" *mestizo* children between Peru and Spain became established practice. Networks of trusted relatives, friends, business partners, and legal proxies became critical for these undertakings, as Spanish wives called for husbands absent in the New World, sometimes forcing them legally to return with their *mestizo* children; or Spanish fathers traveled of their own accord with their *mestizo* offspring to deposit them with relatives in Spain; or alternatively, granted powers of attorney to a sailor or merchant to locate and retrieve them from their indigenous mothers, transporting them to the Peninsula to be raised and educated in distant households.[12] Early indigenous travelers of the 1540s and 1550s likely relied on some of the transatlantic networks forged and expanded by these Indian-Spanish families.[13] Nonetheless, making a transatlantic crossing represented movement on an unprecedented scale and did not always—or perhaps only seldomly—include extensive family networks on the other side. In that sense, early indigenous experiences probably mirrored those of the very first Spaniards who moved to the New World.

Their itineraries generally took indigenous travelers from the main port of El Callao (or other minor ports) to the Isthmus of Panama, with possible stops along the Peruvian coast, and then overland to Nombre de Dios or Portobello. By the early seventeenth century (if not earlier), landowners of the coastal valleys north of Lima were relying on some of the smaller Pacific ports, including Huanchaco, Malabrigo, and Chérrepe, to ship products to distant markets. In Panama, middlemen exchanged flour, wheat, soap, hides, and sugar from these valleys for wine, textiles, and slaves. Indigenous laborers, muleteers, and even small landholders became essential to this renewed seaborne trade early on, even contributing their own products to increase the Pacific shipments. The commercial activities of these coastal dwellers help explain their familiarity with, and participation in, larger oceanic circuits.[14] Indigenous men manned and commanded some of the vessels upon which this intercolonial trade flourished. In the 1670s, Lázaro Llongo, the first mate of the boat *San José* and a native of the port of Paita (near the northernmost city of Piura, on the Peruvian Pacific coast), was regularly making the journey from the port of Huanchaco, Trujillo's harbor and Llongo's hometown, to that of Perico, in the Spanish Main (*Tierra Firme*).[15] Many other natives traversed these seas, likely under very similar conditions.[16] In 1562, Jerónimo, another native from Piura, completed the entire voyage to Spain. In the early seventeenth century, Francisco Mondragón, an indigenous fisherman originally from Huanchaco and a proprietor of two ships, was sailing regularly along the Pacific Rim—and at least once to Panama—for commercial purposes.[17]

These stories and others illustrate the frequency and relative ease with which some Andean subjects moved between ports in Peru, the northern South American mainland, the Isthmus, Cartagena, and beyond.[18] As stated, older connections across the ocean, particularly familial ones forged between Indians and Spaniards in the aftermath of the conquest, might have been the basis for the ease with which indigenous claimants created their own networks and developed their own strategies.[19] Travelers like Álvaro Enríquez, the *limeño* (Lima-born; a native from Lima) tailor who set up shop in Panama in the second half of the seventeenth century and was later brought on board by Chávarri to care for the king's falcons, likely took advantage of these connections, coming into contact with the indigenous sailors that made them possible, perhaps paying men like Llongo to take them to the Isthmus on one of their regular trips or, alternatively, working on board in exchange for passage or even a modest salary.[20]

The round-trip between Seville and the New World usually took nine to ten months, but a journey in the opposite direction could take less time. The voyage between Callao and Panama lasted some three weeks. From harbors in Tierra Firme, most vessels of the royal fleet sailed east to Cartagena, where they usually spent another two or three weeks. Captains replenished food and water supplies, picked up additional passengers, and then went north to Havana. There, the ships united with New Spain's fleet for the sixty-day convoy journey east to the Azores, the Bay of Cádiz, and finally Seville, arriving there in late October or early November.[21] Another twenty or thirty days, or about 340 miles, awaited Andean travelers who made the trip on foot from Cádiz or Seville to Madrid. Securing a return license from the king and the *Consejo de Indias* and having the permit approved by the *Casa de la Contratación* could take an extra two or three months (sometimes significantly more). All in all, undertaking a trip to Spain in the royal convoy and immediately back to the Andes, with new stops along the Peruvian coast as well as a possible final landing in the port of Paita, when Pacific currents and headwinds did not permit continuing to Callao by sea, required about six months and almost twice as long in extremely poor circumstances. The voyage spanned some six thousand miles and, if the traveler had not started his trip in Lima but farther inland—let us say the former imperial seat of Cuzco or the mining mecca of Potosí, both in the southern Andes—then the journey could extend for several additional months. Litigating and petitioning before the king meant a much longer stay, sometimes many years.[22]

Cities in general, but especially urban centers with port outlets linking inter-Andean valleys, highland villages, and the coast, such as Lima, Trujillo, or the now disappeared Saña, offered multiple opportunities for indigenous travelers to devise their trips and decide to join one of the regular ships en route to the Peninsula. Return licenses issued by the *Casa de la Contratación* in Seville reveal that many indigenous travelers claimed to have journeyed from or were returning to prominent Andean cities such as Lima or Trujillo, but also Quito, Guayaquil, and even Cuzco, deep in the southern highlands. The witnesses making declarations in these passenger licenses, moreover, people who had been summoned by the returnees to render their stories credible, were also almost invariably urban residents—old and new—as well as *vecinos* of Seville or some city in the Indies, bound to the travelers by preexisting social relationships.[23]

OF PATRONS AND CLIENTS

Equally telling of their social world, travelers appearing before the ministers of the House often declared that they were *criados*—servants, dependents, or protégés of a Spaniard. These patrons were customarily midranking ministers appointed to serve or already serving in the New World as well as members of the religious orders moving within the empire.[24] In the context of the overseas venture, the term *criado*, which appears regularly in permits and other documents, generally alluded to a client-patron, servant-master, or even employee-employer relationship. Social superiors and their dependents in early modern Spanish societies operated within a general "ethos of clientage" that bonded the two unequal parties at many interlocking levels, embedding interests, loyalties, and relations within highly personalistic bonds.[25]

Formal authorization for the journey could come as a result of these prior connections—commercial, familial, professional, and otherwise.[26] Crown officials were in the position of granting licenses and recommendations to fellow travelers. Sometimes their sole presence made such permits unnecessary, as several individuals voyaging to the royal court alongside viceroys, councilors, and *audiencia* judges experienced firsthand. The officials of the *Casa de la Contratación* in Seville sometimes asked travelers to produce permits, thus hinting at some of the networks behind these trips. In other cases, authorization to travel for some of these *criados* was taken for granted.[27] Take the case of Francisco Ulpo, an "Indian and a native of Peru" (*indio natural del Perú*) who went from Lima to Madrid in the company of *licenciado* Diego García Maldonado, a respected royal minister. While García Maldonado secured his appointment to the *audiencia* of Quito, Francisco Ulpo visited the court "to oversee a certain court case." During a one-week stop in Seville, Francisco stayed with García Maldonado's brother, a scribe based in Lima and a witness in Ulpo's application for a return license.[28]

Relying on connections with Crown officials, other travelers went to Spain to stay. Don Roque Sánchez, a forty-four-year-old noble Indian (*indio principal*) from Saña and the valet (*ayuda de cámara*) of a local Spanish noble, resided in the home of the Count of Alba de Liste in Madrid in the 1660s. The count, a former viceroy of Peru, was probably the person with whom Roque Sánchez voyaged to Spain. Similar networks supported the journey back to Peru. In 1611, Andrés journeyed from his home in Cuzco to Madrid at the service of *oidor* Juan de Villela, recently promoted to the *Consejo de Indias*. Two years later, Andrés requested a return license, this time as a dependent of Jerónimo de Pamones, his fellow traveler to Spain in 1611, who had been appointed *corregidor* of Collaguas, near Arequipa and not too far from Cuzco.[29]

These journeys, under the protection of powerful patrons, were in fact very common.[30] They were not circumscribed to the Andean region.[31] The series of reciprocal exchanges embedded in these relations sustained the transatlantic enterprise. Many such relations predated the trip, while others were constructed, or reactivated, as part of the quest to see the things of Spain. Modern insights about the social links between colonial bigamists and a constellation of partners, relatives, and acquaintances in Mexico and Spain certainly apply to native Andean travelers, although the evidence is not always as readily available. Like other individuals of a similar plebeian status within the emerging Spanish Atlantic world, many travelers counted on the patronage, protection, and friendship of employees, royal ministers, and other benefactors higher up the social ladder. Equally important, the strategic claim of being part of the cohort of a Spaniard, even if unfounded, generally excused travelers from their disregard of the general prohibition against Indians journeying to Spain, while shielding them from any accusations of idleness by the magistrates of the *Casa de la Contratación*. Finally, relationships with councilors and other officials could offer litigants and petitioners a head start. These prior engagements offered the opportunity to talk about cases and aspirations outside the courtroom or seek a private audience, all in an effort to influence the will of ministers and the resolution of cases.

THE FRIARS' CONNECTION

Travel arrangements reveal an interesting yet somewhat predictable array of possibilities, as certain patterns begin to emerge. Certainly, traveling with a colonial official seems to have been ordinary, but other alternatives are discernible in the documents, especially if one focuses on the world of the Catholic Church. If the information contained in passenger licenses issued by the *Casa de la Contratación* during the Habsburg period is to be trusted, individuals journeying to Spain customarily traveled alongside members of the mendicant orders who, as a professional group, regularly traversed the ocean in the sixteenth and seventeenth centuries. Ecclesiastics may have comprised nearly one-third of the total registered emigrants from Spain to America in the first three centuries after the Spanish Conquest.[32] For multiple reasons, many ecclesiastics, especially heads and procurators of orders, often embarked on the opposite journey as well. Moreover, patronage networks *within* the ecclesiastic state, especially those that took the form of the master-dependent relationship between the hierarchies and the lower ranks, were a deep-rooted vehicle for travel, resettlement, and promotion. Given these established patterns, it comes as no surprise that friars would frequently appear in passenger licenses as witnesses verifying Andean travelers' life stories and circumstances.[33]

Ideological as well as pragmatic reasons help us make sense of this pattern of collaboration to cross the ocean, even if a temporary one, between Indians and men of the cloth. The famous controversy about the "perpetuity" (*perpetuidad*) of *encomiendas*, which kept royal officials, encomenderos, native lords, friars, and the king himself busy in the 1550s and 1560s, is an excellent example of the first type of partnership. In 1556, in the midst of the offers and negotiations to influence the sovereign's will on whether to grant *encomiendas* in perpetuity, Don Pedro Topa Yupanqui, of noble Inca descent, journeyed to Spain with the Dominican father Domingo de Santo Tomás, one of the leaders of the "Pro-Indian" party discussed in chapter 3. Two years earlier, Father Tomás de San Martín, another Dominican of the same political faction, counted one Jerónimo de Quiñones, a native Andean from Huamachuco in northern Peru, within the retinue of *criados* returning with him to the New World.[34]

But even the large-scale political mobilization known as the "perpetuity controversy" rested on less visible but older networks of knowledge, communication, and collaboration, progressively forged by Indians and friars since the time of the conquest. Some indigenous travelers of the Habsburg era simply chose to rely on transoceanic networks built by the religious orders. Like other early modern transnational corporations, the orders built these networks to connect their spiritual and material interests across viceroyalties and with Rome or the royal court and the *Consejo de Indias*, the highest court ruling over the Americas and the institution in charge of overseeing royal patronage to the Church. Priests exchanged information about the histories, cultures, and languages of the native inhabitants of the New World, in part obtained from their indigenous informants. Moreover, religious colleges and convents functioned as gathering places for friars on both shores of the Atlantic, especially for official missions. Regular communication existed among convents and colleges, which shared old and new members, library and archival materials, missionary methods, and knowledge about the Indies.[35]

In the realms of litigation and favor-seeking, both areas in which the religious orders were especially involved, transatlantic networks allowed native Andeans to represent their interests before the Council and, with the aid of friars and their connections, circulate news, letters, and petitions within the empire.[36] The links between indigenous groups and subjects, on the one hand, and Dominican friars on the other, which crystallized in the early 1550s during the perpetuity controversy (but never reemerged with the same intensity), illustrate the potential of such alliances. In the coming decades, many indigenous actors relied on the same channels and practices to make their trips to Spain possible.[37]

Even though the pan-Andean spirit of collaborative activism that had developed during the perpetuity controversy did not really last beyond the 1560s, general patterns of Indian-priest support for reaching the royal court, oiled by widespread relations of patronage-dependence, generally did. Travel arrangements to reach the royal court and the legal campaigns that unfolded there, rather than being based on such highly politicized and supralocal controversies as the perpetuity controversy, turned into affairs of a more restricted political and geographical scope. Even when relying on the matrix of social networks forged in the 1550s to reach out to the king, patron-client and teacher-disciple relations among Indians and sympathetic friars, with no political overtones, along with very pragmatic considerations regarding the transatlantic voyage, offer alternative (and perhaps equally important) explanations for certain patterns of support and collaboration based on mutual convenience.

Like royal officials, members of religious orders normally journeyed to the

New World at the expense of the royal treasury, a privilege that could encompass some of their *criados*. Through the *Consejo de Indias* and the *Casa de la Contratación*, the Crown sponsored almost five hundred missionary expeditions during the sixteenth century alone, covering the friars' travel expenses to Seville, donating money to the convents and houses who hosted the friars while in transit, and paying for the fathers' passage fares and provisions.[38] Furthermore, friars were generally exempt from the cumbersome purity of blood investigations, introduced around 1552, which were customarily conducted at the passengers' own expense and in their place of birth.[39] Contrary to most lay travelers, and depending on the order in question, some friars had proven their genealogical purity when entering their institute, thereby becoming exempt from fulfilling this general travel requirement again. This exemption made the trip from Seville or Cádiz more expedient.

Clerics also enjoyed a special privilege permitting them and their retinues to voyage on the galleons of the armada, which accompanied the royal fleet, having to pay only a fixed price of 20 ducats (22 *reales* or 2.75 pesos) for the convoy tax (*avería*).[40] Moreover, given the centrality of their mission, Dominican, Franciscan, Augustinian, and Mercedarian friars as well as Jesuit priests journeying to the New World customarily received funds from the royal treasury in Seville to pay for their travel expenses as well as for those of one dependent. These perks granted to the regulars help explain why placing themselves at the service of a friar was a common way for travelers, Indians and Spanish alike, to guarantee the success of crucial portions of their long journey.[41] Although the overall expenditures associated with crossing the Atlantic Ocean reflected the social standing and specific circumstances of the travelers involved, in the late sixteenth century there are examples of the potentially high costs of voyaging at one's own expense.[42] Traveling between Peru and the Iberian Peninsula could cost anywhere from a few hundred to several thousand pesos.[43]

But securing the trip alongside the fathers was only one portion of the transatlantic enterprise. In Peru as well as in Spain, clergy members also supported individual indigenous and *mestizo* travelers and seekers of royal grace with their influence and institutional protection. The fathers could back up the natives' negotiations with local and metropolitan authorities, as when they agreed to declare in proofs of merit or attest to the religious zeal, linguistic proficiency, or noble ancestry of an indigenous petitioner. Setting their own patronage networks in motion to benefit protégés, clerics could also pen letters of recommendation to different officials in Peru and Spain as well as transport documents and powers of attorney to distant parts of the empire. The renowned *mestizo* priest, preacher, and Quichua expert Don Diego

Lobato de Sosa, the illegitimate offspring of Captain Juan Lobato and Doña Isabel Yaruc Palla (one of the principal wives of Inca Atahualpa), was an early graduate of the Franciscan school of San Andrés in Quito, where he served as chaplain. In 1591, he received letters of recommendation from the provincials and the fathers of Saint Augustine, Saint Francis, and Saint Dominic in Quito, which proved determinant in his ultimately successful campaign for reward at the royal court.[44]

Aside from this type of institutional backing, and in spite of the Crown's regular prohibitions, priests acted as informal solicitors and procurators for indigenous subjects during the Habsburg era.[45] For example, one could rely on a Dominican friar acting in this capacity to reach out to a registered solicitor assisting at the royal court.[46] Other litigants followed a similar legal strategy and chose to empower the chief procurators of the religious orders directly to represent them, no doubt attracted by their strong and wide-reaching connections, institutional savvy, and legal expertise in dealing with the Crown.[47]

Thanks to their influential posts as chaplains and confessors of viceroys and other ministers in America, friars could also grant indigenous subjects access to the main sources of local power and patronage. Perhaps the story of Juan Vélez, a *mestizo* interpreter who entered into the service of the chaplain of Viceroy Count of Nieva in the early 1560s, was not exceptional. At a relatively young age, the Franciscans took Vélez from his native Jauja to Lima to give him a Christian education (*doctrina y escuela*). Through his master the chaplain, Vélez gained access to the count and the palace circle, placing himself on the path to a successful career as official interpreter for the *audiencia*.[48]

Such patron-client and teacher-student relations could extend well beyond the viceroy's court and the City of Kings (Lima) and the viceregal seat. While at the royal court in Madrid, a man named Lorenzo Ayun Chifo won the esteem of Father Buenaventura Salinas y Córdoba, an influential Franciscan, entering into his personal service around 1646. Ayun's connections to the Franciscans dated back many years. As a young "Indian" living first in Trujillo and then in Lima, he had served another member of the order. Father Salinas's sphere of influence, for his part, included the viceregal palace in Lima, where he had served different viceroys almost since childhood, as well as the court in Madrid, where Salinas had been a vocal advocate for the natives of Peru since 1637.[49] Upon being appointed general commissary for his order, Salinas sailed to New Spain in March 1646, accompanied by two friars and his indigenous *criado*. For seven years, Lorenzo Ayun lived in the Franciscan monastery in Mexico City. Probably through Salinas, who was the viceroy's personal confessor for some time, the traveler gained access to New Spain's viceregal circle. Sometime later, Viceroy Count of Alba de Liste (1655–1661), now promoted to the Peruvian seat, incorporated Lorenzo Ayun into his entourage of *criados* and relatives, taking him back to Peru and landing in the port of Paita in 1655.[50] Aside from illustrating the importance of clerics and friars in sustaining these Pacific and Atlantic journeys, the stories of Lobato de Sosa, Vélez, and Ayun point to the centrality of basic learning and semiformal religious education as privileged social spaces where the patron-client networks sustaining native Andean Atlantic experiences were forged and expanded.

BECOMING LITERATE

Often the result of moving into the city and adopting urban mores, the acquisition and later deployment of basic literate skills and more specialized knowledge by an important portion of indigenous society (larger than previously thought and not restricted to the *cacique* class) were concomitant with the rise of a new Indian elite in Lima, capable of taking over some of the posts and symbolic spaces of the colonial Lettered City. Along with long-term urban residence, teacher-student bonds forged within ecclesiastic and civil spheres help to explain the connection between literacy, power, and legal activism at the Habsburg court.[51] Royal officials of the *Casa de la Contratación* often described native travelers as *indios ladinos*.[52] At the very least, this important label pointed to the traveler's proficiency in Castilian (though one must remember that many of them were likely native speakers of Spanish). It also signaled their ability and good disposition to learn, in particular, all things Spanish. Significantly, the notaries of the House who prepared travel licenses in Seville recorded passengers' testimonies without an official interpreter being present.[53]

Although it is difficult to assess the number of travelers who also knew how to read and write, we are certain that some of them did. These travelers' command of the Castilian language—and what contemporary observers perceived as their "Spanish" ways—is another important hint as to the social background and universe of relations among Atlantic travelers. Some travelers started training as church assistants in native towns or nearby cities, receiving early education from members of the clergy. Either independently or in parish schools, native pupils learned elementary arithmetic and basic religious doctrine (the Lord's Prayer, Ave Maria, the Creed, the Sign of the Cross, the Ten Commandments, and how to recite the Sacraments) as well as to read and write by memorizing printed prayers and catechisms.[54] During the so-called First Evangelization of the Andes (1532–1583), priests began to rely on indigenous assistants to fulfill important duties among rural parishioners. Natives that the friars considered especially apt began to occupy the posts of choir-master (*maestro de capilla*), cantor (*cantor*, who also fulfilled other musical posts), schoolteacher (*maestro de escuela*), and sexton (*sacristán*) in rural and suburban parishes. Musicians trained to serve as acolytes, recite the canonical hours, sing in the choir, and play for the liturgy. *Maestros de capilla*, for their part, taught music to the *cantores* and directed them in rehearsals and performances. They also doubled as teachers of primary schooling and Christian doctrine in towns or sometimes the city, teaching students how to read, write, sing, and pray, thereby increasing the avenues to a basic education for many indigenous subjects.[55] *Sacristanes* (sextons or altar boys) helped priests during weddings, baptisms, Mass, and confession, especially when priests were absent. Their example was to inspire the faithful, serving as a model for an emerging Andean Catholicism. One of their most important tasks was to make sure that everyone attended Mass, calling parishioners by ringing the church's bell. Free from tribute and labor services, these parish assistants (*oficiales de doctrina*) quickly created a power structure and a literate elite parallel to, and sometimes overlapping with, that of municipal councils and traditional lineages of *caciques* and noble Indians, for whom special boarding schools (*colegios*) were eventually created in Lima and Cuzco.[56]

Friars in the Andes often targeted some native children and teenagers in their efforts at religious conversion, selecting the best pupils from rural parishes and sheltering them in convent houses and monasteries located in cities. The original idea was to train native students so they could teach future generations in turn.[57] In convent schools such as San Andrés, founded in the Franciscan monastery of San Pablo of Quito in 1552, Indian and *mestizo* students of varying status also learned how to sing, read, write, and preach in Spanish and in the *lengua del Inga*. The idea was that these students would later perform as musicians, interpreters, missionaries, and teachers to other natives inside and outside the school.[58] In 1568, Pedro Juan Antonio, a brilliant student in the Franciscan *colegio* of Tlatelolco (established in Mexico City for the education of Nahua elites), journeyed to Salamanca to study civil and canonical law in its prestigious university. Six years later, this specialist in the Classics originally from Azcapotzalco published a Latin grammar in Barcelona.[59]

The life stories of travelers of a less prominent background similarly illustrate that moving from the countryside to an urban monastery or school opened a series of possibilities for a privileged education. Some natives residing in monasteries in Lima, Quito, and Cuzco, for instance, learned the Christian doctrine. While attending classes and serving the friars inside cloisters, natives learned and practiced arts and crafts. There, they could become sextons, cooks, tailors, gardeners, painters, shoemakers, or carpenters. The 1613 census of the Indian inhabitants of Lima lists some seventy-three natives working inside the monasteries and hospitals of the city. Most were single and in their teens or early twenties. The sons or nephews of *caciques* were few; others were of a more typically artisan, plebeian, or even commoner background. None of them claimed to be a native of Lima, but like many transatlantic travelers of the early seventeenth century, they had moved to the viceregal capital from Andean cities like Trujillo, Huamanga, and Cuzco (or their surrounding Indian villages). Others claimed to be from predominantly indigenous regions such as Huarochirí, Jauja, Huamachuco, and Huaylas. The overwhelming majority were either too young or too far away from their communities of origin to pay tribute; some even claimed not to remember the name of their *caciques*.[60]

In a few instances, moreover, Indians serving in these urban convents took the habit as lay brothers—a privileged status that helped some of them gain voyage to Spain alongside their Spanish spiritual brothers (*hermanos de religión*). In 1615, Father Claudio Ramírez de Sosa, a Franciscan and Viceroy Prince of Esquilache's confessor and "theological advisor," requested a license in Seville to return to Peru with his dependent, Baltasar. Father Sosa had previously traveled with Baltasar, an *indio donado* or lay brother, from Charcas (Upper Peru) to Spain and then to Rome on undisclosed business.[61] At the close of the seventeenth century, Father Francisco Suárez, another lay brother and an *indio de nación*, journeyed to Madrid with Father José de Obregón, procurator-general of the Dominican province of San Juan Bautista of Peru. They parted ways at the royal court, apparently not on very amicable terms, as Obregón left Suárez stranded. Father Francisco had to stay in the Dominican convent of Alcalá de Henares while he awaited the departure of the royal fleet bound to Peru. He traveled via Cádiz at His Majesty's expense. Similar circumstances probably surrounded the earlier journey of Father Bernardo Inga, *presbítero de los padres clérigos menores* (a presbyter for the fathers who had taken minor orders and thus could not celebrate Mass for themselves). Father Bernardo Inga was in Seville in 1690 and corresponded with *mestizo* presbyter and transatlantic advocate Juan Núñez Vela, then residing in Madrid.[62] Father Francisco Suárez's later journey prompted a 1706 royal decree warning viceroys and governors, as well as provincials in New Spain and Peru, not to allow *religiosos indios* (in this context, Indian friars or lay brothers) to travel to Spain.[63]

Similar links to the Franciscans in Peru, Mexico, and Spain facilitated stays of other indigenous travelers at the royal court. Born in a native village in northern Peru, Lorenzo Ayun, mentioned above, began to serve as an altar boy at age eleven. Five years later, Father Fernando de la Carrera, the local priest, made him sexton. Carrera relied on bilingual informants like Lorenzo during daily religious services and for developing sermons and a grammar of the local *Yunga* tongue. Sometime later, Father Carrera entrusted his protégé to Father Juan de Ayllón, an ill-tempered Franciscan residing in the neighboring Spanish city of Saña, to teach Lorenzo how to play the organ and sing for religious occasions.[64] Under the control of this new benefactor, Lorenzo Ayun and other young bilingual classmates studying under Father Ayllón learned how to read and write in Spanish. In 1646, after moving with the friar to the main convent in Lima and having served as a cook, Lorenzo sailed to Spain for the first time.[65]

Beyond convents, parish schools, and the Jesuit school for noble Indians (the *Colegio del Príncipe*, named after Viceroy Prince of Esquilache), the city of Lima offered less structured and less formal (yet equally significant) learning opportunities for Indians and *mestizos*. Although scholars still know very little about how indigenous intellectuals, officials, and other members of the multifaceted urban elite accumulated, transmitted, and deployed specialized knowledge, mechanisms complementary to the familiar pattern of Indian-friar collaboration were definitely at play.[66] Aside from the boarding school for elite Indians ran by the Jesuits, other learning centers and settings for the effective transmission of this type of knowledge were active in late-seventeenth-century Lima.[67]

Seeking similar results, *caciques* and other elite Indians often placed their sons in a notary's office to acquire basic literacy and general legal skills. Less prominent Andeans placed themselves at the service of scribes in exchange for religious and literate education.[68] Other Spanish professionals, including royal ministers and legal specialists, as well as private indigenous and *mestizo* tutors of first letters (basic arithmetic, reading, and writing), also provided instruction to elite and nonelite Indians in Andean colonial cities, expanding opportunities for upward social mobility.[69] Practical experiences and social connections of this type were an important source of knowledge for interpreters, urban militia officers, and other members of the privileged lettered class. As in the case of Spanish scribes (as well as solicitors, attorneys, and young apprentices), Andean natives relied on the old master-disciple model of empirical training, learning mainly by serving in official capacities, sometimes for many years or even for life, gaining considerable knowledge from teachers and peers during their careers.[70]

In sum, gaining privileged access to Lima's officialdom and lettered elite, and becoming part of transatlantic religious circles (and ultimately of extensive networks stretching across the ocean), required the creation and maintenance of patronage ties with priests and bureaucrats, friars, viceroys, supreme justices, and future councilors. In the larger imperial arena, these bonds, along with specific types of knowledge—speaking fluent Spanish, reading, writing, plus a good command of the law—played in favor of native voyagers. They could prove useful on the other side of the ocean in Spain. Journeying to the royal court and gaining access to the king in writing or in person, especially for nonelite urban Indians, was ultimately a matter of knowing the right people.[71]

MUDAR TRAXE Y LENGUAXE

Atlantic journeys were also shaped by older dynamics of rural-urban and urban-urban migration, ultimately tied to broader Atlantic and Pacific world diasporas. In a sense, traveling to Spain from the Andes was an extension of these ongoing displacements. Conditioned by *mita*, the struggle to escape fiscal burdens, the sale or usurpation of community lands, the search for economic opportunities, and the wish to reunite with relatives, *paisanos* (compatriots or countrymen), and friends, the routes out of rural Andean communities and into colonial cities had become well-trodden paths for indigenous peoples in general, and for some Atlantic travelers in particular, by the end of the seventeenth century.[72]

Like many other cities throughout the first century and a half of colonial rule, Lima remained a place for temporary and permanent indigenous migration, especially from the northern and central Andean regions of the Peruvian viceroyalty. Virtually since its foundation in 1535, however, Lima had also served as a nexus for peoples from Central America, the Caribbean, and the Andes at large.[73] Domestic servants, retainers, and dependents of Spanish residents (initially identified by generic terms such as *yanacona* or *sirviente*), as well as indigenous military auxiliaries, interpreters, and other Andean migrants, gradually joined the original inhabitants of the Lima Valley. In the mid- to late 1560s, an average of three thousand temporary workers (*mitayos*), levied from some twelve provinces of Lima's administrative district, joined this displaced population. Gathering in the city every winter in what was called the *mita de plaza*, *mitayos* built bridges and roads, maintained aqueducts, cleaned streets, erected and maintained private houses, tended livestock, and sowed fields for Spanish residents. An increasing number managed to stay beyond their required time of service, however, swelling the ranks of a floating migrant population over which rural traditional and municipal authorities had much less control.[74]

As in other cities, migrants to Lima settled in Indian suburbs, Spanish households, ranches, and the nearby haciendas and Indian villages of the surrounding valleys, becoming retainers, unskilled and skilled wage laborers, artisans, tenant farmers, and domestic and church servants.[75] The streets near the Hospital of Santa Ana (where *mitayos* were often sent to heal) and the Indian ward of Santiago del Cercado, an Indian municipality officially founded and opened in the early 1570s within the city atop an older informal settlement dating back to circa 1568, became likely destinations and places for residence and activity.[76]

This population influx was so important that, by the early seventeenth century, the "Indian" residents of Lima included individuals from multiple parts of the Spanish Empire, predominantly the northern and central regions of Peru but also New Spain, Quito, Chile, the Philippines, and the Portuguese East Indies.[77] According to a recent estimate, moreover, about 70 percent of Lima's "Indians" between 1570 and 1670 were not natives of the city.[78] Only a fifth of the close to two thousand "Indians" registered in the famous tributary census conducted by notary Miguel de Contreras in 1613 identified the city as their place of origin. Of those who provided a date for their arrival, 19 percent claimed to have been in Lima for less than a year, while 42 percent had spent between one and five years there. More than a quarter of these residents claimed to have migrated from important provincial cities, a significant clue as to their familiarity with urban mores, society, and culture. Moving from the Andes to Tierra Firme or Spain was, for many migrants and the children of migrants, an extension of these forced displacements and voluntary movements.[79]

As part of these dynamics, some indigenous migrants and residents found ways to keep the older connections with their home communities alive. These migrants, especially if originally from the highland areas adjacent to Lima, maintained economic and social ties with those staying back home, retaining landholding rights, paying partial or full tribute, and periodically journeying back and forth to visit relatives and townsfolk, particularly during religious festivities. The migrants' networks in the city were oftentimes based on those shared places of origin.[80] Nonetheless, new urban loyalties intersected with the older ethnic identifications pouring into the city in multiple and complex ways. Indigenous migrants and residents created new connections, actively participating in the formation of multiethnic households and neighborhoods.[81] The world of the village and the world of the city were never two totally separated domains but interconnected parts of a continuum of native urban and semiurban experiences under colonial rule.

Upon moving to the city, migrants rebuilt and expanded social networks, acquiring novel positions and tastes within the bustling urban milieu. They also embraced new social identities and placed themselves within new urban hierarchies.[82] The upwardly mobile segments within the larger indigenous urban population came to inhabit a creolized world, characterized by "new attitudes toward language, religion, dress, and the economy."[83] Throughout the sixteenth century, some *indios criollos*, as members of this highly "acculturated" or "naturalized" (and prosperous) segment within the larger indigenous urban population came to be known, became the target of criticisms from other non-Indian urban residents. They condemned *indios criollos* for having abandoned or changed their allegedly true *naturalezas* (in this case, their "nature" and place of origin), permanently acquiring new urban ones. But these criticisms also point to the fact that people in Lima likely perceived *indios criollos* as women and men who shared basic sociocultural features due to similar class, lifestyle, taste, and status. They probably looked a certain way too, as *criollo* came to mark both place of birth and the adoption of creolized forms of cultural and social expression and adaptation to the city.

More important, *criollo* and *naturalizado* could also be terms for self-definition or ascription with a more positive connotation. They could indicate long-term or permanent residence as well as having "roots" in the city, particularly familial ones.[84] Wills drafted by *criollos* and the use (by others) of the term in notarial records suggest that *indios criollos* in the early seventeenth century likely perceived themselves as a separate community in the making, comprising city-born individuals with ties to "multi-ethnic urban institutions," who had grown up speaking Spanish, rather than individuals "born in rural communities, where they would have been integrated into *ayllus* or other kin-based networks."[85] These were some of the multiple ways of being "Indian" in colonial Peru.[86]

The previously unknown report of interpreter-general (*intérprete general*) and defender for the natives (*defensor de los naturales*) Juan Vélez, drafted in 1612 for the eyes of Viceroy Juan de Mendoza y Luna, the Marquis of Montesclaros (1607–1615), offers an exceptional window into the tensions and complexities of these creolized identities. Vélez, himself a migrant of Spanish and Indian ancestry from the Jauja Valley whose ethnicity went generally unmarked by this time, was a firsthand witness, but also a strong critic, of these urban transformations. His perspective, that of an "external" observer discovering, labeling, and denouncing the urban residents of indigenous descent in Lima, helps us anchor the discussion about *indios criollos* and emerging Indian urban elites.[87]

In its detail, Vélez's ethnography is only surpassed by the pages that Felipe

Guaman Poma, another court interpreter, devoted to these *indios criollos* in his *Nueva corónica y buen gobierno*, finished in 1616.[88] According to Vélez, there were more than four thousand *indios* living in the city and its jurisdiction. For some of them, *criollo* worked as a term of self-identification, a sign of social distinction, and a marker of status change. Some had left their towns as children and, to live unrecognized among Spaniards, had transformed their "dress and language" (*traxe y lenguaxe*) to Spanish custom. If found to be *indios*, they called themselves *criollos*, and thus "exempt from paying tribute and from personal service." They defended this transformation by claiming that "they had now naturalized themselves among Spaniards," refusing to aid their "brothers" and others who had remained in their original villages.[89]

Disguising their origin and tributary status, *criollos* dressed "in Spanish clothes" (*en abito de españoles*), thus embracing urban styles. They boasted "silks and linens from Rouen and Holland" instead of wearing the more traditional wool and cotton, which had become markers of rural Indian identity.[90] *Criollos* ate bread and meat, moreover, and preferred wine over corn beer (*chicha*). The men cut their hair short and carried weapons, mainly daggers and swords, without viceregal license—a privilege traditionally granted to *caciques* and noble Indians of certain rank. Both sexes spoke Spanish regularly and dropped or replaced their native surnames to mirror Spanish usage. Claiming to be "creoles, *ladinos*, and men of the trades," they and their offspring refused to fulfill their tribute and labor obligations, claiming to serve no *cacique* at all. Now that this emerging middle sector had left some of the specific cultural and linguistic markers of its rural "Indianness" behind, nothing justified its subjection to these colonial burdens. In early-seventeenth-century Lima, such a claim amounted to a political statement.[91]

For men like interpreter-general Juan Vélez, the author of this report, the prosperous city Indians that he described subverted the proper social order. Vélez sought to convince the viceroy of the urgent need to introduce better mechanisms to count, tax, and control Lima's indigenous population, eventually forcing them to return to their towns of origin. In that sense, he and Miguel de Contreras, the royal scribe in charge of the 1613 census of the Indians of Lima, shared the conviction that changing dress style was merely a tool to evade economic obligations, particularly tribute and *mita*. Yet, as Karen Graubart observes, escaping tribute was rarely the *only* motivating force in adopting "Spanish" dress and lifestyle in Lima and other Andean cities.[92]

Vélez's portrayal, though far from approving, ultimately reveals that ambivalent terms such *criollo* and *ladino* were not just an excuse to escape labor and tribute obligations but also a means to increasingly ascertain "respectable" status within urban society. *Indios criollos*, especially the most prosperous among them, though often of non-*limeño* origin, acquired their new urban "nature" after several years of hard work and permanent residency in the city, serving in religious and secular institutions, buying land in the urban hinterland, accumulating wealth, knowledge, and prestige, and forming new social relations therein. As Vélez declared in 1612, perhaps with a dose of exaggeration, "All or most of them are rich people; many own two or three slaves."[93] Furthermore, for many urban Indians, particularly those who did not attempt to claim a non-Indian identity during the census, *criollo* status also meant a growing sense of being part of a distinct urban order "whose visual culture they deployed as a matter of identity rather than deceit," investing it with new social and political meanings.[94] As they participated in the creation of ethnic identities and social hierarchies, well-off and acculturated Indians redefined their generic "Indianness"—itself a result of blurred, blended, or reimagined prehispanic identities—as a source of prestige and political empowerment.[95]

This emerging urban middle sector, though still a relatively small and exclusive group, was highly visible due to its participation in the religious and civic life of the indigenous community living in Lima.[96] Theirs was the social world of Atlantic travelers such as Gaspar de la Chira, an "Indian dressed as a Spaniard" who signed a contract with the Spaniard Miguel de Angulo in 1597. Gaspar de la Chira was to serve Angulo, a scribe based in Lima, for two years and accompany him to Guatemala on undisclosed business.[97] Exterior signs of acculturation were the most visible marks of these social and cultural transformations, though not necessarily the most profound. For the upper sector of *indios criollos* in particular, full membership and participation in key institutions and mechanisms of power allowed for the re-creation and reassertion of elite urban identities and cultures, calling for the development of what Paul Charney describes somewhat evocatively as "a new sense of belonging."[98] Taking Lima as a case study, it is possible to sharpen the analysis and single out some of these *indios criollos*, follow their trajectories, and reconstruct their social and professional networks in the city and beyond.

As early as 1607, five *limeño* Indians were granting power of attorney to a transatlantic solicitor, putting him in charge of securing copies of the "royal orders, titles, and decrees granted to us" and bringing them back to Lima. The plural "us" (*nos*) here is intriguing, for it reveals a growing sense of a distinct *limeño* identity among these urban Indians.[99] Fast-forward to the end of the

Habsburg era: another illuminating clue as to how this process of elite consolidation crystallized during the seventeenth century—a process that indigenous journeys to Spain constantly mirror—comes from a 1734 power of attorney. This peculiar *poder* was signed by the native urban leadership of Lima
in order to secure a procurator (*procurador*) of their own in the *Audiencia de
Lima* (and hopefully at the royal court), an attorney of their own *nación* to
represent the Indians of the city and the kingdom as a *república*. In the document, Lima's indigenous leaders fashioned themselves as three separate and
hierarchically arranged guilds or estates (*gremios*). In order of preeminence,
the *gremios* that endorsed the legal device were, first, the "military men" or
militia officers of the city; second, the "*caciques* and governors," which included leaders of the adjacent towns and a few Andean provinces beyond the
jurisdiction of the city; and finally, the "master craftsmen" of the guilds of
Indian shoemakers, tailors, and hatters—perhaps the oldest and most prestigious artisan brotherhoods.[100]

The uppermost distinction between "militia officers" and "*caciques* and
governors" highlights the emergence of a new urban upper class somewhat
distinguishable from the traditional Indian aristocracy of the land. Despite
common aspirations for wealth and social prestige, these two groups can be
traced to two interrelated social segments with different sources of wealth, authority, and legitimacy, based on dissimilar mechanisms for self-preservation
and identification. Consider the seventeenth-century Indian notable Don
Felipe Carguamango de la Paz. Although scholars have characterized Don
Felipe as a *curaca* (an alternative term for *cacique*), he self-identified as a native of Cuzco, an urban citizen (*vecino*) of Lima, and an infantry captain of a
hundred-man Indian squadron. As a reward for his services and alleged illustrious ancestry, Don Felipe fulfilled "noble and honorable posts, both political and military" in the city during the 1650s. These posts included that of
trustee (*síndico*) of the Holy Places of Jerusalem and chief urban magistrate
(*alcalde mayor*) of the Indians of Lima. Don Felipe's roots, like those of many
other urban dwellers of indigenous descent, were to be found in disparate
corners of the Peruvian realm. He was the son of Don Alonso Carguamango,
a *vecino* of Cuzco, and Doña Inés Carguachumbi, a noble Indian (*india principal*) of the native village of Santo Domingo of Yauyos, in the highlands east
of Lima. In his letter to the king, Don Felipe further declared, "I am a noble
man amongst those of my kind [*género*] and a descendant of paramount
lords" from Sacsamarca, a town in the southern province of Vilcasguaman,
yet another locale near the Spanish city of Huamanga to which this petitioner
traced part of his multiethnic ancestry.[101]

BEARING ARMS IN THE CITY

As the case of Don Felipe Carguamango demonstrates, bearing arms for the king attracted city Indians who, although prominent, respected, well connected, and wealthy, did not have easy access to the aristocratic title of *cacique* and the accompanying post of *gobernador* of a rural village, *repartimiento*, or province. Military posts and honors sought by urban *indios principales* fell within the prerogatives of viceroys, *audiencia* judges, and ecclesiastic authorities and thus were not subject to traditional mechanisms of communal control. Although captains of Indian military units selected their standard-bearers and sergeants, they too were expected to receive confirmation from members of the palace circle. In the sixteenth century, many self-identified *caciques* also requested such titles at the royal court.[102] Yet, to judge by similar requests made before the Council in the following century, prosperous and influential Indians from Lima and other urban settings (no doubt supported by powerful patrons) increasingly sought military posts and judicial positions. Nobles and nonnobles made up this new military elite. For these prosperous residents, nobility was, in most cases, not a place of departure but a point of arrival. Their selection for office, moreover, owed as much to individual qualifications as to loyalty to the social web of royal servants in which they were bound.

Around 1615, Felipe Guaman Poma, a court interpreter like Juan Vélez and a direct witness to the rise of urban militia companies, criticized the vice-regal appointment of nonnoble captains and sergeants. He described them as "poor," "low-status," and "tribute-paying" commoners rather than lords. Such appointments were a dishonor to the "gentlemen and principal people, lords and pure-blooded captains" and, as such, a disservice to God and king, to the *República de Indios*, to the city, and to the whole kingdom. These complaints were indicative of the fluid social landscape that had developed as Guaman Poma gave the last touches to his work.[103]

In fact, three years earlier, the Lima census registered two commanders of infantry companies. Don Francisco de Sanzoles, "captain of the *naturales*," was a sixty-year-old tailor from the neighboring Jauja Valley. Pedro Blas, the other captain, was a fifty-eight-year-old laborer (*chacarero*) from the city of Trujillo, another important pole of migration to Lima. Blas was also one of the signatories of the 1607 power of attorney for a procurator to secure royal orders and privileges in favor of important *limeño* Indians.[104] By the mid-seventeenth century, a similar military hierarchy had developed in other urban centers. Don Carlos Chimo, a native from the town of Lambayeque and a traveler to the royal court in the mid-seventeenth century, was a master embroiderer in his adopted home—the city of Trujillo—and the sergeant-mayor of the Indians of the neighboring city of Saña.[105]

Felipe Guaman Poma's denunciation of the "poverty" of these individuals reveals more about the chronicler's ideal equation of upper class and nobility than it does about the realities of urban life in the seemingly chaotic City of Kings. Fulfilling military posts in a squadron demanded that the individual be financially well off. Sanzoles, the captain of the Indians in 1613, owned three houses in Lima. Pedro Blas, the other captain, owned one house and a slave.[106] Similar class indicators are found among those who fulfilled these posts a century later. In a letter to the king written in 1726, Don Lorenzo de Avendaño, commissioner-general (*comisario general*) of the Indian mounted battalion of the city for the previous sixteen years, looked back at his military career. At the age of eighteen, Don Lorenzo started serving as corporal (*cabo de escuadra*), rising through the ranks of sergeant and other posts to commissioner-general at the age of twenty-five. All of this he had achieved "without any rent, salary or remuneration whatsoever, besides that of becoming deserving of employing myself at the service of His Majesty." Though sergeants and captains received no pay, they had to feed, outfit, and mobilize the men under their command from their own patrimony. They were, for the most part, wealthy individuals.[107]

Indian infantry and cavalry companies or battalions (*compañías de naturales*) were already developing in sixteenth-century Lima. In 1589, an Indian company welcomed Viceroy Marquis of Cañete during his official entry into the city.[108] By the 1620s, Lima's Indian militia comprised ten infantry squadrons, each with its own captain and sergeant, totaling some five hundred men. To receive Viceroy Marquis of Guadalcázar in 1622, the companies paraded through the city with muskets and pikes, led by their standard-bearer. In 1648, "several troops" of Indians took their oath of loyalty before the newly appointed Viceroy Marquis of Mancera. In 1666, two squadrons of Indians witnessed the ceremony of acclamation of King Charles II. In 1675, when the viceroy summoned all men of Lima who could bear arms, three squadrons of three "nations" (*naciones*)—Indians, free blacks, and mulattos—answered his call. By 1682, Lima's Indian militia included a cavalry company.[109] Captains of these battalions, some of them visitors at the royal court, moved up the ladder of a little-studied military hierarchy. By the late 1650s, the posts of captain of an Indian squadron had become *de número* in Lima, that is, limited to a small number of beneficiaries and with no new admittances until the death or retirement of one captain. This privilege, added to the fact that some captains of the mid-seventeenth century were the sons of previous captains, reinforced reinforced the self-perpetuating nature of this elite urban body.[110]

By the second half of the seventeenth century, the Indian militia had already established its leading position, in terms of power and prestige, within the Indian *gremios* of the city. Military posts offered these urban *indios principales* a legitimate form of corporate representation within the *República de Indios* and, through them, gave expression to the Indians of the city and the kingdom. Indian militia officers were already performing as a *gremio* in 1657. In that year, the "military men" celebrated the Virgin of the Limpia y Pura Concepción as their patron. In front of "clergymen, gentlemen, and many other residents" attending the ceremony at Lima's cathedral, Archbishop Pedro de Villagómez officiated Mass. The viceroy, *audiencia* judges, and members of the city council joined the celebration. They occupied the seats closest to the altar. Filling other privileged seats were the field marshal, the sergeant-mayor, the general sheriff of the Indian cavalry, nine discharged captains of battalions (who paid for the ceremony), and the standard-bearer of the festivity. Only one of these attendants identified himself as a *cacique*. The other seats were reserved for Indian captains, aides, standard-bearers, sergeants of infantry squadrons, plus all "residents of this city and its hinterland," organized according to rank. Once the ceremony was over, the virgin was paraded throughout the city with great splendor.[111]

Given the complex yet understudied urban dynamics of caste, station, and class, the social boundaries separating the different segments of the indigenous upper sector—the "officers," the "*caciques*," and the "artisans"—appear tenuous. The sources reveal, however, that, through marriage, god-parentage, religious affinity, and business associations, the fluid and dynamic sector of urban *indios principales*—some of them probably self-identified as *criollos*—came to incorporate within their ranks some *caciques* and *principales* of the Indian *pueblos* of the Lima Valley. Some women of the local *cacique* class became wives and daughters of prominent urban militiamen and trade and confraternity officers, chief urban magistrates, and official interpreters of the city, opening the doors for the acquisition of the title by ambitious incumbents. As a result, wealthy Indians of commoner stock gained entry into the *cacique* class of the older, and by then well-established, neighboring *pueblos*. It seems, however, that traditional authorities still represented a minority within this group of urban notables by the end of the seventeenth century, at least in Lima.[112] Some have advanced important explanations for the relative marginalization of traditional elites in the public life of the city. Although elites continued to perform governmental tasks in *reducciones*, population decline, gradual loss of land, ecclesiastic attacks on traditional family patterns in the sixteenth century, as well as the appearance of alternative sources of political authority, weakened their position beyond their localities.[113]

ALL ROADS LEAD TO LIMA

The identities of these and other elite urban Indians living in mid-colonial Lima help us pinpoint this process of social differentiation and ascendancy to the pressing viceregal need to devise ways for governing the urban indige-nous population. This was to be accomplished through political and religious intermediaries, preferably dependents familiarized with urban dynamics. This need eventually led to the creation of new posts such as interpreter, *alguacil* (bailiff), and *alcalde* (urban magistrate).[114] Yet, as part of this viceregal policy, recent migrants and their descendants—and not necessarily the *caciques* and *principales* of the Lima Valley—fulfilled these posts in the sixteenth century. At the time of the founding of their *pueblos* in the 1550s and 1560s, Indian lords were granted a much more restricted jurisdiction.[115] By the 1560s, an overarching indigenous authority no longer existed in the Lima Valley. Nor did the Crown resettle or reorganize native immigrants under any *caciques*. Al-though *mitayos* were, at least theoretically, still under the command of ethnic lords at home, they also became partially subject to the authority of other native urban magistrates. These officials were commissioned to tap into the floating labor pool and try to collect some of the tribute owed to the king.[116]

The fact that a significant number of migrants registered in the 1613 census of Lima's Indians declared themselves to be *cacique*-less is indicative of this reshuffling and relocating of political authority. The migrants' responses to the census-takers reflect the waning of some of the old social bonds, as hun-dreds of native residents managed to place themselves beyond the purview of traditional lords. The census rolls identify several individuals who chose to highlight their independent or semi-independent status. Some claimed to recognize no *cacique* because they were too young when they left their home-towns. Perhaps others were too smart to remember the name of their lord, thus avoiding being registered for tributary obligations. As one of the native residents included in the census put it, "The *criollos* [of the city] serve no *ca-cique*; they are entrusted to the royal Crown." The weakening of older loyalties as well as social obligations and ties linking immigrants and leaders of their villages and *repartimientos* of origin helps explain the gradual emergence of imagined political communities such as the all-encompassing *Nación Índica*, historically rooted in Lima but rhetorically decentered and ultimately detached from any particular lineage, community, province, or local tradition.[117]

The trajectories and social constellations of elite indigenous visitors at the Habsburg court add an additional layer of complexity to urban Indian identities by shedding light on the impact that the incorporation of the Andes into the larger Atlantic world had on the process of elite consolidation. Surviving student rolls of the Jesuit boarding schools of El Príncipe (Lima) and San Borja (Cuzco), in theory restricted to the eldest sons of the *caciques* of these two urban jurisdictions and surrounding areas, do not include transatlantic travelers. The fact that even the most prominent members of the travelers' sample are absent from the universe of traditional *cacique* lineages reflected in these lists is in itself significant, revealing how travelers occupied a different social category.[118] Their lives, available to us only in fragmentary form, reveal that military and governmental service, especially as one moved forward into the colonial era, granted elite status and external signs of de facto nobility to well-off urban Indians, making them almost indistinguishable (at least on paper) from a *cacique*, a governor, or a lesser *indio principal* visiting the viceregal court or living in the municipalities of the Lima Valley. Starting in the second half of the sixteenth century, members of the urban elite sector began to mark this status through the strategic adoption, often authorized by direct viceregal decree, of honors, privileges, and institutions initially limited to *caciques* but later opened by the viceroy and judges of the *audiencia* to Indian militia captains, chief magistrates, and interpreters serving representatives of the king within the city and in special commissions beyond its jurisdictional boundaries.[119]

The adoption of privileges such as dressing as Spaniards, riding horses, and carrying swords and daggers in public, as the Crown had allowed *caciques* to do since the early 1550s, is a revealing indicator of the folding together of two initially distinct groups. In 1663, Viceroy Count of Santisteban issued one in a series of edicts banning any Indian, black, or mulatto in the city from carrying swords, daggers, knives, or machetes. Yet, excluded from viceregal prohibition, and therefore authorized to carry those weapons in public, were the "military officers such as captains, ensigns, aides, and sergeants" of the urban companies of Indians, mulattoes, and blacks.[120] By this time, notables like Don Martín Çapuy, a migrant from the northern highlands and a resident of the nearby village of Surco (where he married into a local family), had been enjoying such privileges for decades. Çapuy, the interpreter-general for the *audiencia* and a traveler to the Habsburg court around 1619, testified to the

Consejo de Indias in a petition: "I have always carried myself in the noblest fashion, going about dressed as a Spaniard with sword and dagger by special favor of the viceregal authorities."[121]

A similar indicator of the increasing access of powerful urban Indians to privileges and honors initially conceived for ethnic lords of vassals and the Inca nobility centered in Cuzco is that, by the mid-seventeenth century, some of these elite urban Indians had been able to secure exceptional admittance for their sons in the Jesuit schools for Indian nobles.[122] In 1657, after a life of royal service, Don Felipe Carguamango de la Paz penned a letter to the king. He explained that, after occupying the post of captain for one of Lima's Indian squadrons, he secured a letter of recommendation that later resulted in the viceroy authorizing a place for his son, Don Francisco de Heriza Paz Carguamango, in the school for Indian nobles run by the Jesuit fathers in El Cercado. By his own testimony, Don Francisco, a militia captain like his father and traveler to the king's court in the 1660s, received his education at the school, where the fathers "teach the sons of noble and notable people how to read." In order to be admitted and secure a space, Don Francisco proudly declared, "one must address a petition to and receive a grace from the viceroy." Don Francisco's military superior called him a *criollo* from the City of Kings, son of good and noble parents, thus revealing the positive connotations of the term. Like other members of their social circle in Lima, Don Felipe and his son Don Francisco, both men with tenuous links to Indian regional elites, had direct access to the patronage and favor of the highest authorities of the kingdom. These social bonds were strong enough to reach the Habsburg court.[123]

Schools, courts, municipal councils, and other institutions were vehicles for gaining access to this type of political patronage, serving as a means of social ascendancy for men like Çapuy, Sanzoles, Carguamango, and other self-made *indios principales* who had adopted the viceregal capital as their home. Important in propelling these transformations were the native battalions (probably formed in the late sixteenth century) and, on a lower social level, the Indian religious brotherhoods, organized around the cult of a saint or different manifestations of the virgin, as well as the craft confraternities of masons, stonecutters, carpenters, joiners, tanners, tailors, and shoemakers. It has been suggested that wealthy and influential Indians were drawn to the prestigious urban militia of Lima, perhaps one of the highest honors, because military service to His Majesty was deemed "a credit that could be presented by a person ambitious for other offices."[124] Indeed, the posts of captain and sergeant enjoyed great prestige, and their bearers often held other permanent and temporary offices within the city.

117

URBAN INDIAN MAGISTRATES

Equally important for understanding the rise of a new indigenous elite in Lima, governmental structures aimed at ruling the Indian populations of the city and offering them the means for legal redress began to coalesce in the period between the late 1550s, when the first adjacent *reducciones* (native villages) were established, and the early 1570s, when, as previously explained, Viceroy Francisco de Toledo (1569–1581) sanctioned some previous reforms and instituted new ones. In the city, the accumulation of political power and wealth at the hands of indigenous officials worked hand-in-glove. Alongside came social prestige. Two early sources of political and social influence can be detected within the urban space: partial control over indigenous tribute and labor; and jurisdiction over minor civil and criminal complaints.

During the last decades of the sixteenth century, the city of Lima witnessed the emergence of the model of municipal councils for reorganizing indigenous government, as exemplified in Santiago del Cercado, the earliest center of indigenous civic life and influence in the city. Surrounding native settlements with a more rural profile, such as Surco, La Magdalena, and Miraflores, reproduced this pattern of self-government on a more modest scale.[125] In the early seventeenth century, the aforementioned *Colegio de Caciques*, also known as *Colegio del Príncipe* (school for *caciques* and sons of Indian nobility), came to be founded in El Cercado. Four religious sodalities, a music school and a school for elementary education, a parish church, a prison house, and an Indian court with exclusive jurisdiction over Indian cases were also established in El Cercado from the late sixteenth century onward.[126] Some indigenous denizens of high standing, like the vast majority of the indigenous people of Lima, lived outside El Cercado, in the city proper.[127] In fact, the neighborhood of San Lázaro, north of Lima's main square and across the Rímac River, became another nucleus of indigenous political life in the mid-colonial urban areas (although it probably did not have the status of an Indian municipality until the eighteenth century). There, the prestigious sanctuary of Nuestra Señora de Copacabana (where local notables sometimes held the annual elections of El Cercado's municipal council) and a lay pious house (*beaterio*) for indigenous women of noble descent, both important loci of indigenous power, came to be established during the seventeenth century.[128] These institutional spaces significantly increased the opportunities for social mobility and political influence among leading Indian residents. Masters of craft confraternities and stewards of parishes and religious brotherhoods embraced these opportunities early on. It has been suggested that the town council of El Cercado came to be dominated by artisans in the early 1600s. A rising middle class of artisans and homeowners with political skills and largely unattached to the hereditary aristocracy of the rural *pueblos* was already discernible by the late sixteenth century.[129]

As part of a historical process with important political ramifications, the jurisdiction of urban officials gradually expanded beyond the immediate perimeter of the Indian-dominated El Cercado. Due to judicial, administrative, and policing duties, the officials of El Cercado's municipal council, in particular its two chief magistrates (*alcaldes*) and four aldermen (*regidores*), bailiffs (*alguaciles*), and notary (*escribano*), increased their already significant quotas of authority. The role of indigenous officials of the General Indian Court (*Juzgado General de Indios*), established by Viceroy Luis de Velasco (1596–1604) one year before the end of his term, is a good case in point. Documents from the late eighteenth century attest to the functioning of this special tribunal throughout the Habsburg and Bourbon periods. They also indicate that, though initially set in El Cercado, the jurisdiction that the *Juzgado's* chief magistrate and his salaried staff came to hold was to extend to cases involving not only the larger indigenous population of Lima and its surrounding villages but also temporary residents who flocked to the city from all parts of the kingdom.[130]

The staff of the *Juzgado*, with the Spanish *corregidor* of El Cercado serving as presiding judge, included a scribe—who in the eighteenth century was an Indian—as well as two indigenous *alcaldes*, each with his own *alguacil* (all salaried posts that probably overlapped with those of El Cercado's municipal council). It is possible that the Spanish magistrate, burdened by other duties, delegated the hearing of minor cases to the two Indian *alcaldes*, granting them authority to mete out justice to the Indians of the larger jurisdiction of the Lima district (*corregimiento*) in the name of the king.[131] Moreover, salaried officials assigned since the 1570s to cases pursued by indigenous litigants before the *audiencia*, including the chief interpreter for the Indians (generally a native Andean), but especially the general defenders and the procurators for the Indians, were also to serve in the *Juzgado*.[132]

Early eighteenth-century campaigns to obtain the right to elect indigenous *procuradores* for the *Nación Indica*, led by prominent residents of El Cercado and their *cacique* allies in Lima and Spain, started within the increasingly powerful municipal council, the San Làzaro word (*barrio*), and the *Juzgado*. This was part of an effort to replace Spanish officials with members of Lima's Indian leadership. Individuals occupying posts such as defender or procurator for the Indians certainly drew influence and power from their quasimonopoly over access to justice at this level. As explained in the two previous chapters, Andean litigants from all parts of the vast territory under the control of the *audiencia* converged in the city every year to present cases through legal intermediaries. Defenders and procurators for the Indians, moreover, corresponded regularly with the *Consejo de Indias*, controlling an important channel of direct communication with a no-longer-so-distant Spain. Influential travelers to the Habsburg court—with networks of litigants and solicitors—moved within these governmental spheres and had ties to or were themselves royal officials. In spite of their very small numbers, native urban authorities enjoyed a disproportionate influence within viceregal and *audiencia* circles. They were Guaman Poma's indigenous "licentiates" and "doctors" residing in Lima.

Posts reserved for Indians within the *Juzgado* are but one example of a fluid constellation of indigenous officials granted power and authority—permanent and temporary—over the Indian population of the City of Kings and its countryside villages. Lima's peculiar condition—the only viceregal court in the Andes at the time—seems to have accommodated the concentration of political capital in local officials to a degree unparalleled in other parts of the kingdom of Peru. Viceroys, *audiencia* magistrates, and Spanish councilmen set this process in motion, appointing minor officials to adjudicate Indians' cases in the late 1550s, if not earlier, gradually substituting *cacique* appointees during the next decade.[133] Around 1563, Viceroy Count of Nieva appointed two urban magistrates (*alcaldes*) to resolve criminal and civil complaints among the servant and retainer (*yanacona*) native population. In 1567, the Spanish municipal council (*cabildo*) appointed an indigenous constable (*alguacil*) to keep the city clean with the aid of urban draft workers (*mitayos*) and to mediate disputes between indigenous and nonindigenous residents.[134] During the formal establishment of El Cercado (c. 1570), Diego Ticayo, a court interpreter, received one such viceregal commission, this time with authority over this Indian ward and perhaps beyond. For two years, the appointed bailiff for the native (*alguazil de los yndios*; surely one of the first of his kind) helped assemble natives in the newly designated plots. Not unlike the ecclesiastic bailiffs (*alguaciles de doctrina*) selected for the city, Ticayo also aided in the conversion and religious instruction of new residents, summoning them to Mass, to learn the Christian doctrine, and to punish drunkenness and other excesses. The viceroy and *audiencia* rewarded him with thirty silver pesos.[135]

During the ensuing years, natives from the outskirts were also compelled to resettle in El Cercado, creating openings for new urban appointments. To aid the Spanish urban magistrate for Indians (*corregidor de los naturales*; established in Lima only in 1591), Viceroy Velasco relied on the established chief urban magistrate for Indians (*alcalde mayor de los naturales*). He appointed a well-recommended *indio ladino*, Andrés Ramírez Inga, to the post of chief magistrate of Santiago del Cercado in 1603.[136] The newly powerful Ramírez Inga, former chief municipal magistate (*alcalde*) of El Cercado and seemingly a *cuzqueño* of plebeian origin (no *Don* preceded his name), was perhaps the first of this type in Lima. From the viceroy, he received ample fiscal, administrative, policing, and judicial prerogatives as well as an annual salary of 250 pesos. Velasco bestowed rights to carry the staff of royal justice, make arrests, punish Indians for minor offenses, collect tribute owed to the king, and organize Indian labor (these last two had been traditional attributes of Andean *caciques*). And even though Ramírez Inga was an official of El Cercado, he was expressly granted authority over indigenous residents and chiefs (*caciques*, *segundas personas*, and *mandones*) of the settlements and towns within the district of Lima. The position placed him above municipal judges of the Indian town councils as well, underpinning the strength of the El Cercado authorities—and that of the other magistrates of indigenous Lima in general—within the *República de Indios*. All leaders—traditional and municipal—were expressly commanded by the viceroy to obey Ramírez Inga's orders.[137]

Henceforth, the *alcalde mayor de los naturales* became an important aid to his Spanish counterpart, the *corregidor de los naturales*, for governing indigenous populations in Lima and its valley. Urban magistrates like him had few necessary ties to *ayllus* and *caciques*, and their authority seems to have superseded everyone else within the urban space. In fact, viceregal authorities granted *alcaldes mayores* like Ramírez Inga judicial authority, entrusting them with defending indigenous urban residents from the abuses of *caciques* and colonial officials.[138] They administered justice in summary form, aided litigants in preparing judicial documents, and even heard appeals of rulings made by Indian municipal judges (thus the term "chief" [*general*] included in the title). Surviving examples confirm such prerogatives, also revealing the legal roles played. In his 1576 *probanza* and services, Diego de Figueroa Cajamarca, *alcalde mayor* of Quito and visitor at the Habsburg court in the 1580s and 1590s, claimed he had been a pro bono defender of local Indians, crafting petitions and helping present cases to urban courts.[139] Similarly, in 1657 Don Felipe Carguamango petitioned for the staff of *alcalde mayor* and for "exclusive jurisdiction" to defend the city's Indians.[140]

Key administrative and judicial functions followed this post throughout the Habsburg period.[141] As with military ranks, non-*caciques* from nearby provinces increasingly monopolized the office in Lima.[142] It was a post of high honor coveted by regional elites, who did not hesitate to petition for this title and that of chief bailiff (*alguacil mayor*) directly at the royal court.[143] In Lima, however, the appointments that survive in the record show that incumbents' power, and mechanisms through which colonial authorities empowered them, were different. Their judicial and policing duties, as well as the extended jurisdiction granted to them, placed these officials among those at the top rung of urban indigenous justice. Much more research must be carried out, but perhaps contradictory aims and overlapping functions help explain why alliances between urban *indios principales* and *caciques* visiting the city for legal and other matters proved to be short-term and, it seems, ultimately unstable.

Beyond Crown authorities and indigenous notables benefiting from bureaucratic patronage, the wider populations had little say in these appointments. On the contrary, viceregal authorities chose chief municipal magistrates (*alcaldes ordinaries*), captains, chief urban magistrates (*alcaldes mayores*), and court interpreters from among the well-connected and respected *indios principales* whom they deemed loyal vassals and good Christians, found literate in Castilian, and considered familiar enough with the laws of the kingdom and the unwritten rules of patronage and favor.[144] Bestowing honors and posts increased officials' ability to command respect and obedience. Any recipient enjoyed direct access to the viceregal economy of favor, benefiting from non-*cacique* channels to remain in power.[145] Access to the *Consejo de Indias*, in person or in writing, thanks to these powerful patrons, could mean securing confirmation of a previous appointment or a letter of recommendation addressed to the viceroy in office. In a self-reinforcing pattern, the ability and social connections of *alcaldes mayores*, *intérpretes generales*, *alguaciles*, and *capitanes* translated into appointments and honors for them and their descendants, with even greater access to alternative appointments.[146]

In what seems like another example of the checks-and-balances approach to colonial government for Spain, viceroys and *audiencia* magistrates might prefer to appoint outsiders, *criados*, recent immigrants, and descendants to overtake tasks that rural *caciques* should not fulfill or were not willing to fulfill in the city. Rewarding clients with honors and offices underpinned and later reinforced a new colonial elite status. Such dynamics, in turn, fostered the conditions that turned some of these individuals into travelers to the Habsburg royal court.

FIVE

AT HIS MAJESTY'S EXPENSE

Imperial Quandaries and Indigenous Visitors at Court

For fifteen years, a man who called himself Jerónimo Lorenzo Limaylla ignored the orders of the *Consejo de Indias* commanding him to return to Peru. Limaylla approached the royal palace in mid-July 1664 to appear before the king in writing. He fashioned himself as the legitimate heir to the lordship (*cacicazgo*) of Luringuanca, in the central Andes, and as a claimant who, though unlicensed, had rightfully arrived at the court to appeal an adverse sentence entered by Lima's *Audiencia*. He alleged that the judges had impinged on his blood rights by ruling in favor of his contender, ending a nine-year-long lawsuit and imposing perpetual silence on the matter. He also denounced the magistrates' refusal to send a copy of the proceedings to Spain for a retrial. However, the Council denied this request. Restating that American superior courts were the proper forum for disputes over *cacicazgos*, it advised the king to issue Limaylla a decree upholding his right to seek justice back in Peru.

Philip IV did as he was advised, but he died little more than a year later. Seizing this opportunity, Limaylla beseeched the Queen Regent, Mariana of Austria, to intervene on his behalf. The councilors advised again: "It is inconvenient to allow these *caciques* to appear before us for these matters or to let them await here for the arrival of their court cases." Dismissing the argument, Queen Mariana resolved in January 1666 that, considering how this was "a matter of justice," Limaylla could not be denied the right to plead his case in a public audience. Whether the audience was held by the queen or the Council is unclear, but several months later she signed a decree ordering that the legal dossier be sent from Lima and the case be reopened at no expense for the litigant. The Council, by pronouncing him "miserably poor" (*pobre de solemnidad*), had entitled him to free judicial council and exemption from court costs.

Seven years later, on October 7, 1671, the Council finally ruled against Limaylla's claims to the *cacicazgo*, confirming the *Audiencia's* verdict. However, Limaylla remained at court for another seven years. In early 1678, he started a new round of petitions to fund the publication of two petitions (*memoriales*) and their supporting documents. The Council advised the Crown to order this Andean visitor to board the outgoing fleet immediately, for he was setting a "bad example." The councilors further revealed that, between August 1664 and Christmas 1677, Limaylla had cost the royal coffers more than 80,000 *reales* in the form of twenty-five different royal allowances (*ayudas de costa*), gifts, and alms (*limosnas*). Ignoring the Council's advice once again, the Queen Regent simply responded, "he must be encouraged to leave, assisting him for that object, but without in any way forcing him." Limaylla's fate, whether he finally returned to Peru or stayed in Castile or Andalusia, remains unknown.[1]

IMPERIAL QUANDARIES

Earlier stays of native Andeans at the Habsburg court unfolded within similar tensions and constellations of power. Early royal decrees issued in the 1560s and reissued throughout the colonial period forbade indigenous lords and commoners from seeking favor and redress directly and in person in Madrid.[2] Nevertheless, royal responses to visitors' petitions and to councilors' formal inquiries and dissenting opinions were much more complex and ambiguous. The Crown—i.e., the king and his personal secretaries and advisors—often reminded its ministers of the *Consejo* that, once an Andean visitor had set foot at the royal court and requested royal support and protection, he or she was to be heard and, as in the case of Limaylla, hopefully enticed (as opposed to being ignored or compelled) to return to the New World.

Thus, by managing to appear at the court, indigenous travelers created a safe space for negotiation. This space existed at the crossroads of the king's restricting policies and his duty to defend, reward, and ensure the physical and spiritual welfare of native vassals. As the queen stated in her reply to the Council's "consultation" (*consulta*) regarding Limaylla, there was a fundamental difference between *encaminar buenamente* and *socorrer*, on the one hand, and *usar apremio* on the other. This seemingly subtle distinction between guiding or helping, on the one hand, and forcing or coercing on the other, was central to the nature of the king's claim to authority over Indian vassals. They were free subjects of the Crown of Castile, and thus their return journey had to be of their own will and volition, after justice, protection, and compensation had been properly dispensed. Royal will commanded that, were travelers to request it, the king's officials had to provide for them and cover a significant portion of expenses during their stay in Madrid and return journey from His Majesty's own treasury.

The Habsburg kings' liberality and preferential treatment of diplomats, foreign princes, nobles, and procurators were celebrated by many visitors for the almost two hundred years of their reign. Even so, royal magnanimity only partially explains the legal and political mechanisms that were set in motion by the sudden appearance of Indians in Spain. Building upon numerous precedents, indigenous visitors deployed effective strategies for maneuvering within the imperial judicial sphere and navigating the hazards of royal favor in order to secure patronage. By the 1560s, requesting the Crown's financial aid had become common practice. Such requests were a sophisticated example of how the seemingly powerless, when able to place themselves within the web of social obligations and expectations that held the Habsburg court in place, could profit from the fluid relationships of interdependence that existed between king, councilors, and indigenous vassals.

In 1616, the Aragonese jurist Pedro Calixto Ramírez wrote that being "king" was a "burdensome office" and an "onerous charge" as a way to remember Philip III of the need to respect the *fueros* (special privileges) of the kingdom of Aragon. Even the most absolutist monarch, because of his social position as "king," appeared implicated in coercive networks and interdependencies that were based on the expectations of the subjects and the need to preserve the image of the sovereign. Such interdependencies limited his power of decision and sphere of influence. The same was true, on a lesser scale, for councilors of the Indies and other metropolitan advising bodies. The royal court was the central configuration in the court society, but as in any other power structure, asymmetrical and coercive dependencies prescribed specific modes, means, and boundaries for the king's dominion. The king was a subject of the system of power over which he ruled. He was at the service of the kingdoms; his power did not exist outside that of the realms.[3]

Andean favor-seekers discovered the effects of this political configuration and began participating in it early on. Legal principles and colonial regulations were subordinated to a larger ideal of justice upon which the expectation of loyalty from the Indians was predicated. Given his inalienable duty to give each one his or her due, the monarch was expected to preserve native subjects and communities by doing away with anything or anyone who might place them in harm's way.[4] The Crown was the party most interested in upholding such an ideal (for, in a colonial setting defined by exploitation and discrimination, it was just that). Its legitimacy was rooted in the king's role as supreme judge and protector of the Indians. The idea that natives shall contribute to the "greater good" with their labor and tribute also depended on the court's ability to project an image of the father-king who listens, rewards, and protects. The treatment afforded to Andean sojourners was the conduit by which the king broadcasted this self-image outward.

By declaring themselves "poor" or "miserable," requesting a free passage, petitioning for legal counsel, or appealing to the king's magnanimity to support trips and live according to their *calidad* (overall social standing), Andean visitors were calling for a reassessment of justice, a rebalancing of sorts. Their aim was to establish what was owed to them not as undifferentiated members of a vague category of "Indians," but as individual vassals aware of the differences of birth, station, and merit that separated them from other "Indian" subjects and made their circumstances unique and hopefully more deserving in the eyes of the king. Indians, in their role as political and legal actors, benefited from jurisdictional tensions and legal constructs, which they used to test the limits of the king's claims to absolute power and negotiate what they thought they deserved. Indigenous transatlantic "justice"—the different strategies for self-promotion and the particular and collective interests promoted by visitors at court—resided in the space where the desire to control met the obligation to protect.

NATIVE LORDS AND INDIGENOUS SLAVES IN IBERIA

Native Andean travelers across the Atlantic were later arrivals to one of the least explored historical dramas of the early modern era. During the first decades of European colonization, thousands of Amerindians were forcefully enslaved, uprooted, and taken to Spain and Portugal from homelands in the Caribbean, Mexico, and Central America. The life of these *indios* (as they came to be known) in mid-sixteenth-century Iberia and their struggle for freedom and justice shaped, in profound and sometimes unexpected ways, the experiences of the smaller group of native Andean travelers who were to follow during the next 150 years.[5] For Andean travelers, the struggle did not turn out to be so much a question of slavery versus freedom, as it had been for enslaved *indios* taken to Spain by trickery or force. Although the debate about the legality and morality of Indian servitude and bondage had not been fully settled when the Inca Empire was conquered in the 1530s and 1540s, by the following decade the polemic had started to wane. In principle, and by virtue of their lineage, legal status, and *naturaleza* (birthplace), Indians "from" Peru (or at least perceived to be so) had been declared free from the extreme forms of servitude and bondage that affected natives in earlier contact zones.[6]

One of the issues Andean travelers to Spain faced was how to be legally declared *indio*, a juridical construct that was fundamental to the colonial order and carried with it "elements of both protection and limitation."[7] Here, and with few exceptions, this category placed the recipient—a descendant of the original inhabitants of the New World—within the larger category of "poor and wretched" (*miserable*). Since 1512, but more firmly during the 1520s, Indians began to be afforded the special status of *miserable*, granted to other "legal minors." By the middle of the century, many Spanish jurists and intellectuals equated Indians with children in need of some form of paternal tutelage. Within this construct, the king emerged as the protector and guardian of these perpetual minors.[8] Being so classified granted access to protections and procedural privileges initially enjoyed by freed and wrongfully enslaved Indians thought to be "wandering" the Peninsula, presumably with no (legitimate) master, known occupation, or family ties.[9] Legal frameworks and discourses deployed by the first generation of enslaved Indians in Spain were partially appropriated, reconfigured, and distilled by Andean travelers and their attorneys. Starting in the 1550s, this became part and parcel of their efforts to remain in Spain, negotiate with representatives of the king, and fund an eventual return to the New World—their original *naturaleza*.

Beginning in the Canary Islands and the Near Atlantic before the so-called Discovery, the practice of enslaving local inhabitants and forcing them to journey to Spain quickly expanded to the islands and mainland of the New World.[10] Upon returning from his first voyage in 1493, Christopher Columbus presented Ferdinand and Isabella with six *indios*, including one *cacique* chief brought from the Caribbean Islands to Seville. Three years later, Columbus brought thirty New World natives and sold them for a good profit in local slave markets. In 1495, he dispatched another five hundred *indios* for the same purpose. Others soon followed his example. In 1499, Amerigo Vespucci and Alonso de Ojeda reportedly sold more than 230 Indians in the slave markets of Cádiz. In response, the Crown issued its first piecemeal laws attempting to limit and regulate forced journeys, ordering royal authorities to free those unjustly enslaved. By then, however, European colonizers were capturing, enslaving, and selling American natives by the thousands. Andalusian cities such as Seville, Cádiz, and Cordoba quickly became active markets for this trade.[11]

Quick profits soon merged with religious enterprises and larger imperial designs.[12] During the first decades of the sixteenth century, the Crown accepted the sporadic presence of coerced or semicoerced *indios* other than the formally enslaved in Spain, justifying their displacement in that these visitors—especially if *caciques* and sons of nobles—could receive religious training and learn Castilian, becoming valuable interpreters, agents of the church, and messengers of empire. Columbus himself had pioneered this practice in the Caribbean, after he came into contact with the *cacique* henceforth known as Diego Colón in the island of Guanahaní. Don Diego visited Spain on two occasions, adopting Catholicism and receiving his baptism in Barcelona. Becoming proficient in Castilian, he later interpreted for the influential *extremeño* Nicolás de Ovando, first royal governor of Hispaniola.[13]

As the practice of bringing Indian lords and youths to Spain gained momentum, news and reports about the massive enslavement of other Indians without just cause reached the court. Mounting pressure by champions of the Indian cause such as Bartolomé de las Casas increased the need to justify the legality of these practices vis-à-vis other soon-to-be Atlantic powers. At a time when the larger intellectual debate on whether enslaving the New World inhabitants was just or unjust took center stage, the Crown started to reverse some early policies and to withdraw some slave licenses.[14]

One of the most persuasive arguments opposing this free-for-all of sorts was the death of New World natives (nobles and commoners alike) in Spain. All of the *indios* taken from Hispaniola to Seville in 1515 died within a year. In another case, Don Lorenzo, a Tlaxcalan lord who reached Spain with Hernán Cortés in May 1528, died a year later while waiting in Seville for the next vessel to depart. Like *audiencia* ministers had done with Andean journeys to these courts of appeal, councilors and courtiers linked these deaths and many others, including some high-profile individuals, to the hardships of the voyage across the Atlantic and the drastic change of climate and environment (*naturaleza*) that visitors experienced. Critics pointed to the royal obligation to secure the well-being of the visitors' bodies in Spain and that of their souls in the afterlife. A related argument, tied to Castile's just titles to the Indies, claimed that Indian bondage and coerced dislocation not only burdened the king's conscience but also put his eternal salvation at risk. Furthermore, the conquests of Mexico and Peru quickly problematized the initial picture of the Indian's alleged "rusticity," lack of reason, and natural servitude, raising fundamental questions about the nature of the Indies and the proper treatment of its inhabitants.[15]

These issues, far from theoretical, were raised by the actual presence of Indian nobles and leaders (*indios principales*), servants, and slaves in the Peninsula. Prompted by the Spanish Conquest of the Mexica realm and its aftermath, several Nahua lords like Don Lorenzo from Tlaxcala began journeying to the royal court on their own accord in search of an audience with their new monarch, a practice with deep roots in Mesoamerican, Andean, and European traditions. The kings, now fully aware of the entrenched social hierarchies that existed in the incorporated kingdoms of Mexico and Peru, began to afford nobles a treatment befitting their high status.[16]

SEEKING FREEDOM AND THE KING'S PATRONAGE

Important changes in royal attitudes toward indigenous transatlantic visitors can be detected in the years leading up to the promulgation of the New Laws (*Leyes Nuevas*) in 1542 and, eight years later, in Charles V's general prohibition of indigenous slavery, even in cases of just war or rebellion. Backed by the papacy's official position on the matter, newer dispositions stated more firmly that Indians were not only humans capable of salvation but also vassals of the Crown. Therefore, slavery was incompatible with their nature and political status. Across the ocean, the New Laws limited the contexts in which natives could be "justly" or legally enslaved and sold. Several royal decrees in the 1540s proscribed the inhabitants of the Indies from taking wrongfully enslaved Indians to Spain under any circumstances, even if the natives had allegedly expressed their will to voyage to or remain in the Peninsula. Laws started to ban viceroys, governors, and justices from issuing royal licenses for transporting Indians to the Iberian kingdoms, annulling all previous permits. Penalties for the transgressors included loss of office, high fines, a hundred public lashes, and perpetual banishment from the Indies.[17]

On the opposite shore, the New Laws opened Castilian courtrooms to enslaved Indians who could petition for their freedom and demand that masters present valid title to their bodies. Two royal inspections, conducted in 1543 and 1549, freed more than a hundred enslaved Indians in Seville alone.[18] A repertoire of legal templates, arguments, and doctrines inherited from Roman and canonical law was available to attempt a classification of those wrongly enslaved or tricked into slavery and servitude as well as to justify the king's protection and liberality toward some of these subjects. As some have argued, "Indios in Castile were seen as subordinate, childlike vassals in need of a support system."[19] Accordingly, decrees banning Indian slavery and the slave trade expressed the king's pity and compassion toward the "wretched" Indians who wandered and begged aimlessly throughout the cities and towns of Iberia, with no family, home, or master to employ them.[20] Within a worldview that saw the defense of the poor and destitute as a Christian obligation and an attribute of the sovereign's legitimate authority, a staff of special lawyers, including advocates, procurators, and solicitors as well as the Crown's own prosecutor, was put at the disposition of *indios* who decided to sue their masters in Castile.

Miserables were those who, due to poverty, weakness, ignorance, or fear of repercussion, could not pursue justice by their own means.[21] Widely embraced and strategically exploited by multiple legal actors, the gendered and patriarchal language of poverty and minority as a barrier to attain justice activated royal protection, judicial lenience or flexibility, and free legal counsel. Thus, *indio* litigants in Spain were declared exempt from court costs. Fulfilling its obligation to protect these *indios*, and in an effort to deter the further shipment of Indian slaves to Iberia, the Crown issued an influential decree on November 25, 1552, setting an important precedent: former masters had to pay the return passage of the wrongfully enslaved to their places of origin.[22]

The practice of extending the king's largesse over some indigenous visitors at court, especially nobles from the lands formerly under the control of the Mexica empire, also began to take hold during the formative years leading to the issuing of the New Laws in 1542. Thanks to the strength and appeal of *costumbre*, travelers were to turn the king's proverbial liberality and initial aid into a form of royal obligation, expected by indigenous vassals of different status. The Crown had displayed similar forms of protection and support early on, specifically with some Caribbean visitors who were part of the early evangelizing and acculturating experiments at the turn of the sixteenth century.[23]

Between 1519 and 1521, the year when Tenochtitlan fell, Hernán Cortés dispatched different groups of natives, including six Totonac Indians, to the court as "presents" for Charles V. In 1528, Cortés himself made his first return visit, bringing indigenous servants and slaves in what had already become common practice among European colonizers. Nonetheless, with Cortés also came seven high-ranking Mesoamerican lords—including three sons of the former emperor Moctezuma—and their entourages of relatives and dependents. The emperor placed this particular group under the care of one Father Antonio de Ciudad Rodrigo, ordering that they be given presents and be "well treated" during the return journey. Funds were also made available for the purchase of devotional objects that the lords were to carry to Mexico.[24]

The lords and their retinues spent five months in Seville (though some of them did not survive that long). A royal decree issued in October 1528 commanded the officials of the *Casa de la Contratación* to cover the cost of clothing for each visitor, making sure as well that the lords received more luxurious garb than the lesser Indians. Two additional decrees, issued in March and May 1529, ordered royal officials to provide lodging and rations for the visitors and to pay for their medicines, medical care, passage fares, and provisions from

His Majesty's treasury. The total charges against royal funds amounted to 1,088 gold ducats of 375 *maravedíes* each.[25] Similar expressions of royal liberality toward Mesoamerican and Caribbean lords were to be displayed in the ensuing years.[26]

Slowly but steadily, royal assistance distilled from the judicial arena created opportunities for Indians other than illustrious and noble visitors. Within the *Casa de la Contratación*, the appropriate forum for complaints of enslaved Indians against their unlawful masters, but also before the Council of Indies, which acted as the appellate court in such cases, advocates, prosecutors, and attorneys started to draw on previous or concurrent cases, partially recycling legal doctrines, royal mandates, and court rulings in order to meet the needs of other clients, particularly during the following decades. Their journeys belonged to an era of transition from enslaved to free status for the Indians of the New World. The use of the term *miserable*, in fact as well as in law, and the rhetoric of wretchedness that often accompanied it, which began to appear in lawsuits initiated against slave masters around 1550, folded these two distinct eras into one another. Thanks to the intervention of Crown prosecutors and attorneys, Indian commoners in Spain started to benefit from measures initially intended to protect enslaved *indios* and, because of their high station, native lords and indigenous royalty. Many of these visitors, however, were neither lord nor enslaved.[27]

NEITHER LORD NOR ENSLAVED:
SETTING A PRECEDENT

Early indigenous travelers from the Andes were caught up in this shifting political landscape. Individual cases show that, by the 1550s, legislation banning the trade of enslaved Indians, although very permissive and tentative at first, had started to intertwine with the legal protection and institutionalized generosity increasingly afforded to some of the most noteworthy New World visitors. Between May 1554 and November 1556, the Crown provided four *reales* per day to cover the living expenses of Don Francisco Tenamazcle, an *indio* and a *cacique* of the towns of Noxtlan and Sucxipila, in New Galicia (New Spain), spending a total of 3,528 *reales*. By order of the Council, the treasury reimbursed one Gregorio de Pesquera for 176 *reales* that he spent to provide room and board as well as two servants for the *cacique* abroad. Cristóbal San Martín, a solicitor, also recovered the 132 *reales* that he spent in medical assistance for Don Francisco.[28]

This type of royal support began to be extended to visiting commoners.

In 1555, the Council ordered Francisco Becerra, a *vecino* of Toro near Zamora (Castile), to pay 30 ducats to Francisco Martín, an *indio* and a native of Chincha, a province on the south-central coast of Peru, then sojourning at court. The Council found Becerra guilty of tricking this *indio*, a free vassal after all, into traveling to Spain with him. Francisco Martín had been brought "with deceit," and the master had benefited from his unpaid labor. The punishment was to fund the journey of Francisco, his unnamed wife, and son back to their hometown.[29]

Finding the culprits of "tricking" these *indios* into going to Spain and holding them accountable proved a difficult task, especially if they had left the court already. Tentatively at first, and more firmly after a 1552 order to the Council, the Crown gradually took over some of the obligations previously imposed on former masters, such as paying for the return journey and accommodating travelers in the royal fleet.[30] After the Council granted them a license to return to their native Tlaxcala in 1555, Diego de Santiago and his wife Inés de Collantes, both classified as *indios*, petitioned the king for passage fare and expenses (*pasaje y matalonaje*) for themselves, two children, and one son-in-law. Acknowledging them as "paupers" (*pobres*) without "any real possibility to pay," the king ordered the *Casa de la Contratación* to inquire who had brought Diego and his family to Spain and to charge him for the return journey. If the culprit could not be found, the officers were to convince someone to pay for the journey in exchange for service at sea (another sign of juxtaposing views about the nature of indigenous servitude). As a last resort, the visitors were to be dispatched to Veracruz at His Majesty's expense.[31] Thus, provided royal officials could not identify those guilty of bringing Indians to Spain (something they were seldom able to do), the king was to defray the costs of those who left voluntarily. The House was commanded to grant them full license at no cost for the claimant and his family, setting an important precedent that uncoerced travelers invoked for the next 150 years.[32]

The legal constructs and categories that emerged from the multiple interactions among enslaved Indians, the Crown, and its ministers cast a certain veil of homogeneity over a very complex social reality. Laws pertaining to free and forced visitors generally envisioned *indios* as part of the economic "poor" and socially "wretched." Royal decrees often portray them as "malleable children."[33] But Andean travelers of the 1550s and 1560s, like their predecessors, were of disparate *calidades*. *Indios* living in Spain fell somewhere within a continuum of experiences involving bondage, displacement, and relocation. Moreover, the boundaries between slavery, servitude, and freedom were by no means easy to establish or, even worse for Indian servants treated as slaves, easy to maintain.[34]

Furthermore, imperial legislation up to the seventeenth century did not contemplate the reality of native travelers who journeyed to Spain (as opposed to being "taken" there by others) or sought to return to the New World of their own volition. Laws tasked officials of the House with inquiring which Indians had illegally arrived in the royal fleet to Cádiz, San Lúcar, and other parts of Andalusia, and with investigating who had "brought" these natives to Spain. Indigenous travelers, presented as passive subjects and victims of deceit, "should be given back" their freedom and "be sent" to the Indies at the expense of those who had brought them in the first place.[35] It was in part the unreality of these laws and the lawmakers' inability to distinguish among indigenous travelers that placed justice and reward beyond the realm of *cédulas* (royal orders), viceregal decrees, and local ordinances.

Rather than preventing natives' voluntary journeys to Iberia from distant parts of the empire, dispositions of the early 1550s added an appeal to the king's liberality and protection to the pool of strategies available to a new wave of indigenous visitors. Their engagement with the courts turned early displays of largesse — initially meant for specific individuals of noble descent — into customary practices in a general application, encompassing many other *indios* residing in Spain (whether noble, commoner, or other). Even under harsh conditions, hundreds of Indians had been able to settle permanently in Iberia in the early sixteenth century. Many — including former slaves and servants — had gained freedom, working and prospering as artisans, tailors, cooks, laborers, and domestics in Seville and other cities. They had learned the languages of the land, converted to Christianity, married, and formed families. Thus, they saw little incentive to abandon their new homes. Across the Atlantic and along the Pacific coast, many others were planning the opposite voyage on their own will and at their own peril, though not always at their own expense.

REACHING OUT TO THE KING

By the 1550s, certain bureaucratic mechanisms, part of the regular functioning of the "epistemic setting" of the royal court, were adapted to deal with the first Andean visitors.[36] Within this setting, where imperial knowledge was produced, *consultas* (consultations) became the privileged way in which "information" about these travelers was generated and the validity of their specific requests checked and validated. *Consultas* also became the means to embed the interests of different parties into the decision process. Above all, however, *consultas* bore the traces of the strategies used by visitors to promote their own interests at court and shape imperial legislation

Consultations were the main channel of communication between the *Consejo de Indias* and the Habsburg kings. These brief documents offer a privileged window into the minds of the ministers entrusted with making decisions about these visitors, their identities, and their claims. Although one is not always privy to the Council's internal discussions, one can access some of the legal theories, precedents, and opinions that shaped how the Crown interacted with visitors. It seems unlikely that the councilors "consulted" with a powerful but busy monarch about every single visitor, but the fact that they often made requests that may now seem petty—a few *reales* for clothing or medicine, for instance—reveals the agency of these vassals impacted the workings of the Spanish monarchy at this level.

The Council fulfilled two central roles through the *consulta*. As an advisory body, it aided the monarch in dispensing justice, favor, and recompense by making information and counsel available to him. As a legislative body, it implemented the king's sovereign will, largely informed by the mechanism of the consultation and the subjects' own petitions, by giving that will its specific normative form. A relatively brief, formal inquiry, the consultation was presented or read to the sovereign by one of his personal secretaries. Meant as a dialogue between monarch and ministers, early consultations were oral in form, as they were put directly before King Charles V by one the councilors during periodic audiences. Starting with the reign of his son Phillip II, however, the consultation acquired a written form and a relatively predictable bureaucratic trajectory. A little over four thousand *consultas* exist dating to the sixteenth century. For the seventeenth century, literally tens of thousands were produced and exchanged as the king and his ministers discussed virtually every aspect of the government of the Indies.[37]

Official inquiries regularly began with the Council's internal discussions on a specific matter or affair, often motivated by a formal petition, letter of recommendation, report, or the need to appoint or confirm an official. In *asuntos de indios* (Indian affairs), oftentimes the Council requested the opinion of the Crown prosecutor, a *fiscal* tasked with defending the interests of the Indians in the name of the king. His response was written directly in the *consulta* or on a separate sheet. A secretary then added the outcome of the councilors' own deliberations in a condensed, unitary opinion or recommendation to the sovereign. The *consulta* was forwarded to the monarch to pass judgment. In most cases, His Majesty responded after a few days (sometimes it took three weeks or more) with a brief statement, written in the margins of the advising body's recommendation, at the bottom of it, or on the back of the *consulta*, either in his own hand or that of his private secretaries. Telegraphic phrases such as *está bien, como parece*, or *así*, all meant to convey the king's approval, were the norm.

The document, now bearing the king's resolution, returned to the Council. If further debate or information was required, the *consulta* was subject to a new round of revisions, discussions, and exchanges with other ministers. If not, then parts of the text were incorporated, sometimes verbatim, into a royal order, decree, or official letter. In the case of royal dispositions, the Council drafted the final order and then sent it to the king for signature. Upon receiving the signed document, councilors either dispatched it to the competent authorities or gave it to the interested party—a litigant or favor-seeker, for example—after transcribing its contents into the Council's registry books.[38]

Such was the regular flow of information at this level. Nevertheless, some Andean petitioners reached out directly to the king and secretaries in his inner circle, increasing the chances of success. In a way, this strategy to win royal favor at court was a refined example of "legal wrangling" or "jurisdictional jockeying": exploiting competing or overlapping jurisdictions by pitting one against the other to better advance one's interests.[39] Even so, it is difficult to speak of two separate jurisdictions for king and Council. Both stood for different—but overlapping—power constellations. Even though the royal prosecutor was expected to defend the interests of the Indians *as if they were* His Majesty's own, this official was, after all, a member of the Council. Rather, appealing to the king directly to insert themselves in the flow of information reveals the preference of some claimants for jockeying from one channel of communication to another, seeking the most favorable to their cause.

Within the political culture of the time, a just king, even if he did not equally represent all the subjects, was expected to listen to them. Political bonds and expected loyalties often stemmed from this act of "listening" through *audiencias* or responses to petitions, taking the form of an obligation that the king could reject only at the risk of appearing unfair.[40] Indigenous appeals to listen were performative actions upon which Indians and sovereign founded and constantly re-created the monarchical compact at court.

Instead of following the standard procedure of appearing before the Council in writing so that the Crown prosecutor could give them a legal voice, some Andean visitors chose to present petitions and supporting documents "directly" to the king, with only the royal secretaries as intermediaries, even when the sovereign was temporarily absent from the palace or holding court in another city. In these cases, Andean petitioners, and not the *Consejo de Indias*, initiated the bureaucratic procedure of the consultation. Worded in a language that reminded the monarch of his obligation to hear and defend native vassals, especially if spoken on behalf of other indigenous subjects, these petitions (*memoriales*) were attempts to influence what the king would "hear" first, thereby exerting a degree of control over the production and circulation of official knowledge within the courtly setting.

Brother Calixto de San José's close encounter with King Ferdinand VI in the early eighteenth century illustrates this strategy in a theatrical fashion. An *hermano donado* (lay brother) of the Order of Saint Francis since 1729, Brother Calixto journeyed to Spain unlicensed along with a fellow Franciscan to present Ferdinand with a long, printed plea, the *Representación verdadera*, prepared on behalf of the *Nación Índica* of Peru.[41] The petitioner arrived in Madrid via Buenos Aires and Lisbon on August 22, 1750. That same night, he approached the royal palace to place the document directly in the sovereign's hands. To his disappointment, he was told that the king could only be "seen" on certain days, and only by way of the Council. This was precisely what Brother Calixto was trying to avoid, as he feared the *Representación verdadera* would fall on deaf ears. The following day, after pondering the great challenges involved in "seeing" the king or "talking" to him, Calixto joined the popular procession accompanying His Majesty through the streets of Madrid and into the countryside, where the king was to go hunting. While Ferdinand's carriage was still in motion, Calixto went further into the crowd and beyond a group of soldiers, quickly approached the king's coach, and handed a petition to a passing Ferdinand. As Calixto recalled, the king "had only stuck his head out twice," giving him just enough time to hand over the printed document.

Brother Calixto realized his actions had paid off the following morning. Back at the royal palace, one of the king's personal secretaries informed him that His Majesty and his personal advisers had read the plea and had been greatly moved by its contents. Using the same courtier as a go-between, Brother Calixto introduced himself and his cause to Ferdinand in writing, explaining the reasons for his visit: to alleviate the sufferings of the Indians of Peru. The king, or more likely a secretary, ordered him to rework the contents of this informal declaration into a formal petition, commanding him to bring it, along with the other papers from Peru, to officials of the Council. Cognizant that the king had now been made aware of his case, the diligent procurator delivered the documents to the councilors "without delay," forcing them, at the risk of doing the king a disservice, to listen.[42]

Earlier indigenous petitioners and procurators had developed and perfected Brother Calixto's strategy. In 1646, Don Carlos Chimo arrived at court to denounce several abuses in the name of the Indian commons of Lambayeque, his hometown, where *caciques* and commoners alike had been dispossessed during the Second General Land Inspection of the viceroyalty. Local judges were too afraid, too venal, or too guilty to uphold the king's justice.[43]

The Council took Chimo's denunciations very seriously but warned the king that the traveler's ultimate motivation was to "stay here" (*quedarse aqui*). Responding to a consultation brought about by Chimo's first petition to the king, the councilors and royal prosecutor reminded His Majesty in September that "Indians cannot come to Spain," adding that "if such is the result, they will make their way here daily on their own." Despite Chimo's unlicensed journey, however, the councilors had fulfilled their obligation of supporting him with 200 *reales* to pay for the journey from Madrid to Seville. Moreover, the Council had dispatched royal decrees to the authorities in Peru restating their duty to provide justice, punish usurpers, and ensure the "good treatment" of natives. Copies of these orders were given to Chimo with the hope that their content would encourage him to return to Peru.[44]

Instead of going to Seville to begin the voyage back to the Andes, as he had been instructed, Don Carlos Chimo journeyed across Castile and into Aragon to meet Philip IV at the old capital of Saragossa and present additional complaints. His new *memorial* was forwarded to the Council along with a royal decree ordering it to look further into the matter and "consult" the king again. In their response of November 1646, the councilors simply restated their previous opinion. Half a year later, in June 1647, Chimo, who had returned to Madrid, forced the Council to review his case once again. Alleging to have received a new letter from the "*caciques* and lords of vassals" of Peru, he reached out to the king with a new *memorial*. Both the *memorial* and the letter were sent to the Council, along with the order that the king be "consulted" about Chimo's new claims. In a July 23 consultation, the Council urged His Majesty to dismiss the letter as a forgery (*pareze supuesta*) and to leave the matter in its hands. If Chimo had something else to request, the councilors argued, he should do it by way of the royal prosecutor, his "protector." In their final response, the ministers considered it appropriate to reiterate that "the *cacique*'s disobedience [*contravención*] should be tolerated no longer because his example will lead others to make their way here daily on their own." This time, the king agreed: *como parece*, His Majesty's reply, ordered as the Council had suggested. One can only surmise that Carlos Chimo finally returned to Peru.[45]

Reaching out to the king through his close circle of secretaries and advisers, and not by way of the Council, set the consultation in motion, even if opposed by the councilors or royal prosecutor. Andean claimants took officials to task before the sovereign, making him aware of their presence and affairs at court. By controlling what reached the ears of the king first, they hoped for a potential ally, or at least a counterbalance to the councilors' seemingly total control over bureaucratic procedure.[46] This strategy seemed an effective way to overcome some of the obstacles posed to Andean transatlantic agents and travelers and their affairs in Spain by the Council or American viceroys and *audiencias*, countering the indolence, inactivity, and corruption of royal ministers. By appealing to the monarch directly, Andean visitors placed the councilors in Madrid in the difficult position of having to respond.

HIS MAJESTY'S DILEMMA

Official letters, petitions, *consultas*, and other documents pertaining to Andean travelers often reflect the fundamental tension between the elements of protection and limitation informing the ideological construction of the *indio*. For legal and practical reasons, the Council was glad to see certain visitors return to their *naturalezas*. The king's will that they be aided from funds other than those of the royal household only made things harder for the Council—the main body responsible for providing the funds to entertain or support travelers and to ensure their well-being.[47]

The councilors' dissatisfaction with the nonimplementation of past decrees emphasizing the need to protect the Indians—which in their view made corrupt officials in America responsible for some journeys—is also apparent in the discussions raised by the visit of Andean subjects. The councilors' generally negative disposition toward travelers and their affairs in Spain might also explain why they almost invariably issued the required return license to those requesting one. As tiresome or impertinent as native travelers were in the eyes of councilors, royal ministers seemed unwilling or unable to order their arrest, imprisonment, or forced return. In Chimo's case, for instance, the Council told the king that it had granted the visitor two hundred *reales* to go to Seville, a royal license to cross the Atlantic unmolested, and up to three hundred *reales* in clothes and other personal effects so that he would "invariably" set sail in the royal galleons. Providing this support, however, was *"everything that the Council was able to do* while wishing (as it always wishes) to assist and protect the Indians." The Council fell short of *forcing* Chimo to return.[48]

The perils of a lengthy navigation were real, as the travelers who drafted their wills before crossing the ocean knew well.[49] Compelling Indians to embark on a perilous journey might result in their death at sea—a clear injustice as well as a sign of bad government. After all, Indians were vassals of the

Crown of Castile and possessors of the freedom to set residence in Spain, if such was their wont.[50]

Testing the limits of the Council's power, Indian visitors and their attorneys learned to advance the opposite argument as well: the negative effects of the Iberian "climate" on the health of some of these travelers turned a denied license into a threat to the visitor's life. His or her death, indirectly caused by the Council's refusal to grant a permit, would place an unacceptable burden on the king's conscience, thus betraying the councilors' mandate.[51]

Others stayed at court despite the Council's warnings and reprimands, or even after it had issued money orders (*libranzas*) to pay for travel expenses. In September 1566, Don Sebastián Poma Hilaquita, a grandson of the Inca Atahualpa and a future court interpreter in Lima, was granted a license to travel back to Peru, along with the authorization to voyage without cost in the royal galleons. He did not depart, however, alleging just cause (*justo impedimento*) and necessity (*necessidad*), but without providing the Council with any further details. Almost eight years later, in August 1574, the Council reissued Don Sebastián's permit, granting him the privilege to travel in the royal fleet again and the daily provisions needed at sea. He returned to Lima.[52]

In 1585, Don Alonso Atahualpa, another grandson of Atahualpa (and Don Sebastián Hilaquita's cousin), journeyed to Spain. In 1586, he requested an *ayuda de costa* by pleading for Philip II to "take pity on his extreme poverty" at court. Don Alonso had "nothing to eat, much less the wherewithal to maintain himself in accordance with his station [*calidad*]." He had a series of debts in Madrid that he was unable to honor. In their *consulta*, the councilors opined that Don Alonso could be awarded a one-time allowance of three hundred ducats (some 3,300 *reales*) "to help himself and be able to return." The king agreed.[53] But Don Alonso used the moneys to tend to his debts and for other expenses. In 1587, the king granted him a one-year extension of the original three-year license to remain in Spain with the proviso that "you return to the said province in the first fleet going there from these kingdoms." Don Alonso never left Madrid. The Inca prince died in the public jail, having been imprisoned for numerous unpaid debts.[54]

Similar stories of negotiation involve indigenous sojourners of much lesser status than these Inca royals. Some, including self-described *indios principales*, were able to circumvent orders of the Council and remain at court, turning royal generosity and protection into a significant advantage.[55] Measures taken by the Council in the case of indigenous commoners, though harder to document, reveal a similar dynamic.[56] Although the Council tried to prevent royal largesse from being stretched indefinitely and becoming customary practice, the political strength of the king's image as an all-powerful monarch partially rested on the treatment accorded such visitors, especially if wrongfully convicted, unjustly treated, or destitute. For councilors, successful transatlantic voyages and sojourns, by their very nature, distorted royal liberality and a subject's prerogative to seek direct audience with the monarch. By the 1560s, news about these stays and the king's support were already traveling across the ocean.[57]

Liberality numbered among the princely virtues, but it could also entail a burdensome obligation. This fundamental tension resurfaced in an official exchange about the fate of certain Incas of noble birth. In 1572, following a swift and irregular trial conducted in Cuzco, Viceroy Francisco de Toledo found several Incas of royal descent guilty of treason and lèse-majesté for calling themselves "lords of the land" (*señores de la tierra*). The viceroy forfeited their *encomiendas* and labeled their ancestors "tyrants." Moreover, deeming their presence in Peru too dangerous to the peace and stability of the kingdom, Toledo also decided to root them out and exile the most threatening ones to the king's court, informing the Council about his plan in a letter.[58]

Toledo's intentions did not receive a warm welcome in Madrid. The councilors were not convinced that the charges had been substantiated and suspected an injustice had been committed. The Incas' *fuero* (special privilege) had not been respected and proper procedure had not been followed. Moreover, the Council worried about the royal obligation that was to ensue if Toledo persisted in carrying forward his plan. In a letter written sometime in early 1573, in all likelihood inspired by the Incas' own letters to the sovereign and the influence of their patron at court (licentitate Lope García de Castro, former governor and president of the *Audiencia de Lima*), the Council disagreed with the viceroy. It told Toledo that, by dispatching the prisoners to Spain, he would be doing a great disservice to His Majesty because of the "grief and trouble that would multiply for him." The Incas would have to be entertained at the king's expense for the rest of their days (or at least until the sentence was overruled). Unwilling to displease an already upset Council, Toledo informed the magistrates in another letter that, although he still intended to send the Incas into exile, he was now dispatching them to Mexico, along with a letter addressed to the viceroy requesting him to find a proper way to support the Incas (and thus releasing the king from an onerous obligation).[59]

In this case, it was the Council that reminded royal ministers in the Americas about the fundamental obligation to protect native Andean vassals according to their status and *calidad*. Other *consultas* reminded the king about this obligation, which ultimately depended on the king's own will and reflected his majesty. Seeking royal reward in 1585, Don Alonso Atahualpa requested a *merced* proportionate with his *calidad*, royal lineage, and services. (Philip would grant him an annuity of 3,200 pesos.)[60] At some point in the negotiations, the king had forwarded the corresponding *consulta* to the president of the Council, along with a brief private note inquiring if he deemed the return of the noble petitioner to Quito politically troublesome or dangerous. In his response, the president did not seem especially preoccupied with Don Alonso's return. However, he said he was generally opposed to the journeys of indigenous favor-seekers from Mexico and Peru. At the same time, he admitted that refusing to recompense Don Alonso was against royal justice. In a somehow pessimistic tone, the president wrote, "It has to be done" (*es fuerza que se haga*).[61]

DON MELCHOR GOES TO SPAIN

If travelers could not be forced to return without recompense or redress, imposing the opposite journey from Peru to Spain on someone could likewise be construed as an injustice. As Toledo found out in 1573 when he tried to dispatch the Inca royals to Spain, indigenous vassals could not be rightfully compelled to leave their *naturalezas* and travel to Iberia against their will without proper cause or trial and adequate compensation (especially if the Council feared an injustice).[62] A high-profile case in late-sixteenth-century Peru involved Don Melchor Carlos, the son and heir to one of the Incas sentenced by Toledo in Cuzco. We met Don Melchor at the beginning of the book, when news of his death—in a monastery near Madrid in 1610—reached the Andes. At the turn of the sixteenth century, Melchor was the only direct male descendant through the male line of Emperor Huayna Capac, who the Crown recognized as the last "legitimate" occupant of the Inca throne.

The established interpretation of his famous journey posits that the prince's voyage was the result of Viceroy Luis de Velasco's efforts to protect a weak, naïve, and extravagant Melchor from the Spanish and mestizo vagabonds, poor soldiers, and plotters who fueled his imagination with visions of Inca restoration under Melchor's rule. Melchor's politically charged presence in his native Cuzco—for many, he was the true head of the kingdom—could be used as a justification for rising up in arms against the king in Castile. According to this view, Melchor was too weak or fickle to prevent that from happening. Thus, Viceroy Velasco (1596–1604) left Melchor with no choice but to leave for Spain.[63] A careful reading of the wealth of documents exchanged by the viceroy, the Council, and Melchor's own procurators regarding the Inca scion's journey to Spain and his noteworthy pretensions at court tells a different story, one in which legal agency and careful negotiations between the king and his vassal set the norm for Melchor's life in Spain. This decades-long interaction takes us to the heart of what different historical actors understood as "justice" within the Iberian Atlantic.

In 1582, Doña María de Esquivel, Don Melchor's mother and legal guardian and a native from Trujillo in Extremadura, started her own dealings with the king's courts upon her husband's death in Cuzco. Like other members of third-generation *encomendero* families, Doña María and Don Melchor, then eleven years old, feared that the wealthy *encomienda* granted in 1543 to Melchor's grandfather, Don Cristóbal Paullu Tupac Inca, *and* inherited by his son, Don Carlos Inca, in "second life" in the early 1550s, would now revert to the Crown.[64] The possession of Hatuncana, which yielded some 7,000 ducats of annual rent, was initially confirmed by Viceroy Martín Enríquez (1581–1583), remaining one of the main sources of income for the family. But the viceroy changed his mind soon after, probably pressured to satisfy the multiple claimants awaiting a rent from a vacant *encomienda*. He parceled out Hatuncana, awarding smaller sums to other beneficiaries. From 1583 until 1595, when Melchor finally reached legal majority and took over the family's legal affairs, Doña María's lawyers litigated in Lima to reverse Enríquez's ruling. With the aid of the general defender for the Indians, Melchor took control of the court case before Lima's *Audiencia*. Despite his efforts, however, the family lost the legal battle. He appealed the ruling and placed his case before the *Consejo de Indias*; Melchor hired Gaspar de la Esquina, an experienced *procurador de causas*, to handle the case in Spain.[65]

The Council affirmed the *Audiencia*'s previous ruling on June 10, 1596.[66] Thanks to De la Esquina's excellent connections at court and his post as paupers' attorney (*abogado de pobres*) of the Council, however, Melchor's case reached the king and his secretaries a few days later. De la Esquina requested an astronomical annuity of 30,000 pesos for his client in compensation for the loss of Hatuncana (and, indirectly, the kingdom of Peru). The procurator argued that this *encomienda* should not be subject to the normal rules of inheritance, which limited possession to the original grantee and his immediate successor. Rather, Hatuncana had been a special *merced*, granted to Melchor's grandfather by the king as compensation for ceding an entire kingdom and renouncing any claims to it. Thus, the grant could not expire but was of a perpetual nature.[67]

Ten days after their final verdict, the councilors advised the king in a *consulta* that the services and loyalty of Melchor's forebears and his own *calidad*—an Inca royal and *encomendero* gentleman in Cuzco—deserved a befitting pension or reward. In their judgment: "it seems very just that he be granted some favor." What amount was just, however, the Council could not determine. To establish the appropriate *merced*, Philip requested the new viceroy's opinion about the possibility of granting this benefit (or any other) in perpetuity. A royal order issued on October 31, 1596, commanded him to investigate Melchor's ancestry as well as his *calidad*, form an opinion (*parecer*) on the matter, and send it sealed to the Council. Furthermore, the viceroy was ordered to support (*entretener*) the prince and his household in the meantime.[68]

Don Melchor received news of the royal order sometime before March 1599. He journeyed to Lima and hired a lawyer to see to his case. Through his representative, Melchor requested a provisional grace (*entretenimiento*) according to his noble ancestry and lifestyle, presenting family crests and *encomienda* grants dating back to the 1540s. Melchor also obtained a recommendation from one of the judges of the *Audiencia*, who wrote to Velasco—the new viceroy—in September 1600 in support of Melchor's aspirations.[69] Melchor offered to elaborate a full proof of merit and services in Cuzco, to which Velasco agreed.[70] At this point, perhaps motivated by Velasco's good disposition toward his plea, Don Melchor began to entertain the idea of journeying to Spain to petition the king for a title of nobility—that of count or marquis—a dignity at the royal court, and a coat of arms. In a letter dated November 1, 1600, he told the viceroy that he would arrange his trip to Spain via Lima as soon as he settled his affairs in Cuzco.[71]

As these negotiations were unfolding, Velasco maintained a parallel conversation with the Council. In a letter dated June 1599, he argued for Melchor settling in Spain permanently. Although he believed in Melchor's loyalty, some rumors, letters, and reports had alerted him to the potentially subversive influence that his presence in Cuzco exerted over dissatisfied individuals.[72] The Council agreed: Melchor had to be persuaded to establish his household in Spain, recognizing that his income would have to be commuted for an equivalent one in the Peninsula.[73] Even in a case where a threat to the political order was suspected or seemed imminent, the Crown refrained from forcing this vassal to move to Spain with his family without agreeing first on what kind of reward Melchor, the king, and the Council considered just or appropriate.

With Melchor still in Cuzco, the Council reminded Velasco of the king's obligations. On December 7, 1600, Velasco wrote back informing that Melchor had made up his mind: he would go to Spain to seek royal favor. Nonetheless, he had confided he was (allegedly) unable to pay for the trip or support himself at court. In their response, the councilors restated that the Inca prince should embark to Spain only at his own "will and desire" (*voluntad y gusto*)—that is, as a result of persuasion, the promise of royal reward, and careful political maneuvering on the part of the viceroy—and not by way of compulsion.[74] Velasco reiterated his opinion that Melchor could not be found guilty of any wrongdoing. In the viceroy's view, "there is no reason to compel him [to go to Spain]" other than "the fantasies [*imaginaciones*] of some confused and lost men who have made him the object of their whims."

The Council concurred, authorizing Velasco to support the whole enterprise and to assure Melchor that the king would reward him substantially *if* he finally made the journey across the Atlantic. Melchor left Peru in early May 1602, after obtaining 6,000 ducats for the trip and the right to travel on the royal fleet at His Majesty's expense. He settled in Castile, living between Trujillo, Valladolid, and Madrid in the following years.[75]

The next chapter in Melchor's story unfolded in Valladolid, where the royal court and the Council were residing. A *memorial* presented on June 20, 1603, spelled out his pretensions. On November 7, the king agreed to a perpetual rent of 4,000 ducats—Melchor had requested 10,000—but did not rule on his petition for knighthood. In October 1604, the councilors advised the monarch that, unless Melchor was to receive his perpetual pension, the knighthood of Santiago, and other royal favors, neither they nor His Majesty could rightfully detain him in Spain much longer. They also warned about the dangers of having an enraged or dissatisfied (*descontento y despechado*) Melchor back in Peru. They conceded that only a reward (*merced*) substantial enough to support him and his family "with the decency befitting the great-grandson of the universal lord of Peru" could justly impede his return.[76]

Negotiations did not resume until August 1605, when Melchor's attorney, in an effort to force the Crown to act, told them that Melchor was dissatisfied (*descontento*) and about to request a return license. He argued that Melchor had come to the realization that he would not obtain any additional *mercedes*. The king finally gave in. By April 1607, virtually all of Melchor's requests— including the perpetual pension of 8,500 ducats, a one-time *ayuda de costa* of 8,000 ducats (and another 6,000 ducats to bring his wife to Spain), the courtly dignity of *gentilhombre de boca* of the king, and the knighthood of Santiago—had been granted.[77]

The attitudes of king and Council toward Melchor and his aspirations were not exceptional. On the contrary, they exemplified a common policy— though rarely on such a grand scale—inspired by the need to do what was "just." Don Melchor's transatlantic journeys stemmed from the confluence of imperial anxieties and designs, but decisions were not completely outside the control of Andean petitioners and their attorneys at court. These voyages became a reality only after careful estimation, on the part of litigants, as to how well metropolitan authorities would reward their services, alleviate their hardships, and uphold their privileged status in the Peninsula.[78]

AT HIS MAJESTY'S EXPENSE

Indigenous visitors of varying rank benefited from similar policies and decisions at the Habsburg court, although certainly on a more modest scale and with less notoriety. Throughout the sixteenth and seventeenth centuries, all sorts of *ayudas de costa* were issued to fund journeys and stays at court. The Council earmarked gifts, aids, and contributions to pay for passage fares, daily provisions, and exemption from notarial and administrative fees. Moreover, it reimbursed many individuals in Madrid and Seville, including priests, courtiers, and its own low-ranking bureaucrats for expenses incurred in putting up, "caring for," or "guarding" (*custodiar*) Indian visitors, apparently in their own homes.[79] A survey of *ayudas* over a period of two hundred years reveals the astonishing variety of items paid for, almost in a systematic fashion, by order of the Council, including room and board, charity, medical assistance, marriages, and funerals, along with pensions for the traveler and his relatives, and even funds to print *memoriales* and *privilegios* and prepare *informaciones de méritos y servicios* in Madrid.[80]

His name was Paquiquineo, an Algonquian-speaking *indio cacique* from Jacán (or Ajacán), in what the Spanish termed "La Florida" in the 1550s. In the summer of 1561, the Spanish crew of the *Santa Catalina* "took" twenty-year-old Paquiquineo from his elite home in the Bahía de Santa María (the Virginia side of modern Chesapeake Bay) to Spain. After a short stay in Lagos, Portugal, the travelers arrived in Seville on September 29. Paquiquineo journeyed to court, where Philip II granted him an audience. In February 1562, the king ordered Paquiquineo, now fluent in Spanish, to return to his homeland in the treasure fleet. He was to aid the Dominican fathers with their conversion efforts at La Florida. Paquiquineo traveled to New Spain and then to Mexico City where, after having taken seriously ill, he was baptized, adopting the name "Don Luis de Velasco" after his baptismal sponsor and godfather, the viceroy of New Spain. Following a "miraculous" recovery, Don Luis joined a failed expedition to La Florida, ultimately returning to Spain in 1566, where the king charged the Jesuits with continuing his Christian education.[81]

Between December 1566 and June 1567, when they finally returned to

Jacán to aid the Jesuits in the establishment of a mission, Don Luis and his *indio* dependent were provided full room and board in an inn (*posada*) in Madrid, costing the Crown five *reales* per day (roughly three times the average daily wage of a laborer in New Castile).[82] The Council also provided funds to pay for the labor and materials to manufacture clothes and shoes for Don Luis and his *criado*. The 82.5 pesos so spent amounted to ten times the basic yearly income of a gardener in Castile-León.[83]

The Council also bought Don Luis a new rosary to attend Mass in the appropriate fashion. Every Sunday and on every religious holiday, the *cacique* left the inn to visit the church of Our Lady of Atocha, on the outskirts of the city. Each time, he gave one real, also provided by the Council, to alms. Don Luis also received two *reales* to bequeath a Mass for his soul and one or two *reales* every weekend to distribute among paupers and beggars. At the Crown's expense, Don Luis visited a barbershop once or twice every month (at a cost of one *real* per visit). He also received 16 *maravedíes* (less than one real) to enjoy himself at a theatrical play. Two royal decrees ordered the House of Trade to provide Don Luis with fares and provisions for his trip back to the New World.[84]

Unlike Don Luis de Velasco, Don Diego de Torre was not easily recognized as a *cacique*, but he clearly aspired to attain such a status before the Council. The son of a Spanish conquistador and a prominent figure in local *santafereño* society, Don Diego lay claim to the Muisca *cacicazgo* of Turmequé, in the *audiencia* district of Santa Fe, through his mother, the eldest sister of the *cacique* in office.[85] The *pleito* over the lordship and other affairs brought him to court in 1578. Like Don Melchor Carlos Inca and Don Alonso Atahualpa, two noble expatriates who were also to reside and die in Madrid, Don Diego was "perhaps more familiar with the dinner tables of the Santa Fe elite than with everyday life in a *pueblo de indios*." He was a gentleman "who undoubtedly spent more time writing in educated Spanish and readings the important books of his time than conversing in his mother's language."[86] While at court, however, Don Diego managed to benefit from some of the privileges and protections afforded to the broad category of *indios*. Indeed, some of the documents refer to him as a "cacique Indian" (*indio cacique*).

During his two stays in Madrid—his *mestizo* condition and European upbringing notwithstanding—Don Diego was granted at least twelve different *mercedes* from the royal coffers to properly support himself, his nephew, and a dependent (*criado*) in Madrid. Between April and May 1578, he spent four *reales* daily in his *sustento* (twice the average wage of a laborer in New Castile).[87] The king also authorized 275 pesos for the *cacique's* journey back to Santa Fe. Between 1586 and 1587, during a second stay in the Peninsula, Don

Diego benefitted from several other *mercedes* totaling 843.25 pesos, justified in terms of his "necessity" (*necesidad*) and earmarked as a "subsistence allowance" (*ayuda a sustentarse*) according to his station as a gentleman (*caballero*).

Don Diego died in Madrid. In April 1590, the Council authorized the release of eight pesos for Don Diego's funeral. Juana de Oropesa, his Spanish widow, was granted a perpetual pension of 495 pesos, along with an additional one-time gift of 275 pesos in reward for Don Diego's service. In 1596, six years after Don Diego de Torre's demise, the Council of the Indies awarded the widow 2.75 pesos to help pay for the funeral of her only child with the dispossessed *cacique* of Turmequé.[88]

By the 1660s, the amounts regularly awarded to indigenous favor-seekers had become customary. The travelers' own agency turned what started as an ad hoc response to the first visitors from the Caribbean and Mesoamerica into a general practice.[89] Royal aid also materialized in *limosnas* and *ayudas de costa*, usually to fund stays or return trips. Throughout the seventeenth century, *indios* customarily received 30 ducats (330 *reales* or 41.5 pesos). Some travelers received significantly more.[90] Provided they could establish their *indio* legal status to the satisfaction of the *Casa de la Contratación*, natives also received the *merced* of sailing gratis in the royal fleet—a privilege reserved for colonial officials, soldiers, and priests.[91] Sea captains and officers were to accommodate returning Indians in their ships according to their *calidad* and provide the daily provision of a soldier but no wage (*sueldo*), especially if "poor," an interesting clue as to the Indians' comparable position in the eyes of metropolitan officials. One such traveler, his poverty being of a situational nature, took a Spanish hatmaker, his *criado*, with him to Quito.[92]

Royal support becomes all the more significant if one considers that 30 ducats was not a negligible sum in the early Atlantic world. The transoceanic journey was generally beyond the means of most Iberians. The expenses included notarial and administrative fees, traveling from the emigrant's hometown to Seville and staying there until the fleet departed, and paying for passage, accommodations, and provisions. A comparison between these expenses and the known wages of some occupations in Castile and Andalusia shows that savings from those wages alone were not enough to finance the journey. Emigrants who went on their own account sold their properties, borrowed money, or relied on remittances sent by relatives living overseas.[93]

On board, class, status, and *calidad* generally determined sleeping arrangements, provisions, and even the amount of privacy a passenger could expect during the trip. In many ways, life on board represented a "microcosm" of the social hierarchies of the time.[94] But travel arrangements involving indigenous voyagers sometimes subverted such hierarchies. Iberian passengers paid the 30 or 40 ducats that the king usually granted indigenous visitors to cover the full cost of passage plus provisions in 1580.[95] Three hundred and thirty *reales* represented ten times the monthly wage of an apprentice seaman on the Spanish treasure fleet between 1567 and 1623 and still more than what a pilot, master, or captain earned during that period.[96] Most Iberian voyagers traveled on the deck. The more affluent ones, however, purchased wooden chambers on the top deck, which could house up to four adults, two children, and baggage, for 110 to 165 pesos.[97] In 1665, by contrast, Don Juan de Azabache and Nicolás Flores—"Indians who arrived from Peru"—received 275 pesos each in 1660 for their trip and that of Nicolás's wife and son back home.[98]

Accommodating Indian travelers in the royal fleet had the benefit of helping the Council accomplish its goal of aiding *indios* to return to their *naturalezas*. A journey in the king's armada increased the chances of a safe arrival and prevented native visitors from remaining in Spain or in one of the intermediate stops along the way. In 1678, the *Consejo de Indias* responded to a previous letter from the president of the *Casa de la Contratación* regarding Jerónimo Lorenzo Limaylla's arrival to Seville. Because he arrived too late to embark on the outgoing fleet, the Council feared that he would stay in Spain even longer. It ordered the president of the House to "support" (*entretener*) Jerónimo until he could be placed in the first official ship sailing to Peru. Back in 1671, the councilors had issued an *ayuda de costa* of 200 *reales*, to be given to Limaylla in person in Seville, but he never left. This time, the Council wanted to make sure Limaylla had little option but to return.[99]

THE RHETORIC OF WRETCHEDNESS

By the late 1540s, officials within courtly circles began to identify enslaved and free *indios* or *naturales* as *personas miserables* or *de condición miserable*: "poor" and "miserable" persons with a status of temporal or perpetual legal minority.[100] By subordinating native Andeans to Spaniards, the privileges and protections of the poor and wretched, resignified and demanded in multiple legal forums, became part of the natives' *fuero* (special judicial regime) and *república*. The sovereign was "so far away," the Nahua lords of the polity of Huejotzingo declared in a letter to the king in 1560, and his indigenous subjects were "very poor" and without the means to complete the journey to Spain. By the 1550s, indigenous favor-seekers had incorporated the language of poverty and wretchedness into the repertoire of strategies abroad.[101]

This ascribed inferiority became a tool for empowerment at the royal court. By midcentury, the language of wretchedness and poverty began to appear regularly in connection with the efforts of indigenous travelers to obtain financial backing for their stays and endeavors.[102] The "wretched" argument became an effective strategy especially among *indios naturales* of commoner origin and relatively modest resources, travelers who had little else to offer in terms of the language of privilege, high birth, and service used by noble counterparts.[103] Crown prosecutors and paupers' attorneys who drafted requests to king and Council drew on two important precedents: Mesoamerican and Caribbean lords visiting the court in the first decades of the sixteenth century, and enslaved Indians seeking freedom after the New Laws of 1542. The language of poverty and necessity drew from and fused together both collective experiences.[104]

Metropolitan officials had to assume that, because of their ignorance, feeble nature, or poverty, native commoners lacked the means to pursue justice, and thus they must receive it for free. Even if *caciques* and nobles generally avoided identifying themselves as *indios* or *miserables* in writing, they still had limited access to these privileges. In such cases, ministers seem to have taken a common *indio* status for granted. *Caciques* could also receive legal assistance if they could prove that they were litigating on behalf of their subjects or were too destitute to obtain justice.

This privilege created a significant advantage for certain transatlantic litigants. Imperial courts and attorneys for the poor and wretched, available to indigenous travelers, were hardly available for the bulk of Spanish voyagers, especially if wealthier and more powerful than their Indian legal rivals. In 1666, the royal prosecutor of the Council addressed a petition to the councilors on behalf of Jerónimo Limaylla. As someone lacking any income in Spain, Limaylla should be declared *pobre de solemnidad* (a solemn pauper), which would entitle him to a pauper's attorney and to pursue his lawsuit at no cost. Three witnesses, all *vecinos* of Madrid, corroborated Jerónimo's apparently obvious lack of means. One of them had known Don Jerónimo for a year and could testify that "he is very poor and needy and does not have the wherewithal to maintain himself, so that this witness has often seen him, a poor and shameful beggar, asking for alms from many a person; and this witness has sometimes given him what he could." Despite some doubt, and following the queen's express order, the Council assigned Limaylla a lawyer and admitted the case. His legal opponent back in the Andes, however, was unable to travel or to secure an attorney at court, despite several communications from the Council ordering that he choose his legal counselor. Nor could he, as a *cacique* litigating in a private matter—a *cacicazgo*—have recourse to the "pauper" argument. Considering the cost of transatlantic litigation, free legal assistance represented a significant advantage for Limaylla.[105]

The pauper status assigned to some travelers can be gauged from the sums regularly issued to support ordinary and extraordinary expenses. The source of such royal aids also reflects the perception the councilors had of common Andean visitors as members of the poorer classes. Between the late sixteenth century and the late seventeenth century, native visitors customarily received 30 ducats (330 *reales* or some 41 pesos) in one-time *ayudas de costa* from the Council. While "ordinary" *indios* typically received two *reales* to cover their daily provisions, higher-ranking *caciques* or noble bearers of the honorific title *Don* received double that amount per day.[106] Interestingly, these sums seem to have been the customary aid that the Council dispensed to nonindigenous persons "in need" (*necesidad*).[107]

These funds generally came from the *penas de cámara* (court costs), *penas de estrados* (fees and fines), and *obras pías* (charity) accounts, which were part of the internal budget. Councilors made customary use of these funds to give alms and gifts to convents and hospitals and to support religious services and other charitable endeavors, which is probably how they framed, at least in part, their support to Andean travelers. They also used these funds to grant extraordinary aids (*ayudas extraordinarias de costa*), alms (*limosnas*), and graces (*mercedes*) of different sorts. Gifts and gratuities, in the form of *aguinaldos*, *luminarias*, and *propinas*, were given away during holidays and special occasions, including Christmas, Easter, and New Year's Eve. The beneficiaries were middle- and lesser-ranking officials, *criados*, servants, and other dependents of the Council and court. Poor individuals who depended on this patronage were among the beneficiaries.[108]

The moneys allotted to indigenous visitors generally came from these funds.[109] The internal accounting books of the Council usually recorded individuals of these two groups next to one another. In 1582, Damiana, "La Negra," a humble sweeper of the Council, received 66 *reales* of *limosna* for Holy Easter. That day, Don Pedro de Zama, an *indio* from Peru, received a smaller gift of 5.5 pesos from the same fund, justified in terms of Zama's "poverty and necessity" at court. The religious holiday probably also played a part in fomenting the councilors' generosity.[110] Ancient Regime attitudes toward the poor accepted their social inevitability, but they also constructed them as an opportunity for generosity and benevolence on the part of the powerful and wealthy.[111]

Untangling the rhetoric of the travelers' letters, petitions, and *ayudas de costa* from realities and hardships is a difficult task.[112] Drawing any distinction, however, probably misses the main point. For litigants in criminal cases in Quito from the 1720s onward, for instance, there was little or no relation-ship between a declaration of poverty and a true state of destitution.[113] Simi-larly, "wretchedness" at the royal court could very well be a matter of per-ception and inference as much as an economic reality. Ideally, perceptions of poverty were the result of careful consideration of the status, quality, and services of the individual or lineage in question. How such factors compared to the specific circumstances of other claimants was also relevant. These per-ceptions were shaped by the ideal of allowing someone to live according to his or her station (*calidad*). The central concern of the Council, still conceived as a part of the king's extended household and subject to similar expectations, was how to give each traveler and petitioner his due.

Dealing with "poor" travelers was as much a display of royal largesse and Christian piety as it was an exercise in royal justice. The ideal of fairness behind early modern forms of redistributive justice meant giving to every-one their due equally (*con igualdad*) and proportionately. Proportionality de-manded maintaining what each already had rather than leveling everyone under some ideal of social justice and equality.[114] Recommendations by the Council for a post or dignity in the Americas often bore the mark of what these ministers considered just: viceroys, based on their local knowledge, should employ native Andean visitors "in posts commensurate to the person in question," based on their *calidad*, skills, and merits, no more or less.[115] The king could recompense the same action or tend to the same need differently, depending on who performed the service or requested aid. Redistributive justice, then, was meant to accentuate social differences, not to bridge dis-parate social worlds.

Humbler visitors usually expected aid attuned to their relatively lower class and *calidad* (although they certainly negotiated status if possible). Visi-tors of a higher rank wished for more. More so than with indigenous com-moners, the righteous monarch had to meet this obligation to uphold justice for prominent vassals. Claimants and petitioners of status and wealth could also recast themselves on paper as Incas of noble descent, *caciques*, *vecinos*, prominent *encomenderos*, *pobres de solemnidad*, or even *indios* in need of legal protection, depending on the context and on how such labels suited their aims in court.[116]

In a highly stratified society, the poverty and need of travelers in Spain was of a relative and situational nature. Don Melchor Carlos Inca's ancestors in Cuzco had amassed considerable wealth, including several *chacras* of coca, maize, and chili (*ají*), orchards, textile mills, and houses, and the famous palace of Colcampata that towered over the city.[117] In 1599, a proof of merit and services was prepared to aid Melchor in his quest for recompense. An impressive roster of witnesses, including paramount Spanish conquistadors and *encomenderos*, testified as to Melchor's noble *estofa* (quality, class) and refined upbringing as a noble and a gentleman (*caballero hijodalgo*), placing him among the most illustrious descendants of the Inca emperors *and* the most influential *vecinos encomenderos* of Cuzco.[118]

Despite his wealth, *encomendero* lifestyle, and partial Spanish ancestry, Melchor managed to secure free legal representation by the defender for the Indians in 1595, a strategy generally unavailable to Spanish *vecinos, encomenderos, gente principal,* and *mestizos* who frequented the same urban spaces as Melchor and socialized with him, but who were not considered *indios*. In March 1599, after his case was successfully appealed to the *Consejo de Indias*, Melchor informed Viceroy Velasco that, as a result of his journey from Cuzco to Lima to oversee his lawsuit, "every day my poverty increases." Velasco, the claimant argued, had to determine the appropriate amount based on what "a nobleman like myself" required for his support, for it was only fair that "descendants of those who had and could do so much do not become impoverished, as I am at present."[119]

In Spain, Melchor found himself in a far better position than most indigenous travelers asking for an *ayuda de costa* or the protection of a pauper's attorney. After Melchor's death in October 1610, royal officials auctioned his estate in Cuzco for 20,000 assayed pesos (31,250 pesos of eight).[120] In 1609, Melchor donated 5,500 pesos to Doña Isabel de Peñaloza, a widow from Madrid, for the future dowry of Catalina Gutiérrez de Fonseca (probably an illegitimate offspring of Melchor with the *madrileña*). In his testament, Melchor bequeathed his *criados* with more than 1,650 pesos and a mourning dress of relatively fine quality for each. Melchor granted his jester another 206 pesos, freed his slave, and donated an extra 2,750 pesos and his entire wardrobe to a relative who had accompanied him to Spain. He also donated 137.5 pesos to the School of Saint Agustin in Alcalá and 5,500 pesos for Masses for his soul.[121] Melchor's multiple heirs were expected to honor 2,475 pesos of debts that he had incurred to pay for his attire, his funeral, a golden reliquary, and other unspecified objects and services, all indispensable for maintaining the lifestyle of a prince in exile in Spain.[122]

Don Melchor's "poverty," like that of landowners, merchants, and notable widows who declared themselves poor in late colonial Quito, was grounded less in economic conditions than in their failure to live up to social expectations at court. They were "socially" poor rather than "economically" poor.[123] The ideal order that the Habsburg court was meant to project explains why high-ranking travelers expected the king to provide for a living according to their noble status. Travelers would acquire debts and then ask the king to provide the means to honor them. In 1589, a destitute Alonso Atahualpa died in the royal prison of Madrid for an unmet obligation of 100 pesos.[124] It does not seem like much for someone with 4,800 pesos of annual rent. For his stay at court, Alonso rented a residence in the Puerta de Vega in Madrid and purchased another one. While in Madrid, he received 570 pesos of gold (912 silver pesos) in remittances from his *encomiendas* in America, where he still possessed significant assets.

Alonso's debts in Spain stemmed from his lifestyle and refined manners. His parents had raised him among Spanish *hidalgos* and *encomenderos*, entrusting the dean of Quito's cathedral to teach him "the things that the sons of *hidalgos* should know." He was literate and dressed "like other sons of Spanish *vecinos*." For one of the witnesses in his *probanza*, Don Alonso "is not part Indian, according to his behavior, but a full Spaniard." While he lived in Quito, Don Alonso purchased Spanish-style gloves, clothes, hats, silver ornaments, and even a lute.[125] The need to preserve this lifestyle explains why, in 1586, Alonso petitioned His Majesty for an *ayuda de costa* "according to his *calidad* so that he can pay some debts that he has, bring honor to himself, and return to his land [*tierra*]."[126]

Don Alonso's second cousin, Don Melchor Carlos Inca, who boasted of a similar upbringing among the *vecinos encomenderos* of Cuzco, also contracted important debts in Spain. His perpetual annual pension of more than 11,600 pesos placed him within the lowest rank of the Spanish titled aristocracy.[127] Yet, by 1605 he could no longer sustain his lifestyle or his retinue of ten *criados* in Spain. Aware of Don Melchor's financial difficulties, the Council reminded Philip that 9,625 annual pesos were not enough to support Melchor according to his *calidad*. The Council suggested, instead, a pension ranging from 13,750 to 16,500 pesos. The king replied by awarding Melchor the prestigious knighthood of Santiago plus 2,000 pesos. The council insisted on adding an outstanding request of 11,000 pesos of immediate *ayuda de costa* to finance the prince in Spain, plus 8,250 pesos to bring Melchor's wife and household from Cuzco to the court. The bargain ended up favoring Don Melchor.[128]

Melchor's classic biographer once portrayed the Inca prince as an "ostentatious mestizo," the last in a long line of stubborn and importunate "petty beggars" (*pedigüeños*), constantly pleading for rent and other aids that he nevertheless foolishly expended in Peru and Spain.[129] This portrayal fails to see that the constant demands of the Inca prince and other prominent travelers were not the result of mere stubbornness or excessive ambition. Rather, they were the expected behavior in the Ancient Regime. Not unlike those of the Habsburg king, Melchor's prestige and status as the head of the colonial Inca nobility and one of the paramount *vecinos encomenderos* of Cuzco made little sense without his largesse and ostentation in Peru and Spain. The petit court he maintained in Spain made perfect sense within a society that viewed the equation of wealth, rank, and power as natural and the proverbial object of royal justice. From this perspective, Melchor's famous journey to secure a pension and other privileges was an appeal to the magnanimous king to restore the balance between the Inca's prominent rank and his decreasing patrimony as well as a successful attempt to increase both directly at court.

SIX

WHAT'S IN A NAME?

Impostors, Forgeries, and the Limits of Transatlantic Advocacy

Five years after he stopped holding the post of viceroy of Peru, Don Pedro Álvarez de Toledo, the Marquis of Mancera (1639–1648), still harbored ill feelings against an indigenous traveler to the Spanish court. As he recalled in a petition (*memorial*) addressed to Philip IV in 1653, a handful of well-connected officials and landowners had mounted a defamation campaign while he still held office. These false accusations, Mancera alleged, stemmed from the punishment he meted out to them for defrauding the Royal Exchequer and usurping indigenous communal lands. His enemies circulated malicious reports and satirical pamphlets in Lima and Spain, greatly damaging the viceroy's reputation. Hoping to tarnish his name even further, one opponent journeyed to the court in late 1645 or early 1646, seeking audience with the *Consejo de Indias* and putting forth additional false allegations. To render his complaints credible, the accuser "brought along" an *indio* from Lima to Spain. The viceroy did not even care to record his name, but other documents reveal to us that he was Don Carlos Chimo, the man we met in previous chapters. Mancera warned His Majesty in 1653 that this visitor was won over to the unjust cause and, before the Council, lied about him and the supreme justice of the *Audiencia de Lima* in charge of the Second General Land Inspection in northern Peru.[1]

Some of the events had unfolded according to Mancera's recollections. In 1646, Don Carlos Chimo filed his own petition before the Council, depicting himself as one of the paramount lords (*caciques principales*) of the town of Lambayeque, a sergeant of the Indian company of the neighboring city of Saña, and a descendant of the pre-Hispanic Chimo kings who ruled the northern coastal plains of Peru until the Incas defeated them in the fifteenth century. Don Carlos primarily advocated on behalf of the commons of Lambayeque and other neighboring towns, but he took his advocacy beyond and raised his voice at the behest of "all the *caciques* and lords of vassals and all of the *naturales* of Peru" who had suffered because of Mancera's misrule. He particularly complained about the "violence and tyranny with which the Marquis has oppressed the Indians, depriving them of their lands."[2]

But Mancera was set on exposing Chimo as a fraud. The viceroy claimed to possess information that proved beyond a doubt the false nature of his accusations. The viceroy stated, "This *indio* was a con man, not a *cacique* but a vile man and a *mestizo*, punished and lashed for thievery in Peru." The councilors should have not taken his allegations seriously for that reason. And, even assuming that Chimo possessed a drop of noble blood, Mancera reminded them, he had tainted it with vile labor and infamy.[3]

AN IMPOSTOR ARRIVES AT THE ROYAL COURT?

If, as Mancera alleged, Don Carlos Chimo was an impostor (*supuesto*), what kind of impostor was he? Character assassination was the common currency in early modern Spanish courts, for discrediting the accuser was a way to disprove the accusation. The strategy took advantage of the legal doctrine positing that the degree of truthfulness and trustworthiness of a judicial deposition was not solely dependent on the deponent's relation to what actually happened. Its validity also depended on the individual's credibility, status, religious zeal, and station (*calidad*). Combined with the easy-to-invoke argument that Indians and *mestizos* (individuals of Indian and Spanish ancestry) were particularly prone to lying in courts and bearing false witness, a lowly *calidad* could tip the scales of justice—and ultimately the councilors' opinion—against Don Carlos.[4] Therefore, the fact that Mancera and Don Pedro de Meneses, the supreme justice in charge of the contested land inspection, raised such charges against Don Carlos is not surprising. Nor is it surprising that Chimo became embroiled in a larger plot devised by the viceroy's political enemies to further their own interests and for purposes that had little to do with returning usurped lands to the rightful owners. Neither of these circumstances diminishes the agency displayed by Don Carlos to reach the court on his own and, with the support of other leaders, become instrumental in the Crown's decision to reopen the case so that the complainants against the land judge could meet justice.[5]

Even so, the alternative claims that circulated in Chimo's homeland, in Lima's *Audiencia*, and in the Council about the *cacique*'s "true" *calidad* and *naturaleza* should not be so readily dismissed. These parallel claims raise some intriguing questions about Don Carlos's legitimacy and the basis of his authority as a transatlantic procurator, which this chapter seeks to answer. Such accusations—and similar ones raised against Don Andrés de Ortega Lluncon, Chimo's fellow traveler and his countryman (*paisano*), who filed charges against the local *corregidor* in Spain almost concurrently—were leveled not only by these colonial officials. Claims that discredited the indigenous procurators were seconded by, and in all likelihood partially originated in, a group of indigenous notables (for the most part *caciques, principales,* and governors of the Lambayeque and Trujillo coastal areas). Their testimonies substantiated the accusation that Don Carlos, and especially Don Andrés, were *supuestos* or impersonators of some sort.[6]

Similar accusations were launched against other Andean procurators advocating in local and metropolitan courts around the same time. Thus, although it is crucial to recognize Chimo and Ortega's historical agency by rejecting the idea that Mancera's opponents were simply dictating their words and actions, historicizing such agency should not come at the expense of obliterating the agency of others, particularly that of the *principales* who, from within local indigenous society, opposed the procurators' actions and claims, questioned their capacity for judicial representation, and offered alternative versions of the travelers' social and legal personas.

The crux of Mancera's accusation—the incompatibility between being a *cacique* and being a lowly *mestizo* punished for theft—also deserves further scrutiny. Independent documents produced years before Chimo decided to visit Philip's court help explain the claims of those who questioned Chimo's *cacique* identity. In 1641, Don Carlos Chimo, a thirty-nine-year-old master embroiderer in the city of Trujillo, was sentenced to two hundred public lashes and four years of exile for the sacrilegious crime of stealing an altar front and a set of altar clothes.[7] In looking at the conflicting claims about Chimo's identity, it has been pointed out that it is not a matter of determining which of these two identities is the "real" one. Instead, these identifications are situational, presenting two parallel interpretations. In this view, two scenarios—Chimo the *cacique* and Chimo the migrant artisan—were equally possible, making it necessary for us to discover Chimo's legitimacy within each.[8]

Nonetheless, seeing Chimo's crucible in light of similar transatlantic controversies prompted by analogous sojourns at the Habsburg court opens a third line of inquiry, which this chapter will follow. Chimo's case is not necessarily about possible but mutually exclusive scenarios. One needs not choose between the *cacique* and the artisan of commoner stock, for Mancera's adversary was a master embroiderer, a sergeant, and an *indio principal* from a rural town who now fared well in the colonial city. In the story retold below, Don Carlos Chimo's seemingly conflicting persona—shaped as it was by the rules and expectations of legal representation at the heart of the early modern

Spanish Empire—can be reconciled in terms of the novel realities of indigenous leadership in mid-seventeenth-century Peru. Other stories of transatlantic voyagers and voyages reveal such realities to us. All of them contribute to our understanding of how indigenous elites and plebeians intervened in Spanish courts and crafted similar discourses of self-representation that could speak to legitimacy in a variety of languages.[9]

Like other travelers whose authority, support networks, and legal expertise were wide and strong enough to reach the Spanish court, Chimo was *simultaneously* a *Don*, a master artisan of some means, and a fairly recent migrant from the town of Lambayeque to the multiethnic city of Trujillo. He was an officer in an indigenous battalion, a prestigious post that carried certain governmental duties. Chimo was very *ladino*, probably literate (he could sign his name), and had some family ties to the ruling lineages of the northern Saña-Trujillo region. His corporal punishment and exile were no proof of commoner origin or *mestizo* status, as Mancera wanted the Council to believe. What made the exile, the public lashes, and the temporary imprisonment so insulting (and thus worth fighting against in the courts) was the mismatch between the nature of the punishment and Chimo's self-ascribed status as an *yndio prinçipal*.[10]

Chimo belonged to the colonial native elite of the mid-seventeenth-century northern coast, and in some respects he was not exceptional among his social peers. Chimo's cosmopolitan leadership style, judicial experience, and wide social connections stood out. He was a well-traveled individual who had visited Lima at least once prior to appearing before the *Audiencia* to appeal the 1641 sentence. As a result, he had become knowledgeable about vice-regal legal forums. By setting up shop in Trujillo, moreover, Chimo gained ready access to intermediate ports and networks along the Pacific coast and en route to Spain, which surely facilitated his journey across the ocean.[11] The *cacique*, like the *indio*, was an elastic and negotiable *naturaleza* at the court. The fluidity of categories such as commoner, *cacique*, *mestizo*, and *natural* in an Atlantic setting opened new avenues to power, prestige, and authority for certain travelers. Chimo took advantage of this opportunity, as he embraced—and embodied—the shifting nature of indigenous power in these settings.

Equally important, it was the same social conditions that forged the careers of men like Chimo and made his style of leadership appealing, appropriate, or even necessary, which gave his claims to authority and legitimacy a forever-incomplete nature, subject to challenge on many fronts. The *cacique* template, when deployed in legal settings, still defined leaders in a narrow fashion—those who, because of nobility, paternal inheritance, and high status, enjoyed the Crown's recognition as lords of vassals.[12] As such, the title was incompatible with posing as a lord with no vassals, a *mestizo*, or a tribute-payer—a *parque* or *mitayo*, as Chimo was derogatorily called. Chimo's case demonstrates that the charge of lacking such legal recognition still carried enough weight in court to partially disqualify those who claimed it for themselves but could not, if required, exhibit proper title to it.

Midcolonial Andean procurators operating under the umbrella of *cacique* status never fully resolved this tension. Claims to *cacique* ancestry and legal authority, though necessary to speak to the king from a leadership position within the *República de Indios*, potentially weakened these advocates by making them vulnerable to alternative legal narratives. The charges of falsehood and impersonation launched against Chimo, Ortega, and others show that the legal constraints of the increasingly outdated lord-subject mode for collective representation—that of the *cacique*—threatened to limit transatlantic spokespersons' ability to represent ever-larger political communities. But such constraints only partially contained these leaders' advocacy and activism. Chimo's gradual and perhaps not so subtle shift from being a *cacique principal* of Lambayeque to being an advocate of "all the *caciques*, lords of vassals, and native Indians of Peru" is how this traveler and others who followed a similar trajectory in the second half of the seventeenth century attempted to resolve this tension. These imperial subjects could not ignore established categories, but they could fit within their content, rework them, and even deprive them of any concrete meaning when presenting themselves and representing others in the public arena. Instead of a disingenuous or fake claim, this fundamental rhetorical shift represented a partially fruitful effort to break free from the limitations of an increasingly fossilized model of legal representation within the *República de Indios* while remaining a valid intermediary between the sovereign and his indigenous vassals.

INDIAN BLOOD PURITY AND THE TWO REPUBLICS

Defining Don Carlos Chimo's *cacique* identity in Peruvian and Spanish legal forums in large measure depended on whether he was determined to be an *indio* or a *mestizo*, and a lord or a commoner. Familiar discourses about Indian "blood purity" (*limpieza de sangre*), which resurfaced in the polemics surrounding his journey to Spain, provide a good starting point for this discussion. The deepest roots of Indian *limpieza* or *pureza* lay in the dual framework of *repúblicas*—one of Indians and one of Spaniards—and its important precedents in medieval Iberia.[13] In the wake of the Spanish Conquest, this dual model of two semidiscrete jurisdictions came to be increasingly predicated upon the need to guarantee the proper conversion of indigenous peoples to the Catholic faith, even if such efforts meant physically segregating members of the two *repúblicas* from one another. Although physical separation quickly proved an impossibility, this theoretical scheme, inspired by medieval corporate ideas and fed by New World economic, social, and legal practices, slowly migrated from the religious to the secular sphere. However, it never lost its strong religious overtones.[14] The theory of acknowledging the king's majesty without resistance and voluntary conversion underwrote the constitution of the Republic of Indians: acceptance of God and king had entitled indigenous subjects and their lords to retain certain rights, including possession of lands and limited self-rule and autonomy. The *República de Indios* was to become a legal space where Indians could enjoy royal protection and where certain indigenous administrative and political structures could endure the hardships of the colonial regime, which they helped keep in place.[15]

During the first 150 years of Spanish rule, the *repúblicas* grew to become two distinct, partially overlapping, and mutually dependent jurisdictions under the authority of Crown and Church, each with "natural" lords and authorities, nobles and commoners, and privileges, exemptions, and obligations of their own.[16] The vitality of the *República de Indios* beyond these juridical formulations rests on the fact that it quickly became a coveted site for power and autonomy. Based on this fundamental notion, elite Indians (noble and commoner) and municipal councils carved out autonomous spaces largely devoid of Spanish tutelage and intervention. In these spaces, governors, *cabildo* authorities, and indigenous judges ruled over disparate constituencies and decided issues based on specific circumstances as well as customary laws and practices.[17]

Claims to *limpieza* and nobility among mid- and late-colonial Nahua lords of New Spain show that, stemming from the initial emphasis on true and voluntary conversion as a requisite to maintain chiefly recognition, *caciques* and others aspiring to purity status asserted three competing, overlapping, and often inconsistent understandings of what blood purity meant or entailed.[18] One version emphasized the antiquity of the *caciques'* Catholic lineages. At the earliest opportunity, their ancestors had fully embraced the faith, sometimes virtually upon the arrival of the first missionaries, thus granting their seventeenth- and eighteenth-century descendants de facto, and arguably de jure, Old Christian status. A second discourse extended *limpieza* to encompass pure or clean "Indian" blood, unsullied by mixture with inferior *mestizos* and other *castas* (people of "mixed" African, Spanish, and Indian descent). The eventual influx of Spanish blood—a form of "mixing" especially problematic in the case of people classified as *mestizos* who claimed Indian royal descent—remained ambiguous and multivalent. (*Mestizos*, after all, had been formally banned from becoming *caciques* or inheriting *cacicazgos* since 1576.)[19] A third version of purity pragmatically equated *limpieza* with nobility, life-style, social esteem, and fidelity in the form of significant aid rendered to the Spaniards in the earliest stages of the conquest. Thus, a combination of social markers and royal services made *caciques* inherently superior to the commoners (*indios del común*) and tribute payers (*pecheros*) of their *república*. In this last construction of purity, vile and vulgar activities requiring manual labor, as opposed to honorable professions, tributary exemption, and political and ecclesiastic office, were prominent indicators of common, impure blood.[20]

Among Mexico's indigenous elites, then, primordial piety, blood purity, and high social status—alone or combined in creative ways—foregrounded this emerging language of power and exclusion. In bolstering their own claims, Andean *caciques* (as well as those who, like Carlos Chimo, aspired to have that status recognized at court) resorted to a similar rhetorical repertoire. The available evidence points to an early use of these rhetorical strategies in the Andes, perhaps even earlier than in New Spain, although the reasons are not clear.[21] Some scholars regard the so-called "decree about honors" (*cédula de honores*)—a famous 1697 royal order—as a watershed in the process of appropriation and naturalization of the discourse of purity.[22] But it is worth noting that, in fundamental ways, the decree simply reiterated much older legal formulations that were largely ignored or contested by colonial actors, especially within religious orders. The *cédula* restated that, as long as they could prove blood purity (*limpieza de sangre*) and noble station (*calidad de nobles*), indigenous and *mestizo* descendants of noble Indians (those "whom they call *caciques*") deserved the same preeminence and honors as Castilian *hidalgos*, such as admission to centers of higher learning, military and political offices, and the priesthood. This language of legitimization based on purity had deep roots in the Andes.

Earlier formulations of the intertwined languages of *limpieza* and *hidalguía* inform Juan de Santa Cruz Pachacuti's *Relación de antigüedades de este reino del Perú*, an indigenous history of the Inca kings, finished sometime after 1613. They also inspire the pages of Felipe Guaman Poma's *Nueva corónica y buen gobierno*, finished some three years later.[23] Even earlier forms appear in petitions, passenger licenses, *probanzas*, and proofs of nobility of Andean regional *cacique* and Inca elites (including *mestizos* of partial indigenous ancestry) presented in local and metropolitan forums.[24] The 1697 decree created "new avenues of social inclusion and power for Andeans" by rejecting neophytism—the seemingly perennial status of being a recent convert—as a valid reason to deny noble Indians and *mestizos* the honors owed to their class.[25] Nonetheless, the decree also sanctioned much older mechanisms for upward social mobility within indigenous society. These paths to inclusion and power did not pertain only to the unequal privileges and prerogatives thus far enjoyed by members of the two separate *repúblicas*.[26] These avenues to social ascendancy had already been altering the initial elite composition of the *República de Indios*, slowly undermining traditional barriers separating *caciques* from commoners, the very same barriers that the main promoters of the *cédula* in Spain also sought to dismantle.

Internal rivalries, unmet aspirations, and subtle realignments shaped the specific formulas incorporated in the 1697 decree in significant ways. Although consistent with its strong elitist bias, the generic use of the term *cacique* by the councilors who drafted the *cédula* masked a more complex and fluid—but also highly localized—reality, about which they were unaware or, more likely, which they chose to ignore when preparing the decree. The understandings of purity and nobility that crystallized in the *cédula de honores* could be deceiving. Even though the decree pertained to the indigenous and *mestizo* descendants of *caciques*, its particular language (largely the result of the *"mestizo* gentleman" [*caballero mestizo*] and presbyter Juan Núñez Vela's lobbying at court) strategically blurred the distinction between individuals of old, proven noble ancestry and those who had acquired high social status through means other than birthright, particularly class, occupational mobility, and reinvented genealogies. Some of these paths to wealth, social prominence, and political influence have been explored in previous chapters, especially as they unfolded in Lima, from where Juan Núñez Vela traveled to court and to whose indigenous elite he was as least partially accountable. When viewed from the *opposite* shore, the 1697 decree reflected a highly malleable reality at the top of the *República de Indios*, sanctioning in law what was in many cases already a matter of fact. The *cédula* was in itself a major accomplishment of newly fledged cosmopolitan leaders following in the steps of Chimo, now assimilated into the larger *cacique* class—and not just an empty promise of future legal equality.[27]

THE PAPERS OF DON LORENZO ZAMUDIO EL LUCAYN

This broadening of elite status within the *República de Indios*, which had one of its landmark moments in the royal decree of 1697, became especially noticeable at the Habsburg court. So distant a place from Peru, the court of the late seventeenth century made negotiating rank and status the norm for certain travelers classified as *indios*. Advocating on behalf of the *república* while fulfilling the expectations of the different parties involved became one of the ways to negotiate and secure a stay in Spain. Back in Peru, and beginning in the sixteenth century, the great regional *cacique* lineages witnessed how nonnoble pretenders encroached upon their *fueros* (special privileges), lordships, and estates.[28] Yet, only echoes of their protests reached the king's ears, and not with the periodicity and strength that one would expect. After all, to gain access to the transatlantic channels of communication that helped them advance their interests at the court, Andean aristocrats came to depend on the same indigenous and Spanish intermediaries about whom they sometimes complained.[29]

Before the sovereign and his council, Andean pretenders to *cacique* status resorted to the same argumentative lines identified for New Spain: primordial piety, racial purity, and high social status. But they weighted these elements differently depending on circumstances, social networks, and aspirations, thus reconfiguring and combining them in creative ways. Even when proven or assumed nobility was lacking, some travelers still appealed to these arguments to manufacture privileged status and obtain recognition within the *República de Indios*. Our analysis of the politics of *limpieza de sangre* and the quest for *cacique* status among indigenous visitors now turns to one such case. It is the history of an undetected forgery.

In 1673 or earlier, an invisible hand concocted a set of legal instruments in preparation for the appearance of Don Lorenzo Zamudio El Lucayn at the royal court. In December of that year, a man who went by that name crossed the gates of the royal palace. In an opening *memorial* addressed to the Queen Regent, he identified himself as an *"yndio natural* from the town of San Miguel" in Cajamarca, an important region in the Peruvian northern highlands with lengthy *cacique* lines stretching back to the pre-Inca and Inca periods. Zamudio beseeched the queen and her Council to examine a "certification and inquest" that legitimized his identity and demonstrated his illustrious, purely indigenous, and Catholic ancestry. The petition also pleaded with the queen to order that the documents be examined and validated, so that a decree authorizing Zamudio to enjoy the "privileges and prerogatives" granted upon the "caciques and conquistadors of Peru" could be dispatched to the viceregal authorities. These privileges suited him as the successor of the *caciques* and conquistadores of the Inca realm. Although the specific prerogatives being sought were not spelled out, exemption from tribute and labor dues, as well as social prominence, were probably what the claimant had in mind.[30]

Between April and May 1673, Zamudio oversaw the preparation of the customary *información de testigos*. Five witnesses then residing in Madrid swore to the validity of his claims, corroborating the "truth" of the papers now being shown to them and the authority of the notaries who prepared them. The dossier presented before the Council included two certifications (*certificaciones*) allegedly brought to Madrid from Peru. After reviewing them, the Crown's prosecutor recommended granting the request. On March 12, 1674, the councilors agreed and ruled in Zamudio's favor. The queen signed and issued the corresponding *cédula* three days later.[31] Three months had passed when "Don Lorenzo Zamudio Lucayn[,] Indio" presented another *memorial*, this time requesting the return of his original papers, which he claimed he needed for "other affairs," presumably back in Peru. The councilors agreed again, and on July 26 the scribe of the Council made a literal copy to be kept in the archive, returning the originals to this mysterious visitor.

The first *certificación* sought to establish Lorenzo Zamudio's basic genealogy. He was the *hijo natural*—in this context, seemingly a biological son or a son born out of wedlock—of Don Lorenzo Zamudio and Doña Clara Cajamea de la Chapuma, *caçiques prinçipales* of Cajamarca, where the petitioner's hometown of San Miguel was located. Against the backdrop of the early events of the Spanish Conquest of the Inca Empire and the northern Andes, the narrative endeavored to establish that the petitioner's parents were direct descendants of the very first local *caciques* to pay homage to Charles V, welcome the Catholic faith, and be baptized in Cajamarca in 1535—a mere three years after Pizarro and Atahualpa had their pivotal encounter (Figure 6.1). The second *certificación* further anchored the aspirant's nobility: Lorenzo Zamudio was a descendant "of the noble *caciques* of these kingdoms through all of his paternal and maternal lines." His mother, a "cacique noble woman" (*noble caçica*) named Doña Clara Cajamea Tarrazal, was the daughter of Don Lorenzo Cajamea Tarrazal and Doña Luisa González Inga, "noble offspring" of the *caciques* of Asunción.[32]

Lorenzo Zamudio's *certificación e información* sheds light on how deeply Andean travelers understood the workings of the imperial system of justice, the power of the written word, and especially the authority of notaries—real or imaginary—to create legal discourse and to establish truth. Petitioners knew that records of this sort, often known as "titles" (*títulos*, particularly if authenticated by a notary), were paramount in upholding chiefly privilege and claims to purity in Spain and Peru. Like other colonial records, how-

FIGURE 6.1

The first ambassador of Huascar Inca, Don Martín Guaman Malqui de Ayala. From Felipe Guaman Poma de Ayala, El primer nueva corónica y buen gobierno, *375[377]. Royal Danish Library, GKS 2232 quarto.*

ever, these *cacique* titles partially created the reality that they purported to be merely describing, establishing a series of privileges for posterity.[33] This is how they did it.

The authority of one Juan de Arredondo Albéjar, chief notary (*notario mayor*) of "His Catholic Caesar" Charles V in Burgos (Castile), sustains the impressive claims of Lorenzo Zamudio's first *certificación*. Quite astonishingly, this notary had crossed the ocean to double as one of the captains of "the Conquest now being undertaken in the Mainland and the kingdoms of Peru."[34] Arredondo stops in the midst of conquest to declare, in Cuzco on March 9, 1542, that he was one of the members of a conquest expedition (*entrada*) to the towns of Cajamarca, led in 1535 by "captain-general" Gonzalo Pizarro (presumably Francisco's brother), his lieutenant Captain Villagrán, and "many other conquistadors." The notary-cum-conquistador certifies that, upon reaching the native villages, he began drafting a list of *caciques* "who surrendered without resistance," of which, as Arredondo is careful to emphasize, "there was none."

He also certifies that this list, which he presumably has in front of him, includes the conversion of "the *Caçique Lucayn*," a native of the town of San Miguel, formerly known as Tucapal, and the direct ancestor of the 1673 petitioner. On August 3, 1535, of his own will and out of true love for God, the *cacique* received his baptism in the "church" of San Francisco of Cajamarca, with Captain Alonso Zamudio, a "Spaniard" (*español*) from whom the *cacique* was to take his last name, acting as the godfather.[35]

The notary Arredondo also confirms that, through the voice of an interpreter, Don Juan Zamudio Lucayn and many other "noble lords" (*caciques nobles*) of Cajamarca told the Spaniards that they had been previously informed that the faith of Jesus Christ was the true one. Thus, their conversion was sincere and their understanding of the new religion profound—so much so that they offered to journey to Cuzco and "represent the truth of the Catholic religion to the Inca King." Arredondo finally certifies that, on the same day of August 3, 1535, two of the *cacique*'s close relatives entered the Church: his wife, Guapalqua (christened Doña Isabel de Alvarado Tarrazal, after her godfather, the captain and conquistador Pedro de Alvarado, who also happened to be at the scene), and their legitimate son, the three-year-old Armango. Like his father, Lucayn, he changed his name to "Pedro Zamudio Lucayn" after his godfather, Captain Alonso Zamudio.

To authenticate the second, shorter certification, another notary enters the scene. Mateo de Morán is the royal scribe of the "[Spanish] town and [indigenous] village" (*villa y pueblo*) of San Miguel, in Cajamarca. On March 9, 1648, he certifies that his personal archive contains a "secret inquest" (*información secreta*). Conducted before the local magistrate at the request of the petitioner "Don Lorenzo Çamudio el Lucayn," a *vecino* of the town, this document institutes his noble ancestry on the basis of "a number of old and trustworthy witnesses" who, nevertheless, are not listed. This *certificación* elaborates a succinct yet rhetorically effective family tree that, in only three generations, manages to connect the earlier characters of the first certification with the individuals of the present time (c. 1670). Predictably, the two branches converge on Lorenzo Zamudio Lucayn, our traveler to court and the great-great-grandson of the *cacique* Lucayn who converted to Christianity in 1535. In closing, Morán ratifies the story included in the first *certificación*, emphasizing that the old *cacique* Lucayn and his wife, Isabel de Alvarado, were not merely the first to receive the holy Catholic faith in Cajamarca—they also helped in the conversion of "the other *caciques* and nobles of the kingdom." By so doing, they made their descendant worthy of the king's reward.

These documents were carefully fabricated to mirror the epistemological authority of the Lettered City and the power of writing to convey authenticity and to confer purity. The goal was to re-create chiefly legitimacy and *cacique* status at the royal court and, ultimately, back in Peru. The author paid special attention to scribal and procedural conventions, showing the transcendence of notarial and legal rhetoric for the enterprise of self-fashioning and legitimizing oneself through writing. As some have argued, the notions of "truth" or "falsehood" deployed in this type of documentation were "dependent upon the exigencies of the lettered city, its administrative apparatus, and the legal principles upon which it was founded."[36] Only in a narrow sense were these records forgeries, however, as they were produced from *within* the Lettered City. What set them apart from other documents held in the imperial archive was not necessarily their *manufactured* or *fabricated* nature. They were *false* or *fraudulent* only inasmuch as these papers—contrary to what their possessor claimed—were not the result of an original act of writing or validating by a royal scribe, or another agent of the Crown, authorized to act as such. They were, instead, the result of other, less visible relations of power.[37]

TALES OF CONVERSION, NOBLE ANCESTRY, AND VASSALAGE

This remarkable tale of primordial conversion, noble pre-Hispanic lineages, and loyal vassalage seamlessly conflates several historical and fictional eras and characters, covering them with an aura of credibility. Based on the mastery of a handful of notarial genres, and through the skillful use of historical information and imagination, Zamudio's papers strategically intertwine certain events and individuals, coupling them with information likely obtained from family traditions and other sources of local collective memory.[38] Grounded in the events of the conquest of northern Peru and drawing from a pool of arguments about *limpieza*, the narrative establishes several key facts that provide the juridical basis for Lorenzo Zamudio's aspirations in Madrid. Informing the whole episode is the vernacular story of the earliest possible conversion to Catholicism, which Andean *caciques* and literate Indians had been crafting and advancing as a rhetorical antidote to the stain of neophyte status since the sixteenth century. There were several variations on this central theme: natural lords who accepted king and faith could not be unjustly deprived of authority over native subjects. Echoing these claims, Lorenzo Zamudio's papers identify the petitioner's ancestors as the first to convert.

Cajamarca offers a very appropriate setting. It was where the opening scene of the Spanish Conquest in the Andes unfolded. Within the close universe of the first *certificación*, the 1535 *entrada* represents the original instance of contact between the *caciques nobles* of Cajamarca and a handful of prominent Spanish conquistadors (the convenient outcome of which is the *cacique* Lucayn and his family's conversion). Neither fake nor superficial, but foregrounded on a clear understanding of the tenets of the faith, the Indian lords' smooth acceptance of the new religion turned them into Christians "with no aversion or difficulty whatsoever." Through key conversions and the spiritual bonds they entailed, the *certificaciones* seal Lorenzo Zamudio's noble and old Christian ancestry, establishing them for posterity. The *caciques* made themselves and their descendants anew.

Descent from unsullied indigenous nobility and early fealty to the king intertwine to further uphold Lorenzo Zamudio's claims to Old Christian status. His forebears were all *caciques* or sons and daughters of *caciques* from the towns of San Miguel and Asunción. In the first *certificación*, the Inca emperor himself greets the *cacique* Lucayn as the head of a Christian embassy to a still-unconquered Cuzco. The Inca king welcomes Lucayn "with great love," thankful as he is for his teaching of the faith. The scene at the Inca's magnificent court is meant to corroborate the past sovereign's esteem for the great noble from Cajamarca as well as his nobility and legitimacy according to pre-Hispanic custom.

The journey to Cuzco is simultaneously constructed as an act of service to God and king, charging the narrative with a deeper political message. Throughout his life, this Lucayn was to distinguish himself for many "noteworthy services." The questionnaire that guides the testimonies of Lorenzo Zamudio's witnesses in Madrid states that, after their own formal conversion in the sixteenth century, the petitioner's ancestors "[aided] the Spaniards during the conquests of the said kingdoms." The *caciques'* peaceful recognition of Charles V's legitimate lordship over the Indies, and their efforts to help the Catholic Caesar establish it in the land of the Incas, is testament to the fealty of these lords. Lucayn and his family become loyal vassals and true Christians simultaneously. They had remained so since. They offered no resistance, and thus they were not truly conquered. No just war could have been waged on them.

The authority, legitimacy, and purity of Lucayn and his chiefly lineage is beyond question, as they bear no traces of *mestizo*, Spanish, or *casta* "intruders" (*intrusos*). Lucayn and his descendants quickly learn to live like

Christians, but their blood remains unsullied. His pure Indian lineage notwithstanding, the petitioner in Madrid also besieges the queen to recognize him as a "descendant" of the original Spanish conquistadores of the land. Admission to the body of the Church and fictive kinship are the means by which to solve this apparent contradiction. In the story, the Christian names and surnames given to, or carried by, these individuals are not the result of a potentially damming biological *mestizaje* but of a redeeming religious one. In this legal and historical drama, the Spanish captains Alonso Zamudio and Pedro de Alvarado are the influential godfathers of Lorenzo's forebears, passing on their Spanish surnames to them, and thereby forging strong and symbolically charged bonds of kinship through the power of the Catholic ritual. Any potential doubts that could be cast on Lorenzo's Indian lineage, purity, and nobility because of his Spanish surname are thus quickly dispelled. For the *caciques* whose story the document tells, and especially for the petitioner's earliest direct ancestor Lucayn (the trunk of the chiefly family tree), it meant a rebirth into the true faith and the world inaugurated by the Spanish Conquest that, nevertheless, kept their privileges intact.

Who manufactured these papers? One must of course consider the possibility that Lorenzo Zamudio El Lucayn, or whatever his name was, created them. Be that as it may, several clues scattered throughout the dossier reveal a sophisticated writer, proficient in notarial Spanish and versed in the art of preparing and copying ecclesiastic and scribal records. The evidence points particularly to an *escribano público* (notary) available for hire, some of whom exerted surprising control over "public" archives.[39] The participation of some other literate agent—a *corregidor*'s Spanish or indigenous lieutenant, procurator, parish assistant, schoolteacher, or *cacique*, either from Cajamarca (if one is to believe Zamudio's tale about his family origins) or some other Andean locale mentioned in the story—is also possible.[40]

Land and *cacique* titles and other documents could be forged in America, but Madrid or Seville are likely scenarios as well: a market tied to the Atlantic venture had developed in those two cities to satisfy all sorts of legitimate or illegitimate documentary needs.[41] More generally, in cities like Seville, finding judges, notaries, and royal officials willing to accept bribes and gifts was not uncommon. Witnesses for hire, who swore ad hoc testimonies in exchange for money, offered their services in public plazas and streets, as did genealogy experts who testified favorably during *limpieza de sangre* investigations in exchange for a fee. Forgeries in the form of false testaments, baptismal records, and patents of nobility (*ejecutorias de hidalguía*)—drawn up by unscrupulous notaries in Seville, Granada, and Madrid—were also produced by candidates for office and reward. As forged documents were included in formal investigations and original ones were altered and removed from parish archives and notarial offices, noble reputations were ruined and obscure lineages ennobled.[42]

Understanding that "truth was lodged in the office of the notary," the writer in charge of drafting Lorenzo Zamudio's papers reproduced many state- or church-sanctioned standard forms, rendering them credible by paying great attention to detail.[43] Traces of the underlying early modern genres can still be found in the *certificaciones*.[44] The centrality of scribal authority for manufacturing chiefly legitimacy is also revealed by the fact that the events and characters exist only through the authorized voices of two notaries. The scribes' perspectives on events become indistinguishable from the author's. Scribes are present literally from the time the first word is set on paper. The first *certificación* opens with a familiar formula—"I, JUAN DE ARREDONDO ALBEJAR, CHIEF NOTARY OF THE CATHOLIC CAESAR CHARLES V"—which also evokes the enumeration of royal titles that characterized royal provisions issued by local *audiencias*. The second *certificación* opens with an equivalent phrase. Different scriptural strategies help the author to establish the official identity of these notaries by revealing the ultimate source of their power: the king himself. It is he who confers the authority to authenticate a series of legal truths, which in fact are being created by the supposed original notarial act.[45]

Several inconsistencies seem to have gone undetected, allowing Lorenzo Zamudio's claims to go unchallenged. His proof of merit entered the legal record via a copy (*traslado*), following the regular bureaucratic path that ended in the issuing of a *real cédula* recognizing the privileges of the now noble claimant. After besieging the Lettered City, Lorenzo Zamudio El Lucayn had finally conquered it with a few strokes of a quill. Earlier travelers with similar or even grander aspirations had not always been as fortunate.[46] Despite all the lacunae surrounding this case, one conclusion seems inevitable: the petitioner's need to have these titles prepared in order to obtain royal recognition as a descendant of noble *caciques* and Spanish conquistadors betrays a humbler (perhaps even commoner) origin. There was, in that sense, something authentic concealed in this forgery.

THE LETTERED CITY UNDER SIEGE

Moving from text to context, interesting clues regarding Zamudio's social position and networks in Peru and Spain can be surmised from the five witness depositions included in his proof of merit. Two came from indigenous travelers to Spain, and three came from Spanish residents in Madrid. One thing is certain: Zamudio strategically selected them to fashion himself in writing before the Council and, with the witnesses' support, prompt the councilors to validate the records of this self-made *cacique*. The Spaniards who testified in April 1673 were all *indianos* (people who were from the Indies or had been there) settled in Madrid: Don Roque Sánchez, forty-two, allegedly from the town of San Miguel in Cajamarca but now living at court at the service of Don Juan Enríquez; Martín de Campos, from Concepción in Chile and a member of the household of the Knight of Calatrava Don Juan de Salazar; and Domingo de Torrijos, originally from the village of Asunción in Cajamarca, purportedly the hometown of some of Lorenzo Zamudio's ancestors (and apparently his own). Campos claimed to have met Zamudio and his parents back in San Miguel, during a three-year period when he lived with the local priest, a Franciscan. Sánchez and Torrijos attested to having known Lorenzo and his parents for much longer—about three decades—especially back in their native Cajamarca. They also claimed to have remained in contact with him from the time of his arrival at the court some nine or ten years prior. Moreover, Torrijos "recognized" the signature and personal sign of Mateo de Morán, the alleged notary from San Miguel. That signature and sign led this witness to pronounce Lorenzo's records to be authentic.

Lorenzo Zamudio's two indigenous witnesses are already known to us. They were part of a handful of Andean expatriates residing at the royal court at the time (unlike most of them, however, Zamudio does not appear to have requested a return license).[47] In chapter 4 we met Captain Don Francisco de Heriza Paz Carguamango, the second witness to declare. He was the forty-three-year-old *indio principal* and militia officer who journeyed to court from his native Lima seeking royal recognition of the nobility and services of his forebears. A resident in Madrid in the home of one *doctor* Mijancas, located on the street of Siete Jardines, Heriza testified to have known Zamudio for an astonishing twenty-seven or twenty-eight years—first in Cajamarca and then in Lima, where the witness's parents lodged Zamudio in their own home. Don Francisco further testified that he had never heard anyone challenge Zamudio's noble parentage or elite claims, "and this witness would know otherwise for he is, as he has already declared, a *cacique principal* and a noble descendant of royal blood." On the contrary, Zamudio's ancestors, like Heriza's, "acknowledged and received our holy Roman Catholic faith without resistance, aiding in the conquest that His Catholic Majesty and Caesar made in the kingdoms of Peru." Don Francisco was well aware of the power of these arguments. He had relied on them to construct his own *limpieza* and expound his services only a few years earlier.[48]

Zamudio's other indigenous witness—and in fact the first to offer his testimony before the public notary in Madrid—was Don Jerónimo Lorenzo Limaylla, mentioned in chapter 5, a longtime resident of the city by then. Significantly, this experienced litigant lived in the Calle de la Sartén, in the home of Don Francisco Testa, the chief scribe (*escribano mayor*) of the city council.[49] As explained, Limaylla, who styled himself as a "paramount lord of the province of Jauja" (*cazique prinçipal de la prouiçia de Jauja*) in Zamudio's proof of merit, was the determined petitioner who secured royal support for his long stay at court between 1664 and 1678, in part to litigate for recognition as the legitimate heir to the *cacicazgo* of Luringuanca. Others, however, swore that the witness's real name was Lorenzo Ayun Chifo and that he was an Indian commoner from Reque, a coastal village not far from the cities of Saña and Trujillo in Peru. He had first journeyed to Spain in 1644, after living a few years in Lima with a short-tempered Franciscan and entering into the service of a merchant with whom he traveled to Panama.[50] Limaylla's rivals in court charged him with impersonating the real Limaylla (long deceased by then) and forging parish records and securing false witnesses in Lima, Jauja, and Madrid. He was, in the eyes of his detractors, an early modern trickster, not unlike the famous Martin Guerre, someone who made the life of the scion of one of the most powerful *cacique* lineages of the viceroyalty his own.[51]

This "Don Jerónimo Lorenzo Limaylla," like Captain Francisco de Heriza Carguamango, supported Lorenzo Zamudio's cause in Spain. He testified to have known Zamudio and his parents in Cajamarca, claiming, rather surprisingly, to have some relatives living there (something he never alleged before). Limaylla also declared that he had seen Zamudio in Lima "when he came to Spain" around 1664. Thus, like Carguamango, Limaylla connected Zamudio to the viceregal court, an identification consistent with some of the travel patterns explored in previous chapters. Apparently Carguamango, Limaylla, and Zamudio came to know each other there sometime in the early 1660s, forging propitious alliances that were to serve them well as they lay siege to the Lettered City.[52]

These late-seventeenth-century Andean sojourners shared similar strategies for self-fashioning and self-promotion before the *Consejo de Indias*.[53] Common strategies responded to comparable social position and ascendancy within the *República de Indios*, overlapping support networks and transatlantic advocacy, as well as travelers' own shrewdness to identify previous stories of success and model their own claims after them. In 1669, the alleged "Jerónimo Lorenzo Limaylla" had beseeched the queen to "favor him by making him a *cacique*."[54] Moreover, a year before Zamudio did, Limaylla petitioned the Council for the return of the original *cacique* titles of Luringuanca, claiming to need the papers for other legal affairs.[55] While at the royal court, Don Francisco Heriza Carguamango oversaw the preparation of his own *información de testigos* in 1669, carefully selecting the witnesses who were to make a statement in it (all of them allegedly "trustworthy people and elders of great reputation"). This was necessary, he claimed (like others did before and after him), because he had lost some of the legal records proving his ancestry and services during the long trip across the ocean.[56] Similar cases, some dating to the 1570s, show that the Council was already familiar with this line of argument and that, in some cases, councilors held the petitioner's identity and claims in abeyance until documentary proof was produced.[57]

Heriza Carguamango and those within his close circle were much more fortunate. These Andean travelers shared some of their witnesses in Madrid, calling upon each other and their acquaintances to testify in *probanzas, informaciones*, and other legal proceedings. The *indio principal*, court interpreter, and militia officer Don Pedro Chafo Çavana, a traveler from the town of Lambayeque near Trujillo (but a longtime resident in Lima before departing to Spain around 1662), was one of Carguamango's witnesses in his 1669 *probanza*. Another witness, Don Roque Sánchez, was to render his testimony four years later in Lorenzo Zamudio Lucayn's proof of merit. In the first *probanza*, Don Roque identified himself as a "noble Indian who enjoys the protections, exemptions, and privileges granted to said noble Indians." In the second, his *calidad* went unmarked. Rather than declaring to be a native from Cajamarca, as he was to do in 1673, he claimed in 1669 to be "a native of the place of Saña," for such a provenance was more convenient to support Chafo Çavana's case. Witnesses like Don Roque accommodated their *calidad* and place of residence (*vecindad*) to fit or uphold narratives of the petitioners in a faraway land, dependent as they were almost exclusively on witness testimony.[58]

BECOMING A *CACIQUE* AT THE COURT

Supposedly verifiable documents and depositions successfully entered into the record established the nobility, *cacique* status, and blood purity of many an Andean traveler. For their witnesses, these attributes rested on ancestry, chiefly rank, and royal service. But such qualities were also linked to what one *letrado* witness—a former viceregal secretary and now an *audiencia* attorney—referred to as Don Francisco de Heriza Carguamango's public and positive "acts" of nobility. Zamudio's *certificación* included similar language. It was a circular but effective argument: for some of the witnesses, the Cargua-mangos' uncontested reputation as nobles in Lima proved their pure blood and nobility. In other words, because they had publicly fulfilled "noble and honorable" political and military posts befitting Indian noble residents of Lima, they themselves *must* be nobles. On several occasions, Don Francisco Heriza and his father, Don Felipe Carguamango, had made public displays of their self-ascribed status as *caciques, indios principales*, and *vecinos* of the city of Lima. They had carried weapons, dressed as Spaniards, and openly displayed the manners of behavior expected from the nobles and *principales* of their "nation" (*nación*). Given such open displays of a substantial *calidad* within the *República de Indios*, no one—not even the viceroys presiding over the ceremonies—had objected. Quite the contrary: the king's ministers had sanctioned these displays of nobility by appointing the Carguamangos to different posts of honor reserved for nobles of the *Nación Índica*.

Several witness depositions followed this fundamental line of legal argumentation. For some witnesses, Don Francisco Heriza's admission into the *Colegio de Caciques* (the school for Indian nobles and their children) in El Cercado, thanks to the viceroy's personal recommendation, was clear proof that his claim to nobility had gone unquestioned at the time and therefore had to be true. Witnesses further testified that several viceroys had allowed the Carguamangos to carry swords and daggers in public, allegedly for self-defense, not only because of their military duties but also in recognition of their noble status. Such licenses were a privilege bestowed only upon those considered "patently noble." The *Consejo de Indias* still understood them as such at the close of the seventeenth century. This explains the effectiveness of their arguments at the royal court.[59]

But Herizas and Carguamangos embodied mobility more than nobility. They rose from humbler migrant beginnings in Lima to occupy relevant posts within the *República de Indios*. With their acquired wealth and thanks to patronage from viceroys, secretaries, and other influential ministers in Peru and Spain, Don Francisco Heriza was now seeking formal recognition of noble status before the king. Given that lengthy investigations to be conducted in Peru were seldom practical, how else was the Council to assess the nobility and *cacique* status of men like Zamudio, Heriza, or Limaylla other than relying on scant (or dubious) written records and partial witness testimonies? Royal magistrates in the Andes had developed different mechanisms to legally assess and recognize indigenous noble rank and to grant "titles" to Andeans who could prove their *cacique* status. Witness statements (preferably from elders and Indian nobles), combined with *probanzas* and other written records (parish books, governmental inspections, tributary rolls, and previous titles), helped to establish *cacique* ancestry and hereditary rights based on local knowledge and recognition.[60]

These mechanisms were, nonetheless, hardly available to the magistrates of the *Consejo de Indias* or the *Casa de la Contratación*. With some exceptions, these bureaucrats were not a part of the social milieu in which visitors were recognized or reputed as "Indians" or "*caciques*" in the first place. In a distant royal court, public fame, reputation, and the unchallenged performance of "positive" acts of nobility—calling oneself a *Don* unopposed, for instance— gained importance. These criteria, however, also blurred the line between *being* a *cacique* and *behaving* like one. Accordingly, differentiating between nobles and commoners became an increasingly difficult task over the course of the seventeenth century. In 1648, Don Pedro de Meneses, the justice accused by Carlos Chimo of selling Indian lands to local Spaniards, felt the need to suggest to the king that, if he were to grant permits for Indians to go to Spain, then they should declare their *naturaleza* first. If they were "of the *caciques*," it should be recorded in the license for everyone to know. Apparently, Meneses could not think of alternative ways to safely differentiate between lords and commoners.[61]

Travelers to the royal court could obtain and maintain *cacique* and *principal* status because of the way they called themselves or behaved, on paper and in person, and not only because of birth or formal title. The proper combination of names and surnames, as seen in the case of Don Lorenzo Zamudio El Lucayn, became one of the strategies to convey noble status.[62] Partial or full alteration of given names, family names, and aliases were not necessarily unusual in the Iberian Atlantic. Many women and men took advantage of movement within the Peninsula and immigration across the ocean to change their names and fashion themselves anew, in an attempt to either circumvent travel regulations and restrictions, improve social standing, or escape the long arm of royal justice.[63]

Enter "Don Jerónimo Lorenzo Limaylla." When he left his hometown of Reque in the late 1630s, he was known as "little Lorenzo" (*Lorençillo*) the *sacristanejo*—a young and relatively unimportant altar boy serving the local parish priest. Friars sometimes applied such diminutives—a mix of affection and scorn, and also patronizing—to native youth who were familiarized with Spanish culture, fluent in Castilian, and often at their service.[64] Lorençillo had been christened in 1622 as "Lorenzo de Ayun," although his last name would later appear in a tributary roll as "Aium Chifo." Earlier in life, he dropped the surname "Chifo," which, by reflecting his father's craftsmanship, bespoke a humble origin.[65] Lorenzo adopted the more imposing "Juan Lorenzo Ayllón" in the late 1630s, after moving to the neighboring city of Saña and entering into the personal service of the Franciscan Juan de Ay-llón. It was not uncommon for Indian *criados*, students, and servants to acquire their Spanish masters' surnames.[66] A few years later, in Madrid and in Mexico, Lorenzo went back to "Juan Lorenzo de Ayun," but he added to his name the title *Don* and the equally distinguished "Córdoba," this time after a new patron, Father Buenaventura de Salinas y Córdoba.[67] Some Spanish names and surnames—and, less often, indigenous ones like "Atahualpa"—projected noble ancestry and social prominence before metropolitan authorities in Spain. Travelers could appropriate them, drop them, or even accumulate them, especially if such names were well known and reputed. Other cases reveal an alternative naming strategy: bringing indigenous surnames together to create the effect of a pure, sustained, and even "profuse" noble ancestry—through several family lines—void of blood mixture with the lower sectors.[68]

Perceptions of high status and verification by witnesses and notaries were, in many cases, the result of the travelers' personal appearance, demeanor, and general behavior in public. In Ancient Regime societies, attire "did not just reflect identity, but helped constitute it."[69] Put simply, *caciques* dressed and spoke as such. In the aftermath of the Spanish Conquest, Iberian clothing and weapons, along with fluency and literacy in Castilian, became fundamental markers of elite rank, noble origin, and royal recognition in the Andes. Inca royals, non-Inca lords, and those aspiring to elite status borrowed European fashions that seemed more likely to differentiate them from commoners—indigenous, mestizos, and Spaniards—and, in combination with Andean markers of status, convey chiefly legitimacy and noble rank in the eyes of the Spaniards.[70]

In 1570, a few years after returning to Peru, Don Felipe Guacrapaucar, the noble Andean from Jauja who journeyed to the royal court in 1562 and whose story is partially told in chapter 2, ran into trouble with Viceroy Toledo. During his visit to Jauja, Toledo decried the local inhabitants' "litigiousness" and made Guacrapaucar a paradigmatic example of the frivolous litigant (a social type that would prove very influential in the years to come). Before punishing Don Felipe Guacrapaucar with ten years of exile, a Crown inspector forced the *cacique* to strip off his Spanish clothes—some of them probably acquired in Spain, from where he had brought an harquebus—and put on "Indian" clothing. By the end of the colonial period, certain styles had become so closely associated with cacique elite status that, in the context of the Great Andean rebellion of José Gabriel Tupac Amaru and the Catari brothers, the *cacique* of Tinguipaya, a "noble Indian" (*yndio noble*) could escape the fury of the rebels only by fleeing the town "disguised" as an Indian commoner.[71] Back in 1570, Toledo's sentence against Guacrapaucar, aimed at humiliating the cosmopolitan chief, did not yield the expected results. A few months after, the same inspector saw the *cacique* in Lima, dressed again in Spanish clothes (*habito de español*) and carrying a sword while appealing the sentence before the *Audiencia*.[72]

Early modern courtly cities like Paris and Madrid were fertile ground for what contemporaries perceived as the "confusion and usurpation" of status and rank through clothing. In these urban spaces, attire, much like names and surnames, could both reveal and conceal social position.[73] For many Andean travelers to the royal court—as well as for the *indios criollos* of colonial Lima explored in chapter 4—clothes were one of the paths to ennoblement. The requests of transatlantic travelers for royal money to purchase attire attest to the importance that they ascribed to how they dressed and looked. Available lists of purchases and debts they incurred with local artisans convey the same message. Ideally, the clothes should match the *calidad* and *cacique* status of these visitors, especially given the possibility of meeting the king.[74]

Antonio Criollo, a free black man from Lima and a witness during the legal dispute over the *cacicazgo* of Luringuanca in the 1660s, during Don Jerónimo Lorenzo Limaylla's second stay at the royal court, testified to having come across this litigant several times in Madrid in the mid-1640s, where he spent most of his time wandering the Habsburg royal palace. Every time Antonio ran into him, Limaylla "always conducted himself like the son of a *cacique*" (recall that was precisely what Limaylla wanted recognized at court).[75] Likewise, during his stay in Mexico-Tenochtitlan between 1646 and 1655, the same traveler "was reputed by everyone to be a noble and an *indio principal*." For witnesses other than Antonio Criollo, who swore to have known Limaylla in Mexico, his "behavior" (*proceder*) and "self-esteem" revealed (*muestra*) that he was "indeed a descendant of *caciques*, a noble and distinguished person." In Mexico, Madrid, and in "other parts of Spain," Limaylla had gone about "making it public . . . that he was the son of a *cacique*." Being and behaving, at least on paper, were hard to tell from each other.[76]

Contemporaries attributed the literate and legal skills of many travelers to the experience of visiting the Iberian Peninsula. The transformative power of the Atlantic journey seldom went unnoticed by those who had known these travelers before their journey and would meet them again during their return to Peru. As his brother Don Carlos recounted in 1570, Don Felipe Guacrapaucar, the *cacique* who journeyed to Spain in 1562, became very "litigious" (*pleitista*) after "doing business with *letrados* and learning to write" in various parts of Spain. Twenty years after Guacrapaucar's return, the memories of he "who had been in Spain" and had followed King Philip northeast into the territories of the Crown of Aragon were still fresh in the central Andes.[77]

Lorenzo Ayun Chifo went back to his native village of Reque in 1656, after spending ten years in Lima, Madrid, and Mexico. The town inhabitants did not hide their surprise as Lorenzo described his trip to the "kingdoms of Spain." Now he dressed "as a Spaniard." One of the local residents even testified as having been able to recognize this former sexton in spite of his being "very *ladino*"—in this context, fully proficient in Castilian—and gallantly dressed, with beard, gloves, and a hat to match.[78] Equally impressive was Lorenzo Ayun's arrival in Jauja a few months later, where he was to claim the *cacicazgo* of Luringuanca as Don Jerónimo Lorenzo Limaylla. The imminent return of the old *cacique* Limaylla had been a matter of public discussion and private gossip even before the traveler set foot on the valley. He entered the streets of San Jerónimo, the village where the local *caciques* had resided since the late sixteenth century, accompanied by a group of indigenous men who, like him, went about "very gallantly dressed and wearing gloves." He visited the village of Sincos and likely others on horseback—that is, like a *cacique*.

For many, Lorenzo Ayun's journey to Spain and the skills and manners he acquired during his itinerant life gravitated toward their positive identification of him as the long-gone Limaylla, son of the last undisputed *cacique principal* of Luringuanca. According to some witnesses, people wanted to see him in office "as much because his blood is that of our *caciques* as for his displays of hospitality and respectful and refined manners." A local *principal* declared, "Having seen [Lorenzo] and learned that he came from Spain, he recognizes him as [the heir to the *cacicazgo*], and for the fact that he seems so capable, knowledgeable, and totally apt." Lorenzo Ayun's former *cacique* in Reque, who had gone to great lengths to collect the absentee's tribute for two decades, was less flattering in his assessment. Even he had to admit that Ayun, though an Indian from the *llanos* and clearly not from the highlands of Jauja, had arrived to usurp the *cacicazgo* only "because he is now *ladino* in the Castilian language."[79] An uncommon familiarity with the idioms and accents of the Peninsula must have been one of the most striking effects of the Atlantic journey. Given that Lorenzo had learned to read and write long before these events, however, these witnesses must have been also referring to something else worth noting besides the traveler's proficiency in Castilian. That something else—Lorenzo's cosmopolitanism—set the foundation of his leadership across the ocean.

ANDEAN COSMOPOLITANS

Literacy had always been an important piece of the puzzle. But Limaylla's cosmopolitanism went beyond fluency in Spanish or the ability to read and write in one or more languages, encompassing instead "a familiarity with [the] legal precepts and formulas" of the different documentary genres—letters, titles, petitions, proofs of merit, and services—which sustained the Lettered City and brought colonial and imperial courtrooms to life.[80] Like many other indigenous subjects, from the great *caciques* and Inca royals to the rural *cabildo* officers and urban *indios principales*, transatlantic procurators had an obvious command of spoken and written Spanish. Yet, their power to broker across the ocean also rested on their firsthand knowledge of the official languages of law and empire and (equally important in the Ancient Regime) their personal and occupational relations of patronage and dependency with the lettered "wielders of pen and paper" who guarded the gates of the Lettered City and produced "the order of signs" on which it rested on both sides of the Atlantic.[81] Thus, personal qualifications and social constellations gave Andean procurators and petitioners the tools to create legal truth and fix it in important legal forums such as the *Casa de la Contratación* or the *Consejo de Indias*. This power made cosmopolitan brokers not just literate but also *lettered*.[82]

The relationship between literacy, judicial expertise, and the proliferation of modes for gaining authority and maintaining power within the *República de Indios* shapes a remarkable story that takes us back, albeit temporarily, from the Habsburg court to Charcas (present-day Bolivia). In her 1609 will, Doña Isabel Sisa, a noblewoman (*palla*) of Inca descent from Cuzco, made a striking confession: before she and her husband, Don Domingo Itquilla, moved from the city of La Plata to the nearby village of Santiago de Curi several years prior, people had always considered Domingo a commoner—a tribute-payer from Toropalca, near Potosí—and certainly not a *Don*. The couple had no assets at the time of their marriage in La Paz, let alone any lands upon which to build the family's prosperity. At the time of Isabel's confession, however, Don Domingo was the wealthy and respected *cacique* of Curi.

The couple's luck had started to change thanks to the power of writing. After settling in Curi, Domingo "applied himself to becoming virtuous, acting as a scrivener." He went around town advertising his literate skills. News quickly reached the local *caciques* and *principales* because, it seems, no other indigenous person in Curi knew how to read and write. Aware of the social value of formal writing and notarial conventions, the village authorities agreed to testify before an unsuspecting Crown official that Domingo was their kin and a member of their *ayllu* and therefore eligible to become *cacique principal* and *gobernador*. At their request, Domingo received the title. From his new position, Don Domingo bought individual titles to three plots of land, receiving confirmation from the Crown in the 1590s and attaching them to the lordship and estate (*cacicazgo*) that he hoped to pass down to his descen-

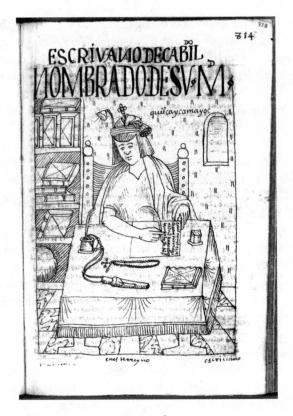

FIGURE 6.2

Scribe of the Municipal Council. From Felipe Guaman Poma de Ayala, El primer nueva corónica y buen gobierno, *814[828]. Royal Danish Library, GKS 2232 quarto.*

dants. Doña Isabel Sisa revealed that her husband, in his own wills, claimed to have inherited the plots from his parents, the alleged *caciques* of Curi. Don Domingo's secret, known to us thanks to Doña Isabel's confession, shows that many unconventional political decisions presenting him as a member of the ruling *ayllu* with full rights to become *cacique* were disguised as routine *cacique* confirmations by Spanish provincial magistrates and other Crown ministers (Figure 6.2).[83]

Although no one but Doña Isabel seems to have disputed Don Domingo's title, internecine struggles and disputes over *cacicazgos* were a recurring event. Intraelite disputes, contradictory *probanzas*, conflicting genealogies, invented ancestors, and the intrusion of indigenous and nonindigenous outsiders in *cacicazgo* politics and chiefly succession became a constant after conquest. They are the "stuff" of which colonial *cacicazgo* politics was made.[84] Despite the impression of continuity of prehispanic political structures and chiefly lines after conquest, *cacique* lineages and *cacicazgo* rights had to be re-created and even reinvented, as indigenous elites throughout the Andes reworked their own pasts and privileges into colonial legal narratives. Such legal narratives, which quickly found in litigation and favor-seeking their raison d'être, translated prehispanic norms, local histories, and institutions into colonial legal notions of *señorío* (lordship), nobility, antiquity, primogeniture, and rightful succession. *Cacique* "titles"—bundles of documents containing a disparate array of oral histories, genealogies, notarial documents, land titles, royal decrees, and proofs of merit—became the cornerstone of this process of reinventing the past to legitimize the present and the future.[85]

Equally important, throughout the colonial period, male and female commoners successfully adopted titles, practices, and strategies once reserved for the elite of pre-Columbian origin.[86] In approaching local *cacique* politics in all of its complexity, Don Domingo Itquilla's rise to the post of *cacique principal* of Curi—hardly a unique case—alerts us to the need to refrain from imposing rigid dichotomies on the sources. In the Andes and across the Atlantic, assertions of legitimacy, the ability to rule, and even *cacique* status were often situational and negotiated. Above all, Andean communities did not speak with one voice, especially about their leaders. The question "is not who was the rightful *cacique* . . . but who was the most appropriate one, and for whom."[87] The complex issue of leadership and legitimacy seems best suited for a case-by-case approach.

Transatlantic experiences had the potential for exacerbating, alleviating, or reconfiguring tensions that were present at the local level. In fact, rivalries inherent in the confrontation of different models of indigenous leadership can be detected in the earliest cases of transatlantic travelers descended from the powerful chiefly lineages. The seventeenth century, however, certainly witnessed the proliferation of partially legitimate, partially contested modes of chiefly and communal authority, access to power, and brokering with the Crown. "Ability" to rule became particularly problematic. "Intruders" of any kind could pose a threat to established *cacique* lineages, political traditions, and local autonomies. Other so-called intruders (like Domingo Itquilla, for example) became, under the right circumstances, important communal assets and, when operating within the proper networks and legal frameworks, even vehicles for reaching the king.

Fulfilling judicial and governmental duties (in particular, prompt and full collection of the king's tribute) demanded enough political adeptness to satisfy the interests and expectations of the main parties involved: Crown officials, *caciques*, and even commoners. Such qualifications took some Andean cosmopolitans very far. In January 1659, Don Francisco Benítez was elected judge-governor (*gobernador*) of Mexico-Tenochtitlan. Obtaining eighty-one of the 132 recorded votes, he won a landslide victory over Don Lorenzo de Santiago, *indio, cacique prinçipal,* and the son of a former governor, who came in third with twenty-one votes. Don Lorenzo objected to Benítez's election on three grounds. First, Don Francisco was not of Mexica-Tenochca or even Nahua descent, let alone of the royal lineage that had dominated the office since the times of the great Moctezuma and the fall of the Mexica capital in 1521. Second, he was not an *indio* but a *mestizo*. Third, and perhaps most suprising, he was a foreigner from the kingdom of Peru—hence the ethnonym "Inga" that followed his Spanish surname.[88]

Indeed, Don Lorenzo argued that Benítez Inga's true *calidad* was that of a *mestizo* from Peru. This was public knowledge and also how he "notoriously" appeared according to his aspect (*aspecto*).[89] Electoral custom and viceregal legislation barred *mestizos*, Spaniards (*españoles*), *mulatos*, and others of mixed origin (*naçion mesclada*) from holding the governorship—or any other post of the *República de Indios*—mandating instead that the governor of Mexico-Tenochtitlan be a legitimately born *indio mero*—a "true" or "pure" Indian, the son of an *indio* and an *india*. Benítez Inga was clearly ineligible.[90]

Benítez Inga contested the second allegation—that he was a *mestizo*—but did not deny that he was a native of Peru. While avoiding applying to himself the *indio* label, he styled himself in writing as a *cacique principal* and a *natural* based on origin and ancestry. His parents were Don Bartolomé Inga and Doña Luisa Ismaquibo, both paramount lords (*caciques principales*) who were properly married in Lima, Don Bartolomé Inga's hometown (Doña Luisa was from Trujillo). Thus, Benítez and his siblings were all born in wedlock. Like his parents, moreover, Benítez Inga was "well-known" and "reputed" as a "pure" or "true" *cacique principal* and a *natural* from Lima, with no stain of mixed ancestry (*generaçion*) or lowly status in his blood. His aspect, public behavior, and noble manners (*bueno y ajustado proceder; compostura*) attested to his *calidad*.[91]

In his defense, Benítez Inga admitted that he had journeyed from Peru to New Spain at the age of thirteen or fourteen, in the company of Captain Alonso Prieto, a ship owner and resident of the port of Callao. Though originally from Peru, he had resided in Mexico City for thirty years, which mitigated his foreign status. During that time, he had been elected governor of the nearby towns of La Asunción de Milpa and San Pedro Atocpan. Therefore, he was clearly qualified; he was *persona hauil capaz y sufiçiente* to become governor of Mexico-Tenochtitlan. The viceregal authorities agreed, appointing Benítez Inga to that office exactly one month after his election, despite his foreign, Peruvian (or more precisely *limeño*) origin.[92]

Several historical lessons can be gleaned from Don Francisco's election. Given that the overwhelming majority of votes favored him, one can contend that the electors in Mexico-Tenochtitlan—past and current officeholders—made the conscious choice of backing this *limeño* because they thought he was the "best" candidate.[93] The formerly hereditary post was now open to elections and thus to novel and highly skilled political actors with enough support and the proper qualifications. The foreign-born Benítez could not appeal to tradition, nativeness, or local lineage. He was, however, able to galvanize the powerful electors of the different wards (*barrios*) and ultimately win the support of Crown officials. Benítez Inga served his term unopposed and was reelected in 1660.[94]

Throughout his political career in New Spain, Benítez learned how to "see, understand, and respond to multiple constituencies who often had competing interests" including the Crown, its royal magistrates, Spanish residents, indigenous *principales*, and the larger native audiences.[95] Benítez Inga clearly fit the bill. Seven years earlier, in 1651, the *principales* and commoners of the city of San Bernardino de Xochimilco and its satellite towns had elected him governor for the following year. In a petition asking the local Spanish magistrate and the viceroy to approve their election, they expressed their "long-held desire" to have Don Francisco Benítez Inga as their governor, especially after they saw how aptly he had served in La Asunción de Milpa. Tribute was the crux of the matter. The two past governors had collected it in full but only delivered part of it, stealing the rest and throwing the community into a 14,000-peso debt. Don Francisco Benítez Inga, by contrast, had managed to guarantee the king's tribute for the whole year of his governorship, perhaps from his own patrimony or through unnamed financial backers. The community of Xochimilco had elected him so he could relieve the commons of the dire consequences of past elite mismanagement: he was to collect the outstanding debt—even if by resorting to judicial means—from past governors.[96]

Thus, obtaining royal decrees and favorable rulings at the king's local and metropolitan courts had become a distinguishing mark of a good Andean leader, cacique or not. Far from the royal palace, the rooms of Lima's *Audiencia*, or the busy courtyards of the *Casa de la Contratación*, perhaps in the yearly meetings of the Indian *cabildo* or during the ritual cleansing of a community's irrigation canal, *cédulas* obtained in Madrid became proof of admittance into the fluid and heterogeneous category of *cacique* or *principal*.[97] Don Felipe Guacrapaucar returned from the royal court in 1564 with so many favorable decrees that they "barely fit in a chest."[98] Very few transatlantic advocates could boast of equal wealth and nobility (Don Felipe was a scion of one of the great regional lineages and the offspring of a rich and powerful great lord [hatun curaca] and a noble Inca woman), yet these new historical actors kept pushing open the gates to the Atlantic. Thanks to the spread of literacy and education and the new opportunities of the colonial city, Don Felipe's legal and literate skills quickly stopped being the exclusive domain of the traditional nobility. Others with more modest backgrounds but fewer ties to a particular office and its formal obligations started procuring cédulas for themselves and others and, in the process, fashioned themselves as transatlantic procurators—if not caciques as well.

The vast ocean had this power to reconfigure identities and elevate social statuses. Were it not for that transformative force, the story of how Lorenzo Ayun Chifo almost became cacique of the Luringuancas in the 1660s could have hardly been possible. Lorenzo's cacique denounced the notion that his long absence in Spain and Mexico had "dignified" his former subject (se hauia hecho graue), so much so that Lorenzo now refused to remove his hat in his presence. Neither the cacique—who held the intriguing title of "gardener of the [viceregal] palace" in Lima—nor the caciques of Luringuanca—where Lorenzo Ayun Chifo was to claim for himself the cacicazgo as Don Jerónimo Lorenzo Limaylla in 1655—considered Ayun to be their peer. For the former, he was a runaway tribute-payer; for the latter, he was a clever impostor, not a highlander (serrano) but a yunga with a different naturaleza (the lowlands [llanos] facing the Pacific Ocean), which he was now trying to legally modify.[99]

During the legal battle for the cacicazgo, multiple loyalties and interests revolved around the crucial issue of mita labor drafts to the dreadful mercury mines of Huancavelica, a royal obligation that the commoners of Luringuanca had endured since 1571.[100] Most likely, some caciques and principales, and perhaps even some commoners, supported Ayun's quest for the cacicazgo because they realized the type of legal advocacy and transatlantic brokerage that he had started at the Habsburg court during the previous decade.[101] In fact, Ayun boasted of having obtained a mysterious cédula granting a general exemption from work at the mines for himself and his subjects.

During the mid-seventeenth century, local native lords found it increasingly hard to collect tribute and to draft mita workers. They complained they were depleting communal funds and their own estate by hiring outside workers to cover for hundreds of tributaries who had simply fled.[102] At this critical juncture, Lorenzo Ayun's claim to possess an original "king's decree" (cédula del Rey) which ordered that "the Indians who became his subjects" would neither pay tribute nor fulfill the Huancavelica *mita*, gained momentum.[103] The *caciques* had sought exoneration since the 1620s, albeit unsuccessfully.[104] To many, the "king's decree" seemingly in the possession of Lorenzo Ayun, obtained directly from His Majesty, was evidence that he had not only made his way to the royal court and "talked" to the king but also managed to obtain the coveted privilege. According to some witnesses, *caciques* and commoners toiling in the mines at the time returned to the valley as soon as they heard about the royal decree. Rather intriguingly, no witnesses—lord or commoner—in favor of or against the incumbent ever claimed to have actually seen the famous *cédula*. By turning the seemingly impossible into something finally within reach, Lorenzo's transatlantic adventures had made his story believable, perhaps even desirable.[105]

The queen never made a *cacique* of Lorenzo Ayun Chifo (or "Jerónimo Lorenzo Limaylla," as he styled himself). In the ensuing years, however, he developed a reputation as an effective *procurador* at the viceregal and royal courts.[106] In 1665, he returned to Spain with *memoriales* that the lords of Tarma and Huamanga—two regions neighboring Jauja—had sent to the king. Apparently, Lorenzo Ayun had told a Franciscan in confidence, "I do not aspire to the *cacicazgo*; all I want is to collect information about the abuses that these Indians receive so I can go back to Spain and put an end to their sufferings." In 1666, colonial authorities in Peru confiscated two letters, written in 1656 and signed by "Don Jerónimo Lorenzo Limaylla," among the possessions of a *cacique* of Huancavelica tried for leading an anti-*mita* and antitribute uprising. In 1677, Limaylla informed the king that he had received letters of attorney from "the rest of the *caciques* of the said kingdom of Peru to appear before Your Majesty ... and represent them as if they were actually present at this court." Throughout the rest of the century, many other self-styled procuradores gathered letters, petitions, and powers of attorney from *caciques* and other Andean clients for legal advocacy at the royal court.[107]

Unlike Don Jerónimo Limaylla, Don Andrés de Ortega Lluncon secured an important *cédula real* during his stay at the royal court (1646–1647). A literate, seasoned *procurador* and tax collector who alternated between Lima and Trujillo, Ortega seemed like the only opportunity for the natives of Lambayeque to oust their abusive *corregidor*. During the months prior to embarking for Spain, he journeyed more than 120 leagues from Lambayeque to Lima to represent the commons in the lawsuit against Don Bernardino de Perales, the corrupt magistrate. But Perales's influential connections at Viceroy Mancera's court were stronger than Ortega's. He neutralized the declarations of several witnesses summoned by Ortega to Lima for the occasion, as well as the letters and other incriminating testimonies gathered by this communal attorney. The lawsuit was arbitrarily dismissed, and Don Andrés was even thrown into jail by order of the viceroy and one of the justices of the *Audiencia*, allies of the defendant. Cognizant of the dangers of litigating "against the powerful," Don Andrés made the decision to leave for Spain "to demand justice for the damages that the natives (*naturales*) suffer due to these tyrannies." Ortega got on board one of the ships of the royal fleet in Callao but could complete his voyage only via the Canary Islands and on an English vessel, after the governor of Havana threw him in jail for five months per the *Audiencia de Lima*'s request.[108]

Andrés de Ortega's advocacy in Spain was, like that of his fellow traveler Don Carlos Chimo, broad and effective. Ortega secured a royal decree in August 1647 ordering that his case be reopened and tried by a new judge appointed in Madrid. Ortega journeyed across southern Spain to meet the judge, Bernardo de Iturrizarra, in Cádiz and to inform him of the charges. Under his protection, Ortega voyaged back to Lambayeque. In January 1648, while still in Tierra Firme (Panama), Ortega formally summoned Iturrizarra to obey the royal decree and start the investigation. He was the first to declare against Perales.[109]

Although Ortega presented himself at court as a "*cacique* and noble tribute collector" (*cacique y pachaca principal*) of the town of Lambayeque, he lacked any formal title. In Madrid, the Council noted that it had no external verification of such a claim. Accordingly, the ministers referred to Ortega as a "*cacique y pachaca principal* (which he says he is)."[110] Information questioning his identity soon arrived from Peru. Although at least thirty *principales* of Lambayeque and the surrounding towns had supported Ortega with letters, petitions, and witness depositions in Lima and Lambayeque, the attacks against Don Andrés's authority to act as an attorney stemmed from within the *República de Indios*. The most direct challenge came from Don Andrés de Azabache. In August 1648, this "*indio cacique principal* [and] governor and *pachaca* of the said town of Lambayeque" appeared before the *corregidor*—his political and business ally—to denounce Ortega as a fraud. Azabache and his witnesses followed a well-known script.

Azabache declared, "It has come to my attention that an *indio* named Andrés de Ortega" had journeyed to Spain "pursuing his own selfish motives" and "incited by powerful people who took him with them." Even worse, Ortega had left owing the tribute he had collected, thus usurping the king's patrimony. Azabache chastised Ortega for lying to king and Council when he claimed he was a *cacique y pachaca principal*. In Spain, he had received honors, *cédulas*, and *mercedes* that he did not deserve. For that, Ortega, a "*parque* Indian, which in Castilian means 'vile and lowly man,' subject to serving the *mita* and paying tribute," deserved punishment. Azabache explained that, although Ortega had been informally named *mandón* or *pachaca* (leader and tribute collector) of the *cacique's parcialidad* (the paramount among the *ayllus*, moieties, or subgroups that coexisted in the town), he was by no means a *cacique* himself. *Caciques* and *corregidores* appointed and removed these *mandones* at will, choosing them for their "due diligence" in the collection of tribute. However, this temporary position entailed neither tributary exemption nor any additional honors. In contrast, an *audiencia* decree proved that Azabache was "the legitimate *cacique* and natural lord of this town."[111]

Five witnesses, among them the chief bailiff of the town and two *pachacas principales*, backed these accusations. In their version of the story, Andrés de Ortega fled to Lima to escape his responsibilities as a tributary and tax collector, stealing His Majesty's tribute, adopting the surname "Ortega," and starting a new life as a tailor. Parish records and tribute rolls brought before the *corregidor* seemingly proved that the defendant "was never called Don Andrés de Ortega, but only 'Andrés.'" Similarly, his father, Diego Lluncon, "did not have the *don* but was a nobody." A 1629 tributary reassessment revealed one "Andres Llancun," an ordinary Indian of commoner stock (*indio ordinario*).[112]

The story was much more complicated, for it rested on a strategic omission on the part of the plaintiff. Andrés de Azabache tried to disqualify Andrés de Ortega by denouncing him as an upstart who had risen from the lower ranks only to betray his mandate and lie to the court about his identity. What he did not mention, however, was that the rise to power of the Azabaches was not substantially different. Like many other local lineages, they claimed descent from the pre-Hispanic rulers of Lambayeque, but Don Andrés de Azabache had started his political career as the *pachaca* of a *parcialidad* other than his own. Moreover, his designation as *cacique principal* of Lambayeque was still a contested issue when he brought his charges against Ortega. Azabache and the Farrochumbis, a powerful local lineage that also traced their ancestors to the period before the Spanish Conquest, were still litigating for the *cacicazgo* before the *Audiencia de Lima*. Although the legal battle was far from over, the *corregidor* Bernardino de Perales arbitrarily selected his friend Azabache to become the titled *cacique* of Lambayeque, no doubt seeking his support in his own conflict with Ortega Lluncon and the other *principales* in Lambayeque, Lima, and Spain. In fact, the governor and several *pachacas* accused Perales of selling *pachaquías* (the title of *pachaca* or tribute collector) to the highest bidder, pointing an accusatory finger at Azabache.[113]

In spite of this seemingly illegitimate path to becoming a *cacique*, Azabache was as capable a leader as his rival Ortega. Personal qualifications, political connections, and a modicum of communal consensus often translated into proven ability to mobilize lower-ranking *caciques*, *principales*, and commoners to properly deliver the king's tribute, guarantee payment of any eventual shortfalls, and, along with exercising ancillary governmental duties, organize the all-important labor drafts. Born in the last decades of the sixteenth century, Azabache was described in 1613 as "an Indian and a good Christian, fluent in Spanish, of the principal ones in the *repartimiento*, capable and apt [for the post]." During that decade, Don Andrés served as interim governor of Lambayeque—in theory ruling over all of the *parcialidades*—while the titled *cacique principal* came of age. In 1624, the local Spanish magistrate praised Azabache's ability to collect the king's tribute on time. In 1618, and again in 1633, he received viceregal authorization to carry a sword and a dagger "in recognition of the fact that he goes about in Spanish clothes and dressed as a Spaniard." Like many *principales* of his class, he served as municipal judge of his town several times in the 1630s and 1640s. Don Andrés's son traveled to the royal court in the late 1650s.[114]

Andrés de Ortega, Azabache's rival in the courts, was equally "able" to rule and represent the commons, although for different reasons. He had left for Lima at a relatively young age. It seems likely that, rather than fleeing, Ortega was put in charge of collecting tribute from absentee Indians in the city. This practice had become fairly common, and it offered interesting opportunities to exercise power beyond the locale. Several midcentury Andean *caciques* were imprisoned for unpaid tribute, which proves that only well-connected and able collectors who enjoyed a high degree of ascendancy among the migrants responsible for these payments were able to fulfill this duty effectively. After Andrés de Ortega returned to Lambayeque in late 1645 or early 1646, the indigenous governor of the town (who was *not* Azabache but one Don Diego Bernardino), his second in command (*segunda persona*), and several *principales* selected him to go back to Lima and file the lawsuit against Bernardino de Perales before the *Audiencia*. There, Ortega dealt with attorneys, interpreters, and scribes as he prepared the detailed list of accusations. It is possible that most *principales* supported Ortega's journey to the royal court, welcoming the king's decree, which showcased the traveler's credentials as a transatlantic and multicommunal procurator. In a letter sent to the king in August 1648, indigenous leaders praised the efficient legal advocacy of captain and *Don* Andrés de Ortega Lluncon, calling him *uno de nuestros prençipales*—one of their own.[115]

CODA: THE PERILS OF LEGAL REPRESENTATION

The interplay between self-identifications and imposed categorizations ultimately configured the royal court as a discursive battleground. Mid-seventeenth-century Andean cosmopolitans and their detractors deployed a series of legal arguments and representations, drawn from a common source dating back to the sixteenth century, to legitimize themselves and discredit rivals. As if in a hall of mirrors, litigants and petitioners, and their supporters and antagonists, invoked inherited discourses about ancestry, nobility, and the ability to rule in order to advocate, accuse, or self-represent before the king. Seemingly contradictory claims about Andean leaders revealed competing interests, fragile intraelite, multiclass and multiethnic alliances, and variable experiences with the realities of colonialism. And yet it was their social position and mediating role, which Crown officials and political rivals criticized as ambiguous, inconsistent, or contradictory, that made these Andean cosmopolitans into transatlantic brokers. Accusations launched against them in Peru and Spain were indicative of deeper social processes that created the possibility for advocates to "see the things of Spain" and represent their own interests and those of others. Usurper, impostor, commoner, foreigner, lowly *mestizo*, and other categorizations stemmed from contending discourses, some of which attempted to invalidate new styles of leadership and novel forms of ethnic and multiethnic prestige and authority; others justified these styles as legitimate and sufficient to negotiate with the king.

Along with personal desire, there was the need, for Ortega Lluncon, Chimo, Limaylla, and others, to style themselves as *caciques* before the king, the Council, and other metropolitan ministers. In a predicament common to other midcolonial leaders, Chimo, by presenting a *cacique* identity on paper, became subject to attacks from *caciques* and indigenous notables governing the jurisdictions over which the petitioner claimed to preside. Because of ancestry, nobility, title to office, and individual interests, some elite Indians felt that Chimo, whom we met at the beginning of this chapter, was not *one of them* and therefore should not speak on their behalf.

Despite the inherent risks, Don Carlos Chimo told the king in a *memorial* of his willingness to "legitimize his person" before the Council, which meant proving with documents that he was specifically who he said he was. Because he failed to produce any written proof, his authority to represent his alleged subjects faded, but it did not completely disappear. The councilors proceeded as was customary with other *unlicensed* and *untitled* travelers, carefully pointing out in their response to the king that Chimo was making his accusations provisionally and pending proper identification as *cacique principal*. This was a legal statement on the part of the *letrados* at the king's court, not a ruse to deny Chimo justice.[116]

Nor were Chimo's claims to *cacique* status a mere exercise at self-promotion. Rather, they were charged with equally relevant juridical meanings. The higher the petitioner's social position along the old lord-vassal spectrum, the stronger his power to represent on a larger scale. Indigenous subjects could legitimately advocate for others and speak for them as long as they could prove membership in the same community, which in turn gave them legal authority to represent collective interests. *Caciques*, as the "natural" lords and spokespersons of the different commons that made up the *República de Indios*, still held this prerogative before the king.[117] Formal title provided access to leadership roles and opportunities for individuals who did not necessarily possess the proper wealth, bloodline, or social standing.[118]

Chimo's self-fashioning thus represented "an effective rhetorical strategy" and a "legal location" from which to speak.[119] Recognition of one's *cacique* status was still a formal requisite to speak to the king on behalf of the commons of Lambayeque and, stretching the traveler's power to represent to its limits, those of nearby towns. Successful forms of individual and collective representation before the monarch and his ministers depended on the proper and effective deployment of such categories of self-representation and legitimization. At the time of Chimo's journey to the royal court, properly accredited *caciques* with *cacicazgos*, no matter how out of touch this formulation may have been with colonial Andean realities, still held the key to political representation within the monarchy.

From a complementary perspective, however, the fluidity of the courtly setting contrasted the seemingly fixed nature of social and legal categories such as *cacique*. Seventy-five years after Francisco de Toledo's far-reaching reforms of the 1570s, this catchall term had become obsolete and insufficient to describe novel and cosmopolitan leaders. Speaking on behalf of native individuals and communities seeking justice was becoming a valid strategy to stay at the court. An emerging caste of procurators-generals started to represent "the Indians" of Peru, even if they were not always members of the specific native group, lineage, or corporate body seeking redress. As they argued in *memoriales*, their power to represent those who had been wronged stemmed from the "blood" that they shared (hence the idea of a common *Nación*). Appropriating, and even subverting, Iberian exclusionist ideas about ancestry and purity and legal categories such as *cacique, indio,* or *república*, transatlantic procurators gradually detached themselves from traditional Indian corporations, turning instead into spokespersons of a more abstract *Nación Índica*.

This gradual shift at the discursive level allowed seventeenth-century transatlantic attorneys to amplify their voices and broaden their representative base. Whereas some procurators-general still spoke on behalf of the Indians of their cities, provinces, and towns, a more encompassing discourse began to emerge from within the viceregal court, likely modeled after the discursive strategies of the General Defender and the General Attorney of the Indians. In Lima, as early as the 1610s, the "native residents of the City of Kings" (in fact, the upper segment of the indigenous urban population) had empowered an attorney to collectively represent them in Madrid.[120] Later testimonies exhibit a pattern of ever-broadening political and legal representation through similar discursive strategies. By declaring to be a descendant from the former lords of the coastal valleys surrounding Trujillo, and not just the *cacique* of Lambayeque, Don Carlos Chimo, who also declared to be speaking in the name of all the *caciques* and *naturales* of Peru, made an encompassing call, one that resonated among the rural and urban indigenous communities that articulated the colonial world.[121] In a 1657 letter to the king, the Lima notables Don Luis and Don Felipe Carguamango made a similar call, claiming to speak on behalf of "the *caciques* of your kingdom."[122] An even broader call came in 1662, when Don Jerónimo Lorenzo Limaylla told the king in a *memorial* of his intent to speak "for the relief of these poor Indians, his brothers."[123] At the royal court, he declared in 1678 to be seeking "some relief for the Indians of the whole kingdom, for the preservation and survival of the noble Indians and the rest."[124] In two *memoriales* prepared in Madrid around the same time, Limaylla also claimed to collectively represent the *caziques* of Mexico and Peru, from whom he had received letters of attorney when he requested the creation of an exclusive military order that, under the protection of Saint Rose of Lima, would bring honor to the two kingdoms and the noble Indians who inhabited them.[125]

Seventeenth-century procurators-general active at the royal court were able to articulate this broader discourse because, by virtue of their voyage to and stay in Spain, they managed to detach themselves from specific native Andean polities and communities and instead invoke more general notions related to common blood and origin (disguising, in the process, important distinctions of class and status). Thus, they began to represent "the Indians of Peru" with varying degrees of success. These mechanisms and strategies to establish chiefly legitimacy were not unique to these travelers. In fact, *caciques* had provided a training ground for the languages of indigenous elite legitimacy since the mid-sixteenth century. And, like the travelers' efforts to present themselves as *caciques* before the king, cacical legitimacy had also been performed and produced in myriad ways in the Andes. The increasing ability of transatlantic procurators to mimic this rhetoric and speak in the name of the whole *República de Indios*, however, was a strategy that *caciques* of the old mold could have hardly followed because their legitimacy and authority were, first and foremost, tied to the *repartimientos* and towns that they ruled and their obligations toward Crown and commoners. *Caciques* had, of course, multiple reasons to visit Lima and enter into contact with potential travelers and transatlantic attorneys but very few real chances to abandon their duties for as long as the venture of "seeing the things of Spain" as a *cacique* of all the Indians—and therefore of none—demanded.

SEVEN

THE GREAT INCA DON LUIS I

In January 1725, more than a century after the 1610 pageant in Cuzco celebrating the beatification of Ignatius, the Inca kings symbolically rose from their pagan graves and paraded once again. On this occasion, however, they walked through the streets of viceregal Lima to commemorate King Philip V's abdication in favor of his son Louis Ferdinand. Stretching back from Huascar to Manco Capac, thirteen men dressed in royal costumes and accompanied by dancers, personal guards, and pages entered the main plaza to salute the royal and ecclesiastic authorities, giving shouts to "the great Inca Don Luis I" as they went around the square tossing silver coins to the populace. Their grandiose procession and public oath of fealty on behalf of the *Nación Índica* of Peru symbolized a seemingly uninterrupted transition from Inca to Spanish history and sovereignty. Many changes lay hidden in this story of dynastic continuity, however. Unlike the 1610 procession honoring the future Jesuit saint, led by Tito Atauchi and others who embodied their direct royal ancestors, the 1725 festivity showed a distinct *limeño* and *norteño* (northerner) accent throughout.[1]

The perception of the Indians of the coastal valleys stretching from Lambayeque and Trujillo to Lima and nearby valleys regarding their own importance and that of their pre-Hispanic ancestors in the history of the Inca Empire, the Spanish Conquest, and the colonial present of the *Nación Índica* became noticeable from the opening day of festivities. The celebration began with the two urban magistrates for the Indians (*alcaldes de los naturales*) of Lima who, escorted by a lieutenant, six footmen, and five guards, entered the square on horseback and paid respects to the viceroy and archbishop. Dancers wore insignias of nobility like the ones allegedly granted by the Chimo Capac, "sovereign of the valleys of Trujillo, Chicama, and their surroundings." This Chimo Capac was, in fact, one of the first characters to approach the representatives of God and king that afternoon, followed by Atum Apo Cuismango, "lord of Pachacamac," a valley immediately south of Lima and seat of one of the greatest pre-Inca shrines in the region. Inca Huascar was only the third to enter, followed by Chuquis Manco, "lord of the valleys of Luna-guaná," also south of the City of Kings.[2]

Members of the Lima Indian elite, among them well-established and re-spected migrants with blood ties to the regional aristocracies of old, repre-sented some of the main characters. Don Francisco Atum Cuismango Saba Capac, the *cacique* of nearby Pachacamac and Lurín, was given the role of pre-Hispanic lord of Pachacamac. Don Valentín Minollulli Xecfunchunpi Falen-pinciam, a "native noble from the valleys of Lambayeque" and proud member of the northern *cacique* families who claimed descent from the Chimo Capac and the pre-Inca nobility, performed as the pan-Andean deity Tunupa.[3] The seemingly plebeian Bartolomé Rodríguez, formerly known as Don Cristóbal Apoalaya, paraded as Lloque Yupanqui, third in the official list of Inca kings. Thirty-five years earlier, Don Cristóbal had fled his hometown in Jauja and moved to Lima, where he changed his name, set up a barbershop, and made a name for himself, apparently renouncing any claims to the *cacicazgo* of his forebears the Apoalayas.[4]

Thus, as they organized the festivities from their base at El Cercado, the indigenous notables and authorities of the "Nation of the Native Peruvians" selected themselves and other Lima residents to perform in this urban dem-onstration of their community's fealty to the Spanish monarchs. As impor-tant, they seamlessly wove claims to leadership and preponderance within the *República de Indios* into the script and performance, carefully shaping their content and messages as well as the order of precedence, dress, and identity of the main characters. The leaders of the *República de Indios* who represented the Indians of the kingdom during the 1725 festivities, while dissociating Inca political legitimacy and symbolism from its original Cuzco context, success-fully reembedded the royal line within a *limeño*-migrant milieu. Their strategy to displace the Inca royals of Cuzco from the top of the *República de Indios* involved both local symbolic representation and transatlantic legal advocacy.[5]

As this book has shown, however, this was hardly a novel strategy. The personal trajectories of some individuals representing past Inca emperors and other characters in eighteenth-century Lima are illustrative of the emer-gence of a hybrid elite that, in turn, significantly shaped, and was significantly shaped by, the broader processes of transoceanic travel and negotiation that the ancestors of the Apoalayas, Minollullis, and others had begun in the mid-sixteenth century.

Imperial reformers of that time increasingly demanded that native An-deans seek justice in the Americas and not in Spain. Bringing royal justice to indigenous towns and municipal councils would stop the unsanctioned displacements of "frivolous" indigenous litigants and claimants. The success-ful insertion of native groups and subjects into the Atlantic system of justice had a much more ambivalent outcome. It encouraged Andean leaders and communities to actively seek justice and legal redress in local, provincial, and viceregal forums, either in person or by proxy, gradually building on a reper-toire of legal strategies and a pool of practices and experiences that gave the early modern world its distinctive character. An economy of local and trans-oceanic litigation developed, connecting legal networks horizontally—within and across ethnicity and region—and vertically—between legal centers and peripheries—in part redesigning the old ecological model of the Andean ver-tical archipelago.

A significant number of letters, petitions, and proofs of merit prepared by, or on behalf of, native Andeans arrived at the Habsburg court through these formal channels, attesting to the natives' quick mastery of the web of Crown protectors and procurators appointed for the defense of the Indians. Hidden behind the public system of legal representation mounted in 1574–1575, there existed parallel networks of informal operators. These agents were often travelers themselves, petitioners and litigants like their clients, priests and laymen, lawyers and nonprofessional practitioners of the law. All of them multiplied the conduits of communication between Indian polities and sub-jects and the king. A great deal of this Atlantic legal network probably lay outside the purview of the Crown. Litigants and favor-seekers often moved in broader social spaces only partially affected by the sanctioned, the official, and the strictly legal.

Indeed, throughout the period covered here, *indios* other than litigants and favor-seekers sailed to Spain from Lima and other cities and ports along the Pacific coast. Many had been born and raised there (or so they declared). A minority within the larger sample of Andean travelers, especially in the six-teenth century, were Inca nobles, *caciques*, or *gobernadores*. During the follow-ing century, many Andean travelers also came from urban worlds and from plebeian, artisan, military, and immigrant backgrounds. Their life stories and the documents they generated hint at a universe of social relations forged with other Indians, *mestizos*, and Spaniards within urban spaces in Peru and Spain, sometimes several years prior to the trip.

These social relations underpinned such Atlantic experiences. Many trav-elers claimed to have journeyed as *criados*, aides, or dependents of a Span-iard, often a priest or royal minister in route to the royal court or about to take up their post in Peru: a *corregidor* but also an *audiencia* judge, a recently appointed councilor, or even a viceroy. The ties of patronage, authority, and dependency that sustained these interactions resurfaced during significant portions of the transatlantic voyage, including the stay in Spain and the direct negotiations with the king's ministers in Seville and Madrid.

The Andean travelers and cosmopolitans did not need an interpreter to appear before metropolitan authorities—in fact, some were themselves court-appointed interpreters for the Indians, militia officers, and minor urban officials with at least a basic knowledge of law and legal procedure. Some had learned how to read and write from priests, officials, scribes, and schoolteachers in part because of the opportunities for social advancement offered within the colonial city. These clues are indicative of their degree of "acculturation," although the term seems insufficient: for some travelers born in cities like Lima or Trujillo, Castilian was probably their first language, and "Spanish ways" were anything but exclusively Spanish. Royal ministers often described individual travelers a *ladino* (or even *muy ladino*), a *"mestizo* Indian" (*indio mestizo*), an "Indian dressed in Spanish clothes" (*indio vestido en hábito de español*), and other expressions suggestive of familiarity with—if not a full immersion and active participation in—hybrid cultural forms and multiethnic institutions that thrived in colonial cities and among urban *indios*. *Ladinos*, too, could be informal practitioners of the law. Hence, the expression *indio de nación*—that is, Indian by way of birth, ancestry, or decent—seems to have marked these travelers as *indios* even though, in the eyes of colonial authorities, they had permanently or temporarily abandoned their *naturalezas* (by moving to the city, for example) and did not necessarily look, sound, or act like "Indians." The creation and use of these terms in itself indicates that renewed forms of *being* Indian were rising.

As a means to physically segregate Indians and Spaniards, the system of two *repúblicas* obviously failed. The social and legal boundaries between the two could be very real, although they were constantly transgressed. On a much deeper sense, however, the *Repúblicas* (plural, uppercase) referred to the existence of two distinct but partially overlapping and mutually dependent jurisdictions (Indian and Spanish), each with certain privileges and obligations of its own. This book reveals the vitality of the *República de Indios* as a partially discrete judicial sphere, an autonomous space largely devoid of Spanish tutelage and intervention where indigenous authorities—rural and urban—ruled according to specific circumstances, as well as how this sphere gradually morphed into a multitude of individual *repúblicas* (municipal councils) and a broad *Nación Índica* based on common ancestry.

Although information is not always available regarding identity, position, and social constellations, travelers who left a larger imprint in the colonial archive in the form of letters, petitions, *memoriales*, and proofs of merit directed to the king and his Council or exchanged between Peru and Spain, belonged to the fluid indigenous (and sometimes *mestizo*) upper class in mid-colonial Peru. *Caciques* and their relatives by birth or marriage are to be expected, but the upper and most visible segment of Andean travelers, in terms of their class, status, and ability to reach out to the king, also came to comprise well-off and well-related urban Indians of a less aristocratic background, thus complicating current narratives that equate travelers with *caciques* of Andean polities.

With more tenuous links to the native aristocracy of old and the indigenous commons they governed, many *criollos, indios prósperos*, and *indios principales* began to control, in the late sixteenth century but increasingly in the seventeenth, some of the most prestigious religious and secular institutions of Indian urban life and government, centered around Lima. Some of the most influential *cabildo*, military, and judicial appointments available to Indians in the colonial city—seat of the *Audiencia* and the viceroy's court—came to be controlled by them as well. The proximity of Andean notables and officials to, and in fact their membership into, the lettered elite gave them privileged political access to the networks and circuits within which peoples, goods, and papers successfully circulated across the empire.

Transatlantic experiences, even if not directly related in time and space, built upon each other. Because of this accumulation of juridical capital, a specialized group of Indian procurators—some of them self-appointed, informal, or unlicensed, others empowered by multiple subjects and communities—started to appear in the mid-seventeenth century. Their ability to represent and mediate went well beyond that of the original community procurators of the 1570s. Whereas communal attorneys still spoke on behalf of Indian *repartimientos* and *pueblos*, travelers with more cosmopolitan orientations and connections eventually strived to replace Spanish procurators for the Indians. The activities of the early transatlantic specialists forecasted the vicissitudes of better-known *procuradores* of the *Nación Índica* at the Bourbon royal court in the eighteenth century, such as Calixto de San José Túpac Inca, Don Vicente Mora Chimo, and Don Juan de Bustamante Carlos Inca.

Operating in urban scenarios in Iberia and the Andes, and therefore physically detached from the traditional rights and obligations of their communities of origin, Indian transatlantic procurators of the late Habsburg period gradually stretched the boundaries of indigenous legal representation. They expanded the Atlantic web further in order to encompass alternative native corporate identities (urban parishes, religious brotherhoods, and Indian battalions, for example) as well as broader imagined communities, such as "the *caciques* of Peru" or the increasingly invoked *Nación Índica*. These individual and collective identifications had not been envisioned in the original legalistic formulation of the *República de Indios* composed of nobles and *caciques*, commoners/tribute payers, and rural municipal authorities. These travelers-procurators were not necessarily the *caciques* of the land or the well-off notables of Inca descent who had made extensive use of the transoceanic system of justice in the sixteenth century. They embodied other forms of being an elite *indio* or *natural* in colonial Peru.

In recent years, scholars have increasingly turned attention to this constellation of literate Andeans who, thanks to their position within the elite of learned men in charge of producing and controlling the language of law and favor in colonial Peru, became administrators, polemicists, and advocates to different individuals and corporations.[6] Yet, the ways in which their participation in the exclusive world of intellectuals and *letrados* affected their relationships with indigenous traditional elites and the vast majority of commoners in Lima and beyond has remained unclear. Andean ethnogenesis must be framed within the important reorientations of power affecting indigenous society, especially in midcolonial Lima, the centerpiece of the Andean system of justice. To a significant degree, social networks and power relations within the indigenous collective known as the *República de Indios* in sixteenth- and seventeenth-century Peru came to be shaped by the political constraints imposed by the church and judiciary. Nevertheless, the *república* also came to be shaped by new opportunities, rivalries, and contradictions from within, sometimes by indigenous wielders of pen and paper—*letrados*, advocates, and intellectuals—and their specific professional and social aspirations. Contrary to its rhetorical appeal, this was an increasingly localized, rather than a vaguely pan-Andean, process (although it had significant urban-rural ramifications that deserve to be fully studied).

Lima's native *letrados*, militia officers, and urban magistrates were particularly well placed to influence and sometimes even to control the circulation of delegates and discourses between centers of power in the Andes and Spain. In their petitions to the king, they aimed at a rhetorical construct that, while extolling the royal services of the *Nación Índica* that they claimed to lead and upholding the honors and prerogatives of its highest members, ultimately placed their own privileged group of legal and political intermediaries, as well as the urban institutions that gave them their collective expression, at the center of indigenous colonial society. This was a new leadership, a composite of Indian officials, officers, and artisans of plebeian roots with important ties to local indigenous elites and often the descendants of migrants from multiple parts of the viceroyalty. By speaking on behalf of the Indians—the *other* Indians—and claiming to defend them from colonial abuse, Lima's urban governing class fashioned itself as the most important interlocutors between the king and his indigenous vassals in the Andes.

As others have noted, imperial structures did not oppress (or liberate) all native subjects equally. On the contrary, the historical experiences of each community within the empire to some extent "depended on its skill and success at negotiating its interests within the courts."[7] The social, administrative, and spatial dimensions of the imperial court system that legal actors built in the sixteenth century—which was ultimately grounded in the economic and political realities of the viceroyalty—played a significant role in shaping when, where, how, and by whom such negotiating skills and legal strategies were deployed, thus determining the degree of "success" that indigenous communities and individual claimants could expect in the courts. The seventeenth century, a period of relative political stability often associated with a "mature" colonial state in the Andes, witnessed a series of discursive struggles *from within* for the control of key official posts from which to gain almost unmediated access to the king's court. Historical actors involved in this process knew that such posts were conduits to channel a novel "voice" claiming to speak on behalf of Peru's *Nación Índica*. From the mid- to late-colonial period, indigenous and *mestizo* travelers to the royal court, as procurators (*procuradores*) or representatives (*diputados*), increasingly claimed to be speaking in the name of larger collectivities.[8] The legal discourses that supported their claims had begun to crystallize in the late sixteenth century, becoming easily identifiable in the eighteenth-century journeys of transatlantic attorneys-general for the Indians who claimed to represent the *Nación Índica* before the king and his Council.[9]

The genesis of this process of elite reconfiguration was firmly anchored in the transformations that Andean societies had experienced in the two previous centuries. Both the traditional indigenous aristocracy ruling over the Andean countryside—those generally labeled *caciques* and *principales*—and the lords of noble Inca descent living in Cuzco and its surroundings failed to articulate a hegemonic discourse capable of enshrining them as heads of the native populations of Peru. Due to novel styles of upward social mobility, leadership, and political legitimacy—which developed simultaneously as a requirement for, and a result of, the process of negotiating directly with the king via the courts—other cosmopolitan native leaders started to appear. The new leadership partially blended with the old aristocracy and, in fact, gradually eroded its power, even as new leaders continued to wear the *cacique* legal mask before king and Council while enshrining their symbolic preeminence within the *República de Indios*. This emerging leadership appropriated some of the self-reproducing mechanisms and performative strategies of the traditional Inca and non-Inca elites they were now displacing, adapting them to their own social setting and refashioning themselves in the Atlantic arena as the legitimate representatives of the *Nación Índica*. It is possible that the transoceanic journeys of late-colonial *Inca* procurators—as well as the revival of Inca imperial memory and cultural symbols in the Cuzco region, which became increasingly visible in artistic genres, public ceremonies, and other forms of Inca *nationalism* over the course of the eighteenth century—was the Inca elite's somewhat belated response to this process of appropriation and displacement.

The main scenario for this process was the multiethnic colonial city, where Indian and *mestizo* intellectuals, interpreters, procurators, and well-off urban leaders from artisan and militia backgrounds reimagined their own political communities and reinvented historical traditions in response to Spanish legal and political theories of corporate selves, including the theory of separate *repúblicas*. Institutional, legal, and social barriers kept prominent members of the *República de Indios* subordinated to the Spanish one, preventing them from accessing honors and privileges enjoyed by the Spaniards until the first half of the eighteenth century. The resulting aspirations laid the initial foundation for the idea of a *Nación Índica* in the seventeenth century, giving its main advocates the legal basis on which to assert their own autonomy from, and partial equality with, the *República de Españoles* (at least as it pertained to the pure-blooded "nobles" of both republics).

Such discourses usually formed in, and were disseminated from, major colonial centers, particularly Lima, where elite urban Indians residing within its walls had more direct access to the theories and institutions of the Lettered City and the officials who upheld it at the viceregal court. From their privileged positions, some of these *lettered* Indians acted as imperial power brokers, legal agents, and solicitors for native leaders and communities litigating in Lima or aspiring to take their cases to the royal court—a place that a handful of procurators were to see with their own eyes. Equally as important, they used the *Nación Índica* as an ideological springboard from which to seize legal control of key Indian urban institutions and colonial posts, thus gaining privileged access to the judicial channels linking the viceregal court with the Habsburg court. The *Nación Índica* that clustered in Lima became a "community of interest"—that is, one of specific interests—seeking to forge, under its leadership, an independent Indian (and only symbolically Inca) *república* in Peru.[10]

Behind this image of unity, however, inner disputes and disagreements over who should be the legitimate spokespersons of the *Nación Índica* constantly undermined collective efforts, even after important battles were won at the king's court. The idea of a *Nación Índica* as a "new and collective identity" or "consciousness," capable of overriding previous identifications and uniting elites, commoners, and everyone in between under a common banner, rested on legal categorizations and rhetorical constructs that did not necessarily translate into "identities"—ethnic or otherwise.[11] Although juridical categories shaped social identities and identifications in colonial and Atlantic scenarios, the strategic deployment of legal categories such as *indio* or *nación* by a specific group for the purposes of self-representation and promotion of class and political interests did not necessarily entail the emergence of a shared "Indian identity," let alone a commonality of goals and aspirations with indigenous commoners and communities experiencing colonialism outside urban centers of power.[12] The voices behind the *Nación Índica* showed an acute self-awareness of inferior status vis-à-vis the *República de Españoles* that negatively affected them and that they adamantly sought to escape. Their means of escape was to embrace the legal advocacy and activism of the *Nación Índica* at large while becoming gatekeepers of its specific contours and hierarchies.

Thus, where some see a "new Indian corporate self," others see a series of "strategies for action." Though an increasingly effective corporate interlocutor with the king, the *Nación Índica* was "not much more than a temporary discursive strategy aimed at a common goal, but inexistent as a real social actor."[13] The eighteenth-century struggle to have the Crown allow for the autonomous appointment of indigenous *procuradores generales* from among the ranks of the *cabildo* of El Cercado—the Indian ward within the city—shows that problems among different factions quickly ensued. The artisan guilds and the militia officers fought to control these appointments, especially after the town council, controlled by the silk weaver (*sederos*) and button maker (*botoneros*) guilds, chose the first *procuradores*. In certain late-colonial instances, moreover, these *cabildo* officials underscored their own prerogative to choose a *procurador*, rejecting the larger community's involvement in deciding who could legally represent the natives.[14] Future studies will likely reveal that, even though the *Nación Índica* officially stood for the whole of the *República de Indios*, indigenous urban institutions quickly developed their own boundary-marking and hierarchy-making strategies, thereby fragmenting the Indian elite of the viceregal seat across occupational, religious, and, it seems, old and new ethnic lines. In that sense, the *Nación Índica* did not develop mechanisms of corporate representation capable of encompassing all potential members and representing their particular interests, an inherent limitation that other colonial corporations experienced as well. Despite pretenses at universalism and common interest, this *national* discourse was likely fragmented and localized, clustered around power centers such as Lima and the viceregal court.

Despite its limitations, this platform for the construction of corporate selves did provide key strategies and mechanisms facilitating the accumulation of legal capital and the development of transoceanic alliances between some *caciques* of the kingdom, the *indios principales* of Lima, and nonindigenous actors such as the mendicant orders and ministers of the Crown. This process, in turn, allowed for the formation of a new class of native *letrado* specialists, who partially replaced their Spanish counterparts in different spheres of colonial life. The privilege to appoint indigenous attorneys-general for the Indians, as well as the right of Indians and *mestizos* to be ordained priests, obtained or confirmed by transatlantic travelers at the royal court, must be understood in terms of this larger historical process. Mainly articulated through the *cacique* legal identity—the one better suited for addressing the king and representing the commoners in writing—this *national* discourse stemmed primarily from a renewed, culturally fluid Indian leadership revolving around colonial institutions such as the Indian municipal council (*cabildo de naturales*), the religious brotherhoods, the office of defender of the Indians (*protectoría de indios*), the urban trades and crafts organizations, and the Indian urban militia.

The credentials of this leadership—sometimes of *cacique* stock, sometimes of tributary, migrant, or *forastero* background, and sometimes of partial Inca ancestry—did not necessarily originate in previous aristocratic forms of authority yet clearly benefitted from appropriating claims to legitimacy, nobility, and pure blood. Rather, that legitimacy came from individuals' privileged access to new sources of power stemming from Peru's role and position within the empire. We might not know enough yet to determine whether the *Nación Índica* constituted a case of new identity, one of legal ventriloquism, or both. Yet, as this book has shown, the mechanisms for social promotion, legal representation, and discursive appropriation that urban Indian aristocracies deployed between the 1720s and 1770s to make their collective voice heard were set in motion by the bold and tenacious cosmopolitans who traversed the ocean in the two preceding centuries and helped to define the particularly Andean meanings of legal advocacy and political negotiation with the king.

NOTES

CHAPTER 1

1. Esquivel y Navia, *Noticias cronológicas*, 2: 11; Romero, "Festividades." On Topa Atauchi: Cobo, *Historia*, 2: bk. 12, chs. 12 & 18. For Incas and Jesuits in Cuzco: Cahill, "Sponsoring," 70–75; Cahill, "The Inca"; Estenssoro, "Construyendo la memoria," 139–140. On Don Melchor in Spain: Casado Arboniés, "El Inca"; Temple, "Azarosa existencia." On his claims that his grandfather Paullu had been Huayna Capac's "only legitimate first-born son" (*unico hijo Primojenito lig[iti]mo*): "Ascendencia de Juan Carlos Inga," 1539–1626, BNE, MS, 20193, 18. On festive representations of the "Inca" and colonial political culture: Espinosa, *El Inca barroco*, 75–85.

2. *nuestro Ynga que es el rey ... y don Melchor se a muerto.* Guaman Poma, *Nueva corónica*, 1120–1122. On the *visita* of Francisco de Ávila, the priest in Guaman Poma's tale: "Petición de Francisco de Ávila," Lima, March 16, 1615, AGI, Lima, 326, 1r–3r (modern pagination); Temple, "Dos documentos."

3. Silverblatt, *Modern Inquisitions*, 177.

4. The phrase comes from a 1542 decree authorizing Don Pedro Moctezuma to return to New Spain. He claimed to have journeyed "only to see the things of Spain" (*solo a ver las cosas de España*). "Pedro, indio," Ocaña, December 27, 1542, AGI, Indiferente, 1963, l. 8, 96v–97r. For variants such as "to see Spain" (*ver España* or *ver a España*): Alaperrine-Bouyer, "Cruzar el océano," 39.

5. Guaman Poma, *Nueva corónica*, 42 (Castile and the Indies), 556–558 (Spaniards born in Castile), 671, 930 (Indians in Spain are *mitmaq*, or foreigners), 963 (the four parts of the world). On Guaman Poma and the larger world: Adorno, "Colonial Reform," 354–355; Adorno, *Guaman Poma*, 89–91; Zavala, "La monarquía." On how images of a world, inhabited by multiple Christian and non-Christians peoples and nations, were conveyed in colonial sermons prepared for the conversion of indigenous peoples: Silverblatt, *Modern Inquisitions*, 112–115. On Philip II and the Spanish "universal monarchy": Fernández Albaladejo, *Fragmentos*, 60–72; Maravall, "El concepto," 66–71; Río Barredo, *Madrid, Urbs Regia*, 75. On English cosmopolitanism in this era of global interactions: Games, *The Web*, 8–13.

6. *Con estos príncipes habla el señor rrey enperador.* Guaman Poma, *Nueva corónica*, 753, 1122; Chimalpahin Cuauhtlehuanitzin, *Annals*, 107, 163, 165, 167. On Chimalpahin's cos-

mopolitanism: Gruzinski, *Las cuatro partes*, 25–49; Schroeder, *Chimalpahin*, 21–22; Tavárez, "Reclaiming the Conquest," 20. On Don Diego Luis in Spain: "Licencia a don Diego Luis Moctezuma para volver a Nueva España," Madrid, November 17, 1576, AGI, Indiferente, 738, n. 242; "100 reales a Don Diego Luis Moctezuma," Madrid, August 14, 1576, AGI, Indiferente, 426, l. 26, 6r–6v; "30 ducados a Don Diego Luis de Montezuma," Madrid, November 10, 1576, AGI, Indiferente, 426, l. 26, 14r.

7. Temple, "Azarosa existencia," 135. In 1533, a son of Emperor Moctezuma was graced with the similar honorific post (*etiqueta real*) of *contino de la casa real*. Díaz Serrano, "La república," 1057.

8. *Recopilación*, bk. 2, tit. 15, law 15. Whenever possible, I have included cases from adjacent *audiencia* districts, such as Quito and Charcas.

9. Games, *The Web*, 10.

10. Matthew, "Facing East"; Mira Caballos, *Indios y mestizos*; Reséndez, *The Other Slavery*; Van Deusen, "Coming to Castile."

11. Don Baltasar Zaman prided himself on having attended the monarch at court, staying in his household for three years. Glave, "Hombres de mar," 19. In a 1656 letter, Lorenzo Ayun claimed to have entered the palace "to kiss the hand of His Majesty" (*a besar la mano a Su Magd.*). "Autos del gobernador de Huancavelica," Huancavelica, 1667, AHMPH, EC, Siglo XVII, l. 1, e. 1, 40r–40v. Don Juan Bustamante Carlos Inca stated that he had placed some documents "into the royal hands of your Majesty" (*en las propias Reales manos de su Magestad*). Cahill, "Becoming Inca," 263–264. For a *cacique* from Riobamba (Quito) who claimed one of his ancestors secured *mercedes* in Spain "by groveling himself at the king's feet" (*prostrado [sic] bajo los pies del rey*): Espinosa, *El Inca barroco*, 47.

12. Díaz, *The Virgin*, 15. On the "royal encounter" and indigenous political culture up to the eighteenth century: Puente Luna, "Into the Heart," ch. 5.

13. Cohen, "Was there an Amerindian Atlantic?," 399.

14. Gruzinski, *Las cuatro partes*, 30–31. By tracing native innovations of *costumbre* (custom) in the late eighteenth century, Bianca Premo also highlights indigenous litigation and legal culture as "not just a defense against modernity but also as constitutive of it." Premo, "Custom Today," 361. Her recent book looks at "ordinary" litigants and how their engagement with the courts came to shape and problematize what is traditionally known as the Enlightenment. Premo, *The Enlightenment on Trial*. Here I push the general process back to the sixteenth century.

15. Similar perspectives and calls for a renewed history of Indians and the Atlantic are presented in Bushnell, "Indigenous America"; Cañizares-Esguerra and Breen, "Hybrid Atlantics," 602; Matthew, "Facing East"; Richter and Thompson, "Severed Connections"; Terraciano, "Voices."

16. The Spanish Habsburgs moved their court temporarily to Valladolid between 1601 and 1606. After the return to Madrid, the city gradually became the undisputed center. On the administration of the monarchy: Brown and Elliott, *A Palace*, 36–38; Kamen, *Philip of Spain*, 178–182; Maqueda Abreu, *La monarquía*, 18–20; Río Barredo, *Madrid, Urbs Regia*, 91–92, 146–151.

17. I have borrowed and slightly modified John Elliott's elegant phrase. Elliott, "The Court," 144–145. On the origins of the conciliar order and its establishment under Charles V: Brendecke, *Imperios*, 126–130; Fernández Albaladejo, *Fragmentos*, 88–100. On the jurisdiction and acvitivities of the Council of the Indies: Encinas, *Cedulario indiano*, 1: 2–15; *Recopilación*, bk. 2, tit. 2 & tit. 3; Schäfer, *El Consejo Real*, 138–141, 184–185. On the mechanisms and channels of communication between Council and vassals: Ross, "Legal Communications," 112; Schäfer, *El consejo real*. On the articulating role of royal and viceregal courts in the second half of the sixteenth century: Maqueda Abreu, *La monarquía*, 20–21; Martínez Millán, "La articulación"; Yun Casalilla, "Introducción."

18. Baber, "Law, Land, and Legal Rhetoric"; Graubart, "Competing Spanish and Indigenous Jurisdictions"; Yannakakis, "Beyond Jurisdictions," 1075 [quote].

19. Cutter, *The Legal Culture*; Espinosa, *El Inca barroco*, 155; Herzog, *Upholding Justice*, 9; Owens, *"By My Absolute Royal Authority"*; Owensby, *Empire*, 32–36. This basic notion of redistributive justice goes back to the thirteenth-century *Siete partidas*, pt. 3, tit. 1, law 3.

20. Earlier works on the subject of Spanish emigrants to the New World overlooked the existence of these indigenous travelers, claiming that they lacked the resources or could not obtain the licenses needed to voyage from the Indies to Spain. Martínez, *Pasajeros de Indias*, 191. Pioneering works about indigenous voyagers from the Andes were overwhelmingly devoted to members of prominent Inca lineages of the early colonial era. Travelers appear as exceptional, picaresque, even picturesque characters. Their deeds in Spain, detached from their broader context, seem like isolated responses to colonial excesses or elite endeavors determined by powerful outside forces, frivolous motivations, or mere chance. See Lohmann, "El señorío," 431–444; Miró Quesada Sosa, *El Inca*; Temple, "Los Bustamante Carlos Inca"; Temple, "Azarosa existencia"; Vargas Ugarte, *Historia (siglo XVII)*, 450–451.

21. Altman, *Emigrants*, 260–261, 275–284. See also Altman, *Transatlantic Ties*. More recent works show "America in Spain" in multiple other ways: Pescador, *The New World*; Van Deusen, *Global indios*; Mangan, *Transatlantic Obligations*.

22. *hecha una Sevilla*. Glave, "La provincia," 476. On how Seville became "almost an extension of the Indies" in the mid-1500s: Mangan, *Transatlantic Obligations*, 99. On native Andeans's "discovery" of Europe and the larger world: Lorandi, *La monarquía*, 18–19.

23. The rarity of nonenslaved indigenous female travelers after the New Laws of 1542 is connected, I suspect, to prevalent ideas about honor, decency, and propriety, as well as to general royal prohibitions against single women traveling from Spain to the Indies, unless they were accompanied by their husbands, sons, and other relatives. For example: "Real cédula para que no den licencia a mujeres solteras para que pasen a Indias." Madrid, February 8, 1575. AGI, Indiferente, 1956, l. 1, 256r. On the idea of journeying "with honor": Mangan, *Transatlantic Obligations*, 112–119.

24. For recent estimates of the number of primarily enslaved Indians who reached Spain immediately after the conquest and up to the New Laws of 1542: Van Deusen, *Global indios*, 207, n. 203; Mira Caballos, *Indios y mestizos*, 107–121. Another scholar has identified 137 *mestizos* or "sons [or children] of an Indian woman" (*hijos de india*) — 25 women and 112 men in total — traveling to Spain from Peru between 1552 and 1585. Alaperrine-Bouyer,

"Cruzar el océano," 9. My own sample includes about a hundred free travelers from the district of the *Audiencia de Lima* to Spain, although fragmentary and anecdotical information points to a larger number. Puente Luna, "Into the Heart," Appendix 1.

25. This situation contrasts with the sample of *mestizo* travelers studied by Alaperrine-Bouyer. According to her, *mestizos* and *hijos de india* from Peru requested these licenses from viceroys and governors during the second half of the sixteenth century, almost always successfully. Travelers had to present the license before the House of Trade in Seville if they wanted to return. If one could not be produced, a new license had to be requested from the Council of the Indies in Madrid. Alaperrine-Bouyer, "Cruzar el océano," 10–12. On the onerous process of obtaining a license: Mangan, *Transatlantic Obligations*, 107–108.

26. For example: Gil-Bermejo García, "Indígenas americanos"; Mira Caballos, "Indios americanos"; Van Deusen, *Global indios*.

27. Burns, "Unfixing Race." On the idea that ethnic identities are constructed "through complex processes of relationality and representation": Wade, *Race and Ethnicity*, 81–82. Africanists and scholars of the African diaspora and the Atlantic slave trade have made significant contributions in this regard. For example: Hawthorne, *From Africa to Brazil*; Miller, "Retention, Reinvention"; Sweet, *Domingos Álvares*; Wheat, *Atlantic Africa*; and the essays included in Bryant, O'Toole, and Vinson, *Africans to Spanish America*.

28. Brubaker and Cooper, "Beyond 'Identity,'" 14–17 (external categorization); Hall, "Introduction," 2–3; Jenkins, "Rethinking Ethnicity," 218 (practical accomplishments); Sweet, "Mistaken Identities?," 283.

29. For an overview of colonial *caciques* and the "elite stratum" within the early *República de Indios*: Garrett, *Shadows*, 34–41. Also useful are the different essays included in Cahill and Tovías, *Elites indígenas*. For a reassessment of the literature: Garrett, "Indigenous Elites." Garrett problematizes the term *cacique* as a catchall title referring to a wide array of offices and individuals with very different status: "while the social space of the Indian elite remained largely unchanged for almost two centuries, the determination of who occupied that space, and possessed its privileges, was constantly challenged and changed." Garrett, *Shadows*, 36, 43–44 (quote).

30. On the complexities of "seeing" *indios* in Spain and the New World at that time: Van Deusen, *Global indios*; Van Deusen, "Seeing Indios," 207–208, 231–232; Rappaport, *The Disappearing Mestizo*, 181–183; Rappaport, "'Asi lo paresçe,'" 629–631. For a sample of labels and descriptors: Forbes, *Africans*. In 2010, I offered some preliminary conclusions: Puente Luna, "Into the Heart," esp. ch. 3. The formal procedure sometimes amounted to "corroborating" the passenger's individual "Indian" identity: Rappaport, *The Disappearing Mestizo*, 193. On the imposition of a *mestizo* identity on some travelers by the House of Trade: Alaperrine-Bouyer, "Cruzar el océano," 16–17.

31. Tavárez, "Legally Indian," 96. For the Peruvian context: Burns, "Unfixing Race"; Cahill, "Colour by Numbers"; Silverblatt, *Modern Inquisitions*, 187–213. The royal license of Andrés de Ortega classified him as "Indian" (*yndio*). The judges of the House granted him the license "without any formal inquest because it is evident that he is Indian" (*sin que de ynformaçion atento que consto ser yndio*). "Información y licencia: Andrés de Ortega," May 30, 1600, AGI, Contratración, 5262a, n. 76.

32. Fisher and O'Hara, "Introduction," 20–22; Van Deusen, "Seeing Indios." As James Sweet observes "there are moments in every life when it is easier to adapt to social expectations of identity than it is to adhere to 'realities.'" Sweet, "Mistaken Identities?," 302. Tamar Herzog makes a similar case for the Spaniards: classification was "often functional rather than logical, pragmatic rather than theoretically sound." Herzog, "Can You Tell," 149.

33. Laclau, *New Reflections*, 33. See also Hall, "Introduction," 4–5; Herzog, "Can You Tell"; Herzog, "The Appropriation."

34. Estenssoro, *Del paganismo*; Premo, *Children of the Father King*, 33–34.

35. A 1598 royal decree granted the *cacique* Don Diego de Figueroa Cajamarca 275 pesos to return to Quito. A 1580 decree had characterized him as a *vecino* of that city and a leader and descendant of the Indian *mitimaes* (colonists) settled in the area by the Inca. The king granted Don Diego a rent of six hundred pesos in *indios vacos* (lit., "vacant Indians"), an award that carried with it the duties of a *vecino encomendero*. "Real cédula al virrey de Perú," Madrid, December 22, 1580, AGI, Quito, 211, l. 2, 61v–62r; "200 ducados para Don Diego," Madrid, November 26, 1598, AGI, Indiferente, 427, l. 31, 61r. For the status of *vecino* and the implications of *vecindad*, which carried with it a series of privileges and responsibilities within a particular Spanish or Spanish American community: Domínguez Compañy, "La condición de vecino"; Herzog, *Defining Nations*, 43–59, 66.

36. Black, *The Limits*, 130–131, 202 (legal positions); O'Toole, *Bound Lives*, 2 (legal locations).

37. For example: Graubart, *With Our Labor*; Mangan, *Trading Roles*; Murillo, Lentz, and Ochoa, *City Indians*; Poloni-Simard, *El mosaico*.

38. Ángel Rama famously defined "the Lettered City" as the specialized social group of *letrados* who enjoyed dominion over "the universe of signs [in the Americas], organized in the service of the monarchies beyond the sea." For Rama, the *letrados* who clustered in important urban centers and viceregal capitals were essential for facilitating "the concentration and hierarchical differentiation of power" in the colonial world. Rama, *The Lettered City*, 16–17.

39. Charles, *Allies*; Dueñas, *Indians*; McDonough, *The Learned Ones*, 3–33; Ramos and Yannakakis, *Indigenous Intellectuals*; Rappaport and Cummins, *Beyond the Lettered City*.

40. Brendecke, *Imperios*; Yannakakis, *The Art*. For discussions of the "imperial turn" in the study of colonial legal processes: Benton, *Law*; Benton, *A Search*; Benton, "Introduction"; Duve, "European Legal History"; Smolenski and Humphrey, *New World Orders*. The power of "peripheries" to shape early modern American empires is discussed in Bushnell and Greene, "Peripheries." For the Spanish monarchy: Yun Casalilla, *Las redes*.

41. Yannakakis, "Beyond Jurisdictions," 1074–1075. I am also building on Renzo Honores's application of the notion of "legal polyphony"—the many-voiced creation of colonial law—to the relationship between colonial litigants, legal professionals, and the ministers of the *real audiencia* of Lima. Honores, *Legal Polyphony*; Honores, *Colonial Legal Polyphony*. I thank Professor Honores for sharing his unpublished work with me.

42. Owens, *"By My Absolute Royal Authority,"* 1, 46–48, 233, 245. See also Dios, *Gracia*; Fernández Albaladejo, *Fragmentos*, 72–85; Pérez Fernández-Turégano, "La administración," 84–86. The landmark work is Kagan, *Lawsuits*. On the rise of *pleitos* about noble

status: Crawford, *The Fight*. Regarding the "legal revolution" in Spain: Amelang, "Barristers and Judges"; Corteguera, *For the Common Good*. Adrián Masters's dissertation in progress shows the direct influence that petitioners and petitions had over the issuing of decrees and other royal orders emanating from Madrid. Masters, "The Lettered Marketplace."

43. The two foundational studies on the impact of law courts and litigation on colonial Andean societies, which highlighted how these engagements aided in the construction of colonial hegemony, are Spalding, *Huarochirí*; Stern, *Peru's Indian Peoples*. See also Honores, "Litigiosidad indígena."

44. Recent assessments of the now significant literature on the subject include Cunill, "La negociación"; Ruiz Medrano, "The Indigenous Population"; Yannakakis, "Indigenous People," 932.

45. Dedieu, "Procesos." For enslaved Indians' engagements with the *Casa de la Contratación* in Seville: Van Deusen, "Seeing Indios"; Van Deusen, *Global indios*. For similar negotiating strategies among artisans in Barcelona: Corteguera, *For the Common Good*. The legal strategies of subjects of African descent, including slaves, free men and women, and militia men, are discussed in Díaz, *The Virgin*; Jouve, *Esclavos*; McKinley, "Fractional Freedoms"; O'Toole, *Bound Lives*; Vinson, *Bearing Arms*. Similar strategies deployed by *mestizos* are analyzed in Duve, "El concilio"; Ruan, "Andean Activism." For women and the intersection of gender ideologies and the law: Black, *The Limits*; Gauderman, *Women's Lives*; Graubart, *With Our Labor*, ch. 3; Premo, "Felipa's Braid."

46. Belmessous, *Native Claims*; Cañizares-Esguerra, "La memoria," 183–185. On the theoretical implications of approaching the construction of early modern states "from below": Blockmans, Holenstein, and Mathieu, *Empowering Interactions*. On colonial state-building in the Andes: Spalding, "Notes on the Formation."

47. Owensby, *Empire*, 24–25; Silverblatt, *Modern Inquisitions*, 195. Jovita Baber draws some of these conclusions from her study of Tlaxcala: Baber, "Empire," 20. Important examples of the growing literature on customary laws and imperial legal regimes include Herzog, "Colonial Law"; Pease, "¿Por qué los andinos ...?"; Yannakakis, *The Art*; Yannakakis, "Costumbre." See also Belmessous, *Native Claims*; Ruiz Medrano and Kellogg, *Negotiation*.

48. Brickhouse, *The Unsettlement*. On Atlantic networks and the circulation of knowledge: Games, *The Web*; Sweet, *Domingos Álvares*. Colonial Andean historiography has made significant advances in this direction. Some of these local, regional, and metropolitan networks are discussed in Dueñas, *Indians*, 31, 37, 59, 65.

49. I have discussed the role of native language interpreters as power brokers: Puente Luna, "The Many Tongues." Ari Zighelboim and David Cahill have shown how Don Juan de Bustamante Carlos Inca, while petitioning at the royal court in the eighteenth century, represented the interests of many social groups before the highest authorities of the monarchy. News of the *mercedes* granted to Bustamante, of Inca and Spanish descent, reached Cuzco, Lima, Río de la Plata, Nueva Granada, and Mexico. Cahill, "Becoming Inca"; Zighelboim, "Un inca."

50. Sweet, "The Quiet Violence," 212. Recent discussions on ethnogenesis, power, and the politics of identity-making include Cohen, "Was there an Amerindian Atlantic?," 408;

Griffin, "A Plea," 238; Hämäläinen, "Lost in Transitions"; Sidbury and Cañizares-Esguerra, "Mapping Ethnogenesis"; Sidbury and Cañizares-Esguerra, "On the Genesis," 242–244. Caroline Cunill and Bartolomé Yun also emphasize the need to bring the research of power back into the study of Atlantic networks. Yun Casalilla, "Introducción," 29; Cunill, "La negociación," 396.

51. Glave, "The 'Republic of Indians' in Revolt," 502.

52. Estenssoro, "Construyendo la memoria," 163. Works that show how, by the end of the eighteenth century, hereditary lords were no longer the embodiment of indigenous collective identities, their traditional role as heads of the lineage, intermediaries with the supernatural, and administrators of the community's resources having greatly diminished, include: Abercrombie, *Pathways*; O'Phelan, *Kurakas*; Penry, "Transformations"; Rasnake, *Domination*; Serulnikov, *Subverting Colonial Authority*; Spalding, *De indio*; Thomson, *We Alone*.

53. Garrett, *Shadows*, 102 (quote); Serulnikov, *Revolution*, 40–41. The Inca nobility of Cuzco shared a corporate identity, their "Incanness" being constantly performed and patrolled through a series of institutions (the *cabildo de los veinticuatro electores*, responsible for electing the Inca royal standard-bearer for the procession of Santiago) and public ceremonies (Corpus Christi). Inca descendants controlled the main *cacicazgos* and towns of the region. Particularly in the city, exclusive membership in this corporation hinged on proof of direct descent from the pre-Hispanic Inca rulers and royal "houses," usually in the form of patents of nobility or reputation. Throughout the seventeenth and eighteenth centuries, urban Inca nobles grew distinct from other *cacique* elites who ruled over the native populations of Peru. Amado Gonzales, "El alférez"; Amado Gonzales, "El Cabildo"; Cahill, "Popular Religion"; Cahill, "The Virgin"; Dean, *Inka Bodies*, 99–109; Garrett, *Shadows*, 52–57, 76.

54. Garrett, *Shadows*, 15, 46, 60, 83; Cahill, "First among Incas"; Cahill, "A Liminal Nobility." After the Spanish Conquest, "The Incas were reworked into a regional noble caste that dominated the Indian pueblos in the area of the Inca heartland, but among whom there was no clear hierarchy or authority binding these communities into a larger, recognized polity." Garrett, *Shadows*, 30. There were, of course, hundreds of colonial Incas of lesser or more informal status, such as descendants of nonroyal Inca lineages and members of the provincial elite, living in provincial towns as well as cities such as Quito and Lima.

55. Graubart, *With Our Labor*, 92–96.

56. "Expediente de la comunidad de Huasicancha," Lima, September 3, 1937, ARJ, PR, Documentos Sueltos, s/c. On similar delegations visiting the presidential palace: Ragas, "Indios en palacio." On delegates and other legal intermediaries in post-Independence Peru: Aguirre, "Tinterillos"; Deustua and Rénique, *Intelectuales*. On Huasicancha's land recuperation campaigns: Smith, *Livelihood*. On similar petitions of community's *apoderados* (attorneys) to the Bolivian president and senate: Abercrombie, *Pathways*, 306–308; Gotkowitz, *A Revolution*.

CHAPTER 2

1. A standard, somewhat problematic, but still useful narrative of the conquest era can be found in Hemming, *The Conquest*, esp. chs. 1–13. For the efforts of Incas and Spaniards to make sense out of these initial encounters: Lamana, *Domination*, ch. 5. On early Inca-Spanish families: Nowack, "Aquellas señoras"; Julien, "Francisca Pizarro." Recent interventions on the subject of early accomodations include Mangan, *Transatlantic Obligations*, esp. ch. 1; Vicuña Guengerich, "Capac Women."

2. Polo Ondegardo, the famous jurist and viceregal adviser, went to Peru in 1543 as an agent of Hernando Pizarro. For the Pizarros's network and access to the Castilian court: Lockhart, *The Men*, 264; Varón, *Francisco Pizarro*, 136–146; Varón and Jacobs, "Peruvian Wealth," 672–673. Powers of attorney granted by the Pizarros to their agents in Spain are included in Congress, *The Harkness Collection*. Despite a 1529 royal prohibition, there were *procuradores de causas* operating in Lima by the late 1530s. Honores, *Legal Polyphony*, ch. 4.

3. "Informaciones: Pablo Tupac Inca," Cuzco, 1540, AGI, Lima, 204, n. 11, 1r. See also Garrett, *Shadows*, ch. 1; Lamana, *Domination*, 160–165, 213–224. For the expeditions into the Collao region: Abercrombie, *Pathways*, 145–147. Paullu's *encomienda* grant, a royal *merced* consisting of the right to collect tribute from indigenous communities, can be found in "Ascendencia de Juan Carlos Inga," 1539–1626, BNE, MS, 20193, 11r–11v. Paullu and his close kin also received the support of ecclesiastic judge Luis de Morales and Licentiate Cristóbal Vaca de Castro, governor of Peru. Levillier, *Gobernantes*, 1: 72.

4. Early examples include "Don Carlos y don Francisco, hijos de Atabalipa. Sobre su sutentaçion," May 16, 1548, AGI, Lima, 566, l. 5, 275v–276r; "Memoria para el muy reverendo y magnífico señor fray Domingo," Lima, 1555, AGI, Lima, 204, n. 23. For the legal activism of the early colonial Inca nobility: Hemming, *The Conquest*, 258–259; Lamana, *Domination*, 218–224; Nowack, "Aquellas señoras," 26; Oberem, "La familia"; Quispe-Agnoli, *Nobles de papel*. On early indigenous litigation in the Andes: Poloni-Simard, "Los indios"; Spalding, *Huarochirí*; Stern, *Peru's Indian Peoples*. The Andes still lag behind New Spain. See Baber, "Native Litigiousness"; Cutter, Mallo, and Pacheco Fernández, "Indians as Litigants"; Kellogg, *Law and the Transformation*; Lira, "El indio"; Owensby, *Empire*; Ruiz Medrano and Kellogg, *Negotiation*; Yannakakis, *The Art*.

5. On the Uchu Incas, see the recent analysis of Quispe-Agnoli, *Nobles de papel*, as well as the previous study of Escobari de Querejazu, *Caciques, yanaconas y extravagantes*, ch. 4. The undated portrait of Tupac Inca Yupanqui, flanked by two of his descendants, as well as the accompanying illuminated family crest were probably commissioned in the early eighteenth century.

6. Recent approaches to early indigenous legal activism before the *audiencia* and the archbishopric of Lima include Charles, "'More *Ladino*'"; Charles, *Allies*; Charles, "Testimonios"; Honores, "Una aproximación"; Honores, "Litigación en la Audiencia Arzopispal"; Honores, "Una sociedad"; Mumford, "Litigation." For transatlantic litigation specifically: Mumford, "Aristocracy"; Dueñas, *Indians*; Puente Luna, "The Many Tongues." On late-colonial litigation: Dueñas, "Cabildos de naturales"; Premo, "Custom Today."

7. There were, of course, notable exceptions. Native Andean and *mestizo* litigants sometimes brought petitions directly to the American *audiencias* and the royal court in order to bypass royal officials. The number of litigants filing petitions directly seems to have increased over time. Dueñas, *Indians*. Moreover, the law expert–client relation often went beyond the initial petition. In that sense, legal writing was "delegated writing," but it also embodied a joint or "composite" agency. Premo, "Agents"; Burns, *Into the Archive*, 125–127.

8. Premo, "Before the Law," 288.

9. Brian Owensby makes a similar point for seventeenth-century Mexico: Owensby, *Empire*, 9.

10. Taylor, "Between Global Process," 162. Owensby notes that, through the legal system, indigenous commoners in New Spain "found greater if still limited opportunities to say 'no' to excessive demands by encomenderos, corregidores, and *principales*, in effect to negotiate the terms of their subjection." Owensby, *Empire*, 40.

11. In the legal terminology of the time, *cacique* usually referred to the title, whereas *gobernador* pertained to the duties associated with the office. Both did not always fall on the same individual. Upon the death of the previous holder of the title, *caciques principales* received the written title from provincial magistrates, later confirmed by the viceroy and the *audiencias*. If a minor, an interim governor was appointed to collect tribute, organize draft labor, and perform other tasks until the *cacique* reached the age of twenty-five. The recognition and appointment of *caciques* of lesser rank, usually called *principales, mandones, pachaca curacas*, and *caciques de tasa*, followed a less bureaucratic and more autonomous and customary procedure still poorly understood. Puente Luna, *Los curacas*, esp. ch. 3; Garrett, *Shadows*, 34–41.

12. Dueñas, *Indians*; Honores, "Litigiosidad indígena"; Honores, "La asistencia jurídica"; Mumford, "Litigation." These works build on previous studies about the *caciques'* adaptation to colonial rule, which included litigation in colonial courts: Murra, "Litigation"; Pease, *Curacas*; Saignes, "De la borrachera."

13. Different works show how litigation, inasmuch as it allowed for the privatization of collective resources, could unleash intracommunal processes of social differentiation and elite consolidation: Garrett, *Shadows*, chs. 4 & 5; O'Phelan, *Kurakas*; Penry, "Transformations"; Puente Luna, *Los curacas*; Ramírez, *The World*; Ramírez, "Rich Man"; Spalding, *De indio*; Spalding, *Huarochirí*; Stern, "The Social Significance"; Stern, *Peru's Indian Peoples*.

14. Salomon, "Guaman Poma's *Sapçi*"; Ramírez, "Land and Tenure"; Puente Luna, "Felipe Guaman Poma."

15. On the shift from the Inca labor-time system to the colonial quota-based tribute: Assadourian, "Los señores."

16. The situation was not necessarily different in Spain, where ultimate success in the courts "depended heavily on whether the claimant had the means to initiate litigation and the will to pursue the lawsuit to its full completion." Crawford, *The Fight*, 104.

17. There are certainly other possible scenarios for the early colonial Andes, which future studies can help to clarify. In some communities, an ever-increasing demand for collective resources to finance litigation, as well as mass migration and the mismanage-

ment of *sapci* funds by indigenous leaders, likely posed serious threats to the preservation of communal forms of social organization and reproduction, causing the fragmentation of ethnic polities into smaller—*pueblo*—units.

18. Tanck de Estrada, *Pueblos*, esp. chs. 1, 2, and 6. For the contributions of Oaxacan commoners to the community treasuries and legal funds: Yannakakis, *The Art*, 37, 120–121.

19. On Inca and Spanish reorganizations of the Jauja valley, which I have somewhat simplified: D'Altroy, *Provincial Power*; Pärssinen, *Tawantinsuyu*, 297–299; Puente Luna, *Los curacas*, ch. 3.

20. In Jauja at this time, "*repartimiento*" was, to a great degree, a synonym of "*encomienda*." In the latter part of the sixteenth century specific groups counted as part of smaller *repartimientos* were resettled in the towns of the three major divisions. Puente Luna, *Los curacas*, ch. 3.

21. "Información sobre los pleitos de Jauja," Concepción, 1570, AGI, Lima, 28A, 63Q. For a full transcription and an analysis of the context of the *Información*: Medelius and Puente Luna, "Curacas."

22. Spalding, *Huarochirí*, esp. ch. 1. Frank Salomon defines *ayllus* as "non-localized, predominantly patrilineal corporate descent groups." He notes that "the term parcialidad denotes the outer face of the corporation, especially its work as a segment of the community," adding further that "the double terminology reflects the institution's role as the hinge connecting kinship to political organization." Andean ayllus shared a series of characteristics, which Salomon synthesizes as follows: "(1) Ayllus are sibling corporations to each other; that is, they owe each other fraternal solidarity. (2) They stand in fixed order. (3) The rank order is one of precedence, not of dominion. (4) Ayllus have separate endowments but coordinated duties." Salomon, *The Cord Keepers*, 57, 59. For further analysis: Isbell, *To Defend*; Platt, "Mirrors."

23. Murra, "El control vertical," 59–115. For Jauja: Jiménez de la Espada, "Relaciones geográficas," 1: 90–95. I thank Jorge Cañizares-Esguerra for pointing out the connection between John Murra's classic model and the efforts displayed by the Huancas to control different ecological-legal niches.

24. Espinoza, "Los huancas"; Murra, "Las etno-categorías." For the apparent survival of some of these *khipus* until the beginning of the seventeenth century: Dávalos de Figueroa, *Primera parte*, 150.

25. The generic term for these specialists in Quechua is *khipucamayuq/quipucamayo* ("knot-maker" or "cord-keeper"). Some *caciques* served as *khipucamayuqs* and vice versa. For the use of *khipus* in legal forums: Brokaw, "La recepción"; Durston and Urioste, "Las peticiones"; Loza, "El *quipu*"; Loza, "El uso"; Platt, "'Without Deceit or Lies'"; Urton, "From Knots."

26. Brokaw, *A History*; Urton, *Signs*. The connection between *khipus* and *sapci* practice in Huarochirí (modern central Peru) has been most recently discussed in Salomon, "Guaman Poma's *Sapçi*."

27. Cuenca ordered northern communities pursuing their cases before the *audiencia* to send two delegates "at the cacique's expense, if the lawsuit is his, or at the community's, if it is brought in the name of the commons [*común*] as a whole." González de San Segundo,

"El doctor," 667. An earlier royal decree addressed to the authorities of Nueva Granada recommends that the Indians raise livestock "en comun o en particular." "Juntas de indios en pueblos formados," Valladolid, October 9, 1549, AGI, Indiferente, 532, l. 1, 28v.

28. The *caciques' hacienda privada* raises interesting questions about the origin of these assets, especially at a time when the boundaries between communal economies and the *caciques'* domestic economies were still ill defined or even indistinguishable. By the 1560s, legal mechanisms to claim and sell communal land were certainly available to *caciques*. Centering her analysis on northern Peru (coastal valleys and highlands), Susan Ramírez includes land within the realm of *sapci*, citing the 1566 testimony of a chief in the Chimú Valley who stated that, prior to that time, land was "a common thing and open to all and which no one could have nor acquire possession." Ramírez, "Land and Tenure." *Hacienda privada*, then, might be an indicator of the early privatization of communal resources. At some point, these *haciendas privadas*, though probably administered by the *caciques*, could have been communally controlled. In the case of the Apoalayas, the paramount lords of Ananguanca, royal grants of two hundred *yanaconas* (retainers), who were to provide domestic labor as well as tend to the lands and livestock assigned to the *caciques*, can be traced back to the 1540s. "Autos ... que contienen el fraude y engaño," 1776, BNP, MS, C2578, 51v.

29. "Francisco Guacrapaucar y Francisco Ticsi Cangaguala," 1600–1602, LIL, LAM-Peru, 10v. *Audiencia* judge Cristóbal Ramírez de Cartagena claimed that Toledo appointed the first Spanish administrators of communal cattle after he discovered "the communal assets of Jauja that the Indians had kept secret." Medelius, "El licenciado," n.p. [2751r].

30. "Información sobre los pleitos de Jauja," 3r–7v, 11r–15r. Some of these same midranking caciques also faced the Apoalayas in the courtrooms individually, funding their lawsuits from their family wealth.

31. It was Don Carlos's father, the old *cacique* Jerónimo Guacrapaucar, who showed the *khipus* of Luringuanca to Cieza in 1549. Medelius and Puente Luna, "Curacas," 63.

32. "Información sobre los pleitos de Jauja," 2v–3v, 7r–8v. The *ayllus* of Luringuanca also litigated among themselves for lands, houses, and other assets. For a sample case: Puente Luna and Solier Ochoa, "La huella."

33. On household and supra-household spheres of production in Central Andean peasant economies: Guillet, "Agrarian Ecology"; Mayer, *The Articulated Peasant*. For the use of key Andean notions of *chuta* or *trecho* for parceling collective tasks among *ayllus* and *ayllu* members: Salomon and Niño-Murcia, *The Lettered Mountain*, 141.

34. Ondegardo, "Notable daño," 289.

35. In the 1570s, the *caciques* and *chinukamana* (the Aymara equivalent of the *khipukamayoq*) of Sacaca, in Charcas, relied on this method to decode their tributary *khipus*, using these tokens to add up the contributions of each of the *parcialidades*. Assadourian, "String Registries"; Fossa, "Two Khipu"; Platt, "'Without Deceit or Lies'"; Urton, "From Knots." The communities of Lucanas followed the same procedure in a lawsuit against the local magistrate. Curatola Petrocchi and Puente Luna, "Contar concertando." For the Andes as a whole: Acosta, *Natural and Moral History*, 344; Vega, *Royal Commentaries*, 124.

36. "Residencia: Gabriel de Loarte," 1575, AGI, Justicia, 463, 239v–240r. Don Juan Hananpicho testified as much. See Andrés Chirinos's analysis of the contributions of

the Huanca lords to the Spaniards between 1532 and 1554, which demonstrates that each *repartimiento* supplied goods and tributaries to the invaders on the basis of variable ratios, though on a much larger scale. Chirinos, *Quipus*, 21–68. Based on his observations among the natives of Paria, in Charcas, Polo Ondegardo explained the decimal rationale behind this procedure: Ondegardo, "Notable daño," 290.

37. "Información sobre los pleitos de Jauja," 10r–11v.

38. During a famous lawsuit opposing the communities of Canta and Chaclla, witnesses declared that a local Spanish *encomendero* had tried to talk Don Francisco Marcapoma into swapping certain *coca* fields belonging to his people the Chacllas for two hundred llamas. The *cacique* initially refused to sell the fields, claiming that the lands belonged to the Chacllas and that "neither would his Indians permit it, because they are poor and have no *chacaras* [plots] of their own to sow, and that they would not consent to have the tracts sold but would demand them [from his heirs]." Rostworowski, *Conflicts*, 156. The *cacique* finally gave in, but, as he told the *encomendero*, the Chacllas filed a complaint to have the sale annulled.

39. Salomon, *The Cord Keepers*, 39, 44–47, 49; Salomon and Niño-Murcia, *The Lettered Mountain*, 141. Inter-*ayllu* responsibilities include annual communitywide canal cleanings, pasture-wall work, and construction of community halls. Available collections of "*khipu*-documents" make the relationship between *khipus* and the control of communal labor abundantly clear: Curatola Petrocchi and Puente Luna, *El quipu colonial*; Pärssinen and Kiviharju, *Textos andinos*.

40. Salomon, *The Cord Keepers*, 3–7, 16–21, 35–36, 168, 188.

41. For the multiple engagements of the people of Huarochirí with the courts: Espinoza, "Los señoríos de Yaucha"; Puente Luna and Honores, "Guardianes de la real justicia"; Rostworowski, *Conflicts*; Salomon, "Collquiri's Dam."

42. "Información sobre los pleitos de Jauja," 3v–5r, 9r–9v. According to Don Antonio Çuniguacra, head of a thousand households in Luringuanca, part of the money was spent on lawyers, procurators, and scribes. In funding their own *pleitos*, the *ayllus* of Atunjauja followed a similar procedure. On Don Felipe Guacrapaucar's voyage: Espinoza, "Los huancas"; Mumford, "Aristocracy."

43. "Armas para Don Felipe Guacrapaucar," Barcelona, March 18, 1564, AGI, Lima, 569, L. 11, 152r. Don Felipe's descendants were still in possession of these plots, located near Ataura and "El Mojón," in the late eighteenth century. Puente Luna and Solier Ochoa, "La huella." Don Felipe's coat of arms is now the emblem of the city of Huancayo.

44. During the trial of Don Felipe, his political enemies claimed that the reason behind this journey and other legal actions was to extort a "a large amount of gold pesos and livestock" from communal endowments. Don Felipe countered these accusations, claiming that this animosity stemmed from his defense of communal herds. It seems that Don Felipe gave the money to a merchant in Seville, but in spite of Felipe's efforts to get the money back, which included endorsing a power of attorney to collect the debt in Spain, it was never returned. "Residencia: Gabriel de Loarte," 238r.

45. Ibid., 237v–240r. The modern *khipus* of Tupicocha figure prominently in similar

audit procedures conducted during annual civic meetings (*huayronas*). Salomon, *The Cord Keepers*, 138, 186, 197-199; Salomon, "Guaman Poma's *Sapçi*," 360-363.

46. "Información sobre los pleitos de Jauja," 2v. The *caciques* and cord keepers who testified at the subsequent trial against Bartolomé Ruiz, Don Felipe Guacrapaucar's associate, also relied on an interpreter. "Residencia: Gabriel de Loarte," 239v-240r.

47. It was likely the Central Quechua dialect spoken in the valley, or perhaps a standardized Inca or colonial variety. Cerrón-Palomino, *Lengua*; Durston, "Standard Colonial Quechua."

48. "Residencia: Gabriel de Loarte," 240v.

49. The Council of the Indies' marginal notes to Lope García de Castro's 1565 ordinances for the good government of the kingdom state that Indians who have children and wives are called "rich," while those with no kin are considered "poor." García de Castro, "Prevenciones," 125. In the late 1560s, Francisco Falcón, a prominent lawyer with a large indigenous clientele, explained this same concept to his Spanish audience in similar terms. Falcón, "Representación," 470.

50. Guaman Poma, *Nueva corónica*, 977.

51. Murra, "Waman Puma," xv; Salomon, "Guaman Poma's *Sapçi*," 353-354.

52. Salomon, "Guaman Poma's *Sapçi*," 356. According to the chronicler Juan de Santa Cruz Pachacuti, who wrote his *Relación* around the same time as Guaman Poma prepared the *Nueva corónica*, Tupac Inca Yupanqui had decreed that each parcialidad had "comunities and sapssi" (*comunidades y sapssi*) for the welfare of the poor. Pachacuti, "Relación," 232.

53. *depocito de la comunidad y sapci*. Guaman Poma, *Nueva corónica*, 822. For similar community (*sapci*) storehouses in colonial Huarochirí, Taylor, *Ritos y tradiciones*, 298.

54. Salomon develops these ideas in a series of important works on the connection between ethnographic *khipus* and civic and ceremonial spaces (which he calls "collca/sapci complexes"). He convincingly argues that these civic-religious infrastructures and spaces came into being in the 1570s, precisely the "ethnographic present" of this chapter. Salomon, *The Cord Keepers*, 140-141; Salomon, "*Collca y Sapçi*"; Salomon, "Los khipus de Rapaz"; Salomon et al., "Khipu from Colony"; Salomon, "Guaman Poma's *Sapçi*," 358. For previous treatments of *sapci* in connection with community reserves: Spalding, *Huarochirí*, 40, 131.

55. Guaman Poma, *Nueva corónica*, 1153.

56. For a comprehensive list of resources typically stored in these deposits: ibid., 247.

57. Ibid., 251, 1159. Further references to the *sapci chacara*, which George Urioste translates as "community fields for planting" (*sementera de comunidad*), can be found in ibid., 911. Diego González Holguín glosses *sapsichacra* as "that which belongs to the community" (*la de la comunidad*). González Holguín, *Vocabulario*, 323. For a series of pioneering articles on *sapci* lands: Murra, "Derechos a las tierras"; Murra, "Una vision indigena"; Murra, "Waman Puma." For a recent reassessment of *sapci* and land: Ramírez, "Land and Tenure."

58. Diego González Holguín's contemporary vocabulary (1608) defines *sapci* as "that which is common to all" (*cosa común de todos*) and "communal work[;] the work of the

community" (*Lauor comun de todos[;] obra de comunidad*). González Holguín, *Vocabulario*, 323, 333. He also includes the following entry: "sapsi ymampas o caquenpas: the goods [or assets], that which belongs to the Community" (*sapsi ymampas o caquenpas: Los bienes o lo que es de comunidad*). It is important to note that González Holguín's work is about the Southern Quechua dialect and not necessarily the Central Quechua dialect spoken in the Jauja valley. Juan de Matienzo also writes about *sapci* in similar terms. Matienzo, *Gobierno del Perú*, 61. For the central contributions of women of different age groups, elders, and orphans to the "community and sapci" (*comonidad y sapci*): Guaman Poma, *Nueva coró-nica*, 449, 910, 917; Rowe, "The Age-Grades."

59. Guaman Poma, *Nueva corónica*, 884, 910. See also one of Garcilaso's laws of the Incas, which he claimed were compiled by Father Blas Valera from ancient *khipu* records: "The law and favor of the so-called poor required that the blind, dumb, lame, and para-lyzed, the aged and infirm, chronic invalids, and others who were unable to till the soil and feed and clothe themselves by their own labors should be maintained from the public stores." Vega, *Royal Commentaries*, 263.

60. "Residencia: Diego de Escobar," 1644, BNP, MS, B1482, 305r–310v.

61. In 1613, the three *repartimientos* of Jauja were collecting funds from the *Caja General de Censos* in Lima to pay for "the sick and the dead whose quotas are not paid by the tribu-taries." "Testimonio de los 500 pesos que Don Lope de Torres pagó a Don Cristóbal Po-maricra," 1613, AGN, CGC, l. 4, d. 21. In 1666, the *cacique principal* Don Carlos Apoalaya, a direct descendant of the namesake who had testified before Toledo's officials in 1570, gave power of attorney to collect 4,752 pesos from the same Caja "on behalf of the *yndios pobres* of the *repartimiento*." The funds originated in a sixteenth-century endowment "for the rescue of the poor tributary Indians." "Poder. Pedro de Garay a Francisco de Jauregui," February 13, 1666, ARJ, PN, 9 (Beltrán), 597r–597v.

62. Guaman Poma, *Nueva corónica*, 555, 977.

63. Viceroy Toledo wrote on the "institutionalized generosity" expected from *caciques* in this context: "si el [pleito] que traían era del común de los indios, les echaba el cacique derramas en mucha cantidad con color de que era para su bien, que él gastaba y consumía en borracheras, presentes e impertinencias." Toledo, "Memorial que Don Francisco de Toledo dio al Rey," 140. Note that Toledo is referring specifically to communal lawsuits.

64. Don Felipe, moreover, had told his brother Don Carlos, "don't demand more trib-ute from the poor Indians than that which they are already obliged to pay, because then they will sue us [the *caciques*]." "Residencia: Gabriel de Loarte," 268v, 283v. Guacrapaucar's supporters attributed his downfall to the fact that he "favors only the poor of the commu-nity, with [the help of] decrees granted by the *Audiencia de Lima*, thus preventing Don Carlos [his brother and *cacique principal* of Luringuanca] from demanding more tribute from the poor Indians than they are obligated to pay." Ibid., 268r.

65. In 1644, the native authorities of Luringuanca listed their "community assets" (*bienes de comunidades*) as "some plots [*chacaras*] and *sabsis* that are worked by the com-munity to pay their tribute in kind." "Residencia: Diego de Escobar," 220v–221r. The use of *sapci* in connection with community assets and deposits is also documented for Caja-

tambo, in the north-central Andes. Duviols, *Procesos*, 485, 491. I thank Susan Ramírez for bringing these references to my attention.

66. In 1657, the *caciques* of Luringuanca lent 10,000 pesos to a Spanish resident of Huamanga. The notary who authorized the transaction pointed out that the funds belonged to "the community of each of the towns of the repartimiento." BNP, AAC, Z1010 [1651], 140r–141v.

67. "Rodrigo de Acosta contra el administrador general," 1626, AGN, CGC, l. 10, d. 4, 14r–14v. The *Caja General de Censos*, not to be confused with the *cajas de comunidad* (communal lockboxes), was a significant fund fed by the communities' tribute remainder and other revenue, under the general supervision of defenders-general and other bucreaucrats in Lima, Cuzco, and other colonial cities. Over the course of the seventeenth century, legal restrictions and endemic corruption made access to these moneys much harder for Andean leaders. Escobedo Mansilla, "Bienes y cajas de comunidad"; Vásquez, "El endeudamiento."

68. Benito, *Libro de visitas*, 255. For the restitutions made by several *encomenderos*: Espinoza, "Los huancas," 393–395; Guaman Poma, *Nueva corónica*, 573; Lohmann, "La restitución." For similar *encomendero* restitutions and the endowment of community herds in Charcas: Abercrombie, *Pathways*, 242. For an estimate of the value of Luringuanca's communal assets in Huamanga: "Venta que hace la comunidad de . . . Lurin Huancas de las tierras de Viñaca y Conoc," 1720, BNP, AAC, Z1010.

69. In 1590, the *caciques* of Atunjauja declared that they supplemented tribute payments in cash with the sale of maize and wheat obtained from "a smallholding owned by the community." This *chacra* was farmed "at everyone's expense." "Residencia: Martín de Mendoza," Jauja, 1591, AGN, JR, l. 8, c. 21, 28r, 32r. For the annual tribute paid by the Luringuancas: Vázquez de Espinosa, *Compendio*, 457.

70. "Información sobre los pleitos de Jauja," 2r, 12r–15r.

71. "Arancel de los mantenimientos," 1569, MNAAH, AH-Ms., 1; Medelius and Puente Luna, "Curacas," 48.

72. Around the same time, Doña Ana Azarpay Coya, a granddaughter of Atahualpa living in Cuzco, claimed to have spent more than 3,000 pesos in securing a land grant from the viceroy. Francisco Sierra de Leguízamo, son of a veteran conquistador who had settled in Cuzco, sought the king's favor at the royal court on two occasions, at an alleged cost of 16,000 pesos. At the close of the seventeenth century, Doña Ana María Fernández Coronel, a Lima resident and, like Doña Ana Azarpay, a descendant of the former Inca rulers, authorized her agents to contract debts of up to 2,000 pesos for representing her at the Habsburg court. "Poder. Ana María Fernández Coronel Coya a Juan de Elisondo," Lima, September 18, 1696, AGN, PN, 1883 (Torre), 27v–28r; Oberem, *Notas*, 228.

73. "Residencia: Gabriel de Loarte," 239v–240r. A clear example comes from a late-eighteenth-century lawsuit brought by the community of Santo Domingo el Real in Chincha against the local priest. Each parish contributed 12 pesos to pay for copies of ecclesiastic tariffs (*aranceles*), to be sent by courier from Lima to Chincha. Sala i Vila, "Gobierno colonial," 151. For similar collections in Oaxaca: Yannakakis, *The Art*, 45, 120–121.

74. "Residencia: Diego de Escobar," 241r–241v. In 1646, the *repartimientos* empowered

a lawyer and former magistrate to request exemption, in Spain, from *mita* duty at the Huancavelica mercury mines. "Gaspar de Escalona Aguero por los Indios de Xauxa," Madrid, January 27, 1647, AGI, Lima, 125. They made similar efforts in the next decade.

75. At the turn of the eighteenth century, the lords and commoners (*prinsipales y comun*) of the town of Abancay, near Cuzco, complained before a land inspector that they were too poor to send a delegation to obtain copies of their original land titles in Lima. As a result, important portions of their community lands were being usurped. "Visitas y composiciones del Marqués de Valdelirios," Cuzco, 1711–1714, AGN, TP, l. 24, c. 454, 309r.

76. For indigenous complaints about the excessive cost of going to court during the eighteenth century: Dueñas, "The Lima Indian *Letrados*," 171. On a *cacique* of the Cuzco region who was engaged in four different communal lawsuits, spending 856 pesos in just two years: Garrett, *Shadows*, 171. For sixteenth-century Yucatán: Cunill, *Los defensores*, 219–222.

77. Juan Vélez, a *mestizo* interpreter for and interim *protector* (public defender) of the Indians, who, for all intents and purposes, served as an informal attorney for the Huancas before the *audiencia*, claimed to have received lands and "young indigenous servants" (*yndios muchachos de seruiçio*) from the *caciques* of the valley, probably in payment for his services. "Méritos y servicios: Juan Vélez," 1615, AGI, Lima, 145.

78. In 1605, Don Pedro Carrillo de Soto Inga agreed to pay Leandro de la Reinaga Salazar, registered lawyer of the *audiencia*, a yearly salary of 60 pesos to represent him before the court. "Salario. Pedro de Mora a Leandro de la Reinaga," Lima, July 7, 1605, AGN, PN, 47 (Aguilar), 798v–799v.

79. Guaman Poma, *Nueva corónica*, 526; Holguín, *Poder*, 153. In 1585, the interpreter-general for the *audiencia* noted that, because of these fees, native litigants ended up spending "more than a Spaniard." "Probanza: Baltasar de la Cruz Azpeitia," 1585, AGI, Lima, 127, 16v–17r. For similar legal fees levied in the *audiencias* of Quito and Mexico City: Bonnett, *Los protectores*; Borah, *Justice*.

80. Herzog, *Upholding Justice*, 153–159. For the presentation of gifts and favors to chancery officials and other magistrates in Spain: Crawford, *The Fight*, 181–182. For other examples of bribes and gifts given by *caciques* and communities: Alaperrine-Bouyer, *La educación*; Monsalve, "Curacas pleitistas."

81. "Memorial. Juan de Zugasti al Consejo," n.d., AGI, Lima, 538. In 1610, Doña Ana María de Loyola Coya donated a gift or bonus (*aguinaldo*) of 2,000 silver ducats to her steward in Spain, apparently an influential man, for expediting her cause before the Council. In March 1611, when the councilors finally reached a favorable verdict, she distributed 1,300 *reales* in gifts among lesser officials. Lohmann, "El señorío," 411–413.

82. "Méritos y servicios: Juan Vélez," n.p.

83. Evidently, holding the *cacique* status, at least on paper, was not incompatible with occupying municipal posts. "Doña Inés de Ribera contra Don Hernando Viça Alaya," Lima, 1579, AGN, DIE, l. 19, c. 93-a. For other examples: Puente Luna, "Felipe Guaman Poma"; Puente Luna and Honores, "Guardianes de la real justicia."

84. Abercrombie, *Pathways*, 242; Díaz Rementería, "El patrimonio." For the earliest projects of establishing community treasuries (*cajas del común*) in the Andes, which date

back to a letter of the Marquis of Cañete to the king written in 1556: Escobedo Mansilla, "Bienes y cajas de comunidad," 468.

85. Abercrombie, *Pathways*, 239. See also Graubart, "Learning from the *Qadi*."

86. Salomon, "Guaman Poma's *Sapçi*," 356. In early modern Castile, municipalities managed their public assets (farmland, forests, water sources, and pasture) independently, through periodic town meetings and the decisions of annually elected judges and councils. Municipal property fell under two distinct juridical categories: *propios*, or property owned by the municipality as a juridical entity, and the commons, public property set aside for the free use of the residents. Nader, *Liberty*, 8–18; Vassberg, *Land and Society*, esp. ch. 2. A few years before Toledo arrived in Peru, licentiate Francisco Falcón, writing on behalf of "the natives of Peru" and noting these parallels, drew a clever comparison between Castilian and native "commons." Falcón, "Representación," 455–459.

87. Puente Luna, "*En lengua de indios*," 78–79.

88. Mumford, *Vertical Empire*, 96–98; Puente Luna, "Felipe Guaman Poma"; Salomon, *The Cord Keepers*, 140–142; Salomon, "*Collca y Sapçi*"; Salomon, "Los khipus de Rapaz." For Toledo's regulations: *Recopilación*, bk. 6, tit. 4, laws 2, 9, 10, and 13; Sarabia Viejo, *Francisco de Toledo*, 1: 1–39, 65–68; 32: 39–46, 59–62, 73–81, 217–266, 409–449. The establishment of community strongboxes and storehouses in Jauja date back to the mid-1560s. Matienzo, *Gobierno del Perú*, 71–75; "Instruçion para el capitán Juan de la Reynaga," 1565, BNE, MS., 1032, esp. instrucciones xxxi, xxxii.

89. With an ethnographic eye, Guaman Poma detects the connection between the steward (*camayoc*), the community deposits (*collca*) and the traditional law of *sapci*, calling him *collca camayoc, común y sapci camayoc*. Guaman Poma, *Nueva corónica*, 193, 284.

90. In 1573, the king ordered Toledo to remove one Gaspar Enríquez de Montalvo, his *criado*, from the office of trustee (*depositario*) of the *bienes de la comunidad* of the Jauja Valley, probably at the request of the indigenous authorities. Encinas, *Cedulario indiano*, 4: 329. In 1575, a Spaniard, Antonio Bello Gayoso, had replaced one Juan de Bardales as steward of communal funds. A few years later, the communities of Jauja offered to contribute 20,000 pesos to the Crown to have them removed. "Méritos y servicios: Juan Vélez," n.p.; Sarabia Viejo, *Francisco de Toledo*, 2: 59–62.

91. Puente Luna, "*En lengua de indios*," 78–79.

92. Besides biannual tributary quotas per se, the money stored in the tribute strongbox covered ordinary expenditures such as the salary of Spanish magistrates, priests, and *caciques*. "Residencia: Martín de Mendoza," 13v, 21r.

93. In 1575, Toledan inspector Diego de Sanabria ordered that the community chest of the town of Tinquipaya, in Charcas, be divided into two chambers, one for the community archive, and another one for moneys from tributes, salaries, fines, and other rents. The archive was to contain Toledo's general ordinances, account ledgers, wills, and future *visita* inspections. Abercrombie, *Pathways*, 242.

94. Inventories of these community archives are discussed in Puente Luna, "*En lengua de indios*," 77 and ff.

95. "Residencia: Gabriel de Loarte," 139r–139v, 257v–258r.

96. The 1566 case against Guacrapaucar lists several *khipucamayoqs* who were also com-

munal accountants (*contadores*). Ibid., 240r–240v. For Huamanga: Curatola Petrocchi and Puente Luna, "Contar concertando," 206. Guaman Poma's ideal representation of a village councilman (*regidor*) depicts him holding a *khipu* and an accounting book.

97. Sarabia Viejo, *Francisco de Toledo*, 2: 219, 242–250. Accountants and stewards seem to have been audited during the investiture of a new Spanish magistrate. "Declaración: Francisco Chaisa y Alonso Yaure," 1579, MNAAH, AH-MS, A353.

98. In 1660, the authorities of Luringuanca appeared before the local magistrate seeking authorization to sell some of their communal lands and houses. After having "discussed among ourselves" (*tratado y conferido entre nossotros*), they reached "a general agreement to sell the said communal assets" (*un aquerdo y comformidad en hacer venta dellos*). ARJ, PN, 2 [1660], 3r–8v. In 1581, The *caciques* of Lucanas and Laramati "came together to celebrate a town hall meeting" (*se juntaron a cauildo*) to discuss the sale of cattle which belonged to the community. Puente Luna, "Felipe Guaman Poma," 33.

99. Municipal (*cabildo*) elections in New Spain were a deeply contested affair, often based on local custom. Owensby suggests, however, that "while technically only caciques and principales actually spoke as voters" on these occasions, "commoners too might have a 'voice' in elections . . . , for their willingness to listen to upstarts, acclaim a gobernador who was being challenged, and applaud or grumble as lawsuits were brought could set the political contexts within which elected officials governed." Owensby, *Empire*, 226.

100. Cárdenas, *La población*, 46–47; Charney, *Indian Society*, 63; Lowry, "Forging an Indian Nation," 133–134.

101. On the "houses and urban plot" (*casas y solar*) of the Indians of Chincha, Huarochirí, and Luringuanca in El Cercado: "Causa sobre el solar de Guanca," Lima, 1612, MNAAH, AH-MS, B29; "Censo que debe pagar el hospital de Santa Ana," Lima, 1579, MNAAH, AH-MS, A182. and ARJ, PN, 7 [1649]. 41v–44r.

102. Puente Luna, "Choquecasa va a la audiencia."

103. Prominent colonial Incas in Cuzco relied on this same strategy. "Donación. Don Mateo Chalco Yupanqui y su mujer," Cuzco, February 21, 1673, ARC, PN, 224 (Mesa), 429r–434v.

104. The *ayllus* of Atunjauja owned houses and shops (*casas y tiendas*) located "underneath the portals of the scriveners" (*devajo de los portales de los escrivanos*). AGN, Caja de Censos, leg. 8, doc. 18 [1585]; leg. 21, doc. 20; AGN, PN, 70 [1568], 1016r–1016v.

105. Charney, "Negotiating Roots." My own survey of Lima's notarial records reveals that this type of arrangement was fairly common.

106. Puente Luna and Honores, "Guardianes de la real justicia," 24–30. The creation of the post of procurator went back to Viceroy Toledo's reforms of the early 1570. Sarabia Viejo, *Francisco de Toledo*, 2: 336. Previous discussions of Andean *procuradores* include Lavallé, *Al filo de la navaja*; Mathis, "Vicente Mora Chimo." For the *apoderados* in colonial Oaxaca: Yannakakis, *The Art*, 37.

107. In 1660, the indigenous authorities of Conchucos, in the north-central Andes, empowered "licentiate" (*licenciado*) Don Juan Causa Huanca, a member of the Allauca Huari municipal council, to collect a debt. "Poder. Los caciques de Conchucos a Juan Causa Huanca," February 12, 1660, AGN, PN (Angulo Estrada), 109, 36r–37r. Don Juan

Puquia, another elected procurator (*procurador deste dicho pueblo elejido en el cavildo y regimiento del*), was appointed defender (*defensor*) of an Indian accussed of idolatry in Pasco in 1617. "[Causa] de hechicero de oficio contra Tomás Parinanca, yndio," Pasco, 1617, AAL, HEI, l. 1, e. 4.

108. Abercrombie, *Pathways*, 244–246; Sarabia Viejo, *Francisco de Toledo*, 218–219, 236.

109. In January 1689, Don Luis Chayguac, principal of the town of Mansiche, was "acclaimed" procurator by "the commons" (*el comun*). "Expediente en nombre de los alcaldes y regidores de Mansiche," Trujillo, December 11–24, 1689, ARLL, CO, l. 268, c. 3216. Twenty-three members of Lambayeque requested the Spanish defender-general to reappoint procurator Don Clemente Anto after his term. *Cabildo* officials, the *cacique*, and others opposed. Ramírez, "Don Clemente." During local elections of native officials in New Spain, commoners were sometimes present, "acclaiming and applauding a particular slate of officers, or grumbling at a controversial choice." Owensby, *Empire*, 213–214.

110. Abercrombie, *Pathways*, 258, 291–293. Alcira Dueñas's ongoing research on late colonial *cabildos* supports this assertion. Anto, the attorney of Lambayeque mentioned earlier, was able to fulfill the duties of his post because he was wealthy and could self-fund litigation. Ramírez, "Don Clemente," 833, 837. Yannakakis finds that local electoral custom varied for Oaxaca, especially after *cabildo* elections became entangled with the developing fiesta-cargo system. In some villages, there existed the custom of "discussing new candidates among the entire común before proposing them for election." Yannakakis, *The Art*, 170, 180.

111. ARJ, PN, 7 [1652], 301r. Don Vicente Mora Chimo styled himself as procurator of the towns of Santiago, Chócope, Cao, and San Esteban, in the Chicama Valley. Mathis, "Une Figure," 378.

112. In 1622, Don Juan Chaupis Condor declared he was "procurator-general" (*procurador general*) of the province of Lampas "with title from the government." "Carta de los curacas de Lampas al Rey," Cajatambo, April 1, 1620, AGI, Lima, 150. Vicente Mora Chimo claimed a similar appointment. Mathis, "Une Figure."

113. Stern, *Peru's Indian Peoples*, 121. For the appointment of annual solicitors in Tlaxcala, who were to reside in Mexico City and represent the Tlaxcalans before the *audiencia*: Celestino and Valencia, *Actas*, ii–v.

114. Bayle, "Cabildos," 10; Sarabia Viejo, *Francisco de Toledo*, 2: 250.

115. An intriguing 1566 letter from one Pedro de Balboa to Lope García de Castro criticizes indigenous men of an unnamed town or *repartimiento* for letting their women do all the agricultural work while they spend the day weaving and drinking with the *caciques* and *principales* in the main plaza, "where they gather every single day to celebrate a *cabildo*" (*donde hazen todos los dias del mundo cauildo*). "Carta. Pedro de Balboa a Lope García de Castro," Lima, January 12, 1566, AGI, Lima, 121, 51r–53v. Balboa's testimony points to the famous *juntas*, traditional gatherings in which indigenous leaders ate and drank with their subjects, distributing food and presents. Guaman Poma, *Nueva corónica*, 449. For this custom in Huarochirí in the mid-seventeenth century: "Informaciones: Pedro de Garay," 1669, AGI, Lima, 259, n. 11, 186v–187r.

116. For a general portrait of the "chief attendants of the church, confraternities, and

hospitals of this kingdom" (*maiordomos de la santa yglecia y de cofrades, hospitales deste rreyno*): Guaman Poma, *Nueva corónica*, 682–683.

117. Evidence available for the 1562 journey of Tlaxcalan leaders to the royal court seems to indicate that certain decisions were reached in this way. "Andrés de Cervera con los indios principales de Tlaxcala," 1573, AGI, Justicia, 1016, r. 5, 644r–644v. In the early 1660s, Agustín Capcha, an ecclesiastic prosecutor, wrote a complaint describing how the principales of the town of Ambar deposed a corrupt *alcalde* and then "entraron a cabildo de consulta" to elect a new one. Rivarola, *Español andino*, 102.

118. Guaman Poma, *Nueva corónica*, 668–669, 831. For examples of petitions of this sort in Quechua: Itier, "Las cartas en quechua"; Durston, "La escritura"; Durston and Urioste, "Las peticiones." For examples in Spanish: Charles, "Testimonios"; Puente Luna, "*En lengua de indios*"; Rivarola, *Español andino*.

119. In 1583, the Tlaxcalans chose their emissaries to the royal court "in the manner customary for the election of native officers." Baber, "Empire"; Gibson, *Tlaxcala*, 168. Tomás López Medel's 1552's ordinances for the towns of Yucatán prescribed a similar procedure. Cunill, *Los defensores*, 92.

120. AGN, Derecho Indígena, Cuad. 128, Leg. 9 [1650], 4r; ARJ, PN, 3 [1640–1641], 849r–851v; 902r–902v; ARJ, PN, 4 [1657], 435v–436v; ARJ, PN, 7 [1649–1651, 1653, 1655], 41v–44r; 65v–67r, 91v–93v, 243r–246v, 306r–307v; ARJ, PN, 9 [1665, 1667], 586r–588v, 601r–603r; ARJ, PN, 13 [1681], 623r–624r; BNP, AAC, Z338 [1650–1652], 811r–811v; BNP, AAC, Z1010 [1651].

CHAPTER 3

1. Matienzo, *Gobierno del Perú*, 87. The early-modern Iberian subjects' freedom to emigrate from one place to another, which Matienzo invoked in his treatise, was limited by the royal expectation for individuals to integrate or insert themselves in a known community. Full personal liberty, for Indians, Spaniards, and other subjects, was considered living "outside the social and religious norms." Herzog, "Naming, Identifying and Authorizing," 191–193.

2. Abercrombie, *Pathways*, 239; Lohmann, *Juan de Matienzo*; Mumford, *Vertical Empire*, 69–71. Juan de Solórzano Pereyra, a prominent jurist and member of the Council of the Indies, expounded similar arguments in a much more erudite fashion in 1648. Solórzano Pereira, *Política indiana*, bk. 2, esp. chs. 1, 5–6, 24. On different theories and debates about indigenous compulsive labor: Glave, "La petición grande"; Sánchez Albornoz, "El trabajo indígena"; Cole, "An Abolitionism." Besides these sanctioned displacements, permanent migration to escape *mita*, tribute, church exactions, and other colonial burdens became part of the Andean social landscape early on, giving rise to the widespread phenomenon of *forasteros* (migrant outsiders) and *forasterismo*. Glave, *Trajinantes*; Powers, *Andean Journeys*; Saignes, *Caciques, Tribute and Migration*; Wightman, *Indigenous Migration*.

3. Owensby, *Empire*, 148.

4. Herzog, "Naming, Identifying and Authorizing," 198–199.

5. On Spanish theories of *naturaleza* or "nativeness" as they applied to the Indians: Herzog, "The Appropriation," 142. Indians were sometimes described as natives "by origin," as opposed to the Spaniards, considered natives "by birth."

6. Gallup-Díaz, *The Door*; Herzog, *Defining Nations*; Studnicki-Gizbert, *A Nation*, 45–46.

7. The title of this chapter is a spin-off of one of Karen Spalding's most famous chapters in *Huarochirí* (1984), where she contends the following: "Although Huarochirí bordered on the metropolis of Lima . . . , capital of a territory that reached the length and breadth of a continent, until the latter part of the eighteenth century the region was not integrated into the European colonial world." Spalding, *Huarochirí*, 169. Although I take a different approach here, in many and profound ways I remain in debt to her ideas and with the questions she posed in her pathbreaking study.

8. The sixteenth-century *extremeño* emigrants to America, the scientific and intellectual communities debating the nature of the New World, the healing communities of Africans and their descendants in Brazil and Portugal, and the Portuguese nation of transatlantic merchants stand as obvious examples. Altman, *Emigrants*; Cañizares-Esguerra, *How to Write*; Studnicki-Gizbert, *A Nation*, 4–11, 94–121; Sweet, *Domingos Álvares*. On early modern organizations and their capacity to create global networks, act as sources of patronage and grace, and influence imperial politics and administration: Roniger and Herzog, *The Collective and the Public*.

9. Eliga Gould's earlier observation that people moving in the cosmopolitan Atlantic world "belonged not to one community but to several" is pertinent here. According to Gould, "those communities together constituted . . . an interconnected yet porous and open-ended whole." Gould, "Entangled Histories," 785–786. In similar terms, Jane Mangan has looked at vertical and horizontal ties across generation, class, and ethnicity in early colonial Peru to argue that "the web of the colonial family was so intricate that no colonial schemes of hierarchy could fully capture it." Mangan, *Transatlantic Obligations*, 133.

10. Scholars have identified some of the vertical and horizontal ties—corporate allegiance, common interest, patronage, servitude, and kinship—bounding Indians in rural and urban settings. Charney, *Indian Society*; Lowry, "Forging an Indian Nation"; Poloni-Simard, *El mosaico*. Jane Mangan reminds us that many early colonial families in Lima and Arequipa "defy categorization into 'indigenous' or 'Spanish,'" for these "blended families" were based on bicultural networks. Mangan, *Transatlantic Obligations*, 121–122.

11. Yanna Yannakakis makes a similar point for colonial Oaxaca. Yannakakis, *The Art*, 123. Indigenous strategies to negotiate with the king shared some of the same principles and mechanisms that nonnative actors—Spaniards, *mestizos*, and Africans—employed to bargain for royal favor: Cunill, "La negociación"; Dedieu, "Procesos." For specific examples: Díaz, *The Virgin*; Goldwert, "La lucha"; Goldwert, "La lucha (continuación)"; Jouve, *Esclavos*; Olaechea Labayen, "Un recurso al Rey"; Ruan, "Andean Activism."

12. Altman, *Emigrants*, 70, 261–262. On the circulation of regional elites within the Spanish empire: Yun Casalilla, "Introducción," 15.

13. Sarabia Viejo, *Francisco de Toledo*, 1: 178.

14. Previous treatments of the "litigious" nature of the native Andeans include Adorno,

"Images"; Alaperrine-Bouyer, "Recurrencias y variaciones"; Charles, "'More *Ladino*'"; Honores, "Una aproximación"; Puente Brunke, "Notas sobre la Audiencia." For similar stereotypes applied to litigants in Spain: Kagan, *Lawsuits.*

15. "Carta. Francisco de Toledo al Consejo de Indias," Lima, August 2, 1570, AGI, Lima, 28a, n. 45, l. 1, 14.

16. According to Polo de Ondegardo, some indigenous elders rented themselves out as witnesses. Lamana, *Pensamiento colonial*, 144. I thank Renzo Honores for this reference.

17. Such criticisms against excessive fees of scribes, prosecutors, advocates, and judges did not come only from secular officials. López-Ocón Cabrera, "Andinología," 107.

18. Numerous contemporary testimonies support this general picture, but Toledo's ideas are emblematic. For him, frivolous litigation stemmed from the "weakness and stupidity of the said *naturales*." It corrupted their customs: "they have been shown to look for false witnesses while the most cunning have usurped the property of others and engaged in skullduggery and tricks that are very harmful to their *repúblicas*." "Ordinances regarding the Lawsuits of the Indians," 1572. AGI, Lima, 29, 132r–152v.

19. Honores, "History, Rhetoric, and Strategy." Honores traces the debate about indigenous litigation to licentiate Ondegardo's 1561 report on Andean tributary practices to the *audiencia*. For Honores, Toledo's main motivation for implementing his reforms was to restrict the power and autonomy of the *caciques*.

20. Three provincials told the king in 1562: "The preservation of the natives is Your Majesty's principal wealth in these lands, and their conversion is God's." Assadourian, "Las rentas," 76.

21. Assadourian, "Las rentas," 78; Assadourian, "Los señores," 349–350; Assadourian, "Acerca del cambio," 4–6; Bakewell, "La maduración"; Cunill, "La negociación," 33. This "dilemma" is also noted in Mumford, *Vertical Empire*, 3. For the economic situation of Philip II's Spain: Kamen, *Spain, 1469–1714*, 166–181.

22. The literature on Indian *reducciones* is vast. Particularly insightful about the establishment of *pueblos* and their connection to the larger *República de Indios* are Abercrombie, *Pathways*, 237–258; Garrett, *Shadows*, 26–30; Mumford, *Vertical Empire*, esp. ch. 2. For up-to-date considerations of the Toledan reforms, the Junta Magna, and the larger colonial project: Merluzzi, *Gobernando los Andes*. Although these scholars offer in-depth discussions of the different religious, economic, and political arguments that reformers advanced since the 1560s to resettle the natives in Iberian-style towns, judicial reform per se is not one of their main concerns.

23. Bakewell, "La maduración"; Goldwert, "La lucha"; Goldwert, "La lucha (continuación)." Angeli, "'¿Buenos e rectos jueces?.'"

24. Borah, *Justice*, 58–59; Cunill, *Los defensores*, 49–66; Cunill, "La negociación"; Owensby, *Empire*. For the tribute reassessments of the 1550s, ordered by the *audiencia* at the indigenous lords' request: Assadourian, "La renta," 120–123; Honores, "History, Rhetoric, and Strategy."

25. Abercrombie, *Pathways*, 239. On how this tradition was implemented in the communities of the Lima Valley: Graubart, "Learning from the *Qadi*"; Graubart, "Compet-

ing Spanish and Indigenous Jurisdictions"; Graubart, "'Ynuvaciones malas.'" In the central Andean highlands: Puente Luna, "*En lengua de indios*"; Puente Luna and Honores, "Guardianes de la real justicia." In colonial Charcas: Mumford, "Las llamas." In Yucatán: Cunill, "'Nos traen tan avasallados'."

26. Graubart, "Competing Spanish and Indigenous Jurisdictions"; Puente Luna and Honores, "Guardianes de la real justicia."

27. Abercrombie, *Pathways*, 237–241; Graubart, "Competing Spanish and Indigenous Jurisdictions"; Graubart, "Learning from the *Qadi*." This earlier history, which is not told here, is tied to debates about the *caciques'* role in the administration of justice and the establishment of the first *alguaciles* (bailiffs) *regidores* (aldermen), and *alcaldes* (town magistrates), mainly during the government of Viceroy Andrés Hurtado de Mendoza, the Marquis of Cañete (1556–1560), in the Lima Valley and Cuzco. Assadourian, "Los señores," 337–338; Espinoza, "El alcalde mayor," 203–204. Cañete famously told the King: "paper and ink are, in my opinion, the weapons with which war is to be waged in this kingdom." "Carta a S.M. del Marqués de Cañete, Virrey del Perú [Lima, November 3, 1556], 300. See also "Instrucciones de Carlos V al Marqués de Cañete." For a recent survey of the pertinent legislation: Robles Bocanegra, "La efigie," ch. 1.

28. Assadourian, "Las rentas," 94; García de Castro, "Carta a S.M. del Licenciado Lope García de Castro [Lima, December 31, 1565]," 116–130; Hurtado de Mendoza, "Carta a S.M. del Marqués de Cañete, Virrey del Perú [Lima, November 3, 1556]," 299.

29. Graubart, "Learning from the *Qadi*."

30. Levillier, *Audiencia de Lima*, 299. During his 1565–1566 tour, Cuenca single-handedly ruled over cases involving *caciques* and commoners. González de San Segundo, "El doctor"; Mumford, *Vertical Empire*, 68–69; Ramírez, "*Amores prohibidos*." Cuenca's 1566 ordinances for the new native towns commanded the creation of the first native municipal councils and the appointment of the first *alcaldes*, aldermen, and scribes on the northern valleys of Trujillo, Chicama, and Lambayeque. González de San Segundo, "El doctor"; Rostworowski, "Algunos comentarios."

31. On the viceroy's 1559 order to create these urban parishes and appoint *alcaldes*: Navarro Gala, *El libro*, 32–36. Their establishment was followed by the appointment of the first indigenous *alcaldes mayores* (chief municipal magistrates) for the city and its surroundings. Along with status, the post carried real powers of oversight over the urban parish *alcaldes*. Espinoza, "El alcalde mayor," 207; Julien, "La organización parroquial," 86; Rowe, "Colonial Portraits," 264.

32. "Carta. Conde de Nieva a SM," Lima, December 26, 1562, AGI, Lima, 28a, n. 35.

33. Examples of early *cuzqueño* litigants can be found in Honores, "History, Rhetoric, and Strategy." *Jueces de naturales* were to hear disputes concerning land boundaries and pastures, cattle, and inheritance, and resolve them summarily. In 1572, Toledo perfected Nieva's idea, detailing the duties of these justices. Sarabia Viejo, *Francisco de Toledo*, 1: 179–182, 223–230.

34. García de Castro, "Prevenciones," 122. Cuenca's *ordenanzas* of 1566 make a very similar point. González de San Segundo, "El doctor," 667.

35. For the *caciques'* campaign against Castro's *corregidores*: Assadourian, "Los señores," 380–392; Mumford, *Vertical Empire*, 64–69. On the shifting alliances of this period: Assadourian, "Las rentas."

36. Matienzo, *Gobierno del Perú*, 87. On Castro's ordinances for the local dispensation of justice: García de Castro, "Prevenciones," 117, 129–130; "Instruçion para el capitán Juan de la Reynaga," 1565, BNE, MS., 1032, esp. ordinance 21. For an overview of the judicial role of the *corregidor*: Lohmann, *El corregidor*, 66–70, 295–311.

37. Puente Luna and Honores, "Guardianes de la real justicia," 22–24; Serulnikov, *Revolution*, 148–156.

38. Guaman Poma, *Nueva corónica*, 505–506, 779, 825. For a comparison with New Spain: Owensby, *Empire*, 227–230.

39. García de Castro, "Carta a S.M. del Licenciado Lope García de Castro."

40. Cunill, "'Nos traen tan avasallados'"; Honores, "History, Rhetoric, and Strategy."

41. Brendecke, *Imperios*; Cunill, "Los intérpretes"; Cunill, "Philip II."

42. Encinas, *Cedulario indiano*, 4: 357–358.

43. Bayle, "El protector," 87, 118; Cunill, *Los defensores*, 49, 79; Lavallé, "Presión colonial," 307; Ruigómez, *Una política indigenista*, 149–150; Schäfer, *El Consejo Real*, 68, 119–120; Cunill, "Fray Bartolomé"; Cunill, "Philip II."

44. The Council of the Indies suggested that native *alcaldes* be appointed by the *corregidor de españoles* or the *audiencia*. Assadourian, "Los señores," 337; Espinoza, "El alcalde mayor," 203–204.

45. A Tlaxcalan delegation led by four prominent lords had sojourned at the royal court around the same time as Guacrapaucar (1562–1563). Between 1563 and 1564, Don Francisco Inga Atahualpa, son of Inca Atahualpa and *encomendero* of the Quito jurisdiction, also stayed at court, accompanied by an entourage of four dependents. "Andrés de Cervera con los indios principales de Tlaxcala," 1573, AGI, Justicia, 1016, r. 5; "Información y licencia: Francisco Inga Atabalipa," 1563, AGI, Contratación, 5537, l. 3.

46. "Real cédula de oficio para que no vengan indios a estos reinos," Madrid, December 10, 1566, AGI, Lima, 569, l. 12, 235r–235v.

47. *Recopilación*, bk. 6, tit. 7, law 27; bk. 29, tit. 26, law 65.

48. "Agrauio que generalmente se haze a los naturales," 1579?, AGI, Indiferente, 1373. I thank Adrian Masters for informing me about this document.

49. "Causa contra Don Bernardino de Perales," 1647, AGI, Lima, 100.

50. "Real cédula al virrey para que provea lo que le pareciere convenir en los pleitos que los indios tratan," Madrid, February 6, 1571, AGI, Lima, 569, l. 13, 244r.

51. Bayle, "El protector," 146.

52. Toledo claimed to have seen this with his own eyes. Among his statements, see "Carta. Francisco de Toledo al Consejo de Indias," 11–12. In 1572, after his tenure in Peru, García de Castro had resumed his duties at the Council.

53. Medelius and Puente Luna, "Curacas"; Sarabia Viejo, *Francisco de Toledo*. On the larger impact of Toledo's inspection, "the most thoroughgoing effort to transform Andean society": Abercrombie, *Pathways*, 237 (quote), 237–258.

54. This prerogative, which was a holdover of *alcaldes* in early modern Spain, extended

to the viceroy's own version of Castro's *jueces de naturales* and *corregidores de indios*. Toledo's ordinances were largely fashioned after Cuenca's ordinances for the native populations of Trujillo, which García de Castro started to apply to the viceroyalty as a whole. Abercrombie, *Pathways*, 242–244; Graubart, "Learning from the *Qadi*"; Lohmann, "Introducción," 1: xxxi–xxxii.

55. Graubart, "'Ynuvaciones malas'"; Graubart, "Competing Spanish and Indigenous Jurisdictions"; Puente Luna, *"En lengua de indios."*

56. According to Guaman Poma, some among the first generation of Andean municipal officials were too young to inspire any respect and therefore to be obeyed. Guaman Poma, *Nueva corónica*, 450. On clerical violence: Charles, "Testimonios," 115–117. On *caciques* and the dispensation of justice up to this time: Graubart, "Learning from the *Qadi*"; Ramírez, *"Amores prohibidos."*

57. Recent reconstructions of the judicial duties of indigenous municipal officials include Burns, "Making Indigenous Archives"; Graubart, "Competing Spanish and Indigenous Jurisdictions"; Dueñas, "The Lima Indian *Letrados*"; Mumford, *Vertical Empire*, 148; Puente Luna and Honores, "Guardianes de la real justicia."

58. Konetzke, *Colección de documentos*, 1: 243–244, 360, 365–366, 451–452; *Recopilación*, bk. 6, tit. 7, laws 1–4, 7. These and other prerogatives of *cacique* status and hereditary Indian nobility—exemption from tribute and personal service—operated through both legislation and custom. Even so, as Garrett notes, "not all caciques were hereditary nobles; nor were all hereditary nobles caciques." Garrett, *Shadows*, 39–43.

59. González de San Segundo, "El doctor," 651; Premo, *Children of the Father King*, 34. Medieval law recognized the Crown's duty to intervene directly in cases involving orphans, widows, the sick, aged, crippled, poor, and the wretched. The goal was to provide summary justice and release subjects from the financial burdens of litigation. Benton, *Law*, 44; Cuena Boy, "El protector"; Cunill, "El indio miserable." This royal obligation provided an influential model for the legal status and treatment of New World natives. *Recopilación*, bk. 6, tit. 10, law 21; Solórzano Pereira, *Política indiana*, bk. 2, chs. 28–29.

60. Based on Castilian tariffs or *aranceles*, the king determined that *caciques* and communities (when acting as corporate entities) paid half of the regular legal fees that non-native litigants paid at the *audiencia*. Commoners litigating as private individuals were supposed to pay none. Borah, *Justice*, 11–15, 93; Cunill, *Los defensores*, 90–106.

61. Prior to Toledo's reforms, native Andeans successfully appealed some of their cases to the Council. For example: Rostworowski, *Conflicts*.

62. Medelius and Puente Luna, "Curacas." Toledo's reforms also compelled native lords to request an official license to appear before the tribunals in Lima, even if litigating on behalf of their subjects. After obtaining the license, they were supposed to remain in their locales and send two able subjects to represent the commons before the high court. Those who disobeyed would lose their case and, if first-time offenders, receive one hundred lashes. A second-time offense merited permanent exile. A third violation would result in perpetual exile from the kingdom. Díaz Rementería, *El cacique*, 133. Needless to say, these orders seem to have been rarely enforced.

63. Owensby, *Empire*, 159.

64. Mumford, *Vertical Empire*, 112. In Toledo's vision, fulfillment of tribute and labor obligations granted native-born town dwellers (*originarios*) access to lands, pastures, and communal resources. Outsiders (*forasteros*) had no such right unless they enrolled as full tribute payers after ten years of permanent residence. Guevara and Salomon, "A 'Personal Visit'"; Mumford, *Vertical Empire*, 112–113; Powers, *Andean Journeys*; Wightman, *Indigenous Migration*.

65. Enríquez, "Carta del virrey Martín Enríquez a S.M.," 66.

66. Medelius, "El licenciado," 2770v.

67. In 1573, Don Carlos Inca, Don Agustín Condemayta, Don Diego Cayo, and other prominent nobles of Inca descent wrote directly to the Council requesting a hearing. They denounced procedural flaws in a lawsuit brought against them by Toledo, who condemned them to perpetual exile. The Incas had previously requested a similar license from the *audiencia*, but the judges denied it. Although the Council also denied the second petition, it ordered the *audiencia* to review the case. "Don Carlos Inca y otros a SM," Lima, 1573. AGI, Lima, 270, 440r-440v.

68. "Memorial. Don Juan Bustamante Carlos Inca a SM," Madrid, November 21, 1759, AVU, MS, v. 35, d. 16.

69. Díaz Rementería, *El cacique*, 149–150, 187; Lohmann, *El corregidor*, 128.

70. Novoa, *The Protectors*, 44–46.

71. Novoa, *The Protectors*, 47. Viceroys at this time appointed twenty-nine *protectorías* in their jurisdiction (which included several *audiencias* apart from Lima), "not counting other protectorates of less importance." Vázquez de Espinosa, *Description*, 776–777, 783–784.

72. Novoa, *The Protectors*, 50–51. Defenders-general, especially if not university-trained, were to consult with the *abogado de indios*. Cases were often presented and handled by *procuradores generales de los Indios* and *agentes* or *solicitadores* (solicitors). Procurators and solicitors were sometimes designated by the defender-general. Some individuals doubled as defenders and procurators. Borah, "Juzgado General"; Borah, *Justice*; Honores, "Litigación en la Audiencia Arzopispal"; Honores, "Una aproximación"; Lavallé, "Presión colonial," 307–308; Puente Brunke, "Notas sobre la Audiencia," 232–239; Ruigómez, *Una política indigenista*, 70–72; Saravia, "La evolución."

73. Examples in sixteenth-century Cuzco include "Poder. Don Francisco Uncaña y otros a García," Cuzco, November 3, 1576, ARC, PN, 20 (Sánchez), 1183r–1183v; "Concierto. Don Miguel Paniura con Don Alonso Cusi Poma," Cuzco, February 10, 1580, ARC, PN, 24 (Sánchez), 131v; "Venta. Isabel Tocto a Juan Rimachi," Cuzco, February 1st, 1595, ARC, PN, 29 (Sánchez), 423r and ff.

74. Saravia, "Los miserables y el protector," 131–196; Lavallé, "Presión colonial," 309–310. For Quito: Bonnett, *Los protectores*, 125. For Yucatán: Cunill, *Los defensores*, 327–329.

75. Ruigómez, *Una política indigenista*, 97.

76. León Pinelo, *Mandó que se imprimiese*, 56–57; Ruigómez, *Una política indigenista*, 109.

77. Examples of these informal legal facilitators include "Poder. Alonso de Efquen a Miguel Chiclayo," Lima, March 1, 1595, AGN, PN, 1 (Aguilar), 637v–638r; "Poder. Diego Minchay y Pedro Guaman a Alonso Guaman," Lima, October 27, 1592, AGN, PN, 19 [1]

(Castillejo), 266r–266v; Vergara, "La población indígena," 213. For interpreters-general, the city of Chachapoyas, and the *Audiencia de Lima*: "Poder. Doña Ana, viuda de Juan Soplin, a Antonio San Martín y Juan Chuquival," Chachapoyas, September 23, 1584, ARA, PN 9 (Ortiz), 163r–163v; "Poder. El cacique, segunda persona y procurador de los pueblos de Chellel y Oliac, a Diego Solsol," December 23, 1587, ARA, PN, 12 (Sánchez Delgado), 255r–255v; and the analysis in Puente Luna, "The Many Tongues," 153–154.

78. Transaction details and agreements behind the scenes often elude us, but here is an example of these legal encounters. In 1596, Antonio de Neira, *procurador de causas* in the *audiencia*, appeared before a notary in Lima as the guarantor of Don Francisco Tantachumbi, the *cacique* of the nearby town of Surco, previously imprisoned for debts. Neira vouched for the *cacique*, offering to pay a significant bail of 700 pesos if Tantachumbi did not return to prison and face trial within thirty days. They had probably reached some kind of agreement for legal representation. "Fianza. Antonio de Neira a favor de Don Francisco Tantachumbi," Lima, January 9, 1596, AGN, PN, 3 (Aguilar), 1211v–1212r.

79. "Poder. Don Pedro de la Cruz a Pedro Ortiz de Valdelomar," Lima, January 9, 1596, AGN, PN, 3 (Aguilar), 24v–25r.

80. Lavallé, "Presión colonial," 131; Cunill, *Los defensores*, 319.

81. "Don Juan de Guzmán contra los caciques de las guarangas de Cajamarca," AGN, DIE, l. 6, c. 78, 113r–114v.

82. "Memorial. Los indios Lucanas a SM," 1624, AGI, Lima, 152; "Real cédula al virrey del Piru remitiendole la pretenssion que tienen los Yndios Lucanes y Vilcas," Madrid, May 28, 1621, AGI, Lima, 583, l. 17, 283v–284r.

83. See, among many other examples, a 1676 letter of the "caciques from the kingdom of Peru" (*caciques del Reyno del Peru*) praising the work of the protector-general. "Documentos sobre el protector Lucas de Segura y Lara," Lima, 1678, AGI, Lima, 172.

84. Sarabia Viejo, *Francisco de Toledo*, 2: 101–112; "Probanza: Baltasar de la Cruz Azpeitia," 1585, AGI, Lima, 127.

85. An example of one such complaint is that of Nicolás Isla Guaman, attorney of the town of Moche. He denounced the defender of the Indians of Trujillo for holding the wages of eighteen workers who had cleaned the city's main irrigation channel. "Nicolás Ysla Guaman, contra don Diego de Escobar," Trujillo, July 5, 1642, ARLL, CO, l. 275, c. 3444.

86. Puente Luna, "Choquecasa va a la audiencia," 145–147.

87. In 1590, the outgoing *corregidor* of Jauja denounced one Rodrigo de Guzmán for "inciting" the Indians to file charges against him. Citing Toledo's ordinances, he urged a magistrate not to accept any petitions unless they came directly from the local defender. "Residencia: Martín de Mendoza," Jauja, 1591, AGN, JR, l. 8, c. 21, 191r–191v.

88. *porque los demas no uzasen yrse a quejar.* For this paragraph and the previous one: "Memorial. Los caciques principales de Chucuito a SM," 1607, AGI, Lima, 138.

89. For the two preceding paragraphs: "Carta de los curacas de Lampas al Rey," Cajatambo, April 1, 1620, AGI, Lima, 150; "Carta de la Condesa de Lemos a S.M.," Madrid, March 7, 1624, AGI, Lima, 155. On the *obraje*: Pereyra Plascencia, "Mita obrajera"; Pereyra Plascencia, "Chiquian."

90. Bernard Lavallé reaches a similar conclusion in his discussion of late-colonial defenders of the Indians in Cajamarca. Lavallé, "Presión colonial," 325. For the "two-way" alliance between Mayas and defenders in Yucatán: Cunill, *Los defensores*, 191–196.

91. In his will, Don Diego Mache, *cacique* of the Chicama valley, refers to lands near his hometown of Santiago, which he purchased "for the benefit (*utilidad*) of justice and the protector." "Testamento. Don Diego Mache," Santiago, 1630, ARLL, PN, 199 (Paz), 198v–202r.

92. A few examples include "Doña Inés de Ribera contra Don Hernando Viça Alaya," Lima, 1579, AGN, DIE, l. 19, c. 93-a; "Poder. Diego Cóndor Guacho Guasca a Baltasar de la Cruz Azpeitia y otro," Lima, June 26, 1582, AGN, PN, 10 (Arias Cortés), 211r–212r.

93. Novoa, *The Protectors*, 48–51.

94. Cunill, "Philip II"; Honores, "Litigiosidad indígena," 202. In 1591, a *cédula* created the post of "protector fiscal," charged specifically with "Indian cases." Two royal *cédulas* (1614 and 1615) ordered the reappointment of a defender-general in the *audiencias* of Lima and Charcas. Puente Brunke, "Notas sobre la Audiencia," 233–239; Ruigómez, *Una política indigenista*, 70–72; Saravia, "Los miserables y el protector."

95. Medelius, "El licenciado," 2757v.

96. "Probanza: Baltasar de la Cruz Azpeitia," 103r–106v. In 1585, Don Carlos Matia, paramount lord (*cacique mayor*) of the *repartimiento* of Allauca Guari, showed his support for the now-suspended defender-general. The *cacique* and his brothers had been waiting seven months in Lima for the *audiencia* to enter a judgment. Though their lawsuits were not worth more than 50 pesos, they had already spent 400 pesos.

97. Velasco, "Carta a S.M. del virrey Luis de Velasco," 34. See also "Los Yndios de las Prouincias del Perú," Lima, 1633, AGI, Lima, 161, 10 and ff. On the First General Land Inspection and the measures taken by Viceroy García Hurtado de Mendoza to deal with the numerous complaints: Glave, "El arbitrio de tierras."

98. After I finished this chapter, I found out about Mauricio Novoa's newly-published study on the *protectores generales* of the *Audiencia de Lima*. His work is the exception that confirms the rule. Novoa, *The Protectors*.

99. Puente Brunke, "Notas sobre la Audiencia." For the life and career of Juan Martínez Rengifo, rapporteur (1565) and attorney (1568) of the *audiencia*, later defender-general of the Indians (1577–1590): Rodríguez Quispe, *Por un lugar*, 53–57. Recent studies of *abogados*, *procuradores*, and *oidores* include Jurado, "Un fiscal"; Honores, "Una sociedad"; Lohmann, "El licenciado Francisco Falcón"; Novoa, *The Protectors*; Puente Brunke, "Sociedad y administración"; Puente Brunke, "'Los vasallos'"; Puente Brunke, "Los ministros de la Audiencia"; Puente Brunke, "Intereses en conflicto"; Puente Brunke, "Codicia y bien público."

100. Don Pedro Fernández de Castro, Count of Lemos and son-in-law of the Duke of Lerma, was president of the Council between 1603 and 1609. His son actively corresponded with the Prince of Esquilache while the latter served as viceroy of Peru. The king's *merced* authorizing the counts to found textile mills (*obrajes*) in Lampas was made in 1617, during Esquilache's tenure. Lohmann, *El conde de Lemos*, 3; Schäfer, *El Consejo Real*, 189, 352.

101. In 1585, several individuals of noble Inca descent petitioned the viceroy to confirm the temporary appointment of one Martín de Bustinza, their "relative" (*pariente*) as their public defender. "Probanza: Baltasar de la Cruz Azpeitia," 117r–119v. Bustinza's predecessor in the post, Don Pedro Suárez de Carvajal, was also of Inca descent through his mother's side and was married to one of Huayna Capac's granddaughters. It is likely that Bustinza and Carvajal were fluent in Quechua.

102. In 1643, Pedro Simaran brought a complaint against his lord, Don Francisco de Azabache Munao Chimo. Through the local defender, Simaran charged this *cacique* of the town of Moche with giving him one hundred lashes for failing to clean a portion of the local irrigation channel. Azabache was imprisoned. Zevallos Quiñones, *Los cacicazgos de Trujillo*, 144.

103. Upon his arrest on charges of witchcraft and idolatry in 1659, Don Rodrigo Rupaychagua, the *cacique* of Huamantanga and an effective litigant in civil and ecclesiastic courts, demanded to know from the ecclesiastic inspector, "with broken words and actions," the reason for his arrest. He threatened the inspector thus: "His Lordship the Viceroy and the General Protector will know about this." Monsalve, "Curacas pleitistas," 171.

104. Several letters, proofs of merit, and *memoriales* attest to the relatively open access of these public procurators to the Council and the royal court. Cuena Boy, "Utilización pragmática"; Cuena Boy, "El protector"; León Pinelo, *Mandó que se imprimiese*; La Reinaga Salazar, *Memorial discursivo*; Torre Villar, *Los pareceres*.

105. For example: "Probanza: Pedro Suárez Carvajal," Cuzco, 1578, AGI, Patronato, 122, n. 1, r. 11, n/fol.

106. Bayle, "El protector," 122–123; Herzog, *Upholding Justice*, 46–47. According to Toledo's ordinances, chief defenders were to have free access to the viceroy at all time. Two days were set aside for consultation among them and defender, the magistrates of the *audiencia*, and the viceroy. Sarabia Viejo, *Francisco de Toledo*, 101–112.

107. On the salaries of defenders-general (between 500 and 1,200 pesos annually): Bayle, "El protector," 103–105; Ruigómez, *Una política indigenista*, 150–151, 203–215; "Los Yndios de las Prouincias del Peru." With the exception of the *oidores*, defenders-general were among the best paid of the *audiencia* ministers in charge of public advocacy for the natives.

108. Escobedo Mansilla, "Bienes y cajas de comunidad," 465–466, 485. Spanish administrators of the *cajas de censos* were supposed to invest these funds in loans and liens (*censos*) against rural and urban real estate.

109. Puente Brunke, "Sociedad y administración," 343; Puente Brunke, "Codicia y bien público," 143–148; Ruigómez, *Una política indigenista*, 80, 147–148. For indigenous complaints about some of these procurators in the eighteenth century: Dueñas, "The Lima Indian *Letrados*."

110. Brendecke, *Imperios*, 289. Observers of the time were very aware of the virtual impossibility of separating "interests" from the "information" arriving from the New World. For example: "Consideraciones," BL, ADD, Ms., 13992, 25r–34v, 32r.

111. On September 30, 1626, defender-general Domingo de Luna informed the Council of "the condition that the Indians of this kingdom enjoy" while reminding it of "the

care with which I comply with the obligations of my office" and his forty years of service. "Cartas de Domingo de Luna a SM," Lima, 1626, AGI, Lima, 156. In another letter, De Luna complained about *corregidores* and *doctrineros*, while recommending one individual for a *corregimiento* and another one for a *doctrina*. "Cartas del protector Domingo de Luna a SM," Lima, 1629, AGI, Lima, 156. He also reminded the Council that the royal treasury owed attorneys and protectors more than 40,000 pesos in back salaries.

112. In 1634, the advocates and procurators for the Indians complained to the viceroy that the royal treasury owed them more than 100,000 pesos for unpaid back salaries. In 1640, they submitted their complaints to the Council. "El Protector abogados, procuradores y otros ministros de los naturales del Peru," 1634–1640, AGI, Lima, 165, 1r–4r. For previous complaints: "Real cédula al virrey y audiencia de Lima," February 13, 1620, AGI, Lima, 583, l. 17, 202v–203v; "Real cédula al virrey del Perú," San Lorenzo, October 23, 1632, AGI, Lima, 583, l. 19, 180v–182r.

113. In a 1627 *memorial*, Alonso de Torres Romero, procurator-general for the Indians, cited past royal regulations, local ordinances, and specific examples from indigenous communities in Lima's countryside, to complain, on behalf of "the natives" (*los naturales*) of the kingdom, of excessive tribute and labor demands, and the leniency and corruption of Spanish *cabildos*, justices, and officials. Torres Romero demanded higher wages, better working conditions, and the enforcement of past orders on behalf of the Indians. Interestingly, he also complained that viceroys and *audiencia* justices refused to grant an audience to the protector and the procurator for the Indians, petitioning the Crown to issue an order that they could not be denied these hearings. "Carta de Alonso de Torres Romero a S.M.," Lima, 1627, AGI, Lima, 159.

114. Several dossiers sent by defenders and attorneys for the Indians can be found among the papers of the Council. See "Carta de Francisco de Valenzuela a S.M.," Lima, July 17, 1644, CVU, MS, v. 35(3), d. 12, 189r and ff; "Carta de Francisco de Valenzuela al Consejo de Indias," Lima, October 23, 1648, AGI, Lima, 167. On the chief interpreters for the Indians in Mexico and Peru and their direct communication with the Council of the Indies: Cunill, "Los intérpretes"; Puente Luna, "The Many Tongues."

115. Consider the dossier of the Yanque and Lari Collaguas who, like the leaders of Lampas, opposed the creation of a textile mill. It includes a petition to the Council signed by the *caciques* and the defender-general of the city of Arequipa, a letter from the said defender, and a power of attorney given to the king's prosecutor in Spain. "Cartas y poderes de los caciques de Collaguas," 1614, AGI, Lima, 144.

116. Dueñas, "The Lima Indian *Letrados*"; Dueñas, *Indians*; Puente Luna, "What's in a Name?" Upon his appointment as *corregidor* of Ibarra (*audiencia* of Quito) in 1666, Antonio de Arenas Florencia Inga, a descendant of Inca Huascar, offered to journey to Spain and represent local *caciques* and communities, as well as other Inca descendants living in Quito, at the royal court. José de Arenas, his brother, had succesfully petitioned for a pension of 600 pesos at the court in 1656. Espinosa, *El Inca barroco*, 33–35; "Expediente de José de Arenas Florencia Inga," Madrid, July 16, 1657, AGI, Lima, 8.

117. Novoa, *The Protectors*, 52–61; Puente Brunke, "Sociedad y administración," 346–347.

118. Don Pablo Tito Uscamayta Inga de Valladares, a *cacique* of the town of Cajamarca,

was the "procurator-general for the Indians" of the province. Instructed by the lords of Cajamarca and accompanied by one Francisco Quispe, he traveled to Spain in 1684 to represent native leaders and commoners before the Council. After a two-month stay in Madrid, he returned to his hometown bearing no fewer than twelve royal decrees addressed to the viceroy and the *audiencia*, as well as a royal order ordering the magistrates of the high court to uphold these decrees and dispense justice as needed. The decrees covered a range of individual and collective demands. "Carta. Don Melchor Carguarayco y Don Juan Bautista Astoquipan a SM," Cajamarca, May 26, 1687, AGI, Lima, 174.

119. A few cases from the eighteenth century signal the appointment of indigenous subjects, *caciques* in particular, as *protectores de indios*. León Fernández, "El protector," 99; Hunefeldt, "Comunidad, curas y comuneros," 14–15.

120. Just the *junta* in Mama (a small village 35 miles east of Lima) brought together 150 *caciques* and *principales* from Lima, Huamanga, and Huánuco. On the *perpetuidad* controversy: Abercrombie, "La perpetuidad traducida"; Assadourian, "Las rentas," 78–81; Assadourian, "Los señores"; Assadourian, "La renta"; Assadourian, "La política"; Goldwert, "La lucha"; Goldwert, "La lucha (continuación)"; Hanke, *The Spanish Struggle*; López-Ocón Cabrera, "Andinología"; Mumford, *Vertical Empire*, 60–68; Mumford, "Aristocracy"; Pereña Vicente, "La pretensión."

121. Alfonso X's *Siete partidas* devoted an entire title with twenty-seven laws to describe the attributions and responsibilities of *personeros* (later called *procuradores* or procurators). *Siete partidas*, pt. 3, tit. 5, esp. laws 1, 2, 10, 13, and 14.

122. *Todo acquello que yo podría hazer y proveer de qualquiera calidad, condiçion que sea en esas dichas provincias si por mi persona las governara.* Fragments of the power of attorney issued by the king to Viceroy Marquis of Montesclaros in 1606 have been transcribed in Latasa Vassallo, *Administración virreinal*, 12.

123. Renzo Honores's survey of notarial instruments in Lima and Potosí shows that letters of attorney granted to *procuradores* and other legal specialists had become widespread by the 1550s. Honores, "Una sociedad," 206–207, 224–225. My own research in the archives of Madrid, Cuzco, and Lima confirms Honores's contention. For an early example: "Poder. Martín Condortarqui y Francisco Urcuni a Martín Álvarez," Arequipa, April 29, 1558, MNAAH, AH-MS, A236.

124. Several examples of these letters of attorney in connection with the First General Land Inspection, all signed in Cuzco and dated in 1596, can be found in ARC, PN 15 (Salas). For Felipe Guaman Poma's involvement in the First General Land Inspection as assistant, interpreter, witness, and (later) informal procurator: Puente Luna, "Cuando el 'punto de vista nativo.'" For an example of a land title obtained by a *cacique* through the procedure described above: "Francisco de Ayusanta Redin con Pedro Lorenzo Astocuri," Lima, 1713, AGI, Escribanía, 519b, 102r–108r. For similar strategies displayed by the Indian authorities in Charcas: Inch, "El mundo letrado."

125. *Recopilación*, bk. 2, tit. 5, law 1; Schäfer, *El Consejo Real*, 68, 119–120.

126. On the procurators and solicitors operating in Madrid: Kagan, *Lawsuits*, 56–59; *Recopilación*, bk. 2, tit. 28, laws 21–19; Schäfer, *El Consejo Real*, 59, 68–69.

127. The Tlaxcalan leaders hired Cervera by virtue of a letter of attorney empowering

them to act as legal agents of the larger community. In Madrid, they transferred it to Juan Gómez de Argomedo, "procurator of the Royal Council of the Indies" (*procurador del Real Consejo de las Yndias*). "Andrés de Cervera con los indios principales de Tlaxcala," 623v, 655r–660v. The Tlaxcalans who formed the 1585 delegation relied on the famous Diego Muñoz Camargo as their "administrador e interpetre [*sic*]." Gibson, *Tlaxcala*, 166–167; Díaz Serrano, "La república." On muncipal coats of arms in Tlaxcala and other regions of New Spain: Haskett, "Paper Shields," 105–107.

128. "Recaudos de los indios de Collaguas," December 8, 1585, AGI, Lima, 131, 17r–17v.

129. "Poder. Doña Isabel de Padilla y otras al Conde de Lemos," Cuzco, April 12, 1616, AHP, PN, 3173 (Recas), 1602r–1607v; "Poder. Doña Isabel de Padilla y otras a Juan Calderón de Robles y otros," Cuzco, March 18, 1621, AHP, PN (Alvarado), 5300, 219r–224v.

130. In 1573, the Indian dependents or retainers (*yanaconas*) of Juan Arias Maldonado, a *vecino* of Cuzco, empowered attorney Francisco de Jerez and Domingo Ros, perhaps a solicitor, to represent them before the *audiencia* and the Council. Two years later, Ros transferred the power back to Juan Arias Maldonado, then on his way to Spain, and to Sebastián de Santander, a procurator in Madrid. Santander later requested exemption from tribute for the *yanaconas* before the Council. "Carta de los indios yanaconas de Juan Arias Maldonado y otros del Cuzco al señor Don Diego de Zúñiga," 1575, AGI, Lima, 123. On the *yanaconas* of Cuzco: Wightman, *Indigenous Migration*, 17–23.

131. In 1651, the *caciques* and tax collectors of Jauja signed a letter of attorney empowering three legal agents planning a trip to Spain: Don Francisco Hati, Don Rodrigo Flores Caxamalqui, and Don Luis Macas, *caciques* of Latacunga (Quito), Canta, and Yauyos (east of Lima), respectively. They were to plea for a twenty-year exemption from work at the Huancavelica mercury mines. "Poder de los caciques y cobradores de Atunjauja, Luringuanca y Ananguanca," October 21, 1651, ARJ, PN, 7 (Carranza), 208r–212r.

132. In the 1550s, the *caciques* of Canta empowered one Father Diego de Valencia for legal representation before the Council. He then transferred the *poder* to a registered procurator in Spain. Rostworowski, *Conflicts*, 88–89.

133. In 1572, Spanish chronicler and Cuzco resident Diego Trujillo gave his *poder* to Don Sebastián Hilaquita, an "Inca notable" (*ynga principal*) residing in Lima and a relative of Don Francisco Atahualpa, to travel to the royal court and obtain confirmation of privileges granted to two grandchildren of Atahualpa, Don Sebastián's relatives. Oberem, *Notas*, 56–57, 176; Espinoza, "La vida," 256–257; Oberem, *Don Sancho Hacho*, 27. A full discussion of the Inca royals who in 1603 gave their *poder* for legal representation at the royal court to their relatives Garcilaso de la Vega Inca, Don Alonso Fernández de Mesa, Don Alonso Márquez Inca de Figueroa, and Don Melchor Carlos Inca is in Puente Luna, "Into the Heart," 73–76; Puente Luna, "Incas pecheros."

134. Puente Luna, "Into the Heart," 73–76.

135. Altman, *Emigrants*, 204; Herzog, *Upholding Justice*, 236. On the flow of news and information about the Iberian Peninsula within New Spain, especially between the city of Mexico and the port of Veracruz: Boyer, "People, Places." On the concept of "legal culture": Burbank, *Russian Peasants*, 5–10.

136. Paso, *Epistolario*, 4: 150–179.

137. "Memoria para el muy reverendo y magnífico señor fray Domingo," Lima, 1555, AGI, Lima, 204, n. 23. Strikingly, Alvarado signs "menor letrado," thus indicating that he was literate and had some legal expertise, but considered himself a dependent (*menor*) of father Domingo.

138. Titu Cusi Yupangui, *History of How the Spaniards*, xv, 5.

139. Titu Cusi Yupangui, *History of How the Spaniards*, xxviii, 159.

140. Otte and Albi Romero, *Cartas privadas*; Earle, "Letters and Love"; Mangan, *Transatlantic Obligations*, 81–83; Martínez Martínez, *Desde la otra orilla*.

141. Lockhart, "Letters and People to Spain"; Lockhart and Otte, *Letters and People*, ix–x; Rama, *The Lettered City*, 33–34.

142. A letter sent from Valladolid informed Garcilaso of the awards given to Melchor Carlos Inca in 1604. Vega, *Royal Commentaries*, pt. 1, bk. 9, ch. 40.

143. Penry, "Letters," 211.

144. Corteguera, *For the Common Good*, 196. On how literally thousands of petitions traveled to the court, see the work in progress by Masters, "The Lettered Marketplace."

145. Brendecke, *Imperios*, 261–263; Encinas, *Cedulario indiano*, 1: 13; *Recopilación*, bk. 3, tit. 16, laws 13 & 16.

146. Espinosa, *El Inca barroco*, 122. Don Carlos Inca sent a letter to the king in 1571, while his father, Don Cristóbal Paullu Inca, received at least one letter from the sovereign in the early 1540s. Cúneo-Vidal, *Historia de las guerras*, 167; Temple, "La descendencia," 166–168.

147. In the mid-seventeenth century, Juan Lorenzo Ayun, a native from Reque, in northern Peru, addressed at least three letters to his kin describing his journeys and legal affairs in Spain and Mexico. "Jerónimo Limaylla con Bernardino Limaylla," 1656–1671, AGI, Escribanía, 514C, 638r–643r.

148. In 1586, Don Alonso Atahualpa, a grandson of Inca Atahualpa residing in Madrid, signed a letter gifting his children still living in Quito some houses and land. He communicated his decision in a letter to his uncle in that city, who was acting as legal guardian of Don Alonso's children. Estupiñán-Freile, "Testamento," 48.

149. Alonso de Mesa wrote to his *mestizo* offspring in Spain from Cuzco at least once a year. "Méritos y servicios: Pedro Márquez Galeote," 1607, AGI, Patronato, 143, n. 2, r. 4; "Información y licencia: Vasco de Mesa," 1569, AGI, Indiferente, 2084, n. 15. Other examples include "Méritos y servicios: Juan Balsa," Cuzco, 1581, AGI, Patronato, 125, r. 7; "Pruebas para la concesión del Título de Caballero de Santiago de Melchor Carlos Inga," Trujillo; Madrid, 1606, AHN, OM-CS, e. 4081, 26v–29r.

150. Itier, "Las cartas en quechua"; Puente Luna, "What's in a Name?," 139–140.

151. "Andrés de Cervera con los indios principales de Tlaxcala," 622r; "Relación de gastos de Alonso Díaz de Guitián," Madrid, AHP, PN (Alvarado), 5300, 219r–224v; Puente Luna, "What's in a Name?," 139–140.

152. "Carta. Don Juan Condorpussa a Doña María Fernández de Cordoba," Arequipa, November 9, 1664, AGI, Lima, 171.

153. Altman, *Emigrants*, 205–206; Studnicki-Gizbert, *A Nation*. Jane Mangan has recently revealed the centrality of family networks for the transatlantic voyage of Spanish,

mestizo, and indigenous spouses, parents, and children in the second half of the sixteenth century. Family connections "proved key at every stage of the voyage." Mangan, *Transatlantic Obligations*, 98.

154. "Información y licencia: Martín Fernández," 1605, AGI, Contratación, 5286, n. 77; "Información y licencia: Pedro Chafo Savana," 1671, AGI, Contratación, 5437, n. 2, r. 20, 6r.

155. "Méritos y servicios: Pedro Márquez Galeote"; Vega, *Royal Commentaries*, pt. 2, bk. 8, ch. 17.

156. In 1587, Don Alonso Atahualpa named Don Diego de la Torre, *cacique* of Turmequé and longtime resident in Spain, as his executor. Jiménez de la Espada, *Relaciones geográficas. Perú*, 3: cxlvii.

157. "Informaciones: Francisco de Heriza," 1669, AGI, Lima, 259, n. 10, 12v.

158. "Jerónimo Limaylla con Bernardino Limaylla," 559r–559v.

159. Jane Mangan has reached a similar conclusion in her remarkable new study of Indian-Spanish transatlantic families of the early colonial era. Mangan, *Transatlantic Obligations*, 13 & ch. 14.

160. Jerónimo Lorenzo Limaylla reminded the Council in a *memorial*: "[The Council] has aided other natives of the Indies who have returned, such as D. Nicolás Flores and D. Andrés de Ortega, and Don Carlos, and many others who received assistance with their expenses." He received 200 *reales*. "Memorial. Don Jerónimo Lorenzo Limaylla a S.M. solicitando una ayuda de costa para volver al Perú," Madrid, December 23, 1671, AGI, Indiferente, 640.

CHAPTER 4

1. On this demand for Andean falcons: León Portocarrero, *Descripción*, 52; Vega, *Royal Commentaries*, bk. 9, ch. 9. For hunting sports and entertainments at the court: Brown and Elliott, *A Palace*. On hunting parties in seventeenth-century Lima that used dogs and falcons: Rostworowski, *Señoríos*, 99. On Chávarri's commission and failed journey: "Francisco Fernández del Castillo con Miguel de Echavarri," 1678, AGI, Escribanía, 1042a. For previous orders to remit falcons to the royal court: "Carta. Arzobispo virrey del Perú a SM," Lima, August 27, 1678, AGI, Lima, 26. Similar orders issued in the 1690s can be found in AGI, Lima 23.

2. "Francisco Fernández del Castillo con Miguel de Echavarri," esp., 29r–37v, 47v. For the delivery in Seville to a member of the royal household: "Suplemento al thesorero general del Conssejo de 60 Doblones," Madrid, August 29, 1679, AGI, Indiferente, 441, l. 29, 373v. On the royal sponsorship offered to Álvaro Enríquez and Andrés Dávila: "100 pesos de vellón para Álvaro Enrique," Madrid, April 6, 1678, AGI, Indiferente, 441, l. 29, 133r; "30 ducados de vellón para Andrés de Avila," Madrid, April 30, 1678, Indiferente, 441, l. 29, 134v–135r.

3. For previous characterizations of transatlantic travelers as *curacas*, *caciques*, or "ethnic lords": Alaperrine-Bouyer, "Enseignements et enjeux"; Buntix and Wuffarden, "Incas y

reyes"; Dueñas, *Indians*; Dueñas, "Ethnic Power"; Lorandi, *Spanish King*; Pease, "Curacas coloniales"; Pease, "Un memorial"; Pease, *Curacas*.

4. On Dávila's request of an inactive posting (*plaza muerta*) in the mounted company of the viceroy's guard: "Memorial. Andrés Dávila a SM," Madrid, May 13, 1678, AGI, Lima, 18. On the viceroy's guard: Lohmann, "Las compañías." The Council recommended Dávila for a soldier post in one of the companies that guarded the port of El Callao. The king approved.

5. Stern, *Peru's Indian Peoples*, 180–182. For a recent critique of the "cultural uprooting," "deculturation," and "isolation" allegedly experienced by all indigenous migrants as they severed ties to *ayllus*, *caciques*, and rural communities: Graubart, *With Our Labor*, 69–70, 123.

6. I am borrowing some of these ideas about creolization and ethnogenesis from David Brown's analysis of Afro-Cuban religions, which is partly based on Stephan Palmié's discussion of ethnogenesis. Brown, *Santería Enthroned*, 27–28, 50.

7. Sidbury and Cañizares-Esguerra, "Mapping Ethnogenesis," 182–184, 198–199. For comparison with African experiences: Miller, "Retention, Reinvention." For previous discussions about the asymmetries of power that characterize interconnected Atlantic systems: Bailyn, *Atlantic History*; Eltis, "Atlantic History"; Canny, "Writing Atlantic History"; Games, "Atlantic History"; Gould, "Entangled Atlantic Histories"; Gould, "Entangled Histories."

8. Mintz and Price, *The Birth*, esp. ch. 1.

9. Sidbury and Cañizares-Esguerra, "Mapping Ethnogenesis," 184.

10. Previous treatments of this segment of the population include Cárdenas, *La población*; Charney, *Indian Society*; Graubart, *With Our Labor*; Lowry, "Forging an Indian Nation"; Murillo, Lentz, and Ochoa, *City Indians*; O'Toole, *Bound Lives*; Poloni-Simard, *El mosaico*; Powers, *Andean Journeys*, 46; Stern, *Peru's Indian Peoples*, 162; Vergara, "Growing up Indian"; Wightman, *Indigenous Migration*.

11. Carrillo, "'La única voz'"; Dueñas, *Indians*; Estenssoro, *Del paganismo*; Glave, "Memoria"; Vergara, "Piedad e interés económico."

12. Alaperrine-Bouyer, "Cruzar el océano," 39–49; Gil, "Los primeros mestizos"; Mangan, "Moving Mestizos"; Mangan, *Transatlantic Obligations*, 54–69; Van Deusen, *Global indios*, 95–96.

13. This was probably the case with Diego Sánchez Macario and his wife Ana de Andrés. Diego was an *yndio* and a *cacique* from the town of San Pedro Pillao (in the central Andean *corregimiento* of Tarma). Ana, whose *calidad* went unmarked, was a native of Arenillas, in Castilla-León, the daughter of Domingo Andrés and Ana Pastora. In 1667, the couple requested a license to return to Peru via Tierra Firme. "Licencia de pasajero de Diego Sánchez Macario, indio, natural de San Pedro Pillao, con su mujer, Ana de Andrés, natural de Arenillas, hija de Domingo Andrés y de Ana Pastora, al Perú," Madrid, January 17, 1667, AGI, Contratación, 5540a, l. 1, 39v.

14. O'Toole, *Bound Lives*, 5–6, 11. On the participation of Africans as crew members and other roles in the Pacific trade system linking Lima with Trujillo, Paita, Guayaquil, and ultimately with the circum-Caribbean and Atlantic systems: Bryant, O'Toole, and

Vinson, *Africans to Spanish America*. On Africans in urban Atlantic spaces: Cañizares-Esguerra, Childs, and Sidbury, *The Black Urban Atlantic*. Colonial movements of peoples, languages, and goods along the coast of Peru relied on much older routes. Some indigenous fishermen and sailors transported salt, flour, maize, and coal from Lima and its surrounding areas to northern ports such as Huanchaco and even to Panama. Ramos, "Language and Society," 24–26.

15. "Juan Francisco de Abellano contra Lázaro Llongo," Trujillo, November 26, 1672, ARLL, CO, l. 200, c. 1380.

16. On "indigenous navigators" along the Ecuadoran coast: Glave, "Hombres de mar." For *trujillano* and *mochica* fishermen settled in coastal valleys between Trujillo and Lima: Rostworowski, *Señoríos*, 129. For Indian fishermen in colonial Lima: Charney, *Indian Society*, 24; Vergara, "'Tan dulce para España,'" 44–45. For indigenous women who owned boats as part of the local fishing industry: Graubart, *With Our Labor*, 74. For the larger movement of peoples from Guatemala, Nicaragua, Venezuela, Tierra Firme, and Mexico to Lima: Van Deusen, "Diasporas," 257.

17. Ramos, "'*Mi Tierra*,'" 136. On Jerónimo, whom a witness identified as the son of Pedro Alonso Marino (a sailor?) and an unnamed Indian woman: "Información y licencia: Jerónimo," 1562, AGI, Contratación, 5537, l. 2, 217v.

18. Other travelers going from South and Central American ports to Spain include Antón (1586–1597), from Tierra Firme, Pedro Çama (1588), from Manta, Agustín (1605), from Puerto Viejo, Juan Bernal (1607), from Santa Marta, and Francisco de Panamá (1614–1619), from Panama. Puente Luna, "Into the Heart," Appendix.

19. Alaperrine-Bouyer, "Cruzar el océano"; Mangan, *Transatlantic Obligations*, 3–4.

20. In 1594, Andrés de Aguilar, *indio ladino*, signed a contract for personal service (*seruicio y soldada*) with Tomás de Zárate, a merchant based in Lima and in route to Spain. "Asiento. Tomás de Zárate con Andrés de Aguilar," Lima, April 12, 1594, AGN, PN, 1 (Aguilar), 355r.

21. Mangan, *Transatlantic Obligations*, 114.

22. For estimates on the duration of the transatlantic journeys of President Pedro de la Gasca (1546–1547), Garcilaso Inca de la Vega (1560–1561), Viceroy Francisco de Toledo (1581), and Father Calixto de San José Tupac Inca (1749–1750): Loayza, *Fray Calixto*, 3; Miró Quesada Sosa, *El Inca*, ch. 4; Varner, *El Inca*, 196–199; Zimmerman, *Francisco de Toledo*, 22–23. For approximate convoy sailing times from and to Andalusian ports: Haring, *Trade and Navigation*; Jacobs, "Legal and Illegal Emigration," 61–69; Phillips, *Six Galleons*, 11–13; Schäfer, *El Consejo Real II*, 372–373. A 1610 report claimed that Spanish litigants and petitioners from the New World spent between three and six years at the royal court. Brendecke, *Imperios*, 343, n. 112.

23. "Información y licencia: Juan de Oleandres," 1631, AGI, Contratación, 5410, n. 12. Andrés de Espinosa, an "Indian" from New Spain who journeyed to the royal court with Viceroy Luis de Velasco in 1614, presented Domingo de Eguiluz Lezama as one of his witnesses. Eguiluz, a *vecino* of Mexico City and temporary resident in Seville, had known Andrés in New Spain and Madrid. Pedro de Ribera, a *vecino* of Puebla de los Ángeles,

claimed to have known Andrés in the Indies and the royal court. "Información y licencia: Andrés de Espinosa," 1614, AGI, Contratación, 5340, n. 41. For additional examples: Puente Luna, "What's in a Name?" Puente Luna, "Into the Heart," 133.

24. These links are especially clear in the case of the official interpreters of Lima's *Audiencia*. Puente Luna, "The Many Tongues." On *mestizos* who journeyed to Spain as *criados* of a Spaniard, sometimes their own father: Alaperrine-Bouyer, "Cruzar el océano," 16–17, 36–37. The situation was not necessarily different among Spanish travelers. By the late sixteenth century, well over half of the male voyagers who went to Peru were servants. Boyd-Bowman, "Patterns of Spanish Emigration," 94.

25. Altman, *Emigrants*, 70, 261, 262; Boyer, *Lives of the Bigamists*, 2–3, 71–78. On the relations and obligations of *familiaridad* or fictive kinship, which bound many an extended Spanish Atlantic family: Mangan, *Transatlantic Obligations*, esp. ch. 4; Premo, "Familiar"; Van Deusen, "The Intimacies." On the complexities of the term *criado* (literally, someone raised in one's home): Van Deusen, "Coming to Castile," 301; Rappaport, *The Disappearing Mestizo*, 126. For a *cacique* of the Muisca town of Turmequé (in Santa Fe) who returned with his European-born servant in 1579: Rappaport and Cummins, *Beyond the Lettered City*, 32.

26. Don Diego de Figueroa, a self-fashioned *cacique* from Huamachuco, journeyed to Spain in 1596 using the permit given to him by the governor of Cartagena. "Don Diego de Figueroa cacique de la Prouincia de Guamachuco," Madrid, October 7, 1598, AGI, Lima, 134. On how family ties and surrogacy "prompted and supported" transatlantic voyages: Mangan, *Transatlantic Obligations*, 6–7.

27. In 1694, Don Francisco Diez, *vecino* of Mérida in Yucatán, asked for a return license for him and Lorenzo Yajo, his Indian servant. "Información y licencia: Francisco Diez de Velasco," Seville, August 14, 1694, AGI, Contratación, 5455, n. 2, r. 14. For another case involving a Spaniard licensed to take Miguel, an Indian from New Spain, to Iberia and back: "Información y licencia: Vicente de Zaldívar," June 21, 1603, AGI, Contratación, 5279, n. 33.

28. "Información y licencia: Francisco Ulpo," Madrid, April 30, 1618, AGI, Contratación, 5363, n. 44; "Información y licencia: Diego Garcia Maldonado," Madrid, June 4, 1624, AGI, Contratación, 5793, l. 1, 373v–374r. On candidates for office who traveled to Madrid to oversee their appointments: Herzog, *Upholding Justice*, 65.

29. "Información y licencia: Jerónimo de Pamones," March 5, 1613, AGI, Contratación, 5332, n. 23.

30. There are other examples. "Información y licencia: Juan Pedro Chuquival," 1593, AGI, Contratación, 5241, n. 2, r. 42; "Información y licencia: Jacinto Ramos Chuquillangui," December 2, 1623, AGI, Contratación, 5386, n. 88.

31. In the sixteenth century, Don Diego Maxixcatzin, governor of Tlaxcala, appeared before the Council accompanied by Juan de Salmerón, an *audiencia* judge. Baber, "Empire," 30. Juan Antonio, an "Indian" from New Spain, traveled to the royal court at the service of Viceroy Luis de Velasco in 1611. "Información y licencia: Juan Antonio, indio," June 21, 1613, AGI, Contratación, 5334, n. 2, r. 11.

32. Phillips, "The Iberian Atlantic," 87. For a similar pattern of travel alongside priests, this time for *mestizos* who left Peru in the late sixteenth century: Alaperrine-Bouyer, "Cruzar el océano," 41.

33. Jerónimo de Alfaro, classified as "Indian," journeyed from New Spain to Madrid as a dependent of a Mercedarian friar in 1628. "Información y licencia: Jerónimo de Alfaro," 1628, AGI, Contratación, 5401, n. 21. For the crucial role of patronage relations and social networks in judicial settings: Herzog, *Upholding Justice*, 127–151.

34. Topa Yupanqui, one of Santo Tomás's informants for the preparation of the first Quechua grammar and vocabulary printed in Spain in 1560, addressed a memorial to Philip in or around 1557. "Méritos y servicios: Don Diego y Don Francisco, hijos naturales del Emperador Atabalipa," 1557, AGI, Patronato, 188, r. 6, 38r–38v; Jiménez de la Espada, *Relaciones geográficas (Perú)*, 3: 95; "Libro de asientos de pasajeros," AGI, Contratación, 5537, l. 1, 9v. John Murra identified this traveler as "Don Mateo Yupanqui." Murra, "'Nos Hazen Mucha Ventaja,'" 79 and ff.

35. Gálvez Peña, "Cronistas peregrinos," 191–192; Mazín, *Gestores de la real justicia*; Martínez-Serna, "Procurators"; Mörner, "La afortunada gestión."

36. Around 1555, Father Domingo de Santo Tomás brought to court a set of instructions given to him by Juan de Alvarado in Lima. The native noble man from Chachapoyas had traveled to Spain with conquistador Alonso de Alvarado in 1544. "Memoria para el muy reverendo y magnífico señor fray Domingo," Lima, 1555, AGI, Lima, 204, n. 23. In 1551, Santo Tomás also presented the request of the Indians of Collao to have their tribute in kind commuted for silver before the emperor. López-Ocón Cabrera, "Andinología," 101.

37. On the relationship dating back to the 1540s among Andean lords, nobles of Inca descent, and Dominican reformers such as Jerónimo de Loaysa, Tomás de San Martín, and Domingo de Santo Tomás in the late 1540s: Hampe Martínez, *Don Pedro de la Gasca*; Olmedo Jiménez, *Jerónimo de Loaysa*; Rostworowski, "La tasa." On the fathers' role as legal advocates and procurators of the Inca nobility in Cuzco, Quito, Lima, and Europe: Guaman Poma, *Nueva corónica*, 183; Hemming, *The Conquest*, 284; Jiménez de la Espada, *Relaciones geográficas. Perú*, 3: cxliii–cxv; Oberem, *Notas*, 168–169; Vega, *Royal Commentaries*, pt. 1, bk. 9, ch. 39.

38. Borges Morán, "El Consejo." On certain occasions, the *Casa de la Contratación* demanded that royal bureaucrats pay for the passage fee of these subordinates (usually, 20 ducats). "Información y licencia: Nuño de la Cueva," 1628, AGI, Contratación, 5352, n. 18.

39. Herzog, "Naming, Identifying and Authorizing," 196–197; Martínez, *Genealogical Fictions*, 128–129. Despite regulations and restricted emigration, many *moriscos* (Muslim converts) managed to make the journey to Spanish America. Cook, *Forbidden Passages*. The need to have a royal license was introduced in 1501. Sánchez Rubio and Testón Núñez, "'Fingiendo llamarse,'" 214.

40. Amounts are given in pesos of eight *reales* each. Whenever a source registers an amount in assayed pesos (12.5 *reales*), golden pesos, or ducats (11 *reales*), I have converted such quantities to ordinary pesos. The golden peso or *castellano* was worth about 1.6 times a silver peso of eight. One peso of eight equaled 272 *maravedíes*, while the golden peso equaled some 435 *maravedíes*.

41. Altman, *Emigrants*, 191; Jacobs, "Legal and Illegal Emigration," 60, 67, 79; *Recopilación*, bk. 6, tit. 14, laws 16–18 (autos 102 and 103); bk. 109, tit. 126, laws 135–139. On friars who traveled unlicensed from Peru to Spain: "Carta. Conde de Alba de Liste a SM," Lima, June 15, 1656, AGI, Lima, 58, n. 107.

42. Two *vecinos* of Cuzco paid 1,170 pesos to a royal official for bringing their relatives from Seville to Lima. Another *vecino* left 1,560 pesos in his will to pay for the journey of two illegitimate sons to Spain. Another Cuzco resident borrowed 2,340 pesos to pay for his voyage to Spain in 1571. "Testamento. Florencio Fernández de Mesa," Cuzco, October 26, 1589, ARC, PN, unnumbered (Sánchez), 1229r; "Obligación. Juan Arias Maldonado a Cristóbal Jiménez," Cuzco, March 24, 1571, ARC, PN, 22 (Sánchez), 441r–441v; Cornejo Bouroncle, "De la vida colonial," 259–263. On this widespread practice: Mangan, *Transatlantic Obligations*, 79–80.

43. Gangotena Jijón, "Documentos históricos"; "Información y licencia: Jorge Fernández de Mesa y Alonso de Mesa," 1584, AGI, Indiferente, 2094, n. 164. In 1559, Captain Garcilaso bequeathed his illegitimate son Gómez Suárez de Figueroa, better known as *El Inca*, 6,400 pesos to travel to and study in Spain. "Testimonio del testamento del capitán Sebastián Garcilaso de la Vega," Cuzco, January 18, 1560, ARC, PN, 1 (Bitorero), 99r–100v.

44. "Don Carlos y don Francisco, hijos de Atabalipa. Sobre su sutentaçion," May 16, 1548, AGI, Lima, 566, l. 5, 275v–276r. See also Gangotena Jijón, "Documentos históricos," 91–92; Oberem, *Notas*, 56–67, 99–102, 121–133, 182, 193–220, 323–324; Vargas Ugarte, *Manuscritos peruanos*, 153.

45. For the royal prohibition that clerics serve as legal agents: *Recopilación*, bk. 1, tit. 14, law 83 (and auto 141); bk. 141, tit. 112, laws 116–118.

46. "'Poder. Don Fernando Tuçi Trapac a fray Pedro de la Serna,'" Madrid, March 12, 1594, AHN, CS, l. 21484.

47. "Poder. Don Juan Guachuri y Doña Juana Esquivel Yupanqui al padre rector y al procurador del Colegio de la Compañía de Jesús de Madrid," Curahuasi (Cuzco), March 16, 1616, AHP, PN, 3173 (Recas), 1596r–1601r. For a similar example involving the Franciscans in Lima: "Poder. Don Sebastián Guacrapaucar y otros a fray Domingo de la Concepción," Lima, October 9, 1686, AGN, CGC, l. 24, d. 4.

48. "Memorial. Juan Vélez a SM," Lima, 1613, AGI, Lima, 143. For the political gains of some of these confessors due to their proximity to the viceroy: León Portocarrero, *Descripción*, 35.

49. Besides being page to different viceroys since age nine, Salinas served the influential post of personal secretary, albeit briefly. He had the exclusive privilege of signing viceregal provisions, orders, and other documents, and of presenting the writings of litigants and petitioners. He also had continuous access to the viceroy's private chambers. Torres Arancivia, *Corte de virreyes*, 84–85; Puente Luna, "What's in a Name?"

50. Two Franciscans acted as witnesses in Lorenzo's travel license, claiming to have known him for many years. "Información y licencia: Lorenzo Ayllón Atahualpa," AGI, Contratación, 5427, n. 3, r. 33; "Información y licencia: Buenaventura de Salinas y Córdoba," May 9, 1646, AGI, Contratación, 5539, l. 3, 78v–79r; "Jerónimo Limaylla con Bernardino Limaylla," 1656–1671, AGI, Escribanía, 514C, 489r–491v, 550r–552r, 924r–926r.

For Buenaventura's role as confessor of the viceroy in Mexico: Riva-Agüero, *La historia*, 256, n. 252. For details on the Count of Alba's trip to Peru: Bradley, *Society, Economy*. In 1535, Don Diego Maxixcatzin, governor of Tlaxcala, used a similar strategy to strengthen his political connections. He sailed on the same ship as the incoming viceroy bound to New Spain. Don Diego "made it a point to become well-acquainted" with the royal minister. Baber, "Empire," 30.

51. Burns, *Into the Archive*; Rappaport and Cummins, *Beyond the Lettered City*.

52. On *indios ladinos* and the multiplicity of roles that they played in colonial society, see Adorno, "The Indigenous Ethnographer"; Aguilar Moreno, "The *indio ladino*"; and Charles, "'More *Ladino*.'"

53. This situation contrasts with earlier ones in which the Council of the Indies summoned court interpreters to interrogate indigenous subjects in the "indio language," inquiring about specific words and phrases. The purpose was to determine their imperial identity and thus elucidate whether they had been justly enslaved. Van Deusen, *Global indios*, 177–180.

54. Durston, *Pastoral Quechua*, 273.

55. In 1626, Don Antonio de Chaves, a native chanter and teacher from the town of Mansiche, signed a contract with the Indian stewards of the Nuestra Señora de la Asunción sodality founded in Trujillo. Besides singing during the masses celebrated in honor of the virgin, Don Antonio was to teach the native children of the city how to "read, write, sing, and play musical instruments." The indigenous authorities of Mansiche, however, demanded that, despite his teaching responsibilities, Don Antonio continue paying tribute. "Expediente seguido por Don Antonio de Chaves," Trujillo, June 6, 1636, ARLL, C-CO, l. 184, e. 1037.

56. Adorno, "Images"; Charles, *Allies*; Baker, *Imposing Harmony*, 194–203, 231; Guaman Poma, *Nueva corónica*; Durston, *Pastoral Quechua*, 291–293; Estenssoro, *Del paganismo*, 463–468; Vergara, "Growing up Indian." In 1588, the Indian town of La Magdalena, immediately west of Lima, had six *cantores* (three cantors proper, one sexton [*sacristán*], a church prosecutor [*fiscal*], and an executioner) but only four municipal officials (one chief magistrate, one scribe, one town steward [*mayordomo del pueblo*] and one bailiff). "Memoria de los oficiales," January 9, 1589, MNAAH, AH-MS, A103.

57. Estenssoro, *Del paganismo*, 41–43. By the early 1550s, the Dominicans had already founded eighteen convents and many schools for the religious training of indigenous subjects. Alaperrine-Bouyer, *La educación*, 47–48; López-Océn Cabrera, "Andinología," 146, n. 156; Vargas, *Fray Domingo*, 38–39.

58. In 1568, Juan Mitima and Don Diego de Figueroa were receiving 35 pesos each for performing these duties. The latter also became *alcalde de doctrina* of the school of San Andrés and, in 1579, *alcalde mayor* of the indigenous population of Quito, before journeying to the Habsburg court to request additional honors. Other sixteenth-century travelers to the royal court, such as Don Francisco Atahualpa, Don Mateo Yupanqui, and Don Pedro de Henao, though of a much higher social standing, had been Don Diego de Figueroa's classmates at the school of San Andrés. Espinoza, "El alcalde mayor," 216–219; Fernández Rueda, "Educación y evangelización," 130–141; Hartmann and Oberem,

"Quito," 109–119; Moreno, *Fray Jodoco Rique*, 263–297; Oberem, *Notas*, 123–130; Ponce Leiva, *Relaciones histórico-geográficas.*

59. Aguilar Moreno, "The *indio ladino*," 155.

60. Cook, *Padrón*, 479–523. For the indigenous church servants and assistants (*indios de iglesia*) in Cuenca: Poloni-Simard, *El mosaico*, 232–236. There, some teachers and cate-chists (*maestros de capilla*) penned the wills of urban Indians. They enjoyed considerable wealth and status. Sometimes, they passed on their ecclesiastic posts to their sons.

61. Esquilache, who was about to sail to Peru to fill his new appointment, certified that Sosa had received a license "so that he can take one companion and one *criado*." "Información y licencia: fray Claudio Ramírez de Sosa," 1615, AGI, Contratación, 5345, n. 46.

62. One of Father Bernardo's letters to Núñez Vela, written in 1690, was printed in Madrid, in all likelihood by the recipient. In the letter, Bernardo Inga outlined different genealogies linking Inca and Spanish royal and noble houses. Núñez Vela used this infor-mation to bolster his own legal campaign, discussed in a later chapter. Several copies of the letter circulated in Mexico and Peru. Macera, *El Inca colonial*; "Carta que escrivió el P. Ber-nardo Inga, Presbytero, de los PP. Clerigos Menores, à D. Iuan Nuñez Vela de Ribera, Pres-bytero, residente en la Corte de Madrid," Seville, January 10, 1690, ARC, CB, t. 3, d. 20.

63. "Real cédula [para que no] vengan a España religiosos indios por compañeros."

64. In Reque around 1644, de la Carrera prepared a systematic description of the colo-nial "Mochica" or "Yunga" language. Carrera, *Arte de la lengua*, 73–74; Durston, *Pastoral Quechua*, 124–125. Juan de Ayllón praised Carrera's *Arte de la Lengua* with a sonnet in-cluded in the prologue. For similar examples of Indian boys sent to Cuzco to receive musi-cal training from a priest, friar, or instructor: Baker, *Imposing Harmony*, 217.

65. "Jerónimo Limaylla con Bernardino Limaylla," 387v–401r, 443r–443v, 447v–449r, 451v–452r, 470r–475v, 648r–649v, 951v; "Confirmación de encomienda de Reque," AGI, Lima, 201, n. 18; Angulo, "Libro de visitas," 234; Cabero, "El capitán," 94; Rostworowski, *Curacas y sucesiones*, 12; Zevallos Quiñones, *Historia*, 22. On father Juan de Ayllón and the Franciscans of Saña: Arroyo, *Los franciscanos*; Tibesar, *Franciscan Beginnings*, 62–63; Var-gas Ugarte, *Vida del siervo*, 21, 120; Zevallos Quiñones, *Historia*, 57–62.

66. Gabriela Ramos has also suggested that "learning did not occur within clearly defined programs and solid institutions, but was instead haphazard … although *colegios* (schools) were important, a good part of education, knowledge, and learning took place elsewhere." Ramos, "Indigenous Intellectuals," 31.

67. The school of Desamparados was created in 1666 to educate the "poor" Indians of the Indian ward of El Cercado. Prior to his journey to Spain, Juan Núñez Vela, the famous *mestizo* presbyter, ran another of these schools, where he taught sixty-five Indian students the Christian doctrine and how to speak, read, and write in Castilian. Viceroy Duke of La Palata had authorized the school at the request of four "natives and residents" (*naturales y recidentes*) of the city, who claimed to speak on behalf of "the other citizens of Lima" (*los demas vessinos de ella*). "Primera paga de 50 pesos a Juan Matheo Gonzales," 1685, AGN, GO-BI 2, l. 92, c. 868; "Provicion que lleba … Diego de Venavente de los niños naturales de la escuela," 1688, AGI, Lima, 174. Another teacher, Mateo González, "natural de aquel Reino," replaced Núñez Vela in his duties.

68. Ramos, "Indigenous Intellectuals," 31; Ramos, "'*Mi Tierra*,'" 134. On native children and youths incorporated into their Spanish masters' extended families: Van Deusen, "The Intimacies"; Vergara, "Growing up Indian."

69. For an in-depth study of these practices and the different learning opportunities that the city of Potosí afforded indigenous subjects: Inch, "El mundo letrado."

70. Guaman Poma's tale about his relationship with Don Cristóbal de León, his "disciple" in the arts of writing and litigation, is instructive in this respect. Guaman Poma, *Nueva corónica*, 498–501, 694.

71. One late example is that of Don Juan Bustamante Carlos Inca's visit to the royal court in the eighteenth century. Ferdinand VI gave Don Juan an audience thanks to the influence of Don Juan's godfather, the Duke of Santisteban. "Memorial. Don Juan Bustamante Carlos Inca a SM," Madrid, November 21, 1759, AVU, MS, v. 35, d. 16, 3–4.

72. Gauderman, *Women's Lives*; Graubart, *With Our Labor*, 13–19; Mangan, *Trading Roles*, 134–158; Powers, *Andean Journeys*; Saignes, *Caciques, Tribute and Migration*; Wightman, *Indigenous Migration*, 107–124; Zulawski, *They Eat from Their Labor*.

73. Cárdenas, *La población*, 28–46; Graubart, *With Our Labor*, ch. 2; Pereyra Plascencia, "Indios y mestizos"; Van Deusen, "Diasporas," 248–249, 256; Vergara, "Growing up Indian." For the more or less constant flow of migrants from the North Coast to Lima: Graubart, "Ethnicity"; Graubart, "The Creolization," 473; O'Toole, *Bound Lives*.

74. Coello, *Espacios de exclusión*, 220–221.

75. Charney, "'Much too worthy …'"; Graubart, *With Our Labor*, 63–65; Vergara, "Migración y trabajo femenino." For Lima's *valles comarcanos*: Graubart, "Competing Spanish and Indigenous Jurisdictions"; Vergara, "'Tan dulce para España.'" For indigenous domestic servants in the southern Andes: Glave, "Mujer indígena"; Wightman, *Indigenous Migration*, 116–118.

76. Van Deusen, "Diasporas," 267; Coello, *Espacios de exclusión*; Ramos, "Indian Hospitals"; Espinoza, "El alcalde mayor," 211.

77. Cook, *Padrón*; Van Deusen, "Diasporas"; Lowry, "Forging an Indian Nation." Though significantly smaller than that of Spaniards, Africans, and *castas* (people of mixed descent), the "Indian" population amounted to about 10 percent of the total inhabitants of Lima and the surrounding valleys, which included several indigenous municipalities such as Surco, Magdalena, and Lati. Charney, *Indian Society*; Rostworowski, *Señoríos*.

78. Ramos, "'*Mi Tierra*,'" 131.

79. Detailed discussions about the Indian population of Lima based on the 1613 census and other data include Charney, *Indian Society*, 11–14; Charney, "El indio urbano"; Lowry, "Forging an Indian Nation," 127–129; Appendix 121; Vergara, "Growing up Indian." Different estimates are presented in Cárdenas, *La población*.

80. Scholars have reached similar conclusions for Trujillo, Cuenca, Quito, Cuzco, and Huamanga. Many *caciques* knew the whereabouts and occupations of Indian absentees living in the city. Artisans and domestic servants, along with shepherds, *mitayos*, and laborers in nearby rural estates and textile mills, sometimes worked under the supervision of a community official. Charney, *Indian Society*, 12; Charney, "Negotiating Roots," 6–8, 14–16; Graubart, *With Our Labor*, 77–78; Poloni-Simard, *El mosaico*; Powers, *Andean*

Journeys, 73; Ramos, "Indigenous Intellectuals"; Ramos, *Death and Conversion*; Salomon, "Indian Women"; Stern, *Peru's Indian Peoples*, 154–155; Vergara, "Growing up Indian," 76–77; Wightman, *Indigenous Migration*, 123.

81. Graubart, *With Our Labor*, 68; Osorio, "*El callejón de la soledad.*"

82. Karen Graubart has traced these changes through the careful reconstruction of the transculturated wardrobes and other elements "of a developing creolized language" among indigenous women and men in Lima and Trujillo. Graubart, *With Our Labor*, 125 (quote), 147–153; Graubart, "The Creolization." The complex interplay between clothing, a central ethnic, class, and social signifier, and colonial identities and subjectivities, particularly in what pertains to traditional Andean elites, has been explored by several authors: Cummins, "We Are the Other," 226; Cummins, "Let Me See!"; Powers, "The Battle for Bodies," 35–44; Rowe, "Colonial Portraits"; Salomon, "Indian Women."

83. Graubart, *With Our Labor*, 62. For the concept of hybridity and its application to colonial Peruvian society: Dean and Leibshon, "Hybridity"; Graubart, "Hybrid Thinking." Older discussions of Andean ethnogenesis and transculturation in relation to internal migration and class mobility include Powers, *Andean Journeys*, 183; Charney, "'Much too worthy …'" Works addressing ethnogenesis in rural contexts include Abercrombie, *Pathways*; Glave, *Vida, símbolos y batallas*; Penry, "Transformations."

84. In 1653, for instance, Francisco Bioho, a free *moreno* from Guinea, fashioned himself at the royal court as as someone "naturalized [*naturalizado*] from age ten in the City of Kings in Peru, where he maintains his home and family." On the "naturalized Indians" (*indios naturalizados*) of Cuenca: Poloni-Simard, *El mosaico*, 208. For the urban property owners (*solareros*) of Trujillo and Lima, indigenous residents who owned a *solar* (a plot of land): Graubart, *With Our Labor*, 80–87.

85. Graubart, "The Creolization," 493; Graubart, "Ethnicity," 192–193.

86. Regarding colonial Quito, Frank Salomon writes, "In 1600 there were probably more different ways to be an urban Indian than there are today." Salomon, "Indian Women," 326.

87. "Memorial de Juan Vélez al Marqués de Montesclaros," Lima, 1612, AGI, Lima, 143. Vélez personally delivered his report to the viceroy's secretary in an effort to warn Montesclaros of the increasing number of *criollos* who, in spite of their "Indian" origin or appearance, embraced Spanish ways to "disguise" themselves as subjects of partial Spanish ancestry, and thus be able to escape fiscal duties. The house-by-house census of Lima's tributaries, undertaken the following year, was likely influenced by Vélez's report. For the life and career of Juan Vélez: Puente Luna, "The Many Tongues," 149–157.

88. Guaman Poma, *Nueva corónica*, 450, 834–922, esp. 871; 1138.

89. "Memorial de Juan Vélez al Marqués de Montesclaros."

90. The "standard" dress for male Indian tributaries in sixteenth-century Lima implied a draped mantle (*manto* or *manta*) and a sleeveless tunic (*unku* or *camiseta*)—or alternatively a shirt and breeches—made of inexpensive cloth. The general costume for their female counterparts consisted of a wraparound skirt or dress (*anaco*), a woven belt (*chumpi*), a wide shawl (*lliclla*) pinned around the shoulders, and increasingly in the seventeenth century, a Spanish-style skirt, a blouse, and a shawl of cheap fabric. Both ward-

robes signaled poverty and tributary status. For urban residents, they were also reminiscent of the rural costume. Graubart, *With Our Labor*, 125–127; Lowry, "Forging an Indian Nation," 222.

91. "Memorial de Juan Vélez al Marqués de Montesclaros." On the importance of eating wheat bread and speaking Spanish for early definitions of "Spanishness" among Spanish-Indian families: Mangan, *Transatlantic Obligations*, 49.

92. Graubart, *With Our Labor*, 134–135. See also Charney, *Indian Society*, 19. Contreras partially disputed, and sometimes even amended, the self-ascriptions of many of his respondents. He registered many men who called themselves "Indians" as such, sometimes stating that they were "wrongly" dressed as Spaniards. In other cases, he registered self-identified *mestizos* with no *cacique* or *ayllu* affiliation as Indians because, being poor, they were dressed "en habito de indio"—presumably cheap, handwoven Indian cloth. Graubart, *With Our Labor*, 135. Similar controversies raised by the ecclesiastic need to classify the *forasteros* of Latacunga are discussed in Powers, "The Battle for Bodies."

93. "Memorial de Juan Vélez al Marqués de Montesclaros."

94. Graubart, *With Our Labor*, 134–135.

95. Pease, "Conciencia"; Pease, "Un memorial."

96. Graubart, *With Our Labor*, 145.

97. Gaspar was to receive 100 pesos every year, food and clean linen clothes every week, medicines and medical assistance, and basic Christian instruction. "Asiento. Miguel de Angulo y Gaspar de la Chira," Lima, December 15, 1597, AGN, PN, 21 (Castillejo), 1042r–1042v.

98. Charney, "A Sense." See also Ramos, "'*Mi Tierra*.'"

99. The signatories were Pedro Blas, Gregorio Hernández, Alonso Pérez de Guadalupe, Sebastián Francisco, and Domingo Huaylas, "native Indians from this City of Kings of Peru" (*yndios naturales desta ciudad de los Rreyes del Piru*). The letter of attorney was drafted in Pedro Blas's residence, in the neighborhood of San Lázaro. "Poder a Juan de Saint Vicente," Lima, May 22, 1607, AGN, PN, 113 (Aparicio), 274r–275v.

100. "Poder … Los militares y caciques principales de este reino y maestros de oficios … a Don Valentín Mino Llulli," El Cercado, October 14, 1734, AGN, PN, 925 (Roldán), 2r–3v.

101. "Carta. Don Felipe Carguamango a SM," Lima, July 26, 1657, AGI, Lima, 169. For previous identifications of Don Felipe as a "cacique": Alaperrine-Bouyer, *La educación*, 311–312; Puente Brunke, "'Los vasallos.'"

102. For example: "Decreto de SM con un memorial de Don Juan Crisostomo Atagualpa," Madrid, August 13, 1664, AGI, Lima, 17.

103. Guaman Poma, *Nueva corónica*, 909–910.

104. Cook, *Padrón*, 282–283, 385. Pedro Blas grew up in the home of his *encomendero*. At the time of the 1613 census, he had been living in Lima for four decades. My efforts to locate Don Francisco de Sanzoles among the members of the *cacique* lineages of the Jauja Valley have been unsuccessful. His Spanish surname might be indicative of early migration to the city and influence of a Spanish patron. Sanzoles had two sons (a dance teacher and a tailor). One Don Juan Curibilca, master tailor and a native of Huamanga, is listed

in 1613 as sergeant-mayor of the Indians of the city. He declared his *cacique* was his own brother. Curibilca and his wife, the daughter of another *cacique*, declared no *hacienda* or family patrimony. Cook, *Padrón*, 101.

105. "Apelación de Don Carlos Chimo," Trujillo, August 19, 1641, ARLL, C-CC, l. 245, e. 2518; O'Toole, "Don Carlos." For Don Vicente Mora Chimo, who was of a similar social background and a traveler to the royal court in the eighteenth century: Mathis, "Vicente Mora Chimo."

106. For comparisons of this family patrimony with that of other well-off Indians (*indios ricos*) living in El Cercado: Harth-Terré, "El esclavo negro," 305; Charney, "'Much too worthy …,'" 93–95.

107. Mathis, "Vicente Mora Chimo," 479–481. Avendaño had won access to the post of governor and *segunda persona* of the town of Miraflores, south of Lima, perhaps through marriage. For another wealthy captain of an indigenous company who in 1653 owned several properties and four slaves: Charney, "'Much too worthy …,'" 95.

108. Salazar, "Relación," 321. El Cercado had its "Captain of the Indians" since the early seventeenth century. Antón de Cepeda, *ladino*, served as such at least between 1609 and 1614. Antón was also the chief magistrate of El Cercado for some time. Lowry, "Forging an Indian Nation," 154.

109. Lowry, "Forging an Indian Nation," 155; Millones, "The Inka's Mask," 17; Mugaburu and Mugaburu, *Chronicle*, 22, 105, 234–235, 268–270; Osorio, *Inventing Lima*, 73–74.

110. This hierarchy seems to have been composed of the following offices: private (*soldado*), corporal (*cabo de escuadra*), sergeant (*sargento*), standard-bearer (*alférez*), and infantry captain (*capitán*), all under the authority a field marshall (*maestre de campo*), sometimes a Spaniard. Overall, it took a soldier some twenty years to become a captain. "Expediente de Pedro Chafo Zavana," 1660–1662, AGI, Lima, 171; "Informaciones de oficio y parte: Pedro Chafo," Madrid, 1664, AGI, Lima, 255, n. 16; "Memorial. Pedro Chafo Çabana a SM," Lima, 1670, AGI, Lima, 26.

111. "Carta. Don Felipe Carguamango a SM." For strinkingly similar performances by *caciques* in colonial Quito, some of whom bore military titles: Espinosa, *El Inca barroco*, 86–88.

112. Reconstructions of some of these lineages can be found in Charney, *Indian Society*, 103, 175–180; Seminario, "Caciques de Lima." Charney, *Indian Society*, 75–80, 103.

113. Ramos, "Indigenous Intellectuals," 24–25; Ramos, *Death and Conversion*; Puente Luna, "The Many Tongues."

114. The 1613 census shows that, by then, there was already a relatively stable structure of native officials to rule over Indian urban subjects. The Spanish scribe commissioned to conduct the census relied on the *alcaldes* for the Indians, an *alguacil mayor* (chief bailiff), and the *mayorales* of each of the parishes of the city. Cook, *Padrón*, 5–10.

115. Puente Luna, "The Many Tongues," 158–159; Ramos, "Indigenous Intellectuals," 25–26.

116. Lowry, "Forging an Indian Nation," 129; Ramos, "Indigenous Intellectuals," 24–26.

117. Cook, *Padrón*, 149, 164, 220, 227, 300, 309, 337, 426. In Cuenca, Indian *forasteros* seem to have shared some of the characteristics of the *indios criollos* of Lima: Poloni-

Simard, *El mosaico*, 122, 199. The idea of "imagined political community" corresponds, of course, to Benedict Anderson's definition of modern nations. Such political communities are *imagined* because its members "will never know most of their fellow-members, meet them, or even hear of them, yet in the minds of each lives the image of their communion." They are imagined as *communities*, moroever, "regardless of the actual inequality and exploitation that may prevail in each." Anderson, *Imagined Communities*, 6–7, 47–65. See also Baber, "Categories," 27–28, 39.

118. The schools should only admit *caciques principales*, legitimate heirs to *cacicazgos*, and *segundas personas*. Some students, however, were brothers and close relatives of *caciques*, Indian nobles without a title, poor native children, and, after the second half of the seventeenth century, even Spaniards. On the Colegio de Caciques (or Colegio del Príncipe) in Lima: Alaperrine-Bouyer, *La educación*, 126–128; Baker, *Imposing Harmony*, 143; Premo, *Children of the Father King*, 92–97; Puente Brunke, "'Los vasallos,'" 464, note 422. The only exception—a former student of these schools visiting Spain—that I have found is that of Don Francisco Cangaguala Limaylla, who entered the School of El Príncipe in August 1674. Two years later, Don Francisco left for Spain in the company of the Jesuit principal. "Testamento de Don Baltassar Ticssi Canga Guala," Concepción, May 14, 1680, ARJ, PN, 13 (Pineda), 605r–611v.

119. Viceroy Count of Lemos (1667–1672) promoted the expansion of the Congregación del Niño Jesús, a religious corporation for the Indians of Lima led by the Jesuits, to honor the *indios* principales and grant them military titles. Vargas Ugarte, *Historia (siglo XVII)*, 345.

120. Mugaburu and Mugaburu, *Chronicle*, 82–83.

121. "Memorial. Martín Çapuy," 1620, AGI, Lima, 150. On Çapuy: Puente Luna, "The Many Tongues," 147–148; Ramos, "Indigenous Intellectuals." Other travelers negotiated this privilege while at the royal court, increasing their social capital before returning to Peru. "Licencia a Hernando Coro de Chaves, indio de Quito, para llevar ciertas armas," AGI, Quito, 211, l. 2, 197r–197v.

122. Alaperrine-Bouyer, *La educación*.

123. "Carta. Don Felipe Carguamango a SM"; "Informaciones: Francisco de Heriza," 1669, AGI, Lima, 259, n. 10.

124. Spalding, *Huarochirí*, 230. See also Lowry, "Forging an Indian Nation," 155.

125. Graubart, "Competing Spanish and Indigenous Jurisdictions"; Graubart, "'Ynuvaciones malas.'"

126. Harth-Terré, "El esclavo negro," 304, 318; Lowry, "Forging an Indian Nation," 131–136, 158. Ran by the Jesuits and with almost as many *cofradías* as the entire city of Trujillo by the end of the sixteenth century, El Cercado was also a center for evangelization in Lima. Graubart, *With Our Labor*, 116.

127. At the beginning of the seventeenth century, El Cercado had a population of about 800 residents. Another 1,500–2,000 permanent indigenous residents lived within the city limits around the same time, operating "autonomously of an explicit indigenous political community." Many other indigenous men and women lived at the city's edges or *arrabales*. Graubart, "'Ynuvaciones malas'"; Vergara, "Piedad e interés económico."

128. Pereyra Plascencia, "Indios y mestizos," 56–57; Ramos, "Nuestra Señora"; Van Deusen, *Between the Sacred*, 140–143. Vergara, "Piedad e interés económico."

129. Graubart, *With Our Labor*, 83; Graubart, "Competing Spanish and Indigenous Jurisdictions." Artisan guilds apparently elected their *alcaldes* as well, thus adding this position to the list of prestigious posts that urban Indians could occupy. Charney, *Indian Society*, 91; Lowry, "Forging an Indian Nation," 252–254. For a similar process of upward mobilty and elite consolidation within the *cofradías* of Sán Lázaro: Mansilla, "Exteriorizando la religiosidad"; Vergara, "Piedad e interés económico." In Cuenca, artisan guilds elected their own *alcaldes*, usually of a plebeian background. Poloni-Simard, *El mosaico*, 328.

130. Borah, "Juzgado General," 131, 141; Cobo, "Fundación de Lima," ch. 28.

131. Borah, "Juzgado General," 137.

132. Honores, "Una sociedad," 110; Lowry, "Forging an Indian Nation," 139–140; Puente Luna, "The Many Tongues." Borah expounds on this special tribunal: Borah, "Juzgado General," 135. The *audiencia* acted as the court of appeal.

133. In October 1550, the magistrates of the *audiencia* appointed two *caciques*, Don Gonzalo of Lima and Don Antonio of Huarochirí, as "aldermen for the Indians" (*regidores de indios*) giving them policing responsibilities such as bringing Indians to mass and authorizing them to carry the staff of royal justice. Don Gonzalo was later appointed bailiff (*alguacil*) of the Indians of the valley, carrying out similar responsibilities. "Elecciones de regidores de indios," Lima, October 20, 1550, AGI, Patronato, 187, r. 14; Rostworowski, "Dos probanzas."

134. Graubart, "Competing Spanish and Indigenous Jurisdictions." A Spanish official eventually replaced this *alguacil* in 1580. For indigenous interpreters and other *alguaciles de la limpieza* appointed by the Spanish *cabildo*: Vergara, "La población indígena," 209–213.

135. "Real cédula sobre los alcaldes de yanaconas de Lima," Madrid, May 3, 1568, AGI, Lima, 578, l. 2, 140v–141r; "Pago de 30 pesos a Diego Ticayo," Lima, July 11, 1570, LOC, HC, Peru, 870 [874], 209–215. Diego Ticayo was already working as court-appointed interpreter for the Indians in 1563. Guillén Guillén, *Versión inca*, 16, 48.

136. "Título de alcalde mayor del Cercado a Andrés Ramírez Ynga," Lima, December 31, 1603, AGN, *Libro de donde se toma razón de lo que su caja del Señor Virrey Juan [sic] de Velasco provee títulos y provisiones, este presente año 1602*, 134r–135r. For the establishment of the office of *corregidor de indios* of El Cercado: Cárdenas, *La población*, 43–44; Lowry, "Forging an Indian Nation," 108.

137. Little is known about Ramírez Inga, but his name hints at a *cuzqueño* origin. His appointment makes it clear that he had previously served in different posts, including *alcalde* of El Cercado.

138. For Don Pedro Zambiza's 1597 title of *alcalde mayor* of Quito: Espinoza, "Los mitmas," 40.

139. "Méritos y servicios: Don Diego de Figueroa Cajamarca," 1590, AGI, Patronato, 132, n. 2, r. 3, n.p. A description of the post appears in Don Diego's 1579 "Título de alcalde sin salario," included in the same dossier. Don Diego acted as *escribano* for the Indians, prepared their petitions, and advocated for them before the authorities. Espinoza, "La vida"; Espinoza, "Los mitmas."

140. "Carta. Don Felipe Carguamango a SM."

141. Appearing before the Council of the Indies in the 1660s, Don Pedro Chafo, interpreter of the *audiencia*, made a request to the staff of *alcalde mayor* of Lambayeque and the right to sit in the municipal council and vote. "Memorial. Pedro Chafo Çabana a SM." Chief urban magistrates and military officials performed similar policing activities: they patrolled the urban space and directed the construction of defensive walls and other public projects. O'Toole, "Fitting In"; "Pablo Olmedo contra Alonso Lucana," Trujillo, 1625, ARLL, C-CC, l. 242, e. 2368; "Gonzalo de la Madre de Dios sobre se les entreguen los arcabuses para armar su compañía," Trujillo, 1686, ARLL, C-CO, l. 206, e. 1494.

142. Evidently, the post of *alcalde mayor* was available to influential *caciques* and lesser *indios principales* in their own provinces and in urban centers. The opposite, however, was not necessarily true. Espinoza, "El alcalde mayor," 259–281; Poloni-Simard, *El mosaico*, 100. For Cuzco and Potosí (where *alcaldes mayores* had duties related to the organization of *mita* labor at the silver mines): Espinoza, "El alcalde mayor"; Julien, "La organización parroquial," 86; Rowe, "Colonial Portraits," 264.

143. "Don Cristóbal Julcapoma, cacique principal de Cajamarca, sobre que se le dé aquel corregimiento," Madrid, 1595, AGI, Lima, 132; "Méritos y servicios: Don Juan Chuquibalqui y otros," Madrid, July 8, 1595, AGI, Lima, 132; "Real cédula al virrey del Perú para que favorezca y ayude a Agustín Guascatanta," Santarén, May 7, 1580, AGI, Lima, 579, l. 6, 60v–61r.

144. "Informaciones: Francisco de Heriza," 1r–2r.

145. A strikingly similar case for the indigenous government of Mexico Tenochtitlan is discussed in Connell, "'De sangre noble.'"

146. Starting in the late sixteenth century, viceroys chose indigenous interpreters for the *audiencia* as temporary judges and assistants in tribute reassessments and land-title confirmation hearings. Occasionally, some interpreters even became administrators of communal funds and interim defenders for the Indians. Puente Luna, "The Many Tongues," 156.

CHAPTER 5

1. *Se le encaminara buenamente a que se vaia socorriendole para ello pero sin usar de apremio alguno.* "Decreto de S.M. con un memorial de D. Ger.mo Limaylla sobre un pleyto q. dize tiene pendiente en lima," Buen Retiro, July 15, 1664, AGI, Lima, 17. On Queen Mariana's final resolution: "Respuesta del Consejo de Indias a SM sobre memoriales de Don Jerónimo Lorenzo Limaylla," Madrid, Mach 26, 1678, AGI, Lima, 12. For a full discussion of the case: Puente Luna, "What's in a Name?," 140–141. Such a decision might have been ideologically connected to Queen Mariana's campaign to free the enslaved Indians of Chile, Mexico, the Philippines, and other parts of the empire during her regency (1665–1675). Reséndez, *The Other Slavery*, 128 and ff.

2. "Ordenanzas de SM para el buen gobierno," Bosque de Segovia, August 15, 1565, BNE, MS, 2987, ordinance 76; *Recopilación*, bk. 6, tit. 7, law 17.

3. Elias, *La sociedad cortesana*, 12, 41, 47–49, 161, 174–177, 184–185, 190–198, 349; Fer-

nández Albaladejo, *Materia de España*, 79, 114. On the limits to royal power and the king's subordination to customary and written law, kingdom, and political community in medieval and early modern Spanish political theory: Fernández Albaladejo, *Fragmentos*; Fernández Albaladejo, *Materia de España*, 65–91. On the seemingly limitless liberality of the later Habsburgs: Río Barredo, *Madrid, Urbs Regia*, 167.

4. "Para Bien al Rey D. Felipe III N.S.," n.d. [1619?], BNCh, SM, Perú, Folletos Coloniales, 8, 3v–4r.

5. On this subject: the in-depth study by Van Deusen, *Global indios*. The story has been more recently retold in Reséndez, *The Other Slavery*, 48–61. African slavery was of course widespread in early-modern Iberia. Ares Queija and Stella, *Negros, mulatos*; Herzog, "How Did Early-Modern Slaves," 1–4.

6. For the enslavement of Indians during the conquest of Peru: Lockhart, *Spanish Peru*, 199–205.

7. Cutter, "The Legal System," 60–61. See also Borah, *Justice*, 91–93.

8. Premo, *Children of the Father King*, 32–34. Premo's seminal work on children, minority, and *miserables* still informs our understanding of indigeneity and legal minority. In recent years, the literature on the Indians' status as perpetual legal children has grown significantly. Important states of the art include Cunill, "El indio miserable"; Duve, "La condición jurídica."

9. Bayle, "El protector"; Castañeda Delgado, "La condición miserable"; Cutter, *The Protector*; Cuena Boy, "Utilización pragmática."

10. Esteban Mira Caballos has documented almost 2,500 enslaved *indios* living in Iberia between 1493 and 1550, although the numbers were definitely much higher. Mira Caballos, *Indios y mestizos*, 111. See also Van Deusen, *Global indios*, 2; Van Deusen, "Seeing Indios." The relevant literature also includes Forbes, *Africans*, 28–32; Franco Silva, *Los esclavos*; Gil-Bermejo García, "Indígenas americanos"; Hanke, *Aristotle*, 50–51; Julián, "Tráfico de indígenas"; Lobo Cabrera, "Esclavos indios"; Mira Caballos, "El envío de indios americanos"; Mira Caballos, *Indios y mestizos*, 43–46, 75–89.

11. As early as 1500, a royal decree ordered Pedro de Torres to free the enslaved Indians that Columbus had sent from the New World to Andalusia and return them to their *naturalezas*. The next year, Queen Isabella qualified *indios* as free vassals. Konetzke, *Colección de documentos*, 1: 4, 7–8, 78–80, 134–136.

12. A handful of early decrees indicate that the prospects of quick financial gain of this flourishing human trade first tempted the Crown, which had the right to receive one-fifth of the slave's purchase value. Konetzke, *Colección de documentos*, 1: 2–4. See also Mira Caballos, "El envío de indios americanos"; Van Deusen, *Global indios*, 5–7, 151 and ff.

13. Hanke, *The First Social Experiments*, 57; Mira Caballos, "La educación"; Mira Caballos, *Indios y mestizos*, 86–90; Mira Caballos, "Indios nobles y caciques"; Mira Caballos, "Caciques guatiaos"; Rojas, "Boletos sencillos."

14. In this summary discussion of shifting royal policies regarding indigenous slavery in the 1530s and 1540s, I follow closely Van Deusen, *Global indios*, esp. ch. 3; Mira Caballos, "De esclavos a siervos."

15. Hanke, *The Spanish Struggle*; Pagden, *The Fall*.

16. Colonial officials claimed that *caciques* sent some of their sons to Cuzco to learn Quechua and become familiar with the ways of the Incas. Matienzo, *Gobierno del Perú*, 21; Ondegardo, "Informe," 203. This information is confirmed in Don Juan Colque Guarache's proofs of merit (1574–1580), among other documents. The paramount lord (*cacique principal*) of the Killaka in Charcas claimed that one of his paternal ancestors traveled to the Inca court in Cuzco as a young man. There, he learned the "general Language" of the Inca. Abercrombie, *Pathways*, 161.

17. Konetzke, *Colección de documentos*, 1: 217, 227–228. See also *Recopilación*, bk. 6, tit. 1, law 16.

18. Between 1530 and 1585, at least 184 enslaved individuals identified as "indios" brought 127 lawsuits against their masters before the Council of the Indies and the *Casa de la Contratación*. Many plaintiffs claimed to be servants and not slaves, petitioning for their freedom. Reséndez, *The Other Slavery*, 55–61; Van Deusen, *Global indios*, 16.

19. Van Deusen, *Global indios*, 117.

20. *Recopilación*, bk. 6, tit. 1, law 17.

21. Solórzano Pereira, *Política indiana*, bk. 2, ch. 28. In this chapter, Solórzano compares Indians to minors and women.

22. *Recopilación*, bk. 6, tit. 1, law 17; Van Deusen, *Global indios*, 19–21, 223.

23. Such was the case of the *cacique* Diego Colón, already mentioned, and his son and namesake, who also sojourned in Spain, fell sick, and died there in August 1506, despite the medical and spiritual care provided by the *Casa de la Contratación* at His Majesty's expense. Gil-Bermejo García, "Indígenas americanos"; Mira Caballos, "Caciques guatiaos," 13–14; Olaechea Labayen, "Experiencias cristianas." Francisco Pizarro continued this old tradition in 1529 by taking Felipillo and Martinillo (later Don Martín Pizarro), his interpreters, to Spain by force. Busto, "Martinillo"; Lockhart, *The Men*, 213–215; Varón, *Francisco Pizarro*, 169.

24. On Cortés and the indigenous visitors: Cline, "Hernando Cortés"; Díaz Serrano, "La república"; Gil-Bermejo García, "Indígenas americanos," 541–544; Rojas, "Boletos sencillos"; Van Deusen, "Coming to Castile." Hernando de Tapia, who had traveled to Spain with Cortés in 1528, remained at the royal court until 1537, benefitting from the king's liberality repeatedly. "4 ducados de oro para Hernando de Tapia," Madrid, October 27, 1535, AGI, Indiferente, 422, l. 16, 231r–231v; "12 ducados para Hernando de Tapia," Valladolid, February 17, 1537, AGI, Indiferente, 422, l. 17, 103r; "20 ducados para el licenciado Juan de Villalobos," Valladolid, February 17, 1537, AGI, Indiferente, 422, l. 17, 105v–106r.

25. A *ducado* was worth 11 *reales* or 374 *maravedíes*. The *real* was a silver coin worth 34 *maravedíes*. Eight *reales* made one *peso de a ocho*. Up to 1598, royal officials minted *vellón* copper coins with an admixture of silver. From the 1650s onward, the Council of the Indies issued *ayudas de costa* in *ducados de vellón* or copper coins. Hamilton, *American Treasure*, 47–48.

26. On the king's magnanimity toward the 1534 Tlaxcalan delegation led by Don Diego Maxixcatzin: Gibson, *Tlaxcala*, 164–165. The Crown spent some 360 *reales* to feed and clothe Don Diego and his two *criados*. "Libramiento de 21263 maravedíes para Francisco

de Arteaga," Madrid, March 18, 1535, AGI, Indiferente, 422, l. 16, 186r; "Libramiento de 13559 maravedíes para Bartolomé de Zárate," Madrid, March 18, 1535, AGI, Indiferente, 422, l. 16, 186r–186v.

27. Van Deusen pinpoints the appearance of the term *miserable* within this universe of cases to a 1549 lawsuit. According to her, the term did not enter legal discourse in Castile until nearly 1550. Van Deusen, *Global indios*, 119–120. Father Bartolomé de las Casas and other ecclesiastics defined Indians as "personas miserables" in a 1545 petition to the king. A 1563 ordinance issued by Philip II uses the term *miserable*, apparently for the first time in the *legislación indiana*. Assadourian, "Fray Bartolomé"; Castañeda Delgado, "La condición miserable," 264–265, 291; Cunill, "El indio miserable," 232–233. Brian Owensby posits that *miserables* and the privileges at law to which they were entitled took a more distinct legal meaning in New Spain toward the end of the sixteenth century. Owensby, *Empire*, 56. For the Andes, Renzo Honores has found an appeal to the *estatuto de miserabilidad* among indigenous claimants, especially when requesting the appointment of a legal tutor and procurator, from 1551. Honores, "History, Rhetoric, and Strategy."

28. "Real cédula para que se entregue 6000 maravedíes a Gregorio de Pesquera," Valladolid, July 14, 1556, AGI, Indiferente, 425, l. 23, 239r; "Mandamiento para que se entregue 12 ducados a Cristóbal de Sanmartín," Valladolid, September 26, 1556, AGI, Indiferente, 425, l. 23, 249r–249v; Mira Caballos, "Indios nobles y caciques," 4.

29. "Real cédula a Francisco Vecerra, vecino de la ciudad de Toro," Valladolid, March 31, 1555, AGI, Indiferente, 425, l. 23, 141r; "Licencia a Martín, indio, y a su mujer, naturales de Perú," Valladolid, February 27, 1555, AGI, Indiferente, 1965, l. 12; "Licencia a Francisco Martín," Valladolid, February 27, 1555, AGI, Indiferente, 1965, l. 12, 336v.

30. Van Deusen, *Global indios*, 223; Mira Caballos, "De esclavos a siervos," 103.

31. "Real cédula a los oficiales de la Casa de la Contratación," Valladolid, July 17, 1555, AGI, Indiferente, 1965, l. 12, 447v–448r; "Información y licencia: Diego de Santiago e Inés de Collantes," AGI, Contratación, 5537, l. 1, 185v.

32. Additional cases in which native subjects decided to return to the Indies and either the Crown or a particular individual defrayed the costs of the journey include "Real cédula a Diego de Loaisa," Valladolid, August 25, 1555, Indiferente, 425, l. 23, 185r–185v; "Carta. Gabriel de Ocaña al presidente y oficiales de la Contratación," Madrid, January 26, 1649, AGI, Indiferente, 436, l. 14, 274r–274v.

33. Van Deusen, *Global indios*, 120.

34. Van Deusen, *Global indios*, 86–88, 106–114.

35. *Recopilación*, bk. 9, tit. 1, law 99.

36. Brendecke, *Imperios*, esp. chs. 3 and 9. Brendecke explains how knowledge production and exchange within metropolitan and colonial epistemic settings was not simply a means for royal magistrates to acquire neutral or impartial information about known and unknown lands and subjects, but also an opportunity for those very subjects to weave their own interests into the information being exchanged at, or among, centers and peripheries. See also Masters, "The Lettered Marketplace."

37. Brendecke, *Imperios*, 232, 464; Heredia Herrera, *Catálogo de las Consultas*; Heredia

Herrera, "Introducción"; Schäfer, *El Consejo Real*, 51, 97–100, 146. I have added my own observations of dozens of *consultas* produced as a response to Indian visitors sojourning at court.

38. See, for instance, "Respuesta del Consejo de Indias a SM sobre memoriales de Don Jerónimo Lorenzo Limaylla." On the officials of the Council during the reign of Philip II: Schäfer, *El Consejo Real*, 111–120, 198–248.

39. Black, *The Limits*, 11; Yannakakis, *The Art*. For similar legal strategies of native litigants in New Spain: Borah, *Justice*, 304–305; Owensby, *Empire*, 6.

40. Brendecke, *Imperios*, 114.

41. On Brother Calixto's life and journey: Bernales Ballesteros, "Fray Calixto"; Loayza, *Fray Calixto*. For a recent reassessment: Dueñas, *Indians*, 65–78.

42. For this paragraph and the preceding one: Loayza, *Fray Calixto*, 53.

43. Glave, "Gestiones." Rachel O'Toole has also reflected on Chimo's social position. O'Toole, "Don Carlos."

44. *Si se da lugar a esta consequençia se bendran cada dia bagando.* "Respuesta del Consejo de Indias a SM sobre los agravios y vejaciones que presenta Don Carlos Chimo," Madrid, November 29, 1646, AGI, Lima, 7; "Consulta al Consejo de Indias sobre el memorial de Don Carlos Chimo," Saragossa, September 14, 1646, AGI, Lima, 15; "Real cédula al virrey del Perú que cuide mucho del buen tratamiento y aliuio de los Indios," Saragossa, July 23, 1646, AGI, Lima, 573, l. 23, 7r–7v.

45. *[No] se deuia tolerar mas la contravençion que hauia tenido el dicho cazique porque a su exemplo se vendrian cada dia otros vagando.* "Respuesta del Consejo de Indias a SM sobre el memorial de Don Carlos Chimo," Madrid, July 23, 1647, AGI, Lima, 7; "Consulta de SM al Consejo de Indias sobre un memorial de Don Carlos Chimo con una carta adjunta," Madrid, June 13, 1647, AGI, Lima, 15; "Respuesta del fiscal al Consejo de Indias sobre el memorial de Don Carlos Chimo," Madrid, June 13, 1647, AGI, Lima, 15.

46. See, for instance, "Decreto de SM con un memorial de Don Juan Crisóstomo Atagualpa," Madrid, August 13, 1664, AGI, Lima, 17; "Decreto de S.M. con una carta de los caciques y gou.es de la ciu.d de Guamanga," Madrid, August 13, 1664, AGI, Lima, 17.

47. For example: "Respuesta del Consejo a VM que vino con un memorial de Don Geronimo Limaylla," Madrid, January 27, 1666, AGI, Lima, 10.

48. *Todo lo que el Consexo pudo hazer deseando (como siempre dessea) aiudar, y Amparar a los Indios.* "Respuesta del Consejo de Indias a SM sobre el memorial de Don Carlos Chimo" (original emphasis).

49. Martínez, *Pasajeros de Indias*, 117–154. Juan Arias Maldonado, the son of Diego Maldonado, a conquistador, and Luisa Palla, an Inca princess, former wife of Atahualpa, and one of the daughters of Huayna Capac, drafted his will in Cuzco a few months before traveling to Spain. Ten years later, he dictated a second (and last) will while attempting to return to Peru. "Testamento. Juan Arias Maldonado," Cuzco, March 25, 1571, ARC, PN, 25 (Sánchez), 487r–490v; "Testamento. Juan Arias Maldonado," Panama, October 2, 1582, ARC, PN, 25 (Sánchez), 1102r–1107v. Similar examples include: "Testamento. Don Francisco de Ampuero," Lima, April 12, 1617, AGN, PN, 2029 (Zamudio), 871r–872r; Lohmann, "El señorío," 392; Oberem, *Notas*, 79.

50. The difficulties of the trip, along with the years of absence that voyagers could expect as a result of their journey, made the return to the Andes uncertain. Different accounts of the perils of the trip can be found in "Consulta del Consejo sobre pretensión de Don Carlos Tito Amaro," Madrid, August 18, 1582, AGI, Lima, 1, n. 44; "Memorial. Diego de Figueroa Cajamarca a SM," Madrid, October 7, 1598, AGI, Lima, 134; "Méritos y servicios: Pedro Márquez Galeote," 1607, AGI, Patronato, 143, n. 2, r. 4.

51. In 1605, Martín Fernández, identified as an *indio* from the Moquegua Valley, on the southern coast of Peru, requested a return license. One of his witnesses supported the petition "because the said Martín Fernández is now sick after having been tempted by this land." Although Martín could not allege just cause for his travel, the officials granted the license. "Información y licencia: Martín Fernández," 1605, AGI, Contratación, 5286, n. 77.

52. "Real cédula a los oficiales de la Casa de Contratación permitiendo a Don Sebastián Poma Hilaquita regresar al Perú," El Pardo, August 10, 1574, AGI, Indiferente, 1968, l. 20, 6v–7r. On Hilaquita and other court interpreters who journeyed to Spain: Puente Luna, "The Many Tongues."

53. "Consulta del Consejo de Indias sobre la merced y ayuda de costa que pide Don Alonso de Atahualpa," Madrid, November 19, 1586, AGI, Indiferente, 741, n. 133.

54. "Prórroga de licencia para volver a Quito a Alonso Atahualpa," San Lorenzo, September 23, 1587, AGI, Quito, 211, l. 2, 201r–202r. On Don Alonso's debtors: "Obligación. Don Alonso Atahualpa con Andrés de Valla," Madrid, July 1, 1587, AHP, PN, 587 (Henao), 1834v; Jiménez de la Espada, *Relaciones geográficas. Perú*, 3: cxlvi–cxlviii.

55. "Libramiento de 30 ducados de vellón a Don Nicolás Tolentín," August 21, 1664, AGI, Indiferente, 439, l. 22, 284r–284v; "Memorial. Don Nicolás de Tolentino Lluchi Moro a SM," Madrid, January 8, 1667, AGI, Lima, 26.

56. "4 ducados para Francisco Hernández," Madrid, September 20, 1595, AGI, Indiferente, 426, l. 28, 222r; "6 ducados para Francisco Hernández," Madrid, April 24, 1607, AGI, Indiferente, 428, l. 33, 5r–5v. Occasionally, the Council took a proactive stance, trying to persuade some of these visitors to depart immediately by granting them more than they had requested. Two such cases involve Don Francisco Atahualpa in the 1560s and Don Juan de Astubarcaya in the 1590s. Oberem, *Notas*, 100; "200 reales para Don Juan de Astubarcaya," Madrid, June 14, 1596, AGI, Indiferente, 426, l. 28, 253v; "Consulta del Consejo de Indias sobre merced de 400 reales a Don Juan de Astubarcay," Madrid, January 18, 1599, AGI, Indiferente, 745, n. 191; "100 reales para Juan de Astubarcaya," Madrid, April 4, 1600, AGI, Indiferente, 427, l. 31, 112r–112v; "Real cédula al gobernador y capitán general de Tierra Firme para que facilite el pase a Perú de Juan de Astubarcay," Aceca, April 29, 1600, AGI, Panamá, 237, l. 13; Mira Caballos, *Indios y mestizos*, 102.

57. In a 1560 letter in Nahuatl, the lords of Huejotzingo, a municipality in New Spain, told Philip that "*we hear and it is said to us* that you are very merciful and humane towards all your vassals; and when there appears before you a vassal of yours in poverty, *so it is said*, then you have pity on him in your very revered majesty, and in God omnipotent you help him." Lockhart and Otte, *Letters and People*, 166 (emphasis added). See also "Flete y matalonaje de Don Pedro y Don Gabriel," Madrid, November 22, 1540, AGI, Indiferente, 1963, l. 7, 219v–220r.

58. The prosecution indicted the prisoners for a series of crimes, including openly proclaiming one of the accused *Capac* or king, aiding the "rebels" of Vilcabamba, and plotting to rise up in arms against His Majesty. Hemming, *The Conquest*, 452–453; Garrett, *Shadows*, 29; Levillier, *Don Francisco de Toledo*, 1: 363–376; Nowack and Julien, "La campaña," 16.

59. *Obligaciones y pesadumbres que se le recrecerían*. Levillier, *Don Francisco de Toledo*, 1: 369–370; 362: xxix–xxx. Although the Incas themselves pleaded to be allowed to appear before King Philip in person, the *Audiencia de Lima* denied their request of a license and they never left Peru. "Don Alonso Tito Atauchi, Don Agustín Tito Condemayta y Don Diego Cayo a SM," Lima, April 18, 1573. AGI, Lima, 270, 442r-443v; "Don Carlos Inca y otros a SM," Lima, April 20, 1573. AGI, Lima, 270, 440r-440v. The judges in Lima did accept their appeal, refusing to execute the sentence until they were heard. The Council tacitly approved the *Audiencia*'s decision by commanding the viceroy to send the court case—and not the Incas—to Spain for final resolution. They were absolved.

60. This recompense came on top of the 1,600 pesos that Don Alonso's father had received after campaigning successfully at court two decades earlier. "Real cédula del virrey del Perú para que de los indios que haya vacos o vacaren, encomiende a Alonso Atahualpa los que renten la cantidad de que se expresa," San Lorenzo, June 30, 1586, Quito, 211, l. 2, 178v–179r; "Real cédula al presidente y oidores de la Audiencia de Quito para que den a Alonso Atahualpa unos indios en encomienda," Madrid, March 5, 1587, AGI, Quito, 211, l. 2, 195r–195v.

61. Jiménez de la Espada, *Relaciones geográficas (Perú)*, 3: 97.

62. *Recopilación*, bk. 6, tit. 1, law 1; Mira Caballos, *Indios y mestizos*, 67–80, 123–124; Van Deusen, *Global indios*. For an early Andean example of the king's refusal to accept the forced journey of his native Andean subjects to Spain: "Real cédula al gobernador y justicias del Perú sobre las indias que traía Rodrigo de Maçuelas de aquella provincia," Valladolid, September 18, 1538, AGI, Lima, 565, l. 3, 49v.

63. For a recent interpretation suggesting that Velasco forced Don Melchor to go to Spain: Rojas, "Boletos sencillos." The author aligns himself with the older literature on the topic. See Lohmann, "El señorío," 431–444; Miró Quesada Sosa, *El Inca*, ch. 4; Rowe, "El movimiento," 358; Temple, "Azarosa existencia," 138–143.

64. "Ascendencia de Juan Carlos Inga," 1539–1626, BNE, MS, 20193, 11r–12r, 40v, 43v, 52v, 93v; "Memoria de las encomiendas de indios del reyno del Peru que el Licenciado de la Gasca mando hacer," 1548, BPR, MS, II-1960 bis, 102v, 158r–159v. On Doña María de Esquivel's legal guardianship: "Obligación. María de Esquivel a Juan López de Prado," Cuzco, November 5, 1592, ARC, PN, 31 (Sánchez), 526r–528r; "Venta. Santiago Chanca Huachos e Inés Poma a Diego Condori," Cuzco, January 21, 1594, ARC, PN, 28 (Sánchez), 31v; "Venta. Jerónima Yacche y otros a Juan Illacuro y Magdalena Yarpay," Cuzco, December 14, 1595, ARC, PN, 4 (Carrera), 761r.

65. "Ascendencia de Juan Carlos Inga," 14r–16r; "Pruebas para la concesión del Título de Caballero de Santiago de Melchor Carlos Inga," Trujillo; Madrid, 1606, AHN, OM-CS, e. 4081; Cúneo-Vidal, *Historia de las guerras*; Temple, "Azarosa existencia." De la Esquina representó los intereses of other prominent Inca nobles—including some of

Melchor's close relatives—as well as those of native communities in Chiapas and even granddaughters of former Mexica and Inca emperors. For example: "Poder. El cabildo del pueblo de Istapa, provincia de Chiapa, a Gaspar de la Esquina y otros," Chiapa, October 29, 1607, AHN, CS, l. 21486.

66. "Melchor Carlos Inga con Pedro de Bustinza," Madrid, June 1–10, 1596, AGI, Escribanía, 953.

67. "Melchor Carlos Inga con Pedro de Bustinza," Madrid, June 1–10, 1596, AGI, Escribanía, 953.

68. "Sobre la merced que podría hacerse a don Melchor Carlos Inga," Madrid, June 20, 1596, AGI, Indiferente, 744, n. 9; "Real cédula a Luis de Velasco, virrey del Perú, para que averigue la calidad y servicios de Melchor Carlos Inca," San Lorenzo, October 31, 1596, AGI, Patronato, 191, r. 20, 1r–1v.

69. "Carta. El licenciado Maldonado de Torres al virrey solicitando merced para Don Melchor Carlos Inga," Lima, September 13, 1600, AGI, Lima, 34, n. 16. This influential magistrate's support and protection continued while Melchor and his descendants lived in Spain. Maldonado took Melchor's son to the royal court, lodging him in his residence in Madrid. He also provided testimony in his proof of merit to become knight of Santiago in 1627. Temple, "Azarosa existencia," 152–153; Temple, "Los testamentos," 636; Lohmann, *Los americanos*, 1: 198–199.

70. "Descendencia y servicios: Melchor Carlos Inca," Cuzco, 1600, AGI, Patronato, 191, r. 20.

71. "Carta. Melchor Carlos Inga al virrey del Perú," Cuzco, November 1, 1600, CVU, MS, v. 18 (10), d. 4, 6–7. Between 1598 and 1602, Don Melchor sent hundreds of pesos to his legal agents in Spain. He also collected debts, sold some lands, and borrowed money in Cuzco and Lima, in part guaranteed by future earnings. "Venta. Don Melchor Carlos Inca, de siete topos de tierra que posee camino de los Andes," Cuzco, June 18, 1600, ARC, PN, 115 (Fuentes), 397r–397v; "Poder y cesión. Melchor Carlos Inca a Francisco de Tordoya Bazán," Cuzco, June 22, 1600, ARC, PN, 119 (Gaitán), 365v–366v; "Poder. Melchor Carlos Inca a Rodrigo de Carvajal," Cuzco, January 16, 1601, ARC, PN, 243 (Olave), 31r–31v.

72. Velasco, "Carta del virrey Luis de Velasco a S.M.," 192–193.

73. Some viceregal authorities disagreed with the Council's interpretation of the dangers posed by Don Melchor. Other cases involving scions of the Inca royal family and the need to have them settle in Spain include the offspring of the Pizarro brothers, the first Marchioness of Oropesa, and Don Melchor Carlos Inca's father, Don Carlos Inca. "Discurso sobre la descendencia y gobierno de los ingas," 1543, BNE, MS, 2010, 57r; Hemming, *The Conquest*, 452 (endnote); Nowack and Julien, "La campaña"; Varón, *Francisco Pizarro*, 101.

74. "Carta del virrey Luis de Velasco a SM," Lima, December 7, 1600, AGI, Lima, 34, n. 21.

75. *No ay mas caussa para compelerle; ymaginaçiones de algunos Hombres desuariados y perdidos que le tienen por blanco donde las ponen y descansan.* "Carta del virrey Luis de Velasco a SM," Lima, June 17, 1601, AGI, Lima, 34, n. 30, 47r–47v, 50v–51r; "Carta. Luis de Velasco a SM," El Callao, May 5, 1602, AGI, Lima, 34, n. 40.

76. "Memoriales de Melchor Carlos Inca," AGI, Lima, 472, n. 6, 132r–132v.

77. "Encomiendas concedidas a los descendientes de los Incas," AGI, Indiferente, 1613, 11r–15v; "Merced de 8000 ducados de renta a Melchor Carlos Inca," Valladolid, January 18, 1606, AGI, Indifernte, 1953, l. 5, 312v–314v.

78. The councilors applied a similar policy with Ana María Lorenza de Loyola Coya, future Marchioness of Oropesa and the niece of Don Melchor, whom Viceroy Velasco dispatched to Spain in April 1603. A few decades before, the Council had encouraged her mother, Doña Beatriz Clara Coya, to settle in Spain with her husband in exchange for a perpetual rent. Beatriz was to make the trip only "of her own will and in no other way." Lohmann, "El señorío," 363; "Merced de 1000 pesos de renta anual a Martín García de Loyola," San Lorenzo, September 16–30, 1577, ARC, CB, t. 3, 114r–120r, 115v.

79. See, for example, "7500 maravedís para Bernabé de la Fuente," Madrid, February 21, 1567, AGI, Indiferente, 425, l. 24, 319v–320r; "50 reales a Pedro Romero," March 31, 1587, Indiferente, 426, l. 27, 156r–156v.

80. "3 ducados para Diego Rodríguez de Narváez," Madrid, May 12, 1535, AGI, Indiferente, 422, l. 16, 201r–201v; "Decreto de SM con un memorial de D. Ger.mo Limaylla, en que supp.ca se le de vna ayuda de costa p.a imprimir dos memoriales," Madrid, July 15, 1677, AGI, Indiferente, 640. For a comprehensive list of travelers and *mercedes*: Puente Luna, "Into the Heart," 331–359.

81. Brickhouse, *The Unsettlement*, ch. 2; Hoffman, *A New Andalucia*, 182–189; Milanich, *Laboring in the Fields*, 97–99.

82. Hamilton, *American Treasure*, 397. For a detailed account of these expenses: Mira Caballos, "Indios nobles y caciques," 5.

83. Hamilton, *American Treasure*, 267–268, 393–397. One must keep in mind that workers whose wages can be estimated on an annual basis also received allowances of meat, bread, and wine, as well as a dwelling.

84. "Real Cédula al presidente de la Audiencia Real de Santo Domingo para que provea del pasaje y matalotaje hasta la Habana a Luis de Velasco," Madrid, June 10, 1567, AGI, Indiferente, 1967, l. 16.

85. Rappaport, *The Disappearing Mestizo*, ch. 4.

86. Rappaport, *The Disappearing Mestizo*, 137.

87. Hamilton, *American Treasure*, 398. Armada sailors around this time received between 65 and 100 *maravedíes* (2 to 3 *reales*) for daily wages and rations. Pérez-Mallaína, *Spain's Men*, 115.

88. This pension was twenty times the annual monetary salary of a miller in Andalusia at that time. Hamilton, *American Treasure*, 399; Puente Luna, "Into the Heart," 337–339. Apparently, Juana de Oropesa had to wait thirty-six years for the perpetual rent to become effective.

89. In 1667, the Council agreed to a request by Andrés Champón, an *indio* from Saña on the Peruvian North Coast, for an *ayuda de costa* "como a los naturales que se reducen a dichos Reynos de Indias." Middle-ranking *caciques* customarily received 3 or 4 *reales* for daily provisions, about twice the average daily wage of a laborer in Castile in 1578. At that time, Spanish soldiers made 1.1 daily *reales*. In 1635, soldiers made between 1.1 and 2 *reales*,

still less than *caciques* and *principales* were granted. Armada sailors, for their part, received between 1 and 2 *reales* in the second half of the sixteenth century. Hamilton, *American Treasure*, 398; Pérez-Mallaína, *Spain's Men*, 115; Phillips, *Six Galleons*, 240.

90. The Council granted Francisco Ulpo, "indio," almost 69 pesos to journey from Madrid to Seville. "50 ducados para Francisco Ulpo," Madrid, April 6, 1618, AGI, Indiferente, 428, l. 35, 44v.

91. In 1582, Don Agustín Guascatanta returned to Peru in the royal armada of Captain Diego Flores de Valdés. "Información y licencia: Agustín Guascatanta," Seville, 1582, AGI, Contratación, 5538, l. 1, 422r.

92. In 1608, Bartolomé Inga y Orosco, perhaps the last grandchild of Atahualpa who traveled to Spain, was authorized to travel in the royal fleet from Madrid to Tierra Firme. He was granted a "plaza de soldado por ser pobre y no tener con que hazer su viaje." Bartolomé received a royal decree for the governor of Tierra Firme to accommodate him in the armada bound to Peru. "Información y licencia: Bartolomé Atabalipa Inca," Seville, 1608, AGI, Contratación, 5307, n. 2, r. 3. Don Sebastián Poma Hilaquita received free passage and a daily ration "like a solider" in 1574, while Sebastián Inquil Yupanqui received passage, ration, and 30 ducats, but no soldier's wage between 1666 and 1667. "Real cédula a los oficiales de la Casa de Contratación permitiendo a Don Sebastián Poma Hilaquita regresar al Perú," El Pardo, August 10, 1574, AGI, Indiferente, 1968, l. 20, 6v–7r; "30 ducados de vellón a Sebastián Inquil Yupanqui," Madrid, October 27, 1666, AGI, Indiferente, 439, l. 23, 213v–214r; "Información y licencia: Sebastián Inquil Yupanqui," Seville, January 12, 1667, AGI, Contratación, 5540A, l. 1, 37v.

93. Jacobs, "Legal and Illegal Emigration," 65–69. For life and work while aboard: Pérez-Mallaína, *Spain's Men*, esp. ch. 4.

94. Mangan, *Transatlantic Obligations*, 117.

95. Jacobs, "Legal and Illegal Emigration."

96. Phillips, *Six Galleons*, 237–240.

97. Altman, *Emigrants*, 189; Jacobs, "Legal and Illegal Emigration," 67.

98. "Libramiento a favor de Don Juan de Açauache y Nicolas Flores," 1660, AGI, Lima, 26. Though exceptional, members of the Inca royal family received substantial *mercedes* to travel to Spain. For example: "Merced de 1000 pesos de renta anual a Martín García de Loyola."

99. "Memorial. Don Jerónimo Lorenzo Limaylla a S.M. solicitando una ayuda de costa para volver al Perú," Madrid, December 23, 1671, AGI, Indiferente, 640; "Carta. Don Francisco Fernández de Madrigal a Don Juan Jiménez de Montalvo," Madrid, August 16, 1678, AGI, Indiferente, 441, l. 29, 177r. For other examples: "100 ducados en vellón para enviar al Perú a Juan Quelpen," Madrid, August 24, 1653, AGI, Indiferente, 437, l. 17, 62r–62v; "Libramiento a favor de Don Juan de Açauache y Nicolas Flores."

100. Nobles and *caciques*, in part because of their own use of this construct to refer to their *indio* subjects but not to themselves, filled an ambiguous position. Baber, "Categories," 37–39. The documentation produced while Torres was in Spain sometimes exhibits a first-person usage (*nosotros*), which seems to imply that Don Diego was being included in the group of *indios*. Rappaport, *The Disappearing Mestizo*, 142.

101. Lockhart and Otte, *Letters and People*, 166. In the Andes, petitioners formulated this fundamental association between being legally and materially "poor" (*pobre*) and being entitled to special privilege and protection directly in Quechua (*uaccha*). Durston and Urioste, "Las peticiones," 384.

102. It is certainly possible that appeals to the Indians' miserable status were being deployed as early as 1545. Assadourian, "Fray Bartolomé," 79.

103. The case of one Juan de Oleandres, an *indio* from Popayán, is fairly representative. In 1631, he petitioned the *Casa de la Contratación* for passage fare and rations arguing that he was "un moço pobre yndio." "Información y licencia: Juan de Oleandres," 1631, AGI, Contratación, 5410, n. 12.

104. In 1567, Lorenzo and Martín, two "yndios prinçipales," traveled from Mexico City to the court at the service of their relative Don Diego Luis Moctezuma (grandson of Emperor Moctezuma). After a few months, Lorenzo and Martín informed the Council that, although they had concluded their affairs at court (*negocios*) and "desired" to return, they were ultimately "hombres estranjeros e de fuera de estos rreynos" and, as such, they could not obtain "fabor ni nadie quien nos ayude para el camino." They were reaching out to His Majesty, "our natural lord," to be granted "sustenance" (*sustento*), a license, and passage fare. Witnesses testified that, although Lorenzo and Martín were of noble descent and close relatives of the Moctezumas, they were "poor" (*pobres*) and had no means "to return or even eat," confirming their dire "necessity." The Council granted them authorization and 16 ducats to travel from Madrid to Seville, where Don Diego Luis Moctezuma awaited. "16 ducados para Lorenzo de Alameda y Martín de Aguilar," Madrid, November 30, 1568, AGI, Indiferente, 425, l. 24, 418v; "Información y licencia: Lorenzo de Alameda y Martín de Aguilar," Madrid, November 21, 1568, AGI, Indiferente, 2051, n. 106. On Don Diego Luis Motezuma: Chipman, *Moctezuma's Children*, 91–95; Jiménez Abollado, "Don Diego Luis Moctezuma."

105. "Jerónimo Limaylla con Bernardino Limaylla," 1656–1671, AGI, Escribanía, 514C, 15–16r.

106. A few *mercedes* of this nature were considerably higher. At the turn of the sixteenth century, the young Doña Ana María Lorenza de Loyola Coya, future Marchioness of Oropesa, enjoyed a royal annuity of 1,000 ducats (11,000 *reales*) for her *provisiones* in Spain. Lohmann, "El señorío."

107. For the sweepers, constables, and doormen (*porteros*) of the *Consejo de Indias*: "Libramientos," Madrid, 1664, AGI, Contaduría, 113a; "Cargo y data del tesorero general de lo recibido y pagado en vellón aplicado a gastos de estrados," Madrid, 1664, AGI, Contaduría, 110.

108. "Data de lo destinado para obras pías," Madrid, 1582–1583, AGI, Contaduría, 41, n. 4, r. 3; *Recopilación*, bk. 2, tit. 25, laws 21–50; Schäfer, *El Consejo Real*, 117, 126, 259, 260, 305.

109. On Easter of 1596, the Council awarded 50 *reales* from the *penas de estrados* fund to a poor and sick Inés Gómez, an *india* from Lima who "came to these kingdoms many years ago." Inés had received similar *limosnas* in the past. "R[elaci]on de las ayudas de

Costa," Madrid, 1596, AGI, Indiferente, 1374. I thank Adrian Masters for bringing this document to my attention.

110. "Registros generalísimos," Madrid, 1581–1588, AGI, Indiferente, 426, l. 27, 174r–174v. For similar examples: "30 ducados de vellón para Andrés Champón," Madrid, January 14, 1667, AGI, Indiferente, 439, l. 23, 247v–248r; "30 ducados de vellón para Don Nicolás de Tolentino," Madrid, January 14, 1667, AGI, Indiferente, 439, l. 23, 247r–247v; "Libramiento de 30 ducados de vellón a Catalina de Araujo," Madrid, December 23, 1666, AGI, Indiferente, 439, l. 23, 247r.

111. In the words of Joan Sherwood, "the poor were there for the benefit of both donor and recipient of charity." Sherwood, *Poverty*, 3.

112. Doubtless, many Indians, free and enslaved, noble and commoner, arrived in Spain to swell the ranks of the poor and destitute. The aforementioned Luis and Martín, from Mexico-Tenochtitlan, faced serious financial straits after their master—the Marquis of El Valle Don Martín Cortés—withdrew his support, finding themselves unable to live according to their *calidad*. "Información y licencia: Lorenzo de Alameda y Martín de Aguilar." Madrid, November 21, 1568, AGI, Indiferente, 2051, n. 106.

113. Among those declared *pobres de solemnidad* by the courts in Quito there were individuals of the propertied classes. Judges declared some of these litigants "notoriously poor" without requesting proof other than their own declaration. Herzog, *Upholding Justice*, 30–31. For the legal use of the poverty argument among Spaniards, *mestizos*, and *castas* in eighteenth-century Quito: Milton, *The Many Meanings*.

114. Brendecke, *Imperios*, 78–82; Fernández Albaladejo, *Fragmentos*, 75; Fernández Albaladejo, *Materia de España*, 101–102.

115. "Memorial. Don Jerónimo Lorenzo Limaylla a SM solicitando una ayuda de costa para volver al Perú," Madrid, December 3, 1671, AGI, Indiferente, 640; "Decreto de SM con un memorial de Don Juan Crisóstomo Atagualpa." Madrid, August 13, 1664, AGI, Lima, 17.

116. Rappaport, *The Disappearing Mestizo*, 139, 168.

117. On the family assets: "Obligación. Hernando Caballero a Don Alonso de Sevilla," Cuzco, April 18, 1560, ARC, PN, 1 (Bitorero), c. 2, 343v–344r; "Carta de concierto. Don Carlos Inga y Pedro Sánchez para hacer un obraje en el asiento de Mohina," Cuzco, October 27, 1571, ARC, PN, 19 (Sánchez), 1593r–1594v. Additional information can be found in Cornejo Bouroncle, "De la vida colonial," 265–266; Glave and Remy, *Estructura agraria*, 49–51; Heffernan, *Limatambo*, 205–231; Puente Brunke, *Encomienda y encomenderos*, 358, 371, 364, 381, 494, 504.

118. "Descendencia y servicios: Melchor Carlos Inca," n.p. For the *encomendero* upbringing of Don Melchor in Cuzco: "Ascendencia de Juan Carlos Inga," 18r and ff.

119. "los decendientes de los que tanto tubieron y pudieron no vengan a pobreça como la que tengo de presente." "Descendencia y servicios: Melchor Carlos Inca," n.p.

120. Temple, "Azarosa existencia," 147.

121. "Donación. Melchor Carlos Inga a Doña Isabel de Peñalosa," Madrid, August 19, 1609, AHP, PN, 2728 (Peña), 714r; Temple, "Los testamentos."

122. "Felipe de Sierra con los bienes de Melchor Carlos Inca," 1616, AGI, Escribanía, 1020a; "Juan Hurtado y Juan de Santiago con los bienes de Melchor Carlos Inca," 1616, AGI, Escribanía, 1020a; "León Vázquez con los bienes de Melchor Carlos Inca," 1616, AGI, Escribanía, 1020a; "Juan Gallego Barba con los acreedores de Melchor Carlos Inca," 1624, AGI, Escribanía 1022a.

123. Milton, "Poverty and the Politics," 599.

124. Jiménez de la Espada, *Relaciones geográficas (Perú)*, 97. On Don Alonso's imprisonment: González Suárez, *Historia general*, 266–269.

125. On Don Alonso's upbringing and family life in Quito: Oberem, *Notas*, 138–153. On his personal and family assets: Estupiñán-Freile, "Testamento." On his affairs in Spain: "Obligación. Don Alonso Atahualpa con Andrés de Valla." On his multiple debts, which totaled at least 8,599 *reales*: Jiménez de la Espada, *Relaciones geográficas (Perú)*, 97.

126. *no tiene parte de indio, según sus obras, sino de español*. "Consulta del Consejo de Indias sobre la merced y ayuda de costa que pide Don Alonso de Atahualpa." Madrid, November 19, 1586, AGI, Indiferente, 741, n. 133.

127. The entailed estate of a gentleman without a title of nobility might yield him only one or two thousand ducats a year. Brown and Elliott, *A Palace*, 106.

128. "Descendencia y servicios: Melchor Carlos Inca," n.p.

129. Temple, "Azarosa existencia," 138–139.

CHAPTER 6

1. Álvarez de Toledo, "Memorial del Marqués de Mancera a SM," 274. On legal battles between Mancera and his opponents: Glave, "Gestiones"; Lohmann, *Inquisidores*, 111.

2. "Consulta al Consejo de Indias sobre el memorial de Don Carlos Chimo," Saragossa, September 14, 1646, AGI, Lima, 15.

3. Álvarez de Toledo, "Memorial del Marqués de Mancera a SM," 274. Following the opinion of the prosecutor, the Council stated, "the nature of this Indian is unruly." "Consulta al Consejo de Indias sobre el memorial de Don Carlos Chimo."

4. Meneses expounds on these doctrines in his own 1648 indictment of Don Carlos Chimo. Based upon Viceroy Francisco de Toledo's ordinances, judges like him equated the depositions of six indigenous witnesses to that of one Spanish witness. "Causa contra Don Bernardino de Perales," 1647, AGI, Lima, 100, 9v. For other judges, the testimony of an indigenous woman was worth one-third of a European man's testimony. Campbell, "Women and the Great Rebellion," 166.

5. Glave, "Gestiones." Several authorities of the town of Paiján, including Don Luis de Mora Chimo, "*cacique* and governor of the entire Chicama Valley," publicly expressed their support. In a letter to the king, they acknowledged Chimo's efforts to secure a new judge and reported his death (whether in Spain or Peru is unknown). "Carta de los caciques principales del pueblo de Paiján a SM," Paiján, 1648, AGI, Lima, 167.

6. Meneses's attacks against Chimo can be found in "Causa contra Don Bernardino de Perales," esp. 7 (second pagination); "Carta de Pedro de Meneses a SM," Lima, March 28,

1650, AGI, Lima, 167. For a summary of the multiple accusations against Chimo, in particular, of being subject to tribute: Glave, "Gestiones," 102–103. An inquest on Chimo was prepared in Lima in July 1648. It is likely the source from where Mancera built his denunciation in 1653. Among the witnesses who raised charges and denied Chimo was a noble Indian (*indio principal*) or a *cacique* were Don Francisco Coscochumbi, an *indio prinçipal* from Lambayeque then litigating for the post of paramount lord (*cacique principal*), and Don Marcelo Minollulli, an *indio* and *pachaca principal* (tribute collector). "Causa contra Don Bernardino de Perales," 35v–50r (second pagination).

7. "Apelación de Don Carlos Chimo," Trujillo, August 19, 1641, ARLL, C-CC, l. 245, e. 2518. On Don Carlos Chimo's previous encounters with colonial authorities: "Declaración de Don Carlos Chimo," Trujillo, February 20, 1640, ARLL, PN, 143 (Escobar), 1r–2r.

8. O'Toole, "Don Carlos," 26; O'Toole, *Bound Lives*, 84–86.

9. Colonial Andean *caciques* faced what Karen Powers called "the leadership dilemma of the period." Their legitimacy existed at a colonial crossroads. Successful leaders legitimized their authority by simultaneously satisfying Spanish and Indian criteria, showing their ability "to fulfill contracts with both the colonial regime and the community." Powers, *Andean Journeys*, 108. See also Martínez, *Autoridades*; Pease, *Curacas*; Powers, "Resilient Lords"; Saignes, "De la borrachera"; Ramírez, *The World*; Ramírez, "The 'Dueño de Indios,'" ch. 6; Spalding, "Resistencia." On the different mechanisms and strategies by which *caciques* presented themselves, established nobility, and performed chiefly legitimacy: Garrett, *Shadows*, 166–179; Graubart, *With Our Labor*, 160–169; Noack, "Caciques, escribanos"; Powers, "A Battle of Wills"; Ramos, "El rastro de la discriminación"; Salomon, "Indian Women," 332.

10. Don Carlos Chimo's procurator in Lima told the *audiencia* that his client had been wronged and insulted with the ruling, "being, as he is, a noble Indian [*yndio principal*]." "Apelación de Don Carlos Chimo."

11. A witness in Chimo's criminal case claimed that the current *cacique* of Lambayeque was Chimo's relative. Another witness claimed to have known Chimo for ten years, first as an artisan in Lambayeque and, for the past six months, as a master embroiderer with a shop in Trujillo's main square. A third witness had known Chimo for three years, first in Lima and then in Lambayeque, Saña, and Trujillo. "Apelación de Don Carlos Chimo."

12. This narrow definition still held true at the close of the Habsburg era. In 1694, colonial officials applied it to deny many "sons and relatives" of the *caciques* of Cajamarca, in northern Peru, exemption from tribute and personal service. In their view, only the oldest sons of titled *caciques* should enjoy the privilege because they were *caciques* "by succession and by right of blood since the time of the gentiles." Argouse, "¿Son todos caciques?," 181. On the different "images" adscribed to *caciques* during the colonial period: Alaperrine-Bouyer, "Recurrencias y variaciones."

13. On the two republics in general: Díaz, "Conjuring Identities," 217; Estenssoro, *Del paganismo*; Garrett, *Shadows*, 25–34; Herzog, *Defining Nations*; Mörner, *Race Mixture*; Owensby, *Empire*, 24. On the connection between the two *repúblicas* and the need to exact tribute from newly conquered Muslim and Jewish populations: Graubart, *With Our Labor*, 9–13; Graubart, "'Ynuvaciones malas.'"

14. Powers, "The Battle for Bodies," 33.

15. Solórzano Pereira, *Política indiana*, bk. 2, ch. 27. On the doctrinal aspects of the dual *república* regime: Levaggi, "República de Indios."

16. Chamberlain, "The Concept"; Mumford, "Francisco de Toledo."

17. Graubart, "Learning from the *Qadi*"; Graubart, "Competing Spanish and Indigenous Jurisdictions"; Puente Luna and Honores, "Guardianes de la real justicia." On the categorization of *caciques* as *hidalgos*: Díaz Rementería, *El cacique*, 97 and ff; Garrett, *Shadows*, 39–40; Luque Talaván, "'Tan príncipes e infantes.'"

18. The basic principles regarding Indian "purity"—the equality of native rulers and nobles with *hidalgos*, the pure blood of Indians as a whole, and the voluntary and contractual nature of the relationship of vassalage with the Crown (based on the acceptance of the king and the Catholic faith)—were consecrated during the sixteenth century. Estenssoro, "Construyendo la memoria," 120; Martínez, *Genealogical Fictions*, 92–95, 107; Powers, "The Battle for Bodies," 33.

19. Díaz Rementería, *El cacique*, 132. There were, of course, many exceptions to this rule. Spaniards and *mestizos* assumed the office by marrying into *cacique* families. Garrett, *Shadows*, 69.

20. Villella, "'Pure and Noble Indians,'" 642–654; Martínez, *Genealogical Fictions*, ch. 4; McDonough, "'Love Lost'"; Townsend, *Malintzin's Choices*, 274.

21. Villella argues that such language of *limpieza* became more common among Nahua lords toward the end of the seventeenth century and later, but Kelly McDonough's analysis of similar claims among individual noble Tlaxcalans reveals that these basic "discursive pillars" to bolster and confirm privileged status were present already in the mid-seventeenth century. McDonough, "'Love Lost'"; Villella, "'Pure and Noble Indians,'" 639, 643. The proof of merit of Don Fernando, one of the descendants of Hernán Cortés and Doña Marina, prepared in the 1590s, includes a similar rhetoric. Townsend, *Malintzin's Choices*, 274.

22. Konetzke, *Colección de documentos*, 3: 66–68. For a doctrinal analysis of the *cédula de honores*: Muro Orejón, "La igualdad." On its implementation in Mexico and the Andes: Carrillo, "'La única voz'"; Dueñas, *Indians*, ch. 6; Glave, "Memoria," 9–12; Villella, "'Pure and Noble Indians,'" 641.

23. In referring to his own ancestors, Santa Cruz Pachacuti describes them thus: "All once principal chiefs in the said province [Canas y Canchis, southeast of Cuzco], and professed Christians in the things of our holy Catholic faith. They were the first chiefs who came to the tambo of Caxamarca to be made Christians." Pachacuti, "An Account," 67; Pachacuti, "Relación," 176. Guaman Poma relies on the *purity* argument when describing his own ancestors, especially his father, whom he presents as Inca Huascar's ambassador before Francisco Pizarro as the conquistador first landed in Tumbes in 1532. Yet, Guaman Poma also extends the argument to include Indians in general, highlighting their being Christian vassals and denouncing the Spanish Conquest as illegitimate. Guaman Poma, *Nueva corónica*, 16, 378–379.

24. "Descendencia y servicios: Melchor Carlos Inca," Cuzco, 1600, AGI, Patronato,

191, r. 20; "Pruebas para la concesión del Título de Caballero de Santiago de Melchor Carlos Inga," Trujillo; Madrid, 1606, AHN, OM-CS, e. 4081; "El memorial de los Mallku," 830–835 (Andean *mallku* equated with *hidalgos*, counts, dukes, and marquises). The *limpieza* of earlier Andean travelers began to be conceptualized in terms of their partial or exclusive "Indian" descent. In passenger licenses, Indian "blood" is understood as "clean" from any Jewish or Muslim stain. "Información y licencia: Vasco de Mesa," 1569, AGI, Indiferente, 2084, n. 15.

25. Dueñas, *Indians*, 153–154 (quote); Estenssoro, *Del paganismo*, 495–498.

26. See, for instance, "Carta que don Iuan Nuñez Vela de Ribera ... à los Cavalleros Indios, provenientes de la Estirpe Regia de los Monarcas del Perù, y à todos los Indios, y Mestizos sus Parientes, y Amigos," Madrid, April 30, 1693, AGI, Lima, 20; "Memorial dado a la Mag.d del Sr. Dn. Carlos II. Por Dn. Geronimo Lorenzo Limaylla," Madrid, n.d. [1678?], BPR, MS, II/2848, 211r–216v.

27. "Memorial de Juan Núñez Vela a SM solicitando una canongía en la Iglesia de Lima," Madrid, November 26, 1690, AGI, Lima, 19. On the simultaneous plea to place Nicolás Ayllón, the Indian tailor, in the altars: Estenssoro, *Del paganismo*, 439–516. Núñez Vela's campaign at court generated a significant amount of documentation and deserves a separate study. Although he spoke in his letters to the Indian and *mestizo* descendants of Inca kings and Spanish conquistadors, his more immediate addressees were the indigenous elites of Lima, particularly those centered on the church of Copacabana in San Lázaro. He was appointed chaplain (*capellán*) of the *iglesia y beaterio* there upon returning from Spain. Buntix and Wuffarden, "Incas y reyes," 164.

28. For example: "Carta de Don Diego Chaiaguilca, cacique principal de Maranga, a SM," Lima?, n.d. [early 1570s]. AGI, Lima, 270, 460r-461v.

29. In a printed *memorial* to Charles II, Don Antonio Collatopa, who fashioned himself as an "Indio Cacique" while at court, complained: "To be a *cacique* is proper to nobility, but the Indian with some assets, being a commoner [*villano*], forces the *corregidor* to make him one, while the Indian who was so because of his lineage finds himself deprived of the title." "Memorial de Antonio Collatopa a SM," Madrid, March 17, 1664, AGI, Lima, 17. Local lords in Cajamarca recognized Don Antonio as a descendant of Huayna Capac. "Carta de varios caciques de Cajamarca a SM," Lima, 1663, AGI, Lima, 17.

30. "Papeles de Don Lorenzo Çamudio El Lucayn," Madrid, 1673, AGI, Lima, 172. Unless otherwise stated, all quotations come from this document, which is not paginated.

31. "Real cédula a favor de Don Lorenzo Zamudio," Madrid, March 15, 1674, AGI, Lima, 586, l. 27, 93v–94r.

32. The selection of the surname "Ynga" for the maternal grandmother sought to highlight a link to Incas of noble descent, of whom there were still many in this northern region. On the widespread use of the ethnonym to legitimate political positions and claim nobility: Lorandi, *De quimeras*, 88–89. On the *cacique* lineages of Cajamarca: Argouse, "¿Son todos caciques?"; Noack, "Caciques, escribanos"; Ramírez, "Don Melchior Caruarayco"; Villanueva Urteaga, "Los curacas de Cajamarca." I have not been able to find any of the individuals mentioned in Lorenzo Zamudio's family tree living in the towns of San

Miguel or Asunción in the 1571–1578 inspections of Cajamarca. Nor have I found any Lucayns fulfilling the post of *cacique* at that time. Rostworowski and Remy, *Las visitas*, 1: 278–279, 289; 272: 366.

33. Guevara and Salomon, "A 'Personal Visit.'" On legal discourse and the production of truth: Burns, "Notaries, Truths, and Consequences."

34. Notaries and *letrados* were of course present in these expeditions of conquest. Lockhart, *The Men*, 258–286; Malagón-Barceló, "The Role." Arredondo's title and his presence in Pizarro's expedition seems far-fetched.

35. Towns such as San Miguel and Asunción, both of which appear in the *certificación*, were not established until the 1560s and 1570s. Hampe Martínez, "Notas sobre población," 69; Noack, "Caciques, escribanos," 218.

36. Rama, *The Lettered City*, 29–31; Rappaport and Cummins, *Beyond the Lettered City*, 171 [quote]. On the "invention" of chiefly legitimacy in Riobamba: Powers, "A Battle of Wills." On how this process unfolded in sixteenth-century Cajamarca: Noack, "Caciques, escribanos."

37. On archives as historical artifacts and the connection between power and writing in notarial settings: Burns, *Into the Archive*.

38. The events are reminiscent of the conquest of the Chachapoyas (1535–1545), during which Captain Alonso de Alvarado played an instrumental role. According to local traditions, Alvarado assigned the first *repartimientos* in 1534–1535, based on information provided by the local lords. Several *caciques* received baptism and took their names (i.e., Juan de Alvarado or Francisco Pizarro Guaman) from their Spanish godfathers. The Spaniards summoned the *caciques* and *principales* and, with the aid of three interpreters, urged them to believe in their god. The *caciques* aided the Spaniards with warriors, porters, and interpreters. "Relaçion de las cossas acaeçidas," Lima, December, 1555, AGI, Patronato, 28, r. 56; Schjellerup, *Incas*, 57–59, 140–145.

39. Dueñas, "The Lima Indian *Letrados*"; Herzog, *Upholding Justice*, 50–52. This is also true for the royal court, where councilors and secretaries kept small private archives in their homes. Brendecke, *Imperios*, 139, 449–450.

40. On the more than capable indigenous municipal scribes of Cajamarca, one of whom drafted more than 350 wills and other documents between 1675 and 1688: Argouse, "¿Son todos caciques?"; Argouse, "Testamentos." On the manufacture and presentation of false or misdated *cacique* records in Mexico and Peru: Cummins, "We Are the Other," 228; Gibson, *The Aztecs*, 162–164. The story of Pedro Villafranca, a *cacique* from Jilotepec who in the eighteenth century made a living by forging land titles for communities of the Mexico and Toluca Valleys, is told in Wood, "Pedro Villafranca." Villafranca could counterfeit sixteenth-century land grants, old maps, and even the signatures of viceroys and their secretaries. He charged 28 *pesos* for a "typical" set including a land grant, an act of possession (*posesión y amparo*), and a map, a total of six folios. Other archivists and forgers in colonial Mexico are discussed in Villa-Flores, "Archivos y falsarios." On the falsification of important royal decrees and other documents in colonial Cuzco: Rowe, "Genealogía y rebelión."

41. Some Spanish emigrants to the New World tried to avoid or mislead the authorities by falsifying official documents or by presenting authentic ones that, nevertheless,

belonged to a different person. People usually purchased these forgeries at the *Casa de la Contratación* or in the nearby plaza of San Francisco, where many notaries and scribes had set up shop. Jacobs, "Legal and Illegal Emigration," 69–71. On Viceroy Count of Chinchón's warning to the Council about favor-seekers with specious claims: "Carta. El Conde de Chinchón al Consejo de Indias," Lima, May 5, 1634, AGI, Lima, 45, n. 4, l. 1, 25.

42. Pike, *Linajudos*, 10–11, 33, 40–46, 101. In 1599, the municipal council of Seville discovered that false assistant constables (*alguaciles*) had been renting emblems that, in fact, bore counterfeit signatures. On the falsification of chronicles and, more generally, the role of historical invention in late sixteenth-century Spain: Olds, *Forging the Past*. On false witnesses in travel licenses to travel to the New World: Sánchez Rubio and Testón Núñez, "'Fingiendo llamarse,'" 228.

43. Rappaport and Cummins, *Beyond the Lettered City*, 171.

44. The second certification is likely based on a conventional notarial certification of a previous writing act, conducted by a petitioner before a local magistrate or *audiencia* (i.e., a secret inquest about someone's ancestors and services to the king), overseen by the *corregidor* or his lieutenants, then stored in the notary's private archive. The idea of a list of the *caciques* who surrendered is probably inspired by similar lists of tributaries and parishioners (*padrones*), routinely prepared during civil and ecclesiastic inspections to certify someone's membership in the community or fulfillment of a civil or religious duty. Some of the headings and stock formulas used in this document, however, indicate that a baptismal certificate is also a likely model for the first certification.

45. Throughout the text, notaries Arredondo and Morán certify, with their signatures and other standard, well-worn forms, that what the characters said and did is true. Especially when making a copy of an older document, notaries often received validation from other higher-ranked notaries, who certified the identity of the scribe and attested to the fidelity of his transcription. Cognizant of the formal steps to certify an alleged 1642 copy of a 1542 certification of a 1535 original, the author ends the first *certificación* with the typical formula. The second certification simply states "authorized by the Council."

46. In 1582, different persons who had resided in Peru for several years assured the Council that a traveler and petitioner who called himself Don Carlos Tito Amaro, though of the lineage of the former lords of Cuzco, was neither the great grandson of Emperor Huayna Capac nor the brother of Don Felipe Tupac Amaru, executed by Viceroy Toledo in 1572. The Council refused to discuss Tito Amaro's alleged merits and military services in America, Africa, and Europe until he produced proper documents. "Consulta del Consejo sobre pretensión de Don Carlos Tito Amaro," Madrid, August 18, 1582, AGI, Lima, 1, n. 44. It is possible that Tito Amaro was among the Incas who left Vilcabamba after this last bastion of Inca imperial power fell in 1572. Nowack and Julien, "La campaña," 29, 35.

47. The group included Don Juan de Azabache and Nicolás Flores, Don Juan Crisóstomo Atahualpa, Don Antonio Collatopa, a *cacique* from Cajamarca, Don Pedro Chafo Zavana, a *principal* from Lambayeque, Don Cristóbal Chudin Bamon, a *cacique* from the town of Chongón in the *audiencia* of Quito, and Don Nicolás Tolentino Lluchi Moro, a *principal*, among others. Puente Luna, "Into the Heart," Appendix.

48. Don Francisco described himself as "Caçique prinçipal, de la Baronia de los Reyes

Yngas, que fueron de los Reynos del Piru en yndias." His last name is spelled indistincively as "Heriza," "Herizo," "Arisa," "Erizo," and "Eriza." In the mid-1700s, the Yauric Arizas held the *cacicazgo* of the *ayllu* Cuzco in the town of Oropesa, a few miles from the city of Cuzco. Garrett, *Shadows*, 88.

49. "Conpulsoria Para Sacar escripturas," Valladolid, June 13, 1665, AHN, NO, c. 294, d. 74.

50. Similar stories of indigenous youth "taken" from their villages by abusive friars and later fleeing from their custody in order to relocate to colonial cities were not uncommon. Guaman Poma, *Nueva corónica*, 969.

51. "Jerónimo Limaylla con Bernardino Limaylla," 1656–1671, AGI, Escribanía, 514C, 543r–570r; Davis, *The Return*, 39; Davis, *Trickster Travels*. During the trial, Limaylla did not deny the existence of Lorenzo Ayun but claimed that "Aillum" had worked in Lima as a tailor until 1648. Then, he had embarked to the inhospitable regions of Chile, where he died. The story of how these two lives intertwined is discussed in detail in Puente Luna, "What's in a Name?" For a similar case of impersonation and name appropriation among the Hati *cacique* lineage of the *audiencia* in Quito: Espinosa, *El Inca barroco*, 93.

52. It is not clear whether the witness is referring to his own journey to Spain or to Zamudio's. The dates match. If, by 1673, Zamudio had spent eight or nine years in Madrid, then he left Lima around 1664. Limaylla traveled to Spain sometime between mid-1663 and mid-1665. Puente Luna, "What's in a Name?," 41.

53. "Self-fashioning" refers to "representation of one's nature or intention in speech." Greenblatt, *Renaissance Self-Fashioning*, 3.

54. "Le hiciese merçed de criarle cassique." *Criar* implies both giving title or appointing and making someone something he is not. "Memorial de Don Jerónimo Lorenzo Limaylla a S.M.," Madrid, March 23, 1673, AGI, Lima, 26. In another *memorial*, presented to the Council in 1671, Limaylla requested unsuccessfully that the Queen make him second-in-command (*segunda persona*) of the paramount lord of Luringuanca. "Memorial. Don Jerónimo Lorenzo Limaylla a SM solicitando una ayuda costa para volver al Perú," Madrid, December 3, 1671, AGI, Indiferente, 640.

55. "Memorial de Don Jerónimo Lorenzo Limaylla a S.M." The titles in question are copied in "Jerónimo Limaylla con Bernardino Limaylla," 34v–63r.

56. "Informaciones: Francisco de Heriza," 1669, AGI, Lima, 259, n. 10, 2r.

57. "Consulta del Consejo sobre pretensión de Don Carlos Tito Amaro," Madrid, August 18, 1582, AGI, Lima, 1, n. 44. Jerónimo Lorenzo Limaylla put forth the same argument when requesting an *ayuda de costa* from the Council. "Decreto de SM con un memorial de Don Jerónimo Limaylla," Madrid, January 20, 1666, AGI, Lima, 17.

58. "Informaciones: Francisco de Heriza," 11r–12v. *Vecindad* implied a social and legal condition that, at least in theory, defined the rights and obligations of permanent Spanish residents exclusively.

59. "Informaciones: Francisco de Heriza," 6r. In denying Pedro Quispe, a traveler to court and a tributary payer from Cajamarca, the privilege to carry a sword and a dagger, the councilors reminded the king that it was an honor reserved for the *caciques* "for being

noble people from that land." "Respuesta del Consejo de Indias a S.M. sobre las pretensiones de Pedro Quispe," Madrid, May 27, 1684, AGI, Lima, 12.

60. See, for example, "Información hecha por Diego de Aguilar Diez a petición de don Gonzalo Mango Misari," Lima, 1597, AGN, DIE, l. 31, c. 622.

61. Glave, "Gestiones," 102–103. For similar misidentifications of indigenous travelers as *mestizos* in the 1570s: "Agrauio que generalmente se haze a los naturales," 1579?, AGI, Indiferente, 1373.

62. On naming practices and the adoption of Spanish surnames for acquiring rank and prestige within the indigenous sphere: Lockhart, Berdan, and Anderson, *The Tlaxcalan Actas*, 21, note 126; Martínez, *Genealogical Fictions*, 108. For a more general reflection on the importance of names as identifiers in early modern Spain and Spanish America: Herzog, "Naming, Identifying and Authorizing."

63. Sánchez Rubio and Testón Núñez, "'Fingiendo llamarse,'" 224.

64. Adorno, "Images," 252–253; Estenssoro, *Del paganismo*, 484–485; Guaman Poma, *Nueva corónica*, 678–679. The Franciscans who ran the School of San Andrés in Quito called Cristóbal Ango, *cacique* of the Caranquis, "Cristobalito." Hartmann and Oberem, "Quito," 118. Some *mestizos* who traveled to Spain in the second half of the sixteenth century were also identified with diminutives such as "Cristobalico" or "Juanico" to signal their *criado* status. Alaperrine-Bouyer, "Cruzar el océano," 36–37.

65. According to the *cacique* of Reque, "'Chifu' means 'spindle whorl,' and his father manufactured them." "Jerónimo Limaylla con Bernardino Limaylla," 951v. Lorenzo's parents belonged to the tributary class.

66. "Jerónimo Limaylla con Bernardino Limaylla," 641r–643r; Salomon, "Indian Women," 333. Nicolás Ayllón, Father Ayllón's favorite indigenous student, substituted his original Yunga last name ("Puicon") for the friar's surname. In Reque and elsewhere, *caciques* could also take the surnames of prominent clergymen.

67. "Jerónimo Limaylla con Bernardino Limaylla," 387v–401r, 443r–475v, 648r–649v. Before the officials of the *Casa de la Contratación* in 1646, Lorenzo Ayun went by the name "Don Lorenzo Ayllón Atagualpa" (or, alternatively, "Don Benito Ayllón Atahualpa"), adopting, albeit temporarily, the name/title of the Inca king who met the Spaniards in 1532. "Información y licencia: Lorenzo Ayllón Atahualpa," AGI, Contratación, 5427, n. 3, R. 33; "Memorial de Don Juan Lorenzo Ayllón a SM," Madrid, April 4, 1646, AGI, Lima, 15.

68. Such were the cases of Don Lorenzo Zamudio El Lucayn and Don Felipe de Heriza Paz Carguamango. This strategy is prominently displayed by the Andean authors of a 1710 *memorial* addressed by the "*naturales* of this kingdom" to the monarch. Glave, "Memoria," 9.

69. Rappaport, *The Disappearing Mestizo*, 52 (quote), 57, 282.

70. Dean, *Inka Bodies*, 112–124; Cummins, "We Are the Other," 211–213; Garrett, *Shadows*, 177–178; Graubart, *With Our Labor*, 133–137; Powers, "The Battle for Bodies"; Rowe, "Colonial Portraits"; Rowe, "El movimiento"; Salomon, *The Cord Keepers*, 115–116. Numerous references of the importance of clothing as a marker of rank and status among the native populations of Peru can be found in Guaman Poma, *Nueva corónica*, 752 and

ff. For a discussion of the social significance of the uniforms worn by the privileged students of the Jesuit schools for Indian nobles: Alaperrine-Bouyer, *La educación*, 166–171.

71. "Autos formados a representación de Juan Evangelista Arque," Tinguipaya, December 11, 1780, ABNB, ALP, SGI-28, 2r. Elizabeth Penry suggests that the Indian clothes mentioned by the *cacique* referred to the *poncho* and the stocking-style cap with earflaps "favored by Andeans" in southern Peru and Charcas. Penry, "Letters," 36.

72. "Residencia: Gabriel de Loarte," 1575, AGI, Justicia, 463, 164r–164v, 282r; "Real cédula para que Don Felipe Guacrapaucar pueda passar al Peru un arcabuz," Barcelona, February 26, 1564, AGI, Lima, 569, l. 11, 137v.

73. Roche, *The Culture of Clothing*, 4, 6–7, 39, 50, 128, 512.

74. Upon his death in Madrid, Don Alonso Atahualpa owed several *reales* to a glove maker, a tailor, a silversmith, and a ribbon maker who had manufactured his hats and general attire while he lived in Madrid. Jiménez de la Espada, *Relaciones geográficas (Perú)*, 3: 97–98.

75. Another witness claimed that Father Buenaventura de Salinas, Limaylla's protector in Spain, "loved him and liked him as a son of a *cacique*." "Jerónimo Limaylla con Bernardino Limaylla," 463v, 514r.

76. "Jerónimo Limaylla con Bernardino Limaylla," 467r–467v, 486r, 491r.

77. "Información sobre los pleitos de Jauja," Concepción, 1570, AGI, Lima, 28A, 63Q, 3v–4r. In a letter penned the same year, the *cacique* of Huarochirí told the *corregidor* that Don Felipe was offering legal counsel to the Indians of Jauja and Huarochirí—"consejos" and "bachellerias" (from *bachiller*, someone with a formal training in law), "telling them that he had studied in Salamanca and Seville." "Residencia: Gabriel de Loarte," 224r.

78. "Jerónimo Limaylla con Bernardino Limaylla," 332r–332v; 655r, 658r, 660r. Many travelers, including Don Felipe Guacrapaucar, Don Sebastián Hilaquita, and Don Juan Chuquival, acted as official interpreters in local inspections and at the *audiencia* upon returning to Peru. Puente Luna, "The Many Tongues."

79. "Jerónimo Limaylla con Bernardino Limaylla," 290r, 298v, 556r, 647r.

80. Rappaport and Cummins, *Beyond the Lettered City*, 19; Rappaport, *The Disappearing Mestizo*, 134, 148–149, 161.

81. Rama, *The Lettered City*, 16–18.

82. In 1570, ten years after returning from Spain and becoming an expert in the art of pursuing justice, Don Felipe Guacrapaucar was denounced by the *audiencia* prosecutor for "making all the Indians with whom he deals and communicates anxious by providing them a bad example and putting ideas in their heads." This "bad example" was Don Felipe's determination to fight the appointment of Crown administrators of communal assets in the courtroom; his "new words" were powerful weapons to preserve local autonomy via the courts. "Residencia: Gabriel de Loarte," 305r.

83. "Se dio a hacer virtuoso y escribir por escritorios." Presta, "De testamentos," 827; Presta, "Doña Isabel Sisa." For a discussion of the term *palla* in this particular colonial context: Presta, "Undressing the *Coya*," 63, n. 48.

84. David Garrett's conclusion about the late-colonial *cacicazgos* of the Cuzco area seems apropos here: "the son of a 'cacique intruso' could easily become the legitimate

'cacique propietario' in the eyes of both tributaries and Spanish officials. As a result, the disruptions that toppled individual cacical dynasties, or large swaths of the cacical elite in a particular region, could give way within one or two generations to dynasties who had occupied the office 'since time immemorial,' and were widely reckoned the legitimate caciques of their communities." Garrett, *Shadows*, 167.

85. The literature on chiefly strategies for self-representation and legitimation before colonial courts is too vast to be included in this note. Particularly insightful works and recent approaches to the subject include, for Quito: Powers, "A Battle of Wills." For the North Coast (Trujillo and Cajamarca): Graubart, *With Our Labor*, 160–169; Noack, "Los caciques"; Noack, "Caciques, escribanos." For Jauja: Puente Luna, *Los curacas*, ch. 3. For Cuzco: Garrett, *Shadows*, ch. 5. Charcas: Abercrombie, *Pathways*, 159–164; Jurado, "'Descendientes de los primeros'"; Morrone, "Legitimidad." On documents as "treasure": Rappaport and Cummins, *Beyond the Lettered City*, 21–24.

86. Presta, "Undressing the *Coya*"; Spalding, "Social Climbers."

87. Rappaport, *The Disappearing Mestizo*, 154.

88. "Confirmación de la elección de Francisco Benítez Inga," Mexico, February 9, 1659, AGNM, RA-I, v. 23, 340r–345v. See also Connell, *After Moctezuma*, 118–126; Estrada Torres, "San Juan Tenochtitlan." In the next paragraphs, I follow Connell's interpretation closely.

89. "Confirmación de la elección de Francisco Benítez Inga," 343r.

90. "Confirmación de la elección de Francisco Benítez Inga," 341v–342r. Connell notes that *mestizos* had previously held office in Mexico-Tenochtitlan. The Crown had been generally unwilling to enforce these laws unless someone disputed the election. Connell, *After Moctezuma*, 123.

91. "Confirmación de la elección de Francisco Benítez Inga," 343v.

92. "Nombramiento de gobernador de Suchimilco en Don Francisco Benítez Inga," Mexico, December 7, 1651, AGNM, RA-I, v. 16, 127r–128v.

93. A "good" governor "had to have the ability to create political networks ..., to find creative ways to collect all tribute, and to do all of this without motivating commoners to petition or giving oppositional political figures the capacity to contest through petition." Connell, *After Moctezuma*, 126.

94. Benítez Inga ran again in 1672 but was defeated by Don Juan de Aguilar. Interestingly, Benítez Inga challenged the right of his competitor to take office by accusing him of being *mestizo*. The strategy did not work. Connell, *After Moctezuma*, 119–120, 171–172; Estrada Torres, "San Juan Tenochtitlan," 76–78.

95. Connell, *After Moctezuma*, 120–126; "Confirmación de la elección de Francisco Benítez Inga," 341r–341v.

96. "Confirmación de la elección de Francisco Benítez Inga," 129r.

97. A list of royal decrees awarded to indigenous travelers during the Hasburg period is included in Puente Luna, "Into the Heart," Appendix 2.

98. "Residencia: Gabriel de Loarte," 257v.

99. "Jerónimo Limaylla con Bernardino Limaylla," 364v–365r, 574v.

100. Puente Luna, "What's in a Name?," ch. 3.

101. In 1646, he filed a petition for the king to exclude the natives of Jauja from compulsory labor at the mines. "Memorial de Don Juan Lorenzo Ayllón a SM." Harsh conditions in Huancavelica were proverbial. In the words of a famous Franciscan, the Indians who worked there "cried tears of blood." Salinas y Córdoba, *Memorial*, 278.

102. On "escaped Indians" (*indios fugados*): "Poder. El corregidor de Jauja y los caciques del repartimiento de Luringuanca a don Marcos Cangauala y don Martín Albachin," AGN, DIE, c. 128, l. 9, 4r.

103. "Jerónimo Limaylla con Bernardino Limaylla," 546r.

104. "Poder de los caciques y cobradores de Atunjauja, Luringuanca y Ananguanca," October 21, 1651, ARJ, PN, 7 (Carranza), 208r–212r.

105. "Jerónimo Limaylla con Bernardino Limaylla," 378r, 445r, 473v–474r, 546r, 575r–575v.

106. Limaylla appears as signatory in several letters sent by different *caciques* to the king from Lima. For example: "Carta de Don Diego Lobo y otros a SM," Lima, November 29, 1662. AGI, Lima, 17.

107. "Jerónimo Limaylla con Bernardino Limaylla," 558r; "Decreto de SM con un memorial de D. Ger.mo Limaylla, en que supp.ca se le de vna ayuda de costa p.a imprimir dos memoriales," Madrid, July 15, 1677, AGI, Indiferente, 640.

108. O'Toole, *Bound Lives*, 85; "Causa contra Don Bernardino de Perales," 1r–3v.

109. "Testimonio de la causa contra Don Bernardino de Perales," Lambayeque, AGI, Lima, 167, 3r–3v, 46r; "Carta de los caciques y pachacas de la prouincia de Saña a SM," Lima, October 25, 1648, AGI, Lima, 167. A sentence against Perales was finally issued in 1655. The Council found him guilty of virtually all of the charges. Glave, "Gestiones," 92.

110. *que dice ser*. "Memorial de Don Andrés de Ortega Lluncon para que se le dé ayuda de costa," Madrid, January 18, 1647, AGI, Contaduría, 188; "Respuesta del Consejo de Indias a una orden de VM sobre memorial de Don Andrés de Ortega Lluncon," Madrid, March 14, 1647, AGI, Lima, 7.

111. "Carta de Francisco de Valenzuela al Consejo de Indias," Lima, October 23, 1648, AGI, Lima, 167.

112. "Carta de Francisco de Valenzuela al Consejo de Indias," 9v, 14v–15r, 18r–19r.

113. "Causa contra Don Bernardino de Perales," 1v. Like Azabache, the *principales* of Lambayeque knew about the *corregidor*'s illegal activities. Because they benefitted from them or had no other choice, they accepted the status quo.

114. *yndio buen cristiano, Ladino ... Y de los prinçipales del[,] suficiente[,] abil.* "Carta de Francisco de Valenzuela al Consejo de Indias," Lima, October 23, 1648, AGI, Lima, 167. See also "Árbol genealógico de Don Martín Farrochumbi," AGN, PL, 13; Lohmann, "Nuevos datos"; Rostworowski, *Curacas y sucesiones*, 43–53; Zevallos Quiñones, *Los cacicazgos de Lambayeque*, 69–71.

115. "Carta de los caciques y pachacas de la prouincia de Saña a SM." In 1655, Don Andrés de Ortega was still *pachaca principal*. He also served as municipal judge. Zevallos Quiñones, *Los cacicazgos de Lambayeque*, 72, n. 24. As a reward for his advocacy in Spain, he received the fine of 2,000 pesos that the Council imposed on Perales. Glave, "Gestiones," 92; O'Toole, "Don Carlos," 33. Moreover, the *audiencia* appointed him *juez de*

aguas of the district of Saña, a post that carried a yearly salary of 140 pesos. "Memorial de Andrés de Ortega Lluncon a SM," September 26, 1668, AGI, Lima, 26.

116. "Respuesta del Consejo de Indias a SM sobre los agravios y vejaciones que presenta Don Carlos Chimo," Madrid, November 29, 1646, AGI, Lima, 7. A similar statement appears in "Respuesta del Consejo de Indias a SM sobre el memorial de Don Carlos Chimo," Madrid, July 23, 1647, AGI, Lima, 7; "Causa contra Don Bernardino de Perales," 1 (first pagination). In several *memoriales* presented at court in 1646 and 1647, Don Carlos styled himself indistinctively as "caçique en el piru," "Caçique principal del pueblo de Lanbayeque y sarjento mayor de la ciudad de Saña del Piru," "Cachique [*sic*] Principal de Lambayeque en el Piru," and "Cacique del pueblo de Lambayeque." "Relación de los gastos para vestir y enviar a Cádiz a Don Carlos Chimo y a Don Andrés de Ortega Lluncon," Madrid, November, 1647, AGI, Contaduría, 188; "Memorial de Don Carlos Chimo a SM solicitando un nuevo juez de tierras," Madrid, July 20, 1647, AGI, Lima, 25.

117. A telling commentary on these rules of judicial representation is Viceroy Toledo's assertion that most commoners in the Peruvian viceroyalty believed that only *caciques* could obtain justice. "Carta. Francisco de Toledo al Consejo de Indias," Lima, August 2, 1570, AGI, Lima, 28a, n. 45, l. 1, 11.

118. Sarreal, "Caciques," 227–228.

119. O'Toole, *Bound Lives*, 2–6, 12; Yannakakis, *The Art*, 156.

120. "Real cédula al Virrey del Piru," Madrid, March 18, 1618, AGI, Lima, 583, l. 17, 96v–97v.

121. O'Toole, "Don Carlos," 26.

122. "Carta de los caziques del Peru a S.M.," Lima, July 3, 1657, AGI, Lima, 169.

123. "Carta de Don Jerónimo Lorenzo Limaylla a S.M.," Lima, January 28, 1662, AGI, Lima, 17. See also Limaylla's "Representacion hecha al Sr. rey Dn. Carlos Segundo por Dn. Geronimo Limaylla," Madrid, n.d. [1662?], BPR, MS, II/2848, 217r–247v.

124. "Decreto de S.M. con un memorial de D. Geronimo Limaylla en que supplica se le de vna ayuda de costa para sustentarse y vestirse," Madrid, February 25, 1678, AGI, Indiferente, 640.

125. "Memorial dado a la Mag.d del Sr. Dn. Carlos II. Por Dn. Geronimo Lorenzo Limaylla"; "Decreto de S.M. con dos memoriales impresos del cacique D. Ger.mo Limaylla s.re las molestias que reciuen los Indios del Peru," Madrid, February 9, 1678, AGI, Indiferente, 640.

CHAPTER 7

1. Fernández de Castro y Bocángel, *Elisio Pervano*, n.p. (Fiesta de los naturales). Louis Ferdinand died before the Lima celebrations took place.

2. Millones, "The Inka's Mask," 18–24; Amino, "Three Faces," 352–353. These performances were, to some degree, inspired by one of Juan Núñez Vela's *memoriales* to the king. On the role of these processions of Inca kings in the construction of a historical narrative that legitimized the colonial authority of Andean *caciques*' Inca descendants: Cummins,

"We Are the Other," 222–224; Estenssoro, *Del paganismo*, 501–503; Estenssoro, "Construyendo la memoria," 133 and ff. On these processions as expressions of Indian fealty and corporate identity: Espinosa, *El Inca barroco*, 75–85.

3. Millones, "The Inka's Mask," 25–27. Minollulli was a standard-bearer and a steward of two Indian religious brotherhoods in Lima. In 1734, he received power of attorney from the different indigenous corporations of the city to act as a liaison between them and the transatlantic procurator Vicente Mora Chimo. The Minollullis, who claimed the *cacicazgo* of Lambayeque in the sixteenth century, established family ties with the Lima *cacique* aristocracy. Carrillo, "'La única voz,'" 33; Rostworowski, *Señoríos*, 98; Zevallos Quiñones, *Los cacicazgos de Lambayeque*, 69.

4. For the 1725 celebration, however, his sisters sent him several items of jewelry, allegedly owned by the family since Inca times, and dispatched *pallas* and *ñustas* (noble women) and other *criados*, all of them richly dressed for Don Cristóbal's theatrical appearance. Puente Luna, *Los curacas*, 265–273.

5. Amino, "Three Faces," 352; Millones, "The Inka's Mask," 20. For the foundational role that the procession played in terms of the *Nación Índica*'s self-presentation strategies: Carrillo, "'La única voz,'" 61; Buntix and Wuffarden, "Incas y reyes," 171.

6. On the importance of memory, history, and artistic representation in the conformation of the *Nación Índica*: Dueñas, *Indians*; Estenssoro, "Construyendo la memoria," 161–163; Glave, "Memoria," 9. In festivals and the colonial image of the Inca: Burga, *Nacimiento de una utopía*; Espinosa, *El Inca barroco*.

7. Baber, "Empire," 38; see also 20–21.

8. Dueñas, *Indians*; Glave, "Gestiones"; O'Toole, "Don Carlos."

9. Carrillo, "'La única voz,'"; Dueñas, *Indians*; Glave, "Memoria"; Lowry, "Forging an Indian Nation"; Mathis, "Vicente Mora Chimo"; Mathis, "Une Figure."

10. Lowry, "Forging an Indian Nation," 1–7, 51, 271–279, 283–289. Before Lowry, John Rowe had made a serious effort to frame native travels to the Spanish court within the first "Inca nationalist cycle" of the mid-seventeenth century. Rowe, "The Incas"; Rowe, "Colonial Portraits"; Rowe, "El movimiento." Others expanded Rowe's thesis, positing that some indigenous travelers became millenarian or Messianic figures. As such, they were recognized by many as the banner of a collective Andean "identity" or "consciousness," supported by utopian dreams of restoring Tawantinsuyu under their leadership. Atlantic voyages were, in this interpretation, landmarks in the formation of this utopian horizon, which helped to redefine a neo-Indian identity in colonial Peru. Klumpp, "El retorno"; Lorandi, *De quimeras*; Pease, "Mesianismo"; Pease, "Conciencia"; Pease, "Un memorial." For a full historiographical assessment: Puente Luna, "Into the Heart," 3–13. For a critique of the paradigm: Espinosa, *El Inca barroco*, 14–18.

11. Brubaker and Cooper, "Beyond 'Identity,'" 14–17; Fisher and O'Hara, "Introduction," 21; Jenkins, "Rethinking Ethnicity," 204. Jovita Baber's analysis of the Tlaxcalans of New Spain supports this assertion. They "did *not* have a *collective identity* as *indios* ... they did not imagine themselves as part of a larger community composed of other natives from the Indies. ... For them, *indios* was strictly a legal category that they could access in order to lay claim to particular rights." Baber concludes, "*Indios* never became a nation—a col-

lective identity or an imagined community for native Americans—but it was a *nación*—a legal category ascribed by the Crown." Baber, "Categories," 27–28, 39.

12. On the interplay between legal identifications and social identities: Baber, "Categories"; Van Deusen, *Global indios*; Fisher and O'Hara, *Imperial Subjects*; Rappaport, *The Disappearing Mestizo*; Silverblatt, *Modern Inquisitions*; Sweet, "Mistaken Identities?"

13. Carrillo, "'La única voz,'" 63. Carlos Espinosa has also noted how Inca sovereigns of colonial processions symbolically reconciled the contradiction between "the existence of a wide [Indian] nation and its lack of a universal symbol." Espinosa, *El Inca barroco*, 106.

14. Premo, "Custom Today," 370.

BIBLIOGRAPHY

ARCHIVES AND ABBREVIATIONS

AAL — Archivo Arzobispal de Lima (Lima)
    HEI — Hechicerías e Idolatrías
ABNB — Archivo y Biblioteca Nacionales de Bolivia (Sucre)
    ALP-SGI — Audiencia de la Plata-Sublevación General de Indios
AGI — Archivo General de Indias (Seville)
    Contaduría — Contaduría y Cuentas
    Contratación — Casa de la Contratación
    Escribanía — Escribanía de Cámara de Justicia
    Indiferente — Indiferente General
    Lima — Audiencia de Lima
    Panamá — Audiencia de Panamá
    Patronato — Patronato Real
    Quito — Audiencia de Quito
AGN — Archivo General de la Nación (Lima)
    CGC — Caja General de Censos de Indios
    DIE — Derecho Indígena y Encomiendas
    GO-BI — Superior Gobierno
    JR — Juicios de Residencia
    PL — Planoteca
    PN — Protocolos Notariales
    TP — Títulos de Propiedad
AGNM — Archivo General de la Nación (Mexico)
    RA-I — Instituciones Coloniales-Real Audiencia-Indios
AHN — Archivo Histórico Nacional (Madrid)
    CS — Consejos
    NO — Nobleza-Osuna
    OM-CS — Órdenes Militares-Caballeros de Santiago
AHMPH — Archivo Histórico de la Municipalidad Provincial de Huancavelica (Huancavelica)
    EC — Expedientes Coloniales

AHP—*Archivo Histórico de Protocolos de Madrid (Madrid)*
    PN—Protocolos Notariales
ARA—*Archivo Regional del Amazonas (Chachapoyas)*
    PN—Protocolos Notariales
ARC—*Archivo Regional del Cuzco (Cuzco)*
    CB—Colección Betancourt
    PN—Protocolos Notariales
ARJ—*Archivo Regional de Junín (Huancayo)*
    PN—Protocolos Notariales
    PR—Prefectura de Junín
ARLL—*Archivo Regional de La Libertad (Trujillo)*
    CO—Corregimiento
    C-CC—Corregimiento-Causas Criminales
    C-CO—Corregimiento-Causas Ordinarias
    PN—Protocolos Notariales
BL—*British Library (London)*
    ADD—Additional Manuscripts
BNCh—*Biblioteca Nacional de Chile (Santiago)*
    SM—Sala Medina
BNE—*Biblioteca Nacional de España (Madrid)*
    MS—Manuscritos
BNP—*Biblioteca Nacional del Perú (Lima)*
    AAC—Archivo Astete Concha
    MS—Manuscritos
BPR—*Biblioteca del Palacio Real (Madrid)*
    MS—Manuscritos
CVU—*Colección Vargas Ugarte de la Universidad Ruiz de Montoya (Lima)*
    MS—Manuscritos
LIL—*Lilly Library (Bloomington)*
    LAM—Latin American Manuscripts
LOC—*Library of Congress (Washington, DC)*
    HC—Harkness Collection
MNAAH—*Museo Nacional de Arqueología, Antropología e Historia del Perú (Lima)*
    AH-MS—Archivo Histórico-Manuscritos

bk	Book	n.	Número
c.	Cuaderno	pt.	Part
ch(s).	Chapter(s)	r.	Registro
d.	Documento	t.	Tomo
e.	Expediente	tit.	Title
l.	Legajo/Libro	v.	Volumen

REFERENCES CITED

Abercrombie, Thomas. *Pathways of Memory and Power: Ethnography and History among an Andean People*. Madison: University of Wisconsin Press, 1998.

————. "La perpetuidad traducida: del 'debate' al Taki Onqoy y una rebelión comunera peruana." In *Incas e indios cristianos: elites indígenas e identidades cristianas en los Andes coloniales*, edited by Jean-Jacques Decoster, 79–120. Cuzco; Lima: Centro de Estudios Regionales Andinos Bartolomé de Las Casas; Asociacion Kuraka; Instituto Francés de Estudios Andinos, 2002.

Acosta, José de. *Natural and Moral History of the Indies*. Durham: Duke University Press, 2002.

Adorno, Rolena. "Images of *indios ladinos* in Early Colonial Peru." In *Transatlantic Encounters: Europeans and Andeans in the Sixteenth Century*, edited by Rolena Adorno and Kenneth Andrien, 232–270. Berkeley: University of California Press, 1991.

————. "Colonial Reform of Utopia? Guaman Poma's Empire of the Four Parts of the World." In *Amerindian Images and the Legacy of Columbus*, edited by René Jara and Nicholas Spadaccini, 346–374. Minneapolis: University of Minnesota Press, 1992.

————. *Guaman Poma: Writing and Resistance in Colonial Peru*. Austin: University of Texas Press, 2000.

————. "The Indigenous Ethnographer: The *indio ladino* as Historian and Cultural Mediation." In *Implicit Understandings: Observing, Reporting, and Reflecting on the Encounters Between Europeans and other Peoples in the Early Modern Era*, edited by Stuart B. Schwartz, 378–402. Cambridge: Cambridge University Press, 1994.

Aguilar Moreno, Manuel. "The *Indio Ladino* as a Cultural Mediator in the Colonial Society." *Estudios de Cultura Náhuatl* 33 (2002): 149–184.

Aguirre, Carlos. "*Tinterillos*, Indians, and the State: Towards a History of Legal Intermediaries in Post-Independence Peru." In *One Law for All? Western Models and Local Practices in (Post-) Imperial Contexts*, edited by Stefan B. Kirmse, 119–151. Frankfurt: Verlag, 2012.

Alaperrine-Bouyer, Monique. "Enseignements et enjeux d'un héritage cacical: le long plaidoyer de Jerónimo Limaylla, Jauja, 1657–1678." In *Les autorités indigènes entre deux mondes: solidarité ethnique et compromission coloniale*, edited by Bernard Lavallé, 103–129. Paris: Université de la Sorbonne Nouvelle, Paris III, 2004.

————. "Recurrencias y variaciones de la imagen del cacique." In *Máscaras, tretas y rodeos del discurso colonial en los Andes*, edited by Bernard Lavallé, 189–209. Lima: Instituto Francés de Estudios Andinos; Pontificia Universidad Católica del Perú; Instituto Riva-Agüero, 2005.

————. *La educación de las elites indígenas en el Perú colonial*. Lima: Instituto Francés de Estudios Andinos, 2007.

————. "Cruzar el océano: lo que revelan los viajes a España de los mestizos peruanos en la segunda parte del siglo XVI." *Histórica* 27, no. 2 (2013): 7–58.

Altman, Ida. *Emigrants and Society: Extremadura and America in the Sixteenth Century*. Berkeley: University of California Press, 1989.

———. *Transatlantic Ties in the Spanish Empire: Brihuega, Spain and Puebla, Mexico, 1560–1620*. Stanford: Stanford University Press, 2000.

Álvarez de Toledo, Pedro. "Memorial que presentó al Rey el Excmo. Sr. Marqués de Mancera en el que alegando méritos y servicios hace relación de muchas cosas particulares que obró en el tiempo que fue virrey del Perú." In *Los virreyes españoles en América durante el gobierno de la Casa de Austria: Perú*, edited by Lewis Hanke and Celso Rodríguez. Vol. 3: 224–278. Madrid: Atlas, 1978.

Amado Gonzales, Donato. "El alférez real de los Incas: resistencia, cambios y continuidad de la identidad inca." In *Elites indígenas en los Andes: nobles, caciques y cabildantes bajo el yugo colonial*, edited by David Cahill and Blanca Tovías, 55–80. Quito: Abya-Yala, 2003.

———. "El Cabildo de los Veinticuatro Electores del Alférez Real Inca de las ocho parroquias cusqueñas." *Allpanchis* 39 (2012): 61–96.

Amelang, James S. "Barristers and Judges in Early Modern Barcelona: The Rise of a Legal Elite." *American Historical Review* 89, no. 5 (1984): 1264–1284.

Amino, Tetsuya. "Three Faces of the Inka: Changing Conceptions and Representations of the Inka during the Colonial Period." In *The Inka Empire: A Multidisciplinary Approach*, edited by Izumi Shimada, 347–361. Austin: University of Texas Press, 2015.

Anderson, Benedict. *Imagined Communities: Reflections on the Origin and Spread of Nationalism*. London; New York: Verso, 2016.

Angeli, Sergio. "'¿Buenos e rectos jueces?': La visita a la Audiencia de Lima por el licenciado Briviesca de Muñatones, 1560–1563." *Jahrbuch für Geschichte Lateinamerikas— Anuario de Historia de América Latina* 50 (2013): 9–27.

Angulo, Domingo. "Libro de visitas. 1593. Diario de la segunda visita pastoral que hizo de su arquidiócesis el ilustrísimo señor don Toribio Alfonso de Mogrovejo, arzobispo de Los Reyes." *Revista del Archivo Nacional del Perú* 1 (1920): 227–279.

Ares Queija, Berta, and Alessandro Stella. *Negros, mulatos, zambaigos: derroteros africanos en los mundos ibéricos*. Seville: Escuela de Estudios Hispano-Americanos; Consejo Superior de Investigaciones Científicas, 2000.

Argouse, Aude. "¿Son todos caciques? Curacas, principales e indios urbanos en Cajamarca (siglo XVII)." *Bulletin de l'Institut Français d'Études Andines* 37, no. 1 (2008): 163–184.

———. "Testamentos de indígenas, ¿una fuente excepcional?: la 'voz del pueblo' y del escribano. Cajamarca, Perú, siglo XVII." *Temas Americanistas* 29 (2012): 200–221.

Arroyo, Luis. *Los franciscanos y la fundación de Chiclayo*. Lima: n.p., 1956.

Assadourian, Carlos Sempat. "Las rentas reales, el buen gobierno y la hacienda de Dios: el parecer de 1568 de fray Francisco de Morales sobre la reformación de las Indias temporal y espiritual." *Histórica* 9, no. 1 (1985): 75–130.

 ———. "Los señores étnicos y los corregidores de indios en la conformación del espacio colonial." *Anuario de Estudios Americanos* 44 (1987): 325–426.

———. "La renta de la encomienda en la década de 1550: piedad cristiana y deconstrucción." *Revista de Indias* 48, no. 182–183 (1988): 109–146.

———. "Acerca del cambio en la naturaleza del dominio sobre las Indias: la mita minera del virrey Toledo, documentos de 1568–1571." *Anuario de Estudios Americanos* 46 (1989): 3–70.

———. "Fray Bartolomé de las Casas obispo: la condición miserable de las naciones indianas y el derecho de la Iglesia (un escrito de 1545)." *Allpanchis* 12, no. 35–36 (1990): 29–104.

———. "La política del virrey Toledo sobre el tributo indio: el caso de Chucuito." In *El hombre y los Andes. Homenaje a Franklin Pease G.Y.*, edited by Javier Flores and Rafael Varón. 2: 741–766. Lima: Pontificia Universidad Católica del Perú, 2002.

———. "String Registries: Native Accounting and Memory According to the Colonial Sources." In *Narrative Threads. Accounting and Recounting in Andean Quipu*, edited by Jeffrey Quilter and Gary Urton, 119–150. Austin: University of Texas Press, 2002.

Baber, Jovita. "Native Litigiousness, Cultural Change and the Spanish Legal System in Tlaxcala, New Spain (1580–1640)." *Political and Legal Anthropology Review* 24, no. 2 (2001): 94–106.

———. "Categories, Self-Representation and the Construction of the *Indios*." *Journal of Spanish Cultural Studies* 10, no. 1 (2009): 27–41.

———. "Empire, Indians, and the Negotiation for the Status of City of Tlaxcala, 1521–1550." In *Negotiation within Domination: New Spain's Indian Pueblos Confront the Spanish State*, edited by Ethelia Ruiz Medrano and Susan Kellogg, 19–44. Boulder: University Press of Colorado, 2010.

———. "Law, Land, and Legal Rhetoric in Colonial New Spain: A Look at the Changing Rhetoric of Indigenous Americans in the Sixteenth Century." In *Native Claims: Indigenous Law Against Empire, 1500–1920*, edited by Sahiha Belmessous, 41–62. Oxford; New York: Oxford University Press, 2012.

Bailyn, Bernard. *Atlantic History: Concept and Contours*. Cambridge: Harvard University Press, 2005.

Baker, Geoffrey. *Imposing Harmony: Music and Society in Colonial Cuzco*. Durham: Duke University Press, 2008.

Bakewell, Peter. "La maduración del gobierno del Perú en la década de 1560." *Historia Mexicana* 39, no. 1 (1989): 41–70.

Bayle, Constantino. "El protector de indios." *Anuario de Estudios Americanos* 2 (1945): 1–175.

———. "Cabildos de indios en la América española." *Missionalia Hispanica* 8, no. 22 (1951): 5–35.

Belmessous, Saliha, ed. *Native Claims: Indigenous Law against Empire, 1500–1920*. Oxford; New York: Oxford University Press, 2012.

Benito, José Antonio, ed. *Libro de visitas de Santo Toribio Mogrovejo, 1593–1605*. Lima: Pontificia Universidad Católica del Perú, 2006.

Benton, Lauren. *Law and Colonial Cultures: Legal Regimes in World History, 1400–1900*. Cambridge; New York: Cambridge University Press, 2002.

———. *A Search for Sovereignty: Law and Geography in European Empires, 1400–1900*. Cambridge; New York: Cambridge University Press, 2010.

———. "Introduction to the AHA Forum 'Law and Empire in Global Perspective.'" *American Historical Review* 117, no. 4 (2012): 1092–1100.

Bernales Ballesteros, Jorge. "Fray Calixto de San José Túpac Inca, procurador de indios y la 'Exclamación reivindicacionista' de 1750." *Historia y Cultura* 6 (1969): 5–35.

Black, Chad. *The Limits of Gender Domination: Women, the Law, and Political Crisis in Quito, 1765–1830*. Albuquerque: University of New Mexico Press, 2010.

Blockmans, Willem Pieter, André Holenstein, and Jon Mathieu. *Empowering Interactions: Political Cultures and the Emergence of the State in Europe, 1300–1900*. Farnham, Surrey, UK; Burlington, VT: Ashgate, 2009.

Bonnett, Diana. *Los protectores de naturales en la Audiencia de Quito, siglos XVII y XVIII*. Quito: FLACSO; Abya-Yala, 1992.

Borah, Woodrow W. "Juzgado General de indios del Perú o juzgado particular de indios de El Cercado de Lima." *Revista Chilena de Historia del Derecho* 6 (1970): 129–142.

———. *Justice by Insurance: The General Indian Court of Colonial Mexico and the Legal Aides of the Half-Real*. Berkeley: University of California Press, 1983.

Borges Morán, Pedro. "El Consejo de Indias y el paso de misioneros a América durante el siglo XVI." In *El Consejo de las Indias en el siglo XVI*, edited by Demetrio Ramos, 181–189. Valladolid: Universidad de Valladolid, 1970.

Boyd-Bowman, Peter. "Patterns of Spanish Emigration to the Indies, 1579–1600." *The Americas* 33, no. 1 (1976): 78–95.

Boyer, Richard E. "People, Places, and Gossip: The Flow of Information in Colonial Mexico." In *La ciudad y el campo en la historia de Mexico*, 143–150. Mexico: Universidad Nacional Autónoma de México, 1992.

———. *Lives of the Bigamists: Marriage, Family, and Community in Colonial Mexico*. Abridged ed. Albuquerque: University of New Mexico Press, 2001.

Bradley, Peter T. *Society, Economy, and Defence in Seventeenth-Century Peru: The Administration of the Count of Alba de Liste (1655–61)*. Liverpool, UK: University of Liverpool, 1992.

Brendecke, Arndt. *Imperios e información: funciones del saber en el dominio colonial español*. Madrid; Frankfurt: Iberoamerica-Vervuert, 2012.

Brickhouse, Anna. *The Unsettlement of America: Translation, Interpretation, and the Story of Don Luis de Velasco, 1560–1945*. Oxford Scholarship Online, 2014.

Brokaw, Galen. *A History of the Khipu*. Cambridge; New York: Cambridge University Press, 2010.

———. "La recepción del quipu en el siglo XVI." In *El quipu colonial: estudios y materiales*, edited by Marco Curatola Petrocchi and José Carlos de la Puente Luna, 119–144. Lima: Pontificia Universidad Católica del Perú, 2013.

Brown, David H. *Santería Enthroned: Art, Ritual, and Innovation in an Afro-Cuban Religion*. Chicago: University of Chicago Press, 2003.

Brown, Jonathan, and John Elliott. *A Palace for a King: The Buen Retiro and the Court of Philip IV*. New Haven: Yale University Press, 2003.

Brubaker, Rogers, and Frederick Cooper. "Beyond 'Identity.'" *Theory and Society* 29, no. 1 (2000): 1–47.

Bryant, Sherwin K., Rachel O'Toole, and Ben Vinson. *Africans to Spanish America: Expanding the Diaspora*. Urbana: University of Illinois Press, 2012.

Buntix, Gustavo, and Luis Eduardo Wuffarden. "Incas y reyes españoles en la pintura colonial peruana: la estela de Garcilaso." *Márgenes. Encuentro y Debate* 4, no. 8 (1991): 151–210.

Burbank, Jane. *Russian Peasants Go to the Court: Legal Culture in the Countryside, 1905–1917.* Bloomington: Indiana University Press, 2004.

Burga, Manuel. *Nacimiento de una utopía: muerte y resurrección de los incas.* Lima: Universidad Nacional Mayor de San Marcos y Universidad de Guadalajara, 2005.

Burns, Kathryn. "Unfixing Race." In *Rereading the Black Legend: The Discourses of Religious and Racial Difference in the Renaissance Empires*, edited by Margaret Greer, Walter Mignolo, and Maureen Quilligan, 188–202. Chicago: University of Chicago Press, 2007.

———. *Into the Archive: Writing and Power in Colonial Peru.* Durham: Duke University Press, 2010.

———. "Making Indigenous Archives: The Quilcaycamayoc of Colonial Cuzco." *Hispanic American Historical Review* 91, no. 4 (2011): 665–689.

Bushnell, Amy. "Indigenous America and the Limits of the Atlantic World, 1493–1825." In *Atlantic History: A Critical Appraisal*, edited by Jack Greene and Philip Morgan, 191–219. Oxford; New York: Oxford University Press, 2009.

Bushnell, Amy, and Jack Greene. "Peripheries, Centers, and the Construction of Early Modern American Empires: An Introduction." In *Negotiated Empires: Centers and Peripheries in the Americas, 1500–1820*, edited by Christine Daniels and Michael Kennedy, 1–14. New York: Routledge, 2002.

Busto, José Antonio del. "Martinillo de Poechos." *Revista Histórica* 28 (1965): 86–102.

Cabero, Marco Aurelio. "El capitán Juan Delgadillo, encomendero de Saña." *Revista Histórica* 2 (1907): 92–117.

Cahill, David. "Popular Religion and Appropriation: The Example of Corpus Christi in Eighteenth-Century Cuzco." *Latin American Research Review* 31, no. 2 (1996): 67–110.

———. "The Inca and Inca Symbolism in Popular Festive Culture: The Religious Processions of Seventeenth-Century Cuzco." In *Habsburg Peru: Images, Imagination and Memory*, edited by Peter T. Bradley and David Cahill, 85–150. Liverpool, UK: Liverpool University Press, 2000.

———. "Sponsoring Popular Culture: The Jesuits, the Incas and the Making of the Pax Colonial." *Journal of Iberian and Latin American Studies* 6, no. 2 (2000): 65–88.

———. "Colour by Numbers: Racial and Ethnic Categories in the Viceroyalty of Peru, 1532–1824." In *From Rebellion to Independence in the Andes: Soundings from Southern Peru, 1750–1830*, 1–14. Amsterdam: Aksant, 2002.

———. "The Virgin and the Inca. An Incaic Procession in the City of Cuzco in 1692." *Ethnohistory* 49, no. 3 (2002): 611–649.

———. "First among Incas: The *Marquesado de Oropesa* Litigation (1741–1780) en Route to the Great Rebellion." *Jahrbuch für Geschichte Lateinamerikas* 41 (2004): 137–166.

———. "A Liminal Nobility: The Incas in the Middle Ground of Late-Colonial Peru." In *New World, First Nations*, edited by David Cahill and Blanca Tovías, 169–195. Brighton, UK: Sussex Academic Press, 2006.

———. "Becoming Inca: Juan Bustamante Carlos Inca and the Roots of the Great Rebellion." *Colonial Latin American Review* 22, no. 2 (2013): 259–280.

Cahill, David, and Blanca Tovías. *Elites indígenas en los Andes: nobles, caciques y cabildantes bajo el yugo colonial.* Quito: Abya-Yala, 2003.

Campbell, Leon. "Women and the Great Rebellion in Peru, 1780–1783." *The Americas* 42, no. 2 (1985): 163–196.

Cañizares-Esguerra, Jorge. *How to Write the History of the New World: Histories, Epistemologies, and Identities in the Eighteenth-Century Atlantic World.* Stanford: Stanford University Press, 2001.

———. "La memoria y el estado: la monarquía de España en el siglo XVI." *Iberoamericana* 14, no. 54 (2014): 177–185.

Cañizares-Esguerra, Jorge, and Benjamin Breen. "Hybrid Atlantics: Future Directions for the History of the Atlantic World." *History Compass* 11, no. 8 (2013): 597–609.

Cañizares-Esguerra, Jorge, Matt Childs, and James Sidbury. *The Black Urban Atlantic in the Age of the Slave Trade.* Philadelphia: University of Pennsylvania Press, 2013.

Canny, Nicholas. "Writing Atlantic History; or, Reconfiguring the History of British America." *Journal of American History* 86, no. 3 (1999): 1093–1114.

Cárdenas, Mario. *La población aborigen del Valle de Lima en el siglo XVI.* Lima: Universidad Nacional Mayor de San Marcos; Consejo Nacional de Investigaciones Científicas, 1989.

Carrera, Fernando de la. *Arte de la lengua yunga de los valles del obispado de Truiillo, con un confesonario [sic] y todas las oraciones cristianas y otras cosas.* Lima: Imprenta Liberal, 1880.

Carrillo, Gonzalo. "'La única voz por donde los yndios pueden hablar': estrategias de la elite indígena de Lima en torno al nombramiento de procuradores y defensores de indios (1720–1770)." *Histórica* 31, no. 1 (2006): 9–63.

Casado Arboniés, Manuel. "El Inca en la Alcalá de Henares de Cervantes. Melchor Carlos Inca y el Colegio-Convento de San Agustín el Real de la Universidad de Alcalá a comienzos del Siglo XVII." *Indagación: Revista de Historia y Arte* 4 (1999): 43–49.

Castañeda Delgado, Paulino. "La condición miserable de los indios y sus privilegios." *Anuario de Estudios Americanos* 28 (1971): 245–335.

Celestino, Eustaquio, and Armando Valencia. *Actas de Cabildo de Tlaxcala, 1547–1567.* Mexico: Archivo General de la Nación; Instituto Tlaxcalteca de la Cultura; Centro de Investigaciones y Estudios Superiores de Antropología Social, 1985.

Cerrón-Palomino, Rodolfo. *Lengua y sociedad en el valle del Mantaro.* Lima: Instituto de Estudios Peruanos, 1989.

Chamberlain, Robert. "The Concept of the Señor Natural as Revealed by Castilian Law and Administrative Documents." *Hispanic American Historical Review* 2, no. 19 (1939): 130–137.

Charles, John. "'More *Ladino* Than Necessary': Indigenous Litigants and the Language Policy Debate in Mid-Colonial Peru." *Colonial Latin American Review* 16, no. 1 (2007): 23–47.

———. *Allies at Odds: The Andean Church and Its Indigenous Agents, 1583–1671.* Albuquerque: University of New Mexico Press, 2010.

———. "Testimonios de coerción en las parroquias de indios: Perú, siglo XVII." In *Los indios ante los foros de justicia religiosa en la Hispanoamérica virreinal*, edited by Jorge Traslosheros and Ana de Zaballa Beascoechea, 111–126. Mexico: Universidad Nacional Autónoma de México, 2010.

Charney, Paul. "El indio urbano: un análisis económico y social de la población india de Lima en 1613." *Histórica* 12, no. 1 (1988): 5–33.

———. "Negotiating Roots: Indian Migrants in the Lima Valley during the Colonial Period." *Colonial Latin American Historical Review* 5, no. 1 (1996): 1–20.

———. "A Sense of Belonging: Colonial Indian Cofradías and Ethnicity in the Valley of Lima, Peru." *The Americas* 54, no. 3 (1998): 379–407.

———. *Indian Society in the Valley of Lima, Peru, 1532–1824*. Lanham, MD: University Press of America, 2001.

———. "'Much too worthy …' Indians in Seventeenth-Century Lima." In *City Indians in Spain's American Empire: Urban Indigenous Society in Colonial Mesoamerica and Andean South America, 1530–1810*, edited by Dana Velasco Murillo, Mark Lentz, and Margarita Ochoa, 87–103. Brighton, UK: Sussex Academic Press, 2012.

Chimalpahin Cuauhtlehuanitzin, Domingo Francisco de San Antón Muñón. *Annals of His Time*. Stanford: Stanford University Press, 2006.

Chipman, Donald E. *Moctezuma's Children: Aztec Royalty under Spanish Rule, 1520–1700*. Austin: University of Texas Press, 2005.

Chirinos, Andrés. *Quipus del Tahuantinsuyo: curacas, Incas y su saber matemático en el siglo XVI*. Lima: Comentarios, 2010.

Cline, Howard. "Hernando Cortés and the Aztec Indians in Spain." *Quarterly Journal of the Library of Congress* 26, no. 2 (1969): 70–90.

Cobo, Bernabé. "Fundación de Lima." In *Obras completas del padre Bernabé Cobo.*, 2: 279–460. Madrid: Atlas, 1956.

———. *Historia del Nuevo Mundo*. 2 vols. Madrid: Atlas, 1964.

Coello, Alexandre. *Espacios de exclusión, espacios de poder: el Cercado de Lima colonial (1568–1606)*. Lima: Pontificia Universidad Católica del Perú; Instituto de Estudios Peruanos, 2006.

Cohen, Paul. "Was there an Amerindian Atlantic? Reflections on the Limits of a Historiographical Concept." *History of European Ideas* 34, no. 4 (2008): 388–410.

Cole, Jeffrey. "An Abolitionism Born of Frustration: The Conde de Lemos and the Potosí Mita, 1667–73." *Hispanic American Historical Review* 63, no. 2 (1983): 307–333.

"Colegio de caciques." *Inca* 1, no. 4 (1923): 779–883.

Congress, Library of. *The Harkness Collection in the Library of Congress. Documents from Early Peru, the Pizarros and the Almagros, 1531–1578*. Washington, DC: US Govt. Print. Off., 1936.

Connell, William. *After Moctezuma: Indigenous Politics and Self-Government in Mexico City, 1524–1730*. Norman: University of Oklahoma Press, 2011.

———. "'De sangre noble y hábiles costumbres': etnicidad indígena y gobierno en México Tenochtitlan." *Histórica* 40, no. 2 (2016): 111–133.

Cook, Karoline P. *Forbidden Passages: Muslims and Moriscos in Colonial Spanish America*. Philadelphia: University of Pennsylvania Press, 2016.

Cook, Noble David, ed. *Padrón de los indios de Lima en 1613*. Lima: Universidad Nacional Mayor de San Marcos, 1968.

Cornejo Bouroncle, Jorge. "De la vida colonial (120 escrituras y datos diversos)." *Revista del Archivo Histórico del Cuzco* 3 (1952): 237–346.

Corteguera, Luis. *For the Common Good: Popular Politics in Barcelona, 1580–1640*. Ithaca, NY: Cornell University Press, 2002.

Crawford, Michael. *The Fight for Status and Privilege in Late Medieval and Early Modern Castile, 1465–1598*. University Park: Pennsylvania State University Press, 2014.

Cuena Boy, Francisco. "El protector de indios en clave romanística: una propuesta del siglo XVII." In *III Congreso Iberoaméricano de Derecho Romano*, edited by César Rascón García, 87–97. León, ES: Universidad de León, 1998.

———. "Utilización pragmática del derecho romano en dos memoriales indianos del siglo XVII sobre el protector de indios." *Revista de Estudios Histórico-Jurídicos* 20 (1998): 107–142.

Cummins, Thomas. "We Are the Other: Peruvian Portraits of Colonial *Kurakakuna*." In *Transatlantic Encounters: Europeans and Andeans in the Sixteenth Century*, edited by Rolena Adorno and Kenneth Andrien, 203–231. Berkeley: University of California Press, 1991.

———. "Let Me See! Reading Is for Them: Colonial Andean Images and Objects 'como es costumbre tener los caciques Señores.'" In *Native Traditions in the Postconquest World*, edited by Elizabeth Hill Boone and Thomas Cummins, 91–148. Washington, DC: Dumbarton Oaks, 1998.

Cúneo-Vidal, Rómulo. *Historia de las guerras de los últimos incas peruanos contra el poder español (1535–1572)*. Barcelona: Maucci, 1925.

Cunill, Caroline. "El indio miserable: nacimiento de la teoría legal en la América colonial del siglo XVI." *Cuadernos Intercambio* 8, no. 9 (2011): 229–248.

———. "Fray Bartolomé de las Casas y el oficio de defensor de indios en América y en la Corte española." In *Nuevos Mundos/Mundos Nuevos* (2012), nuevomundo.revues.org/63939 (accessed January 24, 2017).

———. "La negociación indígena en el Imperio ibérico: aportes a su discusión metodológica." *Colonial Latin American Historical Review* 21, no. 3 (2012): 391–412.

———. *Los defensores de indios de Yucatán y el acceso de los mayas a la justicia colonial, 1540–1600*. Mérida: Universidad Nacional Autónoma de México, 2012.

———. "Los intérpretes de Yucatán y la Corona española: negociación e iniciativas privadas en la fragua del imperio ibérico, siglo XVI." *Colonial Latin American Historical Review* 1, no. 4 (2013): 361–380.

———. "Philip II and Indigenous Access to Royal Justice: Considering the Process of Decision-Making in the Spanish Empire." *Colonial Latin American Review* 24, no. 4 (2015): 505–524.

———. "Nos traen tan avasallados hasta quitarnos nuestro señorío: cabildos mayas, control local y representación legal en el Yucatán del siglo XVI." *Histórica* 40, no. 2 (2016): 49–80.

Curatola Petrocchi, Marco, and José Carlos de la Puente Luna. "Contar concertando: quipus, piedritas y escritura en los Andes coloniales." In *El quipu colonial: estudios y materiales*, edited by Marco Curatola Petrocchi and José Carlos de la Puente Luna, 193–243. Lima: Pontificia Universidad Católica del Perú, 2013.

———, eds. *El quipu colonial: estudios y materiales*. Lima: Pontificia Universidad Católica del Perú, 2013.

Cutter, Charles R. *The Protector de Indios in Colonial New Mexico, 1659–1821*. Albuquerque: University of New Mexico Press, 1986.

———. *The Legal Culture of Northern New Spain, 1700–1810*. Albuquerque: University of New Mexico Press, 1995.

———. "The Legal System as a Touchstone of Identity in Colonial Mexico." In *The Collective and the Public in Latin America: Cultural Identities and Political Order*, edited by Luis Roniger and Tamar Herzog, 57–70. Brighton, UK: Sussex Academic Press, 2000.

Cutter, Charles R., Tomás Mallo, and Daniel Pacheco Fernández. "Indians as Litigants in Colonial Mexico." In *De la ciencia ilustrada a la ciencia romántica: actas de las II Jornadas sobre España y las Expediciones Científicas en América y Filipinas*, edited by Alejandro R. Díez Torre, 21–32. Madrid: Doce Calles, 1995.

D'Altroy, Terence N. *Provincial Power in the Inka Empire*. Washington, DC; London: Smithsonian Institution Press, 1992.

Dávalos de Figueroa, Diego. *Primera parte de la miscelánea austral*. Lima: Antonio Ricardo, 1602.

Davis, Natalie Zemon. *The Return of Martin Guerre*. Camdridge; London: Harvard University Press, 1983.

———. *Trickster Travels: A Sixteenth-Century Muslim between Worlds*. New York: Hill & Wang, 2006.

Dean, Carolyn. *Inka Bodies and the Body of Christ: Corpus Christi in Colonial Cuzco, Peru*. Durham: Duke University Press, 1999.

Dean, Carolyn, and Dana Leibshon. "Hybridity and Its Discontents: Considering Visual Culture in Colonial Spanish America." *Colonial Latin American Review* 12, no. 1 (2003): 5–35.

Dedieu, Jean-Pierre. "Procesos y redes. La historia de las instituciones administrativas de la época moderna, hoy." In *La pluma, la mitra y la espada: estudios de historia institucional en la Edad Moderna*, edited by Juan Luis Castellano, Jean-Pierre Dedieu, and María Victoria López-Cordón, 13–30. Madrid: Marcial Pons, 2000.

Deustua, José, and José Luis Rénique. *Intelectuales, indigenismo y descentralismo en el Perú, 1897–1931*. Cuzco: Centro de Estudios Rurales Andinos Bartolomé de las Casas, 1984.

Díaz, María Elena. *The Virgin, the King, and the Royal Slaves of El Cobre: Negotiating Freedom in Colonial Cuba, 1670–1780*. Stanford: Stanford University Press, 2000.

———. "Conjuring Identities: Race, Nativeness, Local Citizenship, and Royal Slavery on an Imperial Frontier (Revisiting El Cobre, Cuba)." In *Imperial Subjects: Race and Identity in Colonial Latin America*, edited by Andrew Fisher and Scarlett O'Phelan, 197–224. Durham: Duke University Press, 2009.

Díaz Rementería, Carlos. *El cacique en el virreinato del Perú: estudio histórico-jurídico*. Seville: Universidad de Sevilla, 1977.

———. "El patrimonio comunal indígena: del sistema incaico de propiedad al de derecho castellano." In *El aborigen y el derecho en el pasado y el presente*, edited by Abelardo Levaggi, 105–139. Buenos Aires: Universidad del Museo Social Argentino, 1990.

Díaz Serrano, Ana. "La república de Tlaxcala ante el rey de España durante el siglo XVI." *Historia Mexicana* 61, no. 3 (2012): 1049–1107.

Dios, Salustiano de. *Gracia, merced y patronazgo real: la Cámara de Castilla entre 1474 y 1530.* Madrid: Centro de Estudios Constitucionales, 1993.

Domínguez Compañy, Francisco. "La condición de vecino. Su signficación e importancia en la vida colonial hispanoamericana." In *Crónica del VI Congreso Histórico Municipal Interamericano*, 703–720. Madrid: Instituto de Estudios de Administración Local, 1959.

Dueñas, Alcira. "Ethnic Power and Identity Formation in Mid-Colonial Andean Writing." *Colonial Latin American Review* 18, no. 3 (2009): 407–433.

———. *Indians and Mestizos in the "Lettered City": Reshaping Justice, Social Hierarchy, and Political Culture in Colonial Peru.* Boulder: University Press of Colorado, 2010.

———. "The Lima Indian *Letrados*: Remaking the República de Indios in the Bourbon Andes." *The Americas* 72, no. 1 (2015): 55–75.

———. "Cabildos de naturales en el ocaso colonial: jurisdicción, posesión y defensa del espacio étnico." *Histórica* 40, no. 2 (2016): 135–167.

Durston, Alan. "La escritura del quechua por indígenas en el siglo XVII. Nuevas evidencias en el Archivo Arzobispal de Lima." *Revista Andina* 37 (2003): 207–236.

———. *Pastoral Quechua: The History of Christian Translation in Colonial Peru, 1550–1650.* South Bend, IN: University of Notre Dame Press, 2007.

———. "Standard Colonial Quechua." In *Iberian Imperialism and Language Evolution in Latin America*, edited by Salikoko S. Mufwene, 225–243. Chicago: University of Chicago Press, 2014.

Durston, Alan, and George Urioste. "Las peticiones en quechua del curato de Chuschi (1678–1679)." In *El quipu colonial: estudios y materiales*, edited by Marco Curatola Petrocchi and José Carlos de la Puente Luna, 379–440. Lima: Pontificia Universidad Católica del Perú, 2013.

Duve, Thomas. "La condición jurídica del indio y su condición como *persona miserabilis* en el Derecho indiano." In *Un giudice e due leggi: pluralismo normativo e conflitti agrari in Sud America*, edited by Mario G. Losano, 3–33. Milan, IT: Giuffrè, 2004.

———. "El concilio como instancia de autorización: la ordenación sacerdotal de mestizos ante el Tercer Concilio Limense." *Revista de Historia del Derecho* 40 (2010): 1–29.

———. "European Legal History—Global Perspectives." Paper presented at the Colloquium 'European Normativity—Global Historical Perspectives', Max-Planck-Institute, Berlin, September, 2–4, 2013.

Duviols, Pierre, ed. *Procesos y visitas de idolatrías. Cajatambo, siglo XVII.* Lima: Pontificia Universidad Católica del Perú and Instituto Francés de Estudios Andinos, 2003.

Earle, Rebecca. "Letters and Love in Colonial Spanish America." *The Americas* 62, no. 1 (2005): 17–46.

"El memorial de los Mallku y principales de la provincia de los Charcas [1582]." In *Qaraqara-Charka: mallku, inka y rey en la provincia de Charcas (siglos XV-XVII). Histo-*

ria antropológica de una confederación aymara, edited by Tristan Platt, Thérèse Bouysse-Cassagne, and Olivia Harris, 828–846. Lima; La Paz: Instituto Francés de Estudios Andinos; Plural, 2006.

Elias, Norbert. *La sociedad cortesana*. Mexico: Fondo de Cultura Económica, 1996.

Elliott, John. "The Court of the Spanish Habsburgs: A Peculiar Institution?" In *Spain and Its World, 1500–1700: Selected Essays*, 142–161. New Haven: Yale University Press, 1989.

Eltis, David. "Atlantic History in Global Perspective." *Itinerario* 23, no. 2 (1999): 141–161.

Encinas, Diego de. *Cedulario indiano [1596]*. 4 vols. Madrid: Cultura Hispánica, 1945.

Enríquez, Martín. "Carta del virrey … a S.M. [Lima, December 22, 1581]." In *Gobernantes del Perú, cartas y papeles, siglo XVI*, edited by Roberto Levillier. 9: 65–73. Madrid: J. Pueyo, 1921–1926.

Escobari de Querejazu, Laura. *Caciques, yanaconas y extravagantes: la sociedad colonial en Charcas en s. XVI-XVIII*. Lima: Institut Français d'Études Andines, 2005.

Escobedo Mansilla, Ronald. "Bienes y cajas de comunidad en el virreinato peruano." *Revista Internacional de Sociología* 32 (1979): 465–492.

Espinosa, Carlos. *El Inca barroco. Política y estética en la Real Audiencia de Quito, 1630–1680*. Quito: FLACSO, 2015.

Espinoza, Waldemar. "El alcalde mayor indigena en el virreinato del Perú." *Anuario de Estudios Americanos* 17 (1960): 183–300.

———. "Los huancas aliados de la conquista. Tres informaciones inéditas sobre la participación indígena en la conquista del Perú." *Anales Científicos de la Universidad del Centro del Perú* 1 (1971–72): 9–407.

———. "Los señoríos de Yaucha y Picoy en el abra del medio y alto Rimac." *Revista Histórica* 34 (1983–1984): 157–259.

———. "La vida pública de un príncipe inca residente en Quito. Siglos XV y XVI." In *Etnohistoria Ecuatoriana. Estudios y documentos*, 245–286. Quito: Abya-Yala, 1988.

———. "Los mitmas Huayacuntu en Quito o guarniciones para la represión armada, siglos XV y XVI." In *Etnohistoria Ecuatoriana. Estudios y documentos*, 7–63. Quito: Abya-Yala, 1988.

Esquivel y Navia, Diego de. *Noticias cronológicas de la gran ciudad del Cuzco*. 2 vols. Lima: Fundación Augusto N. Wiese, 1980.

Estenssoro, Juan Carlos. *Del paganismo a la santidad: la incorporación de los indios del Perú al catolicismo, 1532–1750*. Lima: Instituto Francés de Estudios Andinos; Pontificia Universidad Católica del Perú, 2003.

———. "Construyendo la memoria: la figura del Inca y el reino del Perú, de la conquista a Túpac Amaru II." In *Los incas, reyes del Perú*, edited by Thomas Cummins, 93–173. Lima: Banco de Crédito, 2005.

Estrada Torres, María Isabel. "San Juan Tenochtitlan y Santiago Tlatelolco: las dos comunidades indígenas de la ciudad de México, 1521–1700." MA thesis, Universidad Autónoma Metropolitana, 2000.

Estupiñán-Freile, Tamara. "Testamento de don Francisco Atahualpa." *Revista Miscelánea Histórica Ecuatoriana* 1 (1998): 8–67.

Falcón, Francisco. "Representación hecha por el licenciado Falcón en concilio provincial, sobre los daños y molestias que se hacen á los indios [c. 1567]." In *Colección de documentos inéditos, relativos al descubrimiento, conquista y organización de las antiguas posesiones españolas de América y Oceanía*. 7: 451–495. Madrid: Imp. de Frías y Compañía, 1867.

Fernández Albaladejo, Pablo. *Fragmentos de monarquía: trabajos de historia política*. Madrid: Alianza, 2007.

———. *Materia de España: cultura política e identidad en la España moderna*. Madrid: Marcial Pons, 2007.

Fernández de Castro y Bocángel, Jerónimo. *Elisio Peruano. Solemnidades heroicas, y festivas demonstraciones de jvbilos, que se han logrado en la muy Noble, y muy Legal Ciudad de los Reyes Lima, Cabeza de la America Austral, y Corte del Perù, en la Aclamacion del Excelso Nombre del muy Alto, muy Poderoso, siempre Augusto, Catholico Monarcha de las Españas, y Emperador de la America Don Lvis Primero N.S. (que Dios guarde.)* ... Lima: Francisco Sobrino, 1725.

Fernández Rueda, Sonia. "Educación y evangelización: el colegio franciscano de caciques de San Andrés." In *Passeurs, mediadores culturales y agentes de la primera globalización en el Mundo Ibérico, siglos XVI-XIX*, edited by Scarlett O'Phelan and Carmen Salazar-Soler, 129–145. Lima: Pontificia Universidad Católica del Perú; Instituto Riva-Agüero; Instituto Francés de Estudios Andinos, 2005.

Fisher, Andrew, and Matthew O'Hara. *Imperial Subjects: Race and Identity in Colonial Latin America*. Durham: Duke University Press, 2009.

———. "Introduction: Racial Identities and Their Interpreters in Colonial Latin America." In *Imperial Subjects: Race and Identity in Colonial Latin America*, 1–37. Durham: Duke University Press, 2009.

Forbes, Jack. *Africans and Native Americans: The Language of Race and the Evolution of Red-Black Peoples*. Urbana; Chicago: University of Illinois Press, 1993.

Fossa, Lydia. "Two Khipu, One Narrative: Answering Urton's Questions." *Ethnohistory* 47, no. 2 (2000): 453–468.

Franco Silva, Alfonso. *Los esclavos de Sevilla*. Seville: Excma. Diputación Provincial de Sevilla, 1980.

Gallup-Díaz, Ignacio. *The Door of the Seas and the Key to the Universe: Indian Politics and Imperial Rivalry in Darien, 1640–1750*. Columbia University Press, 2004.

Gálvez Peña, Carlos. "Cronistas peregrinos: apuntes sobre ideas y hombres de Iglesia. Conexiones culturales entre México y el Perú durante el siglo XVII." In *Iglesia y sociedad en la Nueva España y el Perú*, edited by Alicia Mayer and José de la Puente Brunke, 191–211. Lima: Pontificia Universidad Católica del Perú e Instituto Riva-Agüero 2015.

Games, Alison. "Atlantic History: Definitions, Challenges, and Opportunities." *American Historical Review* 111, no. 3 (2006): 741–757.

———. *The Web of Empire: English Cosmopolitans in an Age of Expansion, 1560–1660*. Oxford; New York: Oxford University Press, 2008.

Gangotena Jijón, Cristóbal. "Documentos históricos: la descendencia de Atahuallpa." *Boletín de la Academia Nacional de Historia* 39, no. 93 (1959): 91–97.

García de Castro, Lope. "Carta a S.M. del Licenciado Castro [Lima, December 31, 1565]."

In *Gobernantes del Perú, cartas y papeles, siglo XVI,* edited by Roberto Levillier. 3: 114–130. Madrid: J. Pueyo, 1921–1926.

———. "Carta a S.M. del Licenciado Castro [Lima, September 23, 1565]." In *Gobernantes del Perú, cartas y papeles, siglo XVI,* edited by Roberto Levillier. 3: 94–130. Madrid: J. Pueyo, 1921–1926.

———. "Prevenciones hechas por el Licenciado Castro para el buen gobierno del reino del Perú y especialmente la conservación e instrucción de los indios [1565]." In *Gobernantes del Perú, cartas y papeles, siglo XVI,* edited by Roberto Levillier. 3: 116–130. Madrid: J. Pueyo, 1921–1926.

Garrett, David. *Shadows of Empire: The Indian Nobility of Cusco, 1750–1825.* Cambridge; New York: Cambridge University Press, 2005.

———. "Indigenous Elites in the Colonial Andes." In *Oxford Bibliographies in Latin American Studies,* www.oxfordbibliographies.com/document/obo-9780199766581/obo-9780199766581-0158.xml (accessed Jan-24-2017).

Gauderman, Kimberly. *Women's Lives in Colonial Quito: Gender, Law, and Economy in Spanish America.* Austin: University of Texas Press, 2003.

Gibson, Charles. *The Aztecs under Spanish Rule: A History of the Indians of the Valley of Mexico.* Stanford: Stanford University Press, 1964.

———. *Tlaxcala in the Sixteenth Century.* Stanford: Stanford University Press, 1967.

Gil-Bermejo García, Juana. "Indígenas americanos en Andalucía." In *Andalucía y América en el siglo XVI,* edited by Bibiano Torres Ramírez and José Hernández Palomo, 536–555. Seville: Escuela de Estudios Hispano-Americanos, 1983.

Gil, Juan. "Los primeros mestizos indios en España: una voz ausente." In *Entre dos mundos: fronteras culturales y agentes mediadores,* edited by Berta Ares Queija and Serge Gruzinski, 15–36. Seville: Escuela de Estudios Hispano-Americanos, 1997.

Glave, Luis Miguel. "Mujer indígena, trabajo doméstico y cambio social en el virreinato peruano del siglo XVII. La ciudad de La Paz y el Sur Andino en 1684." *Bulletin de l'Institut Français d'Études Andines* 16, no. 4 (1987): 39–69.

———. *Trajinantes: caminos indígenas en la sociedad colonial, siglos XVI/XVII.* Lima: Instituto de Apoyo Agrario, 1989.

———. *Vida, símbolos y batallas: creación y recreación de la comunidad indígena. Cuzco, siglos XVI-XX.* Lima: Fondo de Cultura Económica, 1993.

———. "The 'Republic of Indians' in Revolt (c. 1680–1790)." In *The Cambridge History of the Native Peoples of the Americas,* edited by Frank Salomon and Stuart B. Schwartz. III, 2: 502–557. New York: Cambridge University Press, 1999.

———. "Gestiones transatlánticas: los indios ante la trama del poder virreinal y las composiciones de tierras (1646)." *Revista Complutense de Historia de América* 34 (2008): 85–106.

———. "La provincia de Chucuito y sus caciques: el contexto de la correspondencia entre Diego Chambilla y Pedro Matheos." In *Pleitos y riqueza: los caciques andinos en Potosí del siglo XVII,* edited by Ximena Medinaceli, 465–486. Sucre, BO: Archivo y Biblioteca Nacionales de Bolivia, 2010.

———. "Memoria y memoriales: la formación de una liga indígena en Lima (1722–1732)." *Diálogo Andino* 37 (2011): 5–23.

———. "La petición grande de don Gabriel Fernández Guarache y el debate sobre la mita minera en un contexto de crisis colonial." In *Mita, caciques y mitayos: Gabriel Fernández Guarache, memoriales en defensa de los indios y debate sobre la mita de Potosí, 1646–1663*, edited by Roberto Choque Canqui, 177–211. Sucre, BO: Archivo y Biblioteca Nacionales de Bolivia; Fundación Cultural; Banco Central de Bolivia, 2012.

———. "El arbitrio de tierras de 1622 y el debate sobre las propiedades y los derechos coloniales de los indios." *Anuario de Estudios Americanos* 71, no. 1 (2014): 79–106.

———. "Hombres de mar. Caciques de la Costa ecuatoriana en los inicios de la Época Colonial." *Procesos. Revista Ecuatoriana de Historia* 40 (2014): 9–36.

Glave, Luis Miguel, and María Isabel Remy. *Estructura agraria y vida rural en una región andina: Ollantaytambo entre los siglos XVI-XIX*. Cuzco: Centro de Estudios Rurales Andinos Bartolomé de las Casas, 1983.

Goldwert, Marvin. "La lucha por la perpetuidad de las encomiendas en el Perú virreinal, 1550–1600." *Revista Histórica* 22 (1955–1956): 336–360.

———. "La lucha por la perpetuidad de las encomiendas en el Perú virreinal, 1550–1600 (continuación)." *Revista Histórica* 23 (1958–1959): 207–245.

González de San Segundo, Miguel Ángel. "El doctor Gregorio González de Cuenca, oidor de la Audiencia de Lima, y sus ordenanzas sobre caciques e indios principales (1566)." *Revista de Indias* 42, no. 169–170 (1982): 643–668.

González Holguín, Diego. *Vocabulario de la lengua general de todo el Perú llamada lengua quichua, o del Inca*. Lima: Francisco del Canto, 1608.

González Suárez, Federico. *Historia general de la República del Ecuador. Tomo II: El descubrimiento y la conquista (1513–1564)*. Quito: Daniel Cadena A., 1931.

Gotkowitz, Laura. *A Revolution for our Rights: Indigenous Struggles for Land and Justice in Bolivia, 1880–1952*. Durham: Duke University Press, 2007.

Gould, Eliga. "Entangled Atlantic Histories: A Response from the Anglo-American Periphery." *American Historical Review* 112, no. 5 (2007): 1414–1422.

———. "Entangled Histories, Entangled Worlds: The English-Speaking Atlantic as a Spanish Periphery." *American Historical Review* 112, no. 3 (2007): 764–786.

Graubart, Karen. "Hybrid Thinking: Bringing Postcolonial Theory to Colonial Latin American Economic History." In *Postcolonialism Meets Economics*, edited by S. Charusheela and Eiman Zein-Elabden, 215–234. London; New York: Routledge, 2003.

———. *With Our Labor and Sweat: Indigenous Women and the Formation of Colonial Society in Peru, 1550–1700*. Stanford: Stanford University Press, 2007.

———. "The Creolization of the New World: Local Forms of Identification in Urban Colonial Peru, 1560–1640." *Hispanic American Historical Review* 89, no. 3 (2009): 471–499.

———. "Ethnicity." In *The Princeton Companion to Atlantic History*, edited by Joseph Miller, 192–196. Princeton: Princeton University Press, 2014.

———. "Learning from the *Qadi*: The Jurisdiction of Local Rule in the Early Colonial Andes." *Hispanic American Historical Review* 95, no. 2 (2015): 195–228.

————. "Competing Spanish and Indigenous Jurisdictions in Early Colonial Lima." In *Oxford Research Encyclopedia of Latin American History*, latinamericanhistory.oxfordre. com/view/10.1093/acrefore/9780199366439.001.0001/acrefore-9780199366439-e-365 (accessed January 24, 2017).

————. "'Ynuvaciones malas e rreprovadas': Justice and Jurisdiction in the Early Colonial Lima Valley." In *Justice in British, Iberian, and Indigenous America, 1600–1825: The Challenge of Legal Intelligibility*, edited by Brian Owensby and Richard Ross. New York: New York University Press, in press.

Greenblatt, Stephen. *Renaissance Self-Fashioning: From More to Shakespeare*. Chicago: University of Chicago Press, 1980.

Griffin, Patrick. "A Plea for a New Atlantic History." *William and Mary Quarterly* 68, no. 2 (2011): 236–239.

Gruzinski, Serge. *Las cuatro partes del mundo. Historia de una mundialización*. Mexico: Fondo de Cultura Económica, 2010.

Guaman Poma, Felipe. *El primer nueva corónica y buen gobierno*. Edited by Rolena Adorno, John Murra, and Jorge Urioste. Mexico: Siglo Veintiuno, 1992.

Guevara, Armando, and Frank Salomon. "A 'Personal Visit': Colonial Political Ritual and the Making of Indians in the Andes." *Colonial Latin American Review* 3, no. 1–2 (1994): 3–36.

Guillén, Edmundo. *Versión inca de la conquista*. Lima: Milla Batres, 1974.

Guillet, David. "Agrarian Ecology and Peasant Production in the Central Andes." *Mountain Research and Development* 1, no. 1 (1981): 19–28.

Hall, Stuart. "Introduction: Who Needs 'Identity'?" In *Questions of Cultural Identity*, edited by Stuart Hall and Paul Du Gay. London: Sage, 1996.

Hämäläinen, Pekka. "Lost in Transitions: Suffering, Survival, and Belonging in the Early Modern Atlantic World." *William and Mary Quarterly* 68, no. 2 (2011): 219–223.

Hamilton, Earl J. *American Treasure and the Price Revolution in Spain, 1501–1650*. Cambridge: Harvard University Press, 1934.

Hampe Martínez, Teodoro. "Notas sobre población y tributo indígena en Cajamarca (primera mitad del siglo XVII)." *Boletín del Instituto Riva-Agüero* 14 (1986): 65–81.

————. *Don Pedro de la Gasca, 1493–1567: su obra política en España y América*. Lima: Pontificia Universidad Católica del Perú, 1989.

Hanke, Lewis. *The First Social Experiments in America: A Study in the Development of Spanish Indian Policy in the Sixteenth Century*. Cambridge: Harvard University Press, 1935.

————. *The Spanish Struggle for Justice in the Conquest of America*. Philadelphia: University of Pennsylvania Press, 1949.

————. *Aristotle and the American Indians: A Study in Race Prejudice in the Modern World*. London: Hollis & Carter, 1959.

————. *The Spanish Struggle for Justice in the Conquest of America*. Dallas: Southern Methodist University Press, 2002.

Haring, Clarence. *Trade and Navigation between Spain and the Indies in the Time of the Hapsburgs*. Cambridge: Harvard University Press, 1918.

Harth-Terré, Emilio. "El esclavo negro en la sociedad indoperuana." *Journal of Inter-American Studies* 3, no. 3 (1961): 297–340.

Hartmann, Roswith, and Udo Oberem. "Quito: un centro de educación de indígenas del siglo XVI." In *Contribuições à Antropologia em homenagem ao Professor Egon Schaden*, 105–134. São Paulo: Univ. de São Paulo, 1981.

Haskett, Robert. "Paper Shields: The Ideology of Coats of Arms in Colonial Mexican Primordial Titles." *Ethnohistory* 43, no. 1 (1996): 99–126.

Hawthorne, Walter. *From Africa to Brazil: Culture, Identity, and an Atlantic Slave Trade, 1600–1830*. Cambridge; New York: Cambridge University Press, 2010.

Heffernan, Ken. *Limatambo: Archaeology, History, and the Regional Societies of Inca Cusco*. Oxford: Tempus Reparatum, 1996.

Hemming, John. *The Conquest of the Incas*. New York: Harcourt Brace Jovanovich, 1970.

Heredia Herrera, Antonia. *Catálogo de las Consultas del Consejo de Indias*. 2 vols. Madrid: Dirección General de Archivos y Bibliotecas, 1972.

———. "Introducción." In *Catálogo de las consultas del Consejo de Indias*. 1: xii–xvii. Seville: Exma. Diputación Provincial de Sevilla, 1983.

Herzog, Tamar. *Defining Nations: Immigrants and Citizens in Early Modern Spain and Spanish America*. Yale University Press, 2003.

———. *Upholding Justice: Society, State, and the Penal System in Quito (1650–1750)*. Ann Arbor: University of Michigan Press, 2004.

———. "Can You Tell a Spaniard When You See One? 'Us' and 'Them' in the Early Modern Iberian Atlantic." In *Polycentric Monarchies: How Did Early Modern Spain and Portugal Achieve and Maintain a Global Hegemony?*, edited by Pedro Cardim, Tamar Herzog, and José Javier Ruiz Ibáñez, 147–161. Brighton, UK: Sussex Academic Press, 2012.

———. "How Did Early-Modern Slaves in Spain Disappear? The Antecedents." *Republics of Letters* 3, no. 1 (2012): 1–7.

———. "Naming, Identifying and Authorizing Movement in Spain and Spanish America (17–18th centuries)." In *Registration and Recognition: Documenting the Person in World History*, edited by Keith Breckenridge and Simon Szreter, 191–209. Oxford: Oxford University Press, 2012.

———. "Colonial Law and 'Native Customs': Indigenous Land Rights in Colonial Spanish America." *The Americas* 69, no. 3 (2013): 303–321.

———. "The Appropriation of Native Status: Forming and Reforming Insiders and Outsiders in the Spanish Colonial World." *Journal of the Max Planck Institute for European Legal History* 22 (2014): 140–149.

Hoffman, Paul. *A New Andalucia and a Way to the Orient: The American Southeast during the Sixteenth Century*. Baton Rouge: Louisiana State University Press, 1990.

Holguín, Oswaldo. *Poder, corrupción y tortura en el Perú de Felipe II: el doctor Diego de Salinas (1558–1595)*. Lima: Congreso del Perú, 2002.

Honores, Renzo. *Legal Polyphony in the Colonial Andes: Professionals, Litigants, and the Legal Culture in the City of Lima, 1538–1640*. Unpublished manuscript.

———. "Litigiosidad indígena ante la Real Audiencia de Lima, 1552–1598." BA thesis, Pontificia Universidad Católica del Perú, 1993.

———. "La asistencia jurídica privada a los señores indígenas ante la Real Audiencia de Lima, 1552–1570." Paper presented at the XXIV International Congress of the Latin American Studies Association, Dallas, March 27–29, 2003.

———. "Una sociedad legalista: abogados, procuradores de causas y la creación de una cultura legal colonial en Lima y Potosí, 1540–1670." PhD dissertation, Florida International University, 2007.

———. *Colonial Legal Polyphony: Caciques and the Construction of Legal Arguments in the Andes, 1550–1640.* Working Paper; 10–11. Cambridge: International Seminar on the History of the Atlantic World, 1500–1825, 2010.

———. "Litigación en la Audiencia Arzopispal de Lima: abogados y procuradores de causas en la litigación canónica 1600–1650." Paper presented at the conference *Nuevos campos de investigación en la historia de las instituciones eclesiásticas y del Derecho Canónico Indiano*, Lima, 2012.

———. "Una aproximación a la hiperlexia colonial: caciques, cultura legal y litigación en los Andes, 1550–1640." *Nueva corónica* 1 (2013): 1–8.

———. "History, Rhetoric, and Strategy in Early Colonial Andean Litigation, 1552–1574." Paper presented at the Symposium on Latin America in the Early Colonial Period, The Newberry Center for Renaissance Studies, Chicago, April 11, 2015.

Hunefeldt, Christine. "Comunidad, curas y comuneros hacia fines del período colonial: ovejas y pastores indomados en el Perú." *HISLA* 2 (1983): 3–31.

Hurtado de Mendoza, Andrés. "Carta a S.M. del Marqués de Cañete, Virrey del Perú [Lima, November 3, 1556]." In *Gobernantes del Perú, cartas y papeles, siglo XVI*, edited by Roberto Levillier. 1: 292–301. Madrid: J. Pueyo, 1921–1926.

Inch, Marcela. "El mundo letrado de los Lupaca: alfabetización y primeras letras a fines del siglo XVI e inicios del XVII." In *Pleitos y riqueza: los caciques andinos en Potosí del siglo XVII*, edited by Ximena Medinaceli, 507–527. Sucre, Bolivia: Ediciones del Archivo y Biblioteca Nacionales de Bolivia, 2010.

"Instrucciones de Carlos V al Marqués de Cañete, virrey del Perú [1555]." In *Los virreyes españoles en América durante el gobierno de la Casa de Austria: Perú*, edited by Lewis Hanke and Celso Rodríguez. 1: 46–47. Madrid: Atlas, 1978.

Isbell, Billie Jean. *To Defend Ourselves: Ecology and Ritual in an Andean Village.* Prospect Heights, IL: Waveland Press, 1985.

Itier, César. "Las cartas en quechua de Cotahuasi: el pensamiento político de un cacique de inicios del siglo XVII." In *Máscaras, tretas y rodeos del discurso colonial en los Andes*, edited by Bernard Lavallé, 43–73. Lima: Instituto Francés de Estudios Andinos; Pontificia Universidad Católica del Perú; Instituto Riva-Agüero, 2005.

Jacobs, Auke Pieter. "Legal and Illegal Emigration from Seville, 1550–1650." In *"To Make America": European Emigration in the Early Modern Period*, edited by Ida Altman and James Horn, 59–84. Berkeley: University of California Press, 1991.

Jenkins, Richard. "Rethinking Ethnicity: Identity, Categorization and Power." *Ethnic and Racial Studies* 17, no. 2 (1994): 197–223.

Jiménez Abollado, Francisco Luis. "Don Diego Luis Moctezuma, nieto de *Hueytlatoani*, padre de conde: un noble indígena entre dos mundos." *Anuario de Estudios Americanos* 65, no. 1 (2008): 49–70.

Jiménez de la Espada, Marcos. *Relaciones geográficas de Indias. Perú.* 4 vols. Madrid: Tip. de Manuel G. Hernández, 1881–1897.

———. *Relaciones geográficas de Indias. Perú.* 3 vols. Madrid: Atlas, 1965.

Jouve, José Ramón. *Esclavos de la ciudad letrada: esclavitud, escritura y colonialismo en Lima (1650–1700).* Lima: Instituto de Estudios Peruanos, 2005.

Julián, Amadeo. "Tráfico de indígenas esclavos de Santo Domingo a España a fines del siglo XV y en el siglo XVI." In *Bancos, ingenios y esclavos en la época colonial,* edited by Amadeo Julián, 17–58. Santo Domingo, DO: Banco de Reserva de la República Dominicana, 1997.

Julien, Catherine. "La organización parroquial del Cusco y la ciudad incaica." *Tawantinsuyu* 5 (1998): 82–96.

———. "Francisca Pizarro, la cuzqueña, y su madre, la coya Ynguill." *Revista del Archivo Regional del Cusco* 15 (2000): 53–74.

Jurado, Carolina. "'Descendientes de los primeros.' Las probanzas de méritos y servicios y la genealogía cacical. Audiencia de Charcas, 1574–1719." *Revista de Indias* 74, no. 261 (2014): 387–422.

———. "Un fiscal al servicio de Su Majestad: Don Francisco de Alfaro en la Real Audiencia de Charcas, 1598–1608." *Población y Sociedad. Revista Regional de Estudios Sociales* 21, no. 1 (2014): 99–132.

Kagan, Richard L. *Lawsuits and Litigants in Castile, 1500–1700.* Chapel Hill: University of North Carolina Press, 1981.

Kamen, Henry. *Philip of Spain.* New Haven: Yale University Press, 1997.

———. *Spain, 1469–1714: A Society of Conflict.* Harlow, UK; New York: Pearson/Longman, 2005.

Kellogg, Susan. *Law and the Transformation of Aztec Culture, 1500–1700.* Norman: University of Oklahoma Press, 1995.

Klumpp, Kathleen M. "El retorno del Inga, una expresión ecuatoriana de la ideología mesiánica andina." *Cuadernos de Historia y Arqueología* 24, no. 41 (1974): 99–135.

Konetzke, Richard. *Colección de documentos para la historia de la formación social de Hispanoamérica (1493–1810).* 3 vols. Madrid: Consejo Superior de Investigaciones Científicas, 1953–1958.

La Reinaga Salazar, Leandro de. *Memorial discursivo sobre el oficio de protector general de los indios del Pirú.* Madrid: Imprenta Real, 1626.

Laclau, Ernesto. *New Reflections on the Revolution of Our Time.* London; New York: Verso, 1990.

Lamana, Gonzalo. *Domination without Dominance: Inca-Spanish Encounters in Early Colonial Peru.* Durham: Duke University Press, 2008.

———, ed. *Pensamiento colonial crítico: textos y actos de Polo Ondegardo.* Lima; Cuzco: Instituto Francés de Estudios Andinos; Centro Bartolomé de las Casas, 2012.

Las siete partidas. Glosadas por el licenciado Gregorio López [1555]. 3 vols. Madrid: Boletín Oficial del Estado, 1985.

Latasa Vassallo, Pilar. *Administración virreinal en el Perú: gobierno del marqués de Montesclaros, 1607–1615.* Madrid: Centro de Estudios Ramón Areces, 1997.

Lavallé, Bernard. *Al filo de la navaja: luchas y derivas caciquiles en Latacunga, 1730–1790.* Quito: Corporación Editora Nacional, 2002.

Lavallé, Bernard. "Presión colonial y reivindicación indígena en Cajamarca (1785–1820) según el archivo del protector de naturales." In *Amor y opresión en los Andes coloniales,* 304–330. Lima: Instituto Francés de Estudios Andinos, Universidad Ricardo Palma, and Instituto de Estudios Peruanos, 1999.

León Fernández, Dino. "El protector de naturales en la provincia de los Collaguas. Siglo XVIII." *Uku Pacha* 3, no. 5 (2003): 91–107.

León Pinelo, Diego de. *Mandó que se imprimiesse este escrito el Excelentísimo señor Conde de Alva de Aliste, y de Villaflor, grande Castilla, virrey destos Reynos del Peru, en la Iunta, que se ha formado, por cédula de Su Magestad, de 21 de setiembre de 1660 años . . .* Lima: n.p., 1661.

León Portocarrero, Pedro de. *Descripción del virreinato del Perú; crónica inédita de comienzos del siglo XVII.* Rosario, AR: Universidad Nacional del Litoral, 1958.

Levaggi, Abelardo. "República de Indios y República de Españoles en los reinos de Indias." *Revista de Estudios Histórico-Jurídicos* 23 (2001): 419–428.

Levillier, Roberto. *Gobernantes del Perú, cartas y papeles, siglo XVI.* 14 vols. Madrid: Sucesores de Rivadeneyra, 1921–1926.

———. *Audiencia de Lima: correspondencia de presidentes y oidores.* Madrid: J. Pueyo, 1922.

———. *Don Francisco de Toledo, supremo organizador del Perú. Su vida, su obra, 1515–1582.* 2 vols. Madrid: Espasa-Calpe, 1935–1940.

Lira, Andrés. "El indio como litigante en cincuenta años de audiencia, 1531–1580." In *Memoria del X Congreso del Instituto Internacional de Historia del Derecho Indiano,* 765–782. Mexico: Universidad Autónoma de México, 2005.

Loayza, Francisco A. *Fray Calixto Túpak Inka, documentos originales y, en su mayoría, totalmente desconocidos, auténticos, de este apóstol indio, valiente defensor de su raza, desde el año de 1746 a 1760.* Lima: D. Miranda, 1948.

Lobo Cabrera, Manuel. "Esclavos indios en Canarias: precedentes." *Revista de Indias* 43, no. 172 (1983): 515–532.

Lockhart, James. *Spanish Peru, 1532–1560: A Colonial Society.* Madison: University of Wisconsin Press, 1968.

———. *The Men of Cajamarca: A Social and Biographical Study of the First Conquerors of Peru.* 2 vols. Austin: University of Texas Press, 1972.

———. "Letters and People to Spain." In *Of Things of the Indies: Essays Old and New in Early Latin American History,* 81–97. Stanford: Stanford University Press, 1999.

Lockhart, James, Frances Berdan, and Arthur Anderson. *The Tlaxcalan Actas: A Compendium of the Records of the Cabildo of Tlaxcala (1545–1627).* Salt Lake City: University of Utah Press, 1986.

Lockhart, James, and Enrique Otte. *Letters and People of the Spanish Indies, Sixteenth Century.* Cambridge; New York: Cambridge University Press, 1976.

Lohmann, Guillermo. *El conde de Lemos, virrey del Perú.* Madrid: Escuela de Estudios Hispano-Americanos, 1946.

―――. *Los americanos en las órdenes nobiliarias (1529–1900).* 2 vols. Madrid: Consejo Superior de Investigaciones Científicas; Instituto Gonzalo Fernández de Oviedo, 1947.

―――. "El señorío de los marqueses de Santiago de Oropesa en el Perú." *Anuario de Historia del Derecho Español* 19 (1948–1949): 347–458.

―――. "Las compañías de gentileshombres, lanzas y arcabuces de la guardia del virreinato del Perú." *Anuario de Estudios Americanos* 13 (1956): 141–215.

―――. *Juan de Matienzo, autor del "Gobierno del Perú."* Seville: Escuela de Estudios Hispano-Americanos, 1966.

―――. "La restitución por conquistadores y encomenderos: un aspecto de la incidencia lascasiana en el Perú." In *Estudios lascasianos,* 21–89. Seville: Escuela de Estudios Hispano-Americanos, 1966.

―――. "Nuevos datos sobre los linajes de los caciques de Lambayeque y Ferreñafe." *Revista del Museo Nacional* 36 (1969): 102–107.

―――. "El licenciado Francisco Falcón (1521–1587)." *Anuario de Estudios Americanos* 27 (1970): 131–194.

―――. "Introducción." In *Francisco de Toledo: disposiciones gubernativas para el Virreinato del Perú,* edited by María Justina Sarabia Viejo. 1: xiii–lxiii. Seville: Escuela de Estudios Hispano-Americanos; Consejo Superior de Investigaciones Científicas; Monte de Piedad y Caja de Ahorros de Sevilla, 1986–1989.

―――. *Inquisidores, virreyes y disidentes: el Santo Oficio y la sátira política.* Lima: Congreso del Perú, 1999.

―――. *El corregidor de indios en el Perú bajo los Austrias.* Lima: Pontificia Universidad Católica del Perú, 2001.

López-Ocón Cabrera, Leoncio. "Andinología, Lascasismo y humanismo cristiano. La defensa de las sociedades andinas del quechuista fray Domingo de Santo Tomás (1499–1570)." MA thesis, FLACSO―Sede Ecuador, 1987.

Lorandi, Ana María. *De quimeras, rebeliones y utopías: la gesta del inca Pedro Bohorques.* Lima: Pontificia Universidad Católica del Perú, 1997.

―――. *Spanish King of the Incas: The Epic Life of Pedro Bohorques.* Pittsburgh: University of Pittsburgh Press, 2005.

―――. "La monarquía española como espacio global entre los siglos XVI y XVII. La contradicción entre el concepto restringido de 'lo andino' y su inclusión en una dimensión planetaria." *Boletín del Instituto Riva-Agüero* 33 (2006): 13–23.

Lowry, Lyn. "Forging an Indian Nation: Urban Indians under Spanish Colonial Control (Lima, Peru, 1535–1765)." PhD dissertation, University of California, 1991.

Loza, Beatriz. "El *quipu* y la prueba en la práctica del Derecho de Indias, 1550–1581." *Historia y Cultura* 26 (2000): 11–37.

Loza, Carmen Beatriz. "El uso de los quipus contra la administración colonial (1550–1600)." *Nueva Síntesis* 7–8 (2001): 59–93.

Luque Talaván, Miguel. "'Tan príncipes e infantes como los de Castilla'. Análisis histórico-jurídico de la nobleza indiana de origen prehispánico." *Anales del Museo de América* 12 (2004): 9–34.

Macera, Pablo. *El Inca colonial.* Lima: Universidad Nacional Mayor de San Marcos, 2006.

Malagón-Barceló, Javier. "The Role of the Letrado in the Colonization of America." *The Americas* 18, no. 1 (1961): 1–17.

Mangan, Jane E. *Trading Roles: Gender, Ethnicity, and the Urban Economy in Colonial Potosí.* Durham: Duke University Press, 2005.

———. "Moving Mestizos in Sixteenth-Century Peru: Spanish Fathers, Indigenous Mothers, and the Children in Between." *William and Mary Quarterly* 70, no. 2 (2013): 273–294.

———. *Transatlantic Obligations: Creating the Bonds of Family in Conquest-Era Peru and Spain.* New York: Oxford University Press, 2016.

Mansilla, Judith. "Exteriorizando la religiosidad: los 'indios ricos' en su lucha por el manejo de la capilla de la Virgen de Copacabana." Paper presented at the VII Congreso Internacional de Etnohistoria, Lima, August 4–7 2008.

Maqueda Abreu, Consuelo. *La monarquía de España y sus visitantes: siglos XVI al XIX.* Madrid: Dykinson, 2007.

Maravall, José Antonio. "El concepto de monarquía en la Edad Media española." In *Estudios de historia del pensamiento español,* 1: 51–73. Madrid: Cultura Hispánica, 1983.

Martínez-Serna, J. Gabriel. "Procurators and the Making of the Jesuits' Atlantic Network." In *Soundings in Atlantic History: Latent Structures and Latent Currents, 1500–1830,* edited by Bernard Bailyn, 181–209. Cambridge; London: Harvard University Press, 2009.

Martínez, José Luis. *Pasajeros de indias: viajes trasatlanticos en el siglo XVI.* Mexico: Fondo de Cultura Económica, 1999.

Martínez Cereceda, José Luis. *Autoridades en los Andes: los atributos del señor.* Lima: Pontificia Universidad Católica del Perú, 1995.

Martínez, María Elena. *Genealogical Fictions: Limpieza de Sangre, Religion, and Gender in Colonial Mexico.* Stanford: Stanford University Press, 2008.

Martínez, María del Carmen. *Desde la otra orilla: cartas de Indias en el Archivo de la Real Chancillería de Valladolid (siglos XVI-XVIII).* León, ES: Universidad de León, 2007.

Martínez Millán, José. "La articulación de la Monarquía española a través de la Corte: Consejos territoriales y Cortes virreinales en los reinados de Felipe II y Felipe III." In *Las cortes virreinales de la Monarquía española: América e Italia,* edited by Francesca Cantù, 39–63. Rome: Viella, 2008.

Masters, Adrian. "The Lettered Marketplace: Writing the King in the 16th-Century Spanish Empire." Paper presented at the Southwest Seminar on Colonial Latin American History, Texas Christian University, Fort Worth, TX, October 13–15, 2016.

Mathis, Sophie. "Une Figure de la Première Globalisation de L'Amérique Espagnole: Vicente Mora Chimo ou l'itinéraire original d' un cacique hispanisé de la côte nord du Pérou à la Cour d'Espagne au début du XVIIIe siècle." PhD dissertation, Université de Poitiers, 2008.

———. "Vicente Mora Chimo, de 'indio principal' a 'procurador general de los indios del Perú': cambio de legitimidad del poder autóctono a principios del siglo XVIII." *Bulletin de l'Institut Français d'Études Andines* 37, no. 1 (2008): 199–215.

Matienzo, Juan de. *Gobierno del Perú con todas las cosas pertenecientes a él y a su historia.* Paris: Ministére des Affairs Etrangéres, 1967.

Matthew, Laura E. "Facing East from the South: Indigenous Americans in the Mostly Iberian Atlantic World." In *The Atlantic World*, edited by D'Maris Coffman, Adrian Leonard, and William O'Reilly, 79–99. London: Routledge, 2015.

Mayer, Enrique. *The Articulated Peasant: Household Economies in the Andes.* Boulder: Westview Press, 2002.

Mazín, Óscar. *Gestores de la real justicia: procuradores y agentes de las catedrales hispanas nuevas en la corte de Madrid.* Mexico: Colegio de México, 2007.

McDonough, Kelly. *The Learned Ones: Nahua Intellectuals in Postconquest Mexico.* Tucson: University of Arizona Press, 2014.

———. "'Love Lost': Class Struggle among Indigenous Nobles and Commoners of Seventeenth-Century Tlaxcala." *Mexican Studies/Estudios Mexicanos* 32, no. 1 (2016): 1–28.

McKinley, Michelle. "Fractional Freedoms: Slavery, Legal Activism, and Ecclesiastical Courts in Colonial Lima, 1593–1689." *Law and History Review* 28, no. 3 (2010): 749–790.

Medelius, Mónica. "El licenciado Cristóbal Ramírez de Cartagena: relator, fiscal y oidor de la Audiencia de Lima. Su Memorial de 1591." *Surandino Monográfico* 3, no. 2 (2013): 63–92.

Medelius, Mónica, and José Carlos de la Puente Luna. "Curacas, bienes y quipus en un documento toledano (Jauja, 1570)." *Histórica* 28, no. 2 (2004): 35–82.

Merluzzi, Manfredi. *Gobernando los Andes. Francisco de Toledo virrey del Perú (1569–1581).* Lima: Pontificia Universidad Católica del Perú, 2014.

Milanich, Jerald. *Laboring in the Fields of the Lord: Spanish Missions and Southeastern Indians.* Washington, DC: Smithsonian Institution Press, 1999.

Miller, Joseph. "Retention, Reinvention, and Remembering: Restoring Identities through Enslavement in Africa and under Slavery in Brazil." In *Enslaving Connections: Changing Cultures of Africa and Brazil during the Era of Slavery*, edited by José Curto and Paul Lovejoy, 81–121. Amherst, MA: Humanity Books, 2004.

Millones, Luis. "The Inka's Mask: Dramatisation of the Past in Indigenous Colonial Processions." In *Andean Art: Visual Expression and Its Relation to Andean Beliefs and Values*, edited by Penny Dransart, 11–32. Aldershot; Brookfield: Avebury, UK: 1995.

Milton, Cynthia. "Poverty and the Politics of Colonialism: 'Poor Spaniards,'" Their Petitions, and the Erosion of Privilege in Late Colonial Quito." *Hispanic American Historical Review* 85, no. 4 (2005): 595–626.

———. *The Many Meanings of Poverty: Colonialism, Social Compacts, and Assistance in Eighteenth-Century Ecuador.* Stanford: Stanford University Press, 2007.

Mintz, Sidney, and Richard Price. *The Birth of African-American Culture: An Anthropological Perspective.* Boston: Beacon Press, 1992.

Mira Caballos, Esteban. "Indios americanos en el reino de Castilla (1492–1550)." *Temas Americanistas*, no. 14 (1998).

———. "El envío de indios americanos a la Península Ibérica: aspectos legales (1492–1542)." *Studia Historica. Historia Moderna*, no. 20 (1999): 201–216.

———. "La educación de indios y mestizos antillanos en la primera mitad del siglo XVI." *Revista Complutense de Historia de América* 25 (1999): 51–66.

———. *Indios y mestizos americanos en la España del siglo XVI*. Madrid; Frankfurt: Iberoamericana-Vervuert, 2000.

———. "Indios nobles y caciques en la Corte real española, siglo XVI." *Temas Americanistas* 16 (2003): 1–6.

———. "Caciques guatiaos en los inicios de la colonización: el caso del indio Diego Colón." *Iberoamericana* 4, no. 16 (2004): 7–16.

———. "De esclavos a siervos: amerindios en España tras las Leyes Nuevas de 1542." *Revista de Historia de América*, no. 140 (2009): 95–109.

Miró Quesada Sosa, Aurelio. *El Inca Garcilaso*. Madrid: Instituto de Cultura Hispánica, 1948.

Monsalve, Martín. "Curacas pleitistas y curas abusivos: conflicto, prestigio y poder en los Andes coloniales, siglo XVII." In *Elites indígenas en los Andes: nobles, caciques y cabildantes bajo el yugo colonial*, edited by David Patrick Cahill and Blanca Tovías, 159–174. Quito: Abya-Yala, 2003.

Moreno, Agustín. *Fray Jodoco Rique y fray Pedro Gocial, apóstoles y maestros franciscanos de Quito (1535–1570)*. Quito: Abya Yala, 1998.

Mörner, Magnus. "La afortunada gestión de un misionero del Perú en Madrid en 1578." *Anuario de Estudios Americanos* 19 (1962): 247–275.

———. *Race Mixture in the History of Latin America*. Boston: Little, 1967.

Morrone, Ariel. "Legitimidad, genealogía y memoria en los andes meridionales: los Fernández Guarachi de Jesús de Machaca (pacajes, siglos XVI-XVII)." *Memoria Americana* 18, no. 2 (2010): 211–237.

Mugaburu, Josephe de, and Francisco de Mugaburu. *Chronicle of Colonial Lima: The Diary of Josephe and Francisco Mugaburu, 1640–1697*. Norman: University of Oklahoma Press, 1975.

Mumford, Jeremy. "Litigation as Ethnography in Sixteenth-Century Peru: Polo de Ondegardo and the Mitimaes." *Hispanic American Historical Review* 88, no. 1 (2008): 5–40.

———. "Aristocracy on the Auction Block: Race, Lords, and the Perpetuity Controversy of Sixteenth-Century Peru." In *Imperial Subjects: Race and Identity in Colonial Latin America*, edited by Andrew Fisher and Matthew O'Hara, 35–59. Durham: Duke University Press, 2009.

———. "Francisco de Toledo, admirador y émulo de la 'tiranía' inca." *Histórica* 35, no. 2 (2011): 45–67.

———. *Vertical Empire: The General Resettlement of Indians in the Colonial Andes*. Durham: Duke University Press, 2012.

———. "Las llamas de Tapacarí: un documento judicial de un alcalde de indios en la Audiencia de Charcas, 1580." *Histórica* 40, no. 2 (2016): 171–185.

Muro Orejón, Antonio. "La igualdad entre indios y españoles: la real cédula de 1697." In *Estudios sobre política indigenista en América*, 365–386. Valladolid, ES: Universidad de Valladolid, 1975.

Murra, John. "Las etno-categorías de un *khipu* estatal." In *Formaciones económicas y políticas del mundo andino*, 243–254. Lima: Instituto de Estudios Peruanos, 1975.

———. "El control vertical de un máximo de pisos ecológicos en la economía de las sociedades andinas." In *Formaciones económicas y políticas del mundo andino*, 59–115. Lima: Instituto de Estudios Peruanos, 1975.

———. "Derechos a las tierras en el Tawantinsuyu." *Revista de la Universidad Complutense* 28, no. 117 (1980): 273–287.

———. "Una visión indígena del mundo andino." In *Felipe Guaman Poma de Ayala. Nueva crónica y buen gobierno*, edited by Rolena Adorno, John V. Murra, and Jorge Urioste. il-lxiii. Madrid: Historia 16, 1987.

———. "'Nos Hazen Mucha Ventaja': The Early European Perception of Andean Achievement." In *Transatlantic Encounters: Europeans and Andeans in the Sixteenth Century*, edited by Kenneth Andrien and Rolena Adorno, 73–89. Berkeley, Los Angeles: University of California Press, 1991.

———. "Waman Puma, etnógrafo del mundo andino." In *Felipe Guaman Poma de Ayala. El primer nueva corónica y buen gobierno*, edited by Rolena Adorno, John V. Murra, and Jorge Urioste. xiii-xix. Mexico: Siglo Veintiuno, 1992.

———. "Litigation over the Rights of 'Natural Lords' in Early Colonial Courts in the Andes." In *Native Traditions in the Postconquest World*, edited by Elizabeth Hill Boone and Thomas Cummins, 55–62. Washington, DC: Dumbarton Oaks, 1998.

Nader, Helen. *Liberty in Absolutist Spain: The Habsburg Sale of Towns, 1516–1700*. Baltimore: Johns Hopkins University Press, 1990.

Navarro Gala, Rosario. *El libro de protocolo del primer notario indígena (Cuzco, siglo XVI)*. Madrid; Frankfurt: Iberoamericana-Vervuert, 2015.

Noack, Karoline. "Los caciques ante el notario. Transformaciones culturales en el siglo XVI." In *América bajo los Austrias: economía, cultura y sociedad*, edited by Héctor Noejovich, 191–204. Lima: Pontificia Universidad Católica del Perú, 2001.

———. "Caciques, escribanos y las construcciones de historias: Cajamarca, Perú, siglo XVI." In *Elites indígenas en los Andes: nobles, caciques y cabildantes bajo el yugo colonial*, edited by David Cahill and Blanca Tovías, 213–227. Quito: Abya-Yala, 2003.

Novoa, Mauricio. *The Protectors of Indians in the Royal Audience of Lima: History, Careers and Legal Culture, 1575–1775*. Leiden; Boston: Brill/Nijhoff, 2016.

Nowack, Kerstin. "Aquellas señoras del linaje real de los Incas: vida y supervivencia de las mujeres de la nobleza inca en el Perú en los primeros años de la Colonia." In *Elites indígenas en los Andes: nobles, caciques y cabildantes bajo el yugo colonial*, edited by David Patrick Cahill and Blanca Tovías, 17–53. Quito: Abya-Yala, 2003.

Nowack, Kerstin, and Catherine Julien. "La campaña de Toledo contra los señores naturales andinos: el destierro de los Incas de Vilcabamba y Cuzco." *Historia y Cultura*, no. 23 (1999): 15–81.

O'Phelan, Scarlett. *Kurakas sin sucesiones: del cacique al alcalde de indios (Perú y Bolivia 1750–1830)*. Cuzco: Centro Bartolomé de Las Casas, 1997.

O'Toole, Rachel. "Don Carlos Chimo del Perú: ¿del común o cacique?" *Secuencia* (2011): 11–41.

———. *Bound Lives: Africans, Indians, and the Making of Race in Colonial Peru*. Pittsburgh: University of Pittsburgh Press, 2012.

———. "Fitting In: Urban Indians, Migrants, and Muleteers in Colonial Peru." In *City Indians in Spain's American Empire: Urban Indigenous Society in Colonial Mesoamerica and Andean South America, 1530–1810*, edited by Dana Velasco Murillo, Mark Lentz, and Margarita Ochoa, 148–171. Brighton, UK: Sussex Academic Press, 2012.

Oberem, Udo. *Notas y documentos sobre miembros de la familia del Inca Atahualpa en el siglo XVI*. Guayaquil, EC: Casa de la Cultura Ecuatoriana, 1976.

———. "La familia del Inca Atahualpa bajo el dominio español." In *Contribución a la etnohistoria ecuatoriana*, edited by Segundo Moreno Yáñez and Udo Oberem, 153–226. Otavalo, EC: Instituto Otavaleño de Antropología, 1981.

———. *Don Sancho Hacho: un cacique mayor del siglo XVI*. Quito: CEDECO; Abya-Yala, 1993.

Olaechea Labayen, Juan Bautista. "Experiencias cristianas con el indio antillano." *Anuario de Estudios Americanos* 26 (1969): 18–113.

———. "Un recurso al Rey de la primera generación mestiza del Perú." *Anuario de Estudios Americanos* 35 (1975): 155–186.

Olds, Katrina B. *Forging the Past: Invented Histories in Counter-Reformation Spain*. New Haven: Yale University Press, 2015.

Olmedo Jiménez, Manuel. *Jerónimo de Loaysa, O.P., pacificador de Españoles y protector de Indios*. Granada, ES: Universidad de Granada, Salamanca, 1990.

Ondegardo, Polo de. "Informe del licenciado Juan [sic] Polo Ondegardo al licenciado Briviesca de Muñatones sobre la perpetuidad de las encomiendas en el Peru [1561]." In *Pensamiento colonial crítico. Textos y actos de Polo Ondegardo*, edited by Gonzalo Lamana, 139–204. Cuzco: Centro de Estudios Regionales Andinos Bartolomé de Las Casas; Instituto Francés de Estudios Andinos, 2012.

———. "Las razones que movieron a sacar esta relación y notable daño que resulta de no guardar a estos indios sus fueros [1571]." In *Pensamiento colonial critico. Textos y actos de Polo Ondegardo*, edited by Gonzalo Lamana, 217–330. Cuzco: Centro de Estudios Regionales Andinos Bartolomé de Las Casas; Instituto Francés de Estudios Andinos, 2012.

Osorio, Alejandra B. "*El callejón de la soledad*: Vectors of Cultural Hybridity in Seventeenth-Century Lima." In *Spiritual Encounters: Interactions between Christianity and Native Religions in Colonial America*, edited by Nicholas Griffiths and Fernando Cervantes, 198–229. Lincoln: University of Nebraska Press, 1999.

———. *Inventing Lima: Baroque Modernity in Peru's South Sea Metropolis*. New York: Palgrave Macmillan, 2008.

Otte, Enrique, and Guadalupe Albi Romero. *Cartas privadas de emigrantes a Indias, 1540–1616*. Mexico: Fondo de Cultura Económica, 1993.

Owens, J. B. *"By My Absolute Royal Authority": Justice and the Castilian Commonwealth at the Beginning of the First Global Age.* Rochester, NY: University of Rochester Press, 2005.

Owensby, Brian. *Empire of Law and Indian Justice in Colonial Mexico.* Stanford: Stanford University Press, 2008.

Pachacuti, Juan de Santa Cruz. "Relación de antigüedades deste reino del Perú." In *Antigüedades del Perú*, edited by Henrique Urbano and Ana Sánchez, 171–269. Madrid: Historia 16, 1992.

———. "An Account of the Antiquities of Peru." In *Narratives of the Rites and Laws of the Yncas*, edited by Clements R. Markham, 67–120. Farnham, UK: Ashgate Publishing, 2010.

Pagden, Anthony. *The Fall of Natural Man: The American Indian and the Origins of Comparative Ethnology.* Cambridge; New York: Cambridge University Press, 1982.

Pärssinen, Martti. *Tawantinsuyu: The Inca State and Its Political Organization.* Helsinki: Finnish Historical Society, 1992.

Pärssinen, Martti, and Jukka Kiviharju. *Textos andinos: corpus de textos khipu incaicos y coloniales.* 2 vols. Madrid: Instituto Iberoamericano de Finlandia y Universidad Complutense, 2004–2010.

Paso, Francisco del. *Epistolario de Nueva España, 1505–1818.* 16 vols. Mexico: Antigua Librería Robredo, de J. Porrúa e hijos, 1939–1942.

Pease, Franklin. "Mesianismo andino e identidad étnica: continuidades y problemas." *Cultura* 5, no. 13 (1982): 57–71.

———. "Conciencia e identidad andinas. Las rebeliones indígenas del siglo XVIII." *Cahiers des Amériques Latines*, no. 29–30 (1984): 41–60.

———. "Curacas coloniales: riqueza y actitudes." *Revista de Indias* 48, no. 182–183 (1988): 87–107.

———. "Un memorial de un curaca del siglo XVII." *Boletín del Instituto Riva-Agüero* 17 (1990): 197–205.

———. "¿Por qué los andinos son acusados de litigiosos?" In *Derechos culturales*, edited by Marco Borgui et al., 27–37. Lima: Pontificia Universidad Católica del Perú; Universidad de Friburgo, 1996.

———. *Curacas, reciprocidad y riqueza.* Lima: Pontificia Universidad Católica del Perú, 1999.

Penry, S. Elizabeth. "Transformations in Indigenous Authority and Identity in Resettlement Towns of Colonial Charcas (Alto Peru)." PhD dissertation, University of Miami, 1996.

———. "Letters of Insurrection: The Rebellion of the Communities." In *Colonial Lives: Documents on Latin American History, 1550–1850*, edited by Richard Boyer and Geoffrey Spurling, 201–215. New York; Oxford: Oxford University Press, 2000.

Pereña Vicente, Luciano. "La pretensión a la perpetuidad de las encomiendas en el Perú." In *Estudios sobre política indigenista española en América*, 427–469. Valladolid, ES: Universidad de Valladolid, 1976.

Pereyra Plascencia, Hugo. "Mita obrajera, idolatría y rebelión en San Juan de Churín (1663)." *Boletín del Instituto Riva-Agüero*, no. 13 (1984–1985): 209–244.

———. "Indios y mestizos en la Lima de los siglos XVI y XVII." *Cielo Abierto* 11, no. 32 (1985): 49–57.

———. "Chiquián y la región de Lampas entre los siglos XVI y XVII: una hipótesis sobre el origen de las campañas de extirpación de idolatrías en el Arzobispado de Lima." *Boletín del Instituto Riva-Agüero*, no. 16 (1989): 21–54.

Pérez-Mallaína, Pablo. *Spain's Men of the Sea: Daily Life on the Indies Fleets in the Sixteenth Century*. Baltimore: Johns Hopkins University Press, 1998.

Pérez Fernández-Turégano, Carlos. "La administración de justicia en la España de los Austrias a la luz de los relatos de los viajeros extranjeros." In *La monarquía de España y sus visitantes: siglos XVI al XIX*, edited by Consuelo Maqueda Abreu, 81–121. Madrid: Dykinson, 2007.

Pescador, Juan Javier. *The New World Inside a Basque Village: The Oiartzun Valley and Its Atlantic Emigrants, 1550–1800*. Reno: University of Nevada Press, 2003.

Phillips, Carla Rahn. *Six Galleons for the King of Spain: Imperial Defense in the Early Seventeenth Century*. Baltimore: Johns Hopkins University Press, 1986.

———. "The Iberian Atlantic." *Itinerario* 23, no. 2 (1999): 84–106.

Pike, Ruth. *Linajudos and Conversos in Seville: Greed and Prejudice in Sixteenth- and Seventeenth-Century Spain*. New York: Peter Lang, 2000.

Platt, Tristan. "Mirrors and Maize: The Concept of Yanantin among the Macha of Bolivia." In *Anthropological History of Andean Polities*, edited by John Murra, Nathan Wachtel, and Jacques Revel, 228–259. Cambridge; New York; Paris: Cambridge University Press, 1986.

———. "'Without Deceit or Lies': Variable Chinu Readings during a Sixteenth-Century Tribute-Restitution Trial." In *Narrative Threads: Accounting and Recounting in Andean Khipu*, edited by Jeffrey Quilter and Gary Urton, 225–265. Austin: University of Texas Press, 2002.

Poloni-Simard, Jacques. "Los indios ante la justicia. El pleito como parte de la consolidación de la sociedad colonial." In *Máscaras, tretas y rodeos del discurso colonial en los Andes*, edited by Bernard Lavallé, 177–188. Lima: Instituto Francés de Estudios Andinos; Pontificia Universidad Católica del Perú; Instituto Riva-Agüero, 2005.

———. *El mosaico indígena: movilidad, estratificación social y mestizaje en el corregimiento de Cuenca (Ecuador) del siglo XVI al XVIII*. Quito: Abya-Yala, 2006.

Ponce Leiva, Pilar. *Relaciones histórico-geográficas de la Audiencia de Quito, s. XVI-XIX. Tomo 1, s. XVI*. Madrid: Consejo Superior de Investigaciones Científicas, 1991.

Powers, Karen. "Resilient Lords and Indian Vagabonds: Wealth, Migration, and the Reproductive Transformation of Quito's Chiefdoms, 1500–1700." *Ethnohistory* 38 (1991): 225–249.

———. *Andean Journeys: Migration, Ethnogenesis, and the State in Colonial Quito*. Albuquerque: University of New Mexico Press, 1995.

———. "The Battle for Bodies and Souls in the Colonial North Andes: Intraecclesiastical Struggles and the Politics of Migration." *Hispanic American Historical Review* 75, no. 1 (1995): 31–56.

———. "A Battle of Wills: Inventing Chiefly Legitimacy in the Colonial North Andes."

In *Dead Giveaways: Indigenous Testaments of Colonial Mesoamerica and the Andes*, edited by Susan Kellogg and Matthew Restall, 183–213. Salt Lake City: University of Utah Press, 1998.

Premo, Bianca. *Children of the Father King: Youth, Authority, and Legal Minority in Colonial Lima*. Chapel Hill: University of North Carolina Press, 2005.

———. "Before the Law: Women's Petitions in the Eighteenth-Century Spanish Empire." *Comparative Studies in Society & History* 53, no. 2 (2011): 261–289.

———. "Familiar: Thinking Beyond Lineage and Across Race in Spanish Atlantic Family History." *William and Mary Quarterly* 70, no. 2 (2013): 295–316.

———. "Custom Today: Temporality, Customary Law, and Indigenous Enlightenment." *Hispanic American Historical Review* 94, no. 3 (2014): 355–379.

———. "Felipa's Braid: Women, Culture, and the Law in Eighteenth-Century Oaxaca." *Ethnohistory* 61, no. 3 (2014): 497–523.

———. "Legal Writing, Civil Litigation, and Agents in the Eighteenth-Century Spanish Imperial World." In *Oxford Research Encyclopedia of Latin American History*. latinameri canhistory.oxfordre.com/view/10.1093/acrefore/9780199366439.001.0001/acrefore-97 80199366439-e-247 (accessed March 11, 2017).

———. *The Enlightenment on Trial. Ordinary Litigantes and Colonialism in the Spanish Empire*. New York: Oxford University Press, 2017.

Presta, Ana María. "De testamentos, iniquidades de género, mentiras y privilegios: doña Isabel Sisa contra su marido, el cacique de Santiago de Curi (Charcas, 1601–1608)." In *El hombre y los Andes. Homenaje a Franklin Pease G.Y.*, edited by Rafael Varón and Javier Flores. 2: 817–829. Lima: Pontificia Universidad Católica del Perú, 2002.

———. "Undressing the *Coya* and Dressing the Indian Woman: Market Economy, Clothing, and Identities in the Colonial Andes, La Plata (Charcas), Late Sixteenth and Early Seventeenth Centuries." *Hispanic American Historical Review* 90, no. 1 (2010): 41–74.

———. "Doña Isabel Sisa: A Sixteenth-Century Indian Woman Resisting Gender Inequalities." In *The Human Tradition in Colonial Latin America*, edited by Kenneth Andrien, 33–50. Wilmington, DE: Scholarly Resources, 2002.

Puente Brunke, José de la. *Encomienda y encomenderos en el Perú: estudio social y político de una institución colonial*. Seville: Excma. Diputación Provincial de Sevilla, 1992.

———. "Sociedad y administración de justicia: los ministros de la Audiencia de Lima." In *XI Congreso del Instituto Internacional de Historia del Derecho Indiano*, 335–349. Buenos Aires: Instituto de Investigaciones de Historia del Derecho, 1997.

———. "'Los vasallos se desentrañan por su rey': notas sobre quejas de curacas en el Perú del siglo XVII." *Anuario de Estudios Americanos* 55, no. 2 (1998): 459–473.

———. "Los ministros de la Audiencia y la administración de justicia en Lima (1607–1615)." *Revista de Estudios Histórico-Jurídicos* 23 (2001): 429–439.

———. "Intereses en conflicto en el siglo XVII: los agentes de la administración pública frente a la realidad peruana." In *El hombre y los Andes. Homenaje a Franklin Pease G.Y.*, edited by Javier Flores and Rafael Varón. 2: 947–962. Lima: Pontificia Universidad Católica del Perú, 2002.

———. "Notas sobre la Audiencia de Lima y la 'protección de los naturales' (siglo XVII)."

In *Passeurs, mediadores culturales y agentes de la primera globalización en el Mundo Ibérico, siglos XVI-XIX*, edited by Scarlett O'Phelan and Carmen Salazar-Soler, 231–248. Lima: Pontificia Universidad Católica del Perú; Instituto Riva-Agüero; Instituto Francés de Estudios Andinos, 2005.

———. "Codicia y bien público: los ministros de la audiencia de Lima seiscentista." *Revista de Indias* 66, no. 236 (2006): 133–148.

Puente Luna, José Carlos de la. "What's in a Name? An Indian Trickster Travels the Spanish Colonial World." MA thesis, Texas Christian University, 2006.

———. *Los curacas hechiceros de Jauja. Batallas mágicas y legales en el Perú colonial.* Lima: Pontificia Universidad Católica del Perú, 2007.

———. "Cuando el 'punto de vista nativo' no es el punto de vista de los nativos: Felipe Guaman Poma y el problema de la apropiación de tierras en el Perú colonial." *Boletín del Instituto Francés de Estudios Andinos* 37, no. 1 (2008): 123–149.

———. "Felipe Guaman Poma de Ayala, administrador de bienes de comunidad." *Revista Andina* 47 (2008): 9–51.

———. "Into the Heart of the Empire: Indian Journeys to the Habsburg Royal Court." PhD dissertation, Texas Christian University, 2010.

———. "The Many Tongues of the King: Indigenous Language Interpreters and the Making of the Spanish Empire." *Colonial Latin American Review* 23, no. 2 (2014): 143–170.

———. "Choquecasa va a la audiencia: cronistas, litigantes y el debate sobre la autoría del Manuscrito quechua de Huarochirí." *Histórica* 39, no. 1 (2015): 139–158.

———. *"En lengua de indios y en lengua española*: cabildos de naturales y escritura alfabética en el Perú colonial." In *Visiones del pasado. Reflexiones para escribir la historia de los pueblos indígenas de América*, edited by Ana Luisa Izquierdo de la Cueva, 51–113. Mexico: Universidad Nacional Autónoma de México, 2016.

———. "Incas pecheros y caballeros hidalgos: la desintegración del orden incaico y la génesis de la nobleza incaica colonial en el Cuzco del siglo XVI." *Revista Andina* 54 (2016): 9–63.

Puente Luna, Jose Carlos de la, and Renzo Honores. "Guardianes de la real justicia: alcaldes de indios, costumbre y justicia local en Huarochirí colonial." *Histórica* 40, no. 2 (2016): 11–47.

Puente Luna, José Carlos de la, and Víctor Solier Ochoa. "La huella del intérprete: Felipe Guaman Poma de Ayala y la primera composición general de tierras en el virreinato del Perú." *Histórica* 30, no. 2 (2006): 7–29.

Quispe-Agnoli, Rocío. *Nobles de papel: identidades oscilantes y genealogías borrosas en los descendientes de la realeza inca.* Madrid; Frankfurt: Iberoamericana-Vervuert, 2016.

Ragas, José. "Indios en Palacio. Emisarios indígenas, Gobierno central y espacios de negociación en Perú (c. 1860–1940)." *Argumentos* 8, no. 2 (2014): 30–35.

Rama, Ángel. *The Lettered City.* Durham: Duke University Press, 1996.

Ramírez, Susan. "The 'Dueño de Indios': Thoughts on the Consequences of the Shifting Bases of Power of the 'Curaca de los Viejos Antiguos' under the Spanish in Sixteenth-Century Peru." *Hispanic American Historical Review* 67, no. 4 (1987): 575–610.

———. *The World Upside Down: Cross-Cultural Contact and Conflict in Sixteenth-Century Peru*. Stanford: Stanford University, 1996.

———. "Rich Man, Poor Man, Beggar Man, or Chief: Material Wealth as a Basis of Power in Sixteenth-Century Peru." In *Dead Giveaways: Indigenous Testaments of Colonial Mesoamerica and the Andes*, edited by Susan Kellogg and Matthew Restall, 215–248. Salt Lake City: University of Utah Press, 1998.

———. "Don Clemente Anto, procurador del común del pueblo de Lambayeque." In *El hombre y los Andes. Homenaje a Franklin Pease G.Y.*, edited by Javier Flores and Rafael Varón. 2: 831–840. Lima: Pontificia Universidad Católica del Perú, 2002.

———. "Don Melchior Caruarayco: A Kuraka of Cajamarca in Sixteenth-Century Peru." In *The Human Tradition in Colonial Latin America*, edited by Kenneth Andrien, 22–34. Wilmington, DE: Scholarly Resources, 2002.

———. "*Amores prohibidos*: The Consequences of the Clash of Juridical Norms in Sixteenth-Century Peru." *The Americas* 62, no. 1 (2005): 47–63.

———. "Land and Tenure in Early Colonial Peru: Individualizing the *Sapci*, 'That Which Is Common to All.'" *The Medieval Globe* 2, no. 2 (2016): 33–71.

Ramos, Gabriela. "Nuestra Señora de Copacabana, ¿devoción india o intermediación cultural?" In *Passeurs, mediadores culturales y agentes de la primera globalización en el Mundo Ibérico, siglos XVI-XIX*, edited by Scarlett O'Phelan and Carmen Salazar-Soler, 163–179. Lima: Pontificia Universidad Católica del Perú; Instituto Riva-Agüero; Instituto Francés de Estudios Andinos, 2005.

———. *Death and Conversion in the Andes: Lima and Cuzco, 1532–1670*. South Bend, IN: University of Notre Dame Press, 2010.

———. "Language and Society in Early Colonial Peru." In *History and Language in the Andes*, edited by Paul Heggarty and Adrian J. Pearce, 19–38. New York: Palgrave Macmillan, 2011.

———. "'*Mi Tierra*' Indigenous Migrants and Their Hometowns in the Colonial Andes." In *City Indians in Spain's American Empire: Urban Indigenous Society in Colonial Mesoamerica and Andean South America, 1530–1810*, edited by Dana Velasco Murillo, Mark Lentz, and Margarita Ochoa, 128–147. Brighton, UK: Sussex Academic Press, 2012.

———. "Indian Hospitals and Government in the Colonial Andes." *Medical History* 57, no. 2 (2013): 186–205.

———. "Indigenous Intellectuals in Andean Colonial Cities." In *Indigenous Intellectuals: Knowledge, Power, and Colonial Culture in Mexico and the Andes*, edited by Gabriela Ramos and Yanna Yannakakis, 21–38. Durham; London: Duke University Press, 2014.

———. "El rastro de la discriminación. Litigios y probanzas de caciques en el Perú colonial temprano." *Fronteras de la Historia* 21, no. 1 (2016): 66–90.

Ramos, Gabriela, and Yanna Yannakakis. *Indigenous Intellectuals: Knowledge, Power, and Colonial Culture in Mexico and the Andes*. Durham; London: Duke University Press, 2014.

Rappaport, Joanne. "'Asi lo paresçe por su aspeto': Physiognomy and the Construction of Difference in Colonial Bogotá." *Hispanic American Historical Review* 91, no. 4 (2011): 601–631.

———. *The Disappearing Mestizo: Configuring Difference in the Colonial New Kingdom of Granada*. Durham: Duke University Press, 2014.

Rappaport, Joanne, and Thomas Cummins. *Beyond the Lettered City: Indigenous Literacies in the Andes*. Durham: Duke University Press, 2012.

Rasnake, Roger Neil. *Domination and Cultural Resistance: Authority and Power among an Andean People*. Durham: Duke University Press, 1988.

"Real cédula a los virreyes, presidentes, audiencias, gobernadores y provinciales de las religiones de ambos reinos del Perú y Nueva España, que no permitan vengan a España religiosos indios por compañeros, ni en otra forma [1706]." In *Cedulario Americano del siglo XVIII. Colección de disposiciones legales indianas desde 1680 a 1800, contenidas en los cedularios del Archivo General de Indias*, edited by Antonio Muro Orejón. 2: 185. Seville: Escuela de Estudios Hispano-Americanos; Consejo Superior de Investigaciones Científicas, 1969.

Recopilación de leyes de los reinos de las Indias. Madrid: Julián de Paredes, 1680.

Reséndez, Andrés. *The Other Slavery: The Uncovered Story of Indian Enslavement in America*. Boston; New York: Houghton Mifflin Harcourt, 2016.

Richter, Daniel, and Troy Thompson. "Severed Connections: American Indigenous Peoples and the Atlantic World in an Era of Imperial Transformation." In *The Oxford Handbook of the Atlantic World, c. 1450–c. 1850*, edited by Nicholas Canny and Philip Morgan, 493–515. Oxford; New York: Oxford University Press, 2011.

Río Barredo, María José del. *Madrid, Urbs Regia. La capital ceremonial de la Monarquía Católica*. Madrid: Marcial Pons, 2000.

Riva-Agüero, José de la. *La historia en el Perú*. Madrid: Maestre, 1952.

Rivarola, José Luis. *Español andino: textos de bilingües en los siglos XVI y XVII*. Madrid; Frankfurt: Iberoamericana-Vervuert, 2000.

Robles Bocanegra, Javier Enrique. "La efigie del rey en el corregidor de indios: cultura política y poder real de una magistrado en el proceso de consolidación del Estado virreinal durante el régimen del gobernador Lope García de Castro, Perú 1564–1569." BA thesis, Universidad Nacional Mayor de San Marcos, 2015.

Roche, Daniel. *The Culture of Clothing: Dress and Fashion in the "Ancien Régime."* Cambridge; New York: Cambridge University Press, 1994.

Rodríguez Quispe, David. *Por un lugar en el cielo: Juan Martínez Rengifo y su legado a los jesuitas 1560–1592*. Lima: Universidad Nacional Mayor de San Marcos, 2005.

Rojas, José Luis de. "Boletos sencillos y pasajes redondos. Indígenas y mestizos americanos que visitaron España." *Revista de Indias* 69, no. 246 (2009): 186–206.

Romero, Carlos. "Festividades del tiempo heroico del Cuzco." *Inca* 1, no. 2 (1923): 447–454.

Roniger, Luis, and Tamar Herzog. *The Collective and the Public in Latin America: Cultural Identities and Political Order*. Brighton, UK: Sussex Academic Press, 2000.

Ross, Richard. "Legal Communications and Imperial Governance: British North America and Spanish America Compared." In *The Cambridge History of Law in America*, edited by Michael Grossberg and Christopher Tomlins. 1: 104–143. Cambridge; New York: Cambridge University Press, 2008.

Rostworowski, María. *Curacas y sucesiones: costa norte*. Lima: Minerva, 1961.

——. "Algunos comentarios hechos a las Ordenanzas del doctor Cuenca." *Historia y Cultura* 9 (1975): 119–154.

——. *Señoríos indígenas de Lima y Canta*. Lima: Instituto de Estudios Peruanos, 1978.

——. "Dos probanzas de Don Gonzalo: curaca de Lima (1555–1559)." *Revista Histórica* 33 (1981–1982): 105–173.

——. "La tasa ordenada por el licenciado Pedro de La Gasca (1549)." *Revista Histórica* 24 (1983–1984): 53–102.

——. *Conflicts over Coca Fields in XVIth-Century Peru*. Lima; Ann Arbor: Instituto de Estudios Peruanos; University of Michigan Press, 1988.

Rostworowski, María, and Pilar Remy. *Las visitas a Cajamarca, 1571–72/1578: documentos*. 2 vols. Lima: Instituto de Estudios Peruanos, 1992.

Rowe, John. "El movimiento nacional inca del siglo XVIII." *Revista Universitaria* 7 (1954): 17–47.

——. "The Incas under Spanish Colonial Institutions." *Hispanic American Historical Review* 37 (1957): 155–199.

——. "The Age-Grades of the Inca Census." In *Miscellanea Paul Rivet octogenario didacta*, edited by Pablo Martínez del Río and P. Bosch-Gimpera, 499–522. Mexico: Universidad Nacional Autónoma de México, 1958.

——. "Colonial Portraits of Inca Nobles." In *The Civilizations of Ancient America*, edited by Sol Tax, 258–268. New York: Cooper Square Publishers, 1967.

——. "El movimiento nacional inca del siglo XVIII." In *Los incas del Cuzco: siglos XVI, XVII, XVIII*, 345–371. Cuzco: Instituto Nacional de Cultura, 2003.

——. "Genealogía y rebelión en el siglo XVIII: algunos antecedentes de la sublevación de José Gabriel Thupa Amaro." In *Los incas del Cuzco: siglos XVI, XVII, XVIII*, 379–395. Cuzco: Instituto Nacional de Cultura, 2003.

Ruan, Felipe E. "Andean Activism and the Reformulation of Mestizo Agency and Identity in Early Colonial Peru." *Colonial Latin American Review* 21, no. 2 (2012): 209–237.

Ruigómez, Carmen. *Una política indigenista de los Habsburgo: el protector de indios del Perú*. Madrid: Ediciones de Cultura Hispánica, 1988.

Ruiz Medrano, Ethelia. "The Indigenous Population and Justice System in Central Mexico and Oaxaca." In *Oxford Bibliographies in Latin American Studies*, www.oxfordbibliog raphies.com/view/document/obo-9780199766581/obo-9780199766581-0106.xml (accessed January 24, 2017).

Ruiz Medrano, Ethelia, and Susan Kellogg. *Negotiation within Domination: New Spain's Indian Pueblos Confront the Spanish State*. Boulder: University Press of Colorado, 2010.

Saignes, Thierry. *Caciques, Tribute and Migration in the Southern Andes: Indian Society and the Seventeenth-Century Colonial Order*. London: University of London, 1985.

——. "De la borrachera al retrato: los caciques andinos entre dos legitimidades (Charcas)." *Revista Andina* 9 (1987): 139–170.

Sala i Vila, Nuria. "Gobierno colonial, iglesia y poder en Perú, 1784–1814." *Revista Andina* 21 (1993): 133–161.

Salazar, Antonio Bautista de. "Relación sobre el periodo de gobierno de los virreyes don Francisco de Toledo y don García Hurtado de Mendoza [1596]." In *Colección de docu-

mentos inéditos, relativos al descubrimiento, conquista y organización de las antiguas posesiones españolas de América y Oceanía, edited by Luis Torres de Mendoza. 8: 212–421. Madrid: Imprenta de Frías y Compañía, 1867.

Salinas y Córdoba, Buenaventura de. *Memorial de las historias del nuevo mundo Pirú.* Lima: Universidad Nacional Mayor de San Marcos, 1957.

Salomon, Frank. "Indian Women of Early Colonial Quito as Seen Through Their Testaments." *The Americas* 44, no. 3 (1988): 325–341.

———. "Collquiri's Dam: The Colonial Re-Voicing of an Appeal to the Archaic." In *Native Traditions in the Postconquest World*, edited by Elizabeth Hill Boone and Thomas Cummins, 265–293. Washington, DC: Dumbarton Oaks, 1998.

———. *The Cord Keepers: Khipus and Cultural Life in a Peruvian Village.* Durham: Duke University Press, 2004.

———. "*Collca y Sapçi*: una perspectiva sobre el almacenamiento inka desde la analogía etnográfica." *Boletín de Arqueología PUCP* 8 (2005): 43–57.

———. "Guaman Poma's *Sapçi* in Ethnographic Vision." In *Unlocking the Doors to the Worlds of Guaman Poma and His Nueva Corónica*, edited by Rolena Adorno and Ivan Boserup, 355–396. Copenhagen: Museum Tusculanum Press, 2015.

Salomon, Frank, Carrie Brezine, Reymundo Chapa, and Víctor Falcón Huayta. "*Khipu* from Colony to Republic: The Rapaz Patrimony." In *Their Way of Writing: Scripts, Signs, and Pictographies in Pre-Columbian America*, edited by Elizabeth Hill Boone and Gary Urton, 353–378. Washington, DC: Dumbarton Oaks Research Library and Collection, 2011.

Salomon, Frank et al. "Los khipus de Rapaz en casa: un complejo administrativo-ceremonial centroperuano." *Revista Andina* 43 (2006): 59–92.

Salomon, Frank, and Mercedes Niño-Murcia. *The Lettered Mountain: A Peruvian Village's Way with Writing.* Durham: Duke University Press, 2011.

Sánchez Albornoz, Nicolás. "El trabajo indígena en los Andes; teorías del siglo XVI." In *Historia económica y pensamiento social: estudios en homenaje a Diego Mateo del Peral*, edited by Nicolás et al. Sánchez Albornoz. Madrid: Alianza; Banco de España, 1983.

Sánchez Rubio, Rocío, and Isabel Testón Núñez. "'Fingiendo llamarse ... para no ser conocido.' Cambios nominales y emigración a Indias (siglos XVI-XVIII)." *Norba. Revista de Historia* 21 (2008): 213–239.

Sarabia Viejo, María Justina, ed. *Francisco de Toledo: disposiciones gubernativas para el Virreinato del Perú.* 2 vols. Seville: Escuela de Estudios Hispano-Americanos; Consejo Superior de Investigaciones Científicas; Monte de Piedad y Caja de Ahorros de Sevilla, 1986–1989.

Saravia, Iván. "La evolución de un cargo: la Protectoría de Indios en el virreinato peruano." *Revista de Ciencias Humanas y Sociales de la Universidad del Sur* 4, no. 1 (2011–2012): 27–56.

———. "Los miserables y el protector. Evolución de la protectoría de indios en el virreinato peruano, siglo XVI-XVIII." BA thesis, Universidad Nacional Mayor de San Marcos, 2012.

Sarreal, Julia. "Caciques as Placeholders in the Guaraní Missions of Eighteenth Century Paraguay." *Colonial Latin American Review* 23, no. 2 (2014): 224–251.

Schäfer, Ernst. *El Consejo Real y Supremo de las Indias: su historia, organización y labor administrativa hasta la terminación de la Casa de Austria*. Madrid: Imp. M. Carmona, Sevilla, 1935.

———. *El Consejo Real y Supremo de las Indias: su historia, organización y labor administrativa hasta la terminación de la Casa de Austria*. Seville: Escuela de Estudios Hispano-Americanos, 1947.

Schjellerup, Inge. *Incas y españoles en la conquista de los chachapoya*. Lima: Pontificia Universidad Católica del Perú; Instituto Francés de Estudios Andinos, 2005.

Schroeder, Susan. *Chimalpahin and the Kingdoms of Chalco*. Tucson: University of Arizona Press, 1991.

Seminario, Miguel. "Caciques de Lima, Carabayllo, Huacho, Lunahuaná y Huachipa." *Revista del Archivo General de la Nación* 19 (1999): 183–190.

Serulnikov, Sergio. *Subverting Colonial Authority: Challenges to Spanish Rule in Eighteenth-Century Southern Andes*. Durham: Duke University Press, 2003.

———. *Revolution in the Andes: The Age of Túpac Amaru*. Durham: Duke University Press, 2013.

Sherwood, Joan. *Poverty in Eighteenth-Century Spain: The Women and Children of the Inclusa*. Toronto; Buffalo: University of Toronto Press, 1988.

Sidbury, James, and Jorge Cañizares-Esguerra. "Mapping Ethnogenesis in the Early Modern Atlantic." *William and Mary Quarterly* 68, no. 2 (2011): 181–208.

———. "On the Genesis of Destruction, and Other Missing Subjects." *William and Mary Quarterly* 68, no. 2 (2011): 240–246.

Silverblatt, Irene. *Modern Inquisitions: Peru and the Colonial Origins of the Civilized World*. Durham: Duke University Press, 2004.

Smith, Gavin. *Livelihood and Resistance: Peasants and the Politics of Land in Peru*. Berkeley: University of California Press, 1991.

Smolenski, John, and Thomas J. Humphrey. *New World Orders: Violence, Sanction, and Authority in the Colonial Americas*. Philadelphia: University of Pennsylvania Press, 2005.

Solórzano Pereira, Juan de. *Politica indiana*. Madrid: D. Díaz de la Carrera, 1648.

Spalding, Karen. "Social Climbers: Changing Patterns of Mobility among the Indians of Colonial Peru." *Hispanic American Historical Review* 50, no. 4 (1970): 645–664.

———. *De indio a campesino: cambios en la estructura social del Perú colonial*. Lima: Instituto de Estudios Peruanos, 1974.

———. "Resistencia y adaptación: el gobierno colonial y las elites nativas." *Allpanchis* 17–18 (1981): 5–22.

———. *Huarochirí: An Andean Society under Inca and Spanish Rule*. Stanford: Stanford University Press, 1984.

———. "Notes on the Formation of the Andean Colonial State." In *State Theory and Andean Politics: New Approaches to the Study of Rule*, edited by Christopher Krupa and David Nugent, 213–233. Philadelphia: University of Pennsylvania Press, 2015.

Stern, Steve. "The Social Significance of Judicial Institutions in an Exploitative Society: Huamanga, Peru, 1570–1640." In *The Inca and Aztec States, 1400–1800: Anthropology and*

History, edited by George Collier, Renato Rosaldo, and John Wirth, 289–320. New York: Academic Press, 1983.

―――. *Peru's Indian Peoples and the Challenge of Spanish Conquest: Huamanga to 1640*. Madison: University of Wisconsin Press, 1993.

Studnicki-Gizbert, Daviken. *A Nation upon the Ocean Sea: Portugal's Atlantic Diaspora and the Crisis of the Spanish Empire, 1492–1640*. Oxford; New York: Oxford University Press, 2007.

Sweet, James. "Mistaken Identities? Olaudah Equiano, Domingo Álvares, and the Methodological Challenges of Studying the African Diaspora." *American Historical Review* 114 (2009): 279–306.

―――. *Domingos Álvares, African Healing, and the Intellectual History of the Atlantic World*. Chapel Hill: University of North Carolina Press, 2011.

―――. "The Quiet Violence of Ethnogenesis." *William and Mary Quarterly* 68, no. 2 (2011): 209–214.

Tanck de Estrada, Dorothy. *Pueblos de indios y educación en el México colonial, 1750–1821*. Mexico: El Colegio de México, 1999.

Tavárez, David. "Legally Indian: Inquisitorial Readings of Indigenous Identity in New Spain." In *Imperial Subjects: Race and Identity in Colonial Latin America*, edited by Andrew Fisher and Matthew O'Hara, 81–100. Durham: Duke University Press, 2009.

―――. "Reclaiming the Conquest: An Assessment of Chimalpahin's Modifications to *La conquista de México*." In *Chimalpahin's Conquest: A Nahua Historian's Rewriting of Francisco López de Gómara's* La conquista de México, edited by Susan Schroeder et al., 17–34. Stanford: Stanford University Press, 2010.

Taylor, Gérald, ed. *Ritos y tradiciones de Huarochirí*. Lima: Instituto Francés de Estudios Andinos; Banco Central de Reserva del Perú; Universidad Particular Ricardo Palma, 1999.

Taylor, William B. "Between Global Process and Local Knowledge: An Inquiry into Early Latin American Social History, 1500–1900." In *Reliving the Past: The Worlds of Social History*, edited by Olivier Zunz, 115–190. Chapel Hill: University of North Carolina Press, 1985.

Temple, Ella Dunbar. "Dos documentos inéditos peruanos." *Revista Histórica* 11 (1937): 324–334.

―――. "Los Bustamante Carlos Inca. La familia del autor del Lazarillo de ciegos caminantes." *Mercurio Peruano* 28, no. 243 (1947): 283–305.

―――. "Azarosa existencia de un mestizo de sangre imperial incaica." *Documenta* 1, no. 1 (1948): 112–156.

―――. "La descendencia de Huayna Capac: don Carlos Inca." *Revista Histórica* 17 (1948): 134–179.

―――. "Los testamentos inéditos de Paullu Inca, don Carlos y don Melchor Carlos Inca. Nuevos datos sobre esta estirpe incaica y apuntes para la biografía del sobrino del Inca Garcilaso de la Vega." *Documenta* 2, no. 1 (1949–50): 630–651.

Terraciano, Kevin. "Voices from the Other Side: Native Perspectives from New Spain, Peru, and North America." In *The Oxford Handbook of the Atlantic World, c. 1450–c. 1850*, edited by Nicholas Canny and Philip Morgan, 252–270. Oxford; New York: Oxford University Press, 2011.

Thomson, Sinclair. *We Alone Will Rule: Native Andean Politics in the Age of Insurgency.* Madison: University of Wisconsin Press, 2002.

Tibesar, Antonine. *Franciscan Beginnings in Colonial Peru.* Washington, DC: Academy of American Franciscan History, 1953.

Titu Cusi Yupangui, Diego de Castro. *History of How the Spaniards Arrived in Peru.* Translated by Catherine Julien. Dual-language ed. Indianapolis: Hackett, 2006.

Toledo, Francisco de. "Memorial que … dio al Rey Nuestro Señor del estado en que dejó las cosas del Perú después de haber sido virrey y capitán general por trece años, que comenzaron en 1569." In *Los virreyes españoles en América durante el gobierno de la Casa de Austria: Perú*, edited by Lewis Hanke and Celso Rodríguez. 1: 128–149. Madrid: Atlas, 1978.

Torre Villar, Ernesto de la. *Los pareceres de don Juan de Padilla y Diego de León Pinelo acerca de la enseñanza y buen tratamiento de los indios.* Mexico: Universidad Nacional Autónoma de México, 1979.

Torres Arancivia, Eduardo. *Corte de virreyes. El entorno del poder en el Perú del siglo XVII.* Lima: Pontificia Universidad Católica del Perú, 2006.

Townsend, Camilla. *Malintzin's Choices: An Indian Woman in the Conquest of Mexico.* Albuquerque: University of New Mexico Press, 2006.

Urton, Gary. "From Knots to Narratives: Reconstructing the Art of Historical Record-Keeping in the Andes from Spanish Transcriptions of Inka Khipus." *Ethnohistory* 45, no. 3 (1998): 409–438.

———. *Signs of the Inka Khipu: Binary Coding in the Andean Knotted-String Records.* Austin: University of Texas Press, 2003.

Van Deusen, Nancy. *Between the Sacred and the Worldly: The Institutional and Cultural Practice of Recogimiento in Colonial Lima.* Stanford: Stanford University Press, 2001.

———. "Diasporas, Bondage, and Intimacy in Lima, 1535–1555." *Colonial Latin American Review* 19, no. 2 (2010): 247–277.

———. "The Intimacies of Bondage: Female Indigenous Servants and Slaves and Their Spanish Masters, 1492–1555." *Journal of Women's History* 24, no. 1 (2012): 13–43.

———. "Seeing Indios in Sixteenth-Century Castile." *William and Mary Quarterly* 69, no. 2 (2012): 205–234.

———. "Coming to Castile with Cortés: Indigenous 'Servitude' in the Sixteenth Century." *Ethnohistory* 62, no. 2 (2015): 285–308.

———. *Global Indios: The Indigenous Struggle for Justice in Sixteenth-Century Spain.* Durham; London: Duke University Press, 2015.

Vargas, José María. *Fray Domingo de Santo Tomás, defensor y apóstol de los indios.* Quito: n.p., 1937.

Vargas Ugarte, Rubén. *Manuscritos peruanos del Archivo de Indias.* Lima: Impr. La Prensa, 1938.

———. *Historia del Perú. Virreinato (siglo XVII).* Buenos Aires: Imp. López, 1954.

————. *Vida del siervo de Dios Nicolás Ayllón o por otro nombre Nicolás de Dios, natural de Chiclayo*. Buenos Aires: Imp. López, 1960.

Varner, John Grier. *El Inca: The Life and Times of Garcilaso de la Vega*. Austin: University of Texas Press, 1968.

Varón, Rafael. *Francisco Pizarro and His Brothers: The Illusion of Power in Sixteenth-Century Peru*. Norman; London: University of Oklahoma Press, 1997.

Varón, Rafael, and Auke Pieter Jacobs. "Peruvian Wealth and Spanish Investments: The Pizarro Family during the Sixteenth Century." *Hispanic American Historical Review* 67, no. 4 (1987): 657–695.

Vásquez, Gladys. "El endeudamiento de Felipe II y el virreinato del Perú: de las cajas de comunidad a la Caja General de Censos de Indios de Lima (1556–1600)." In *El Perú en la época de Felipe II*, edited by Javier Campos, 111–128. Seville: Estudios Superiores de El Escorial, 2014.

Vassberg, David E. *Land and Society in Golden Age Castile*. Cambridge; New York: Cambridge University Press, 1984.

Vázquez de Espinosa, Antonio. *Description of the Indies*. Washington, DC: Smithsonian Institution Press, 1968.

————. *Compendio y descripción de las Indias Occidentales*. Madrid: Atlas, 1969.

Vega, Garcilaso Inca de la. *Royal Commentaries of the Incas and General History of Peru*. Austin: University of Texas Press, 1966.

Velasco, Luis de. "Carta a S.M. del virrey ... en razón del gobierno temporal de las provincias del Perú [Lima, April 10, 1597]." In *Gobernantes del Perú, cartas y papeles, siglo XVI*, edited by Roberto Levillier, 14: 26–35. Madrid: J. Pueyo, 1921–1926.

————. "Carta del virrey ... a S.M. con relación de lo sucedido en Chile después de la muerte del gobernador Martín García de Loyola [Lima, June 15, 1599]." In *Gobernantes del Perú, cartas y papeles, siglo XVI*, edited by Roberto Levillier, 14: 191–193. Madrid: J. Pueyo, 1921–1926.

Velasco Murillo, Dana, Mark Lentz, and Margarita Ochoa. *City Indians in Spain's American Empire: Urban Indigenous Society in Colonial Mesoamerica and Andean South America, 1530–1810*. Brighton, UK: Sussex Academic Press, 2012.

Vergara, Teresa. "Migración y trabajo femenino a principios del siglo XVII: el caso de las indias en Lima." *Histórica* 21, no. 135–157 (1997).

————. "'Tan dulce para España y tan amarga y esprimida para sus naturales': Lima y su entorno rural. S. XVI y XVII." *Diálogos* 1 (1999): 39–56.

————. "La población indígena." In *Lima en el siglo XVI*, edited by Laura Gutiérrez Arbulú, 175–224. Lima: Pontificia Unversidad Católica del Perú, 2005.

————. "Growing Up Indian: Migration, Labor, and Life in Lima (1570–1640)." In *Raising an Empire: Children in Early Modern Iberia and Colonial Latin America*, edited by Ondina E. González and Bianca Premo, 75–106. Albuquerque: University of New Mexico Press, 2007.

————. "Piedad e interés económico: la cofradía de San Crispín y Crispiniano de los zapateros indígenas de Lima (1634–1637)." In *Iglesia y sociedad en la Nueva España y el*

Perú, edited by Alicia Mayer and José de la Puente Brunke, 151–171. Lima: Pontificia Universidad Católica del Perú; Instituto Riva-Agüero, 2015.

Vicuña Guengerich, Sara. "Capac Women and the Politics of Marriage in Early Colonial Peru." *Colonial Latin American Review* 24, no. 2 (2015): 147–167.

Villa-Flores, Javier. "Archivos y falsarios: producción y circulación de documentos apócrifos en el México borbónico." *Jahrbuch für Geschichte Lateinamerikas* 46 (2009): 19–41.

Villanueva Urteaga, Horacio. "Los curacas de Cajamarca." In *Historia de Cajamarca*, edited by Fernando Silva Santisteban, Waldemar Espinoza Soriano, and Rogger Ravines, 337–342. Cajamarca, PE: Instituto Nacional de Cultura; Corporación de Desarrollo de Cajamarca, 1985.

Villella, Peter B. "'Pure and Noble Indians, Untainted by Inferior Idolatrous Races': Native Elites and the Discourse of Blood Purity in Late Colonial Mexico." *Hispanic American Historical Review* 91, no. 4 (2011): 633–663.

Vinson, Ben. *Bearing Arms for His Majesty: The Free-Colored Militia in Colonial Mexico.* Stanford: Stanford University Press, 2001.

Wade, Peter. *Race and Ethnicity in Latin America.* Chicago: Pluto Press, 1997.

Wheat, David. *Atlantic Africa and the Spanish Caribbean, 1570–1640.* Chapel Hill: University of North Carolina Press, 2016.

Wightman, Ann M. *Indigenous Migration and Social Change: The Forasteros of Cuzco, 1570–1720.* Durham: Duke University Press, 1990.

Wood, Stephanie. "Pedro Villafranca y Juana Gertrudis Navarrete: falsificador de títulos y su viuda, Nueva España, siglo XVIII." In *La lucha por la supervivencia en la América colonial*, edited by David Sweet and Gary Nash, 472–485. Mexico, 1987.

Yannakakis, Yanna. *The Art of Being In-between: Native Intermediaries, Indian Identity, and Local Rule in Colonial Oaxaca.* Durham: Duke University Press, 2008.

———. "Costumbre: A Language of Negotiation in Eighteenth-Century Oaxaca." In *Negotiation within Domination: New Spain's Indian Pueblos Confront the Spanish State*, edited by Ethelia Ruiz Medrano and Susan Kellogg, 137–171. Boulder: University Press of Colorado, 2010.

———. "Indigenous People and Legal Culture in Spanish America." *History Compass* 11, no. 11 (2013): 931–947.

———. "Beyond Jurisdictions: Native Agency in the Making of Colonial Legal Cultures." *Comparative Studies in Society and History* 57, no. 4 (2015): 1070–1082.

Yun Casalilla, Bartolomé. "Introducción. Entre el imperio colonial y la monarquía compuesta. Élites y territorios en la Monarquía Hispánica (ss. XVI y XVII)." In *Las redes del imperio: élites sociales en la articulación de la Monarquía Hispánica, 1492–1714*, edited by Bartolomé Yun Casalilla, 11–35. Madrid; Seville: Marcial Pons; Universidad Pablo de Olavide, 2009.

———, ed. *Las redes del imperio: élites sociales en la articulación de la Monarquía Hispánica, 1492–1714.* Madrid; Seville: Marcial Pons; Universidad Pablo de Olavide, 2009.

Zavala, Silvio. "La monarquía del mundo según Guaman Poma de Ayala." *Cuadernos Americanos* 37, no. 3 (1978): 119–125.

Zevallos Quiñones, Jorge. *Los cacicazgos de Lambayeque.* Trujillo, PE: Gráfica Cuatro, 1989.

———. *Los cacicazgos de Trujillo*. Trujillo, PE: Fundación Alfredo Pinillos Goycochea, 1992.

———. *Historia de Chiclayo (siglos XVI, XVII, XVIII y XIX)*. Lima: Minerva, 1995.

Zighelboim, Ari. "Un inca cuzqueño en la corte de Fernando VI: estrategias personales y colectivas de las elites indias y mestizas hacia 1750." *Histórica* 34, no. 2 (2010): 7–62.

Zimmerman, Arthur. *Francisco de Toledo: Fifth Viceroy of Peru, 1569–1581*. Caldwell, UK: Caxton Printers, 1938.

Zulawski, Ann. *They Eat from Their Labor: Work and Social Change in Colonial Bolivia*. Pittsburgh: University of Pittsburgh Press, 1995.

INDEX

Page numbers followed by f indicate illustrations.

City of Kings. *See* Lima

Ciudad Rodrigo, Antonio de, 130

class stratification: and blood purity discourse, 191; and *Nación Índica*, 200–201; and native ethnogenesis, 91–92; and patronage, 16; and *República de Indios*, 14; and transatlantic litigation, 196–197

clergy, 61, 83, 100, 102–103, 114, 269n66

clothing. *See* dress

coats of arms. *See* *escudos*

cobradores (indigenous tribute collectors), 26. *See also* native tax collectors

cofradías (sodalities), 248n126

Cohen, Paul, 6

Colegio de Caciques (School for Noble Indians). *See* Colegio del Príncipe

Colegio del Príncipe (Jesuit boarding school for noble Indians in Lima), 105, 116, 118, 174, 248n118. *See also* education

Colegio de Tlatelolco, 103

Collaguas, 97, 232n115

Collantes, Inés de, 132

Collatopa, Antonio, 265n29, 267n47

collcas (community welfare deposits), 34, 219n88. *See also* *sapci*

Colón, Diego, 128, 252n23

colonialism: and Andean cosmopolitans, 189; and Andean traditions, 19, 37; and indigenous self-government, 18; and legal networks, 14; and litigation, 56; and *Nación Índica*, 200–201

colonial processions, 1, 275n13

Columbus, Christopher, 127, 251n11

commercial networks, 94–95, 96

communal assets: as contingency funds, 35; and fiduciary responsibilities, 24–25; and Felipe Guacrapaucar's expenses, 33; and *hacienda privada*, 213n28; and legal fees, 75; and litigation, 27; sale of, 220n98; stewards of,

219n90; and Toledo's 1570 investigation, 28–29. *See also* *sapci*

communal labor: and *ayllus*, 26; and *sapci*, 34–35

communal lands, 18, 75, 155, 220n98

community treasuries. *See* *cajas de comunidad*

Condemayta, Agustín, 228n67

Congregación del Niño Jesús (religious confraternity), 248n119

Consejo de Indias (Council of the Indies): and Alonso Atahualpa, 141; and *cabildos*, 47; and Melchor Carlos Inca, 142–145, 152; and *cédula de honores* (1697), 162; and Carlos Chimo's petition, 137, 155–156; and consultations regarding visitors, 134–135; and cosmopolitan brokers, 179; cost of access to, 40; and defenders-general, 78; and elite status, 116–117, 175; and enslaved Indians, 252n18; and ethnic classification, 10–11; and exiled Inca nobles' petition (1573), 228n67; and expenses of indigenous visitors, 146–147; and financial aid to travelers, 258–259n89; and funding of return journeys, 138–139, 255n56; and Huanca legal activism, 25–26; and humble petitioners, 8; and indigenous officials, 122; and indigenous procurators, 120; indigenous recourse to, 67; and indigenous travelers, 17, 145; and labor drafts, 71; and legal networks, 58; and legal reforms, 62; and legal staff, 82; and license to carry weapons, 174; and military posts, 112; and native litigation, 61–62; and Pizarro clan, 20; and power of attorney, 80; and religious orders, 99; and rhetoric of wretchedness, 260n104; and secular defense of indigenous subjects (1551, 1563), 63; and self-representation, 172–173; and slavery investigations, 242n53;

Enríquez, Martín (viceroy 1581–1583), 68, 142
Enríquez de Montalvo, Gaspar, 219n90
escribanos (notaries), 180f; and early modern identities, 169–170, 179–180; of El Cercado, 119; and forged documents, 266–267n41; Pedro de Gante on, 62; and indigenous litigation, 58; as *indios ricos*, 92; and legal expenses, 40; and Lettered City, 12; as private legal providers, 78; and public legal assistance, 69; and rented housing, 44; and Spanish conquest, 266n34; and Spanish language, 102; and Zamudio papers, 164–167, 267n45
escudos (coats of arms): and Melchor Carlos Inca, 143; and *Consejo de Indias*, 67; and Felipe Guacrapaucar, 33, 214n43; and Paullu Tupac Inca, 21; petitions for, 7; and Tlaxcalan delegates, 82, 233–234n127; and transatlantic networks, 5; and Uchu Inca lineage, 21, 210n5. *See also* patents of nobility
Espinosa, Andrés de, 97, 238–239n23
Esquilache, Prince of (viceroy 1615–1621), 71, 104, 105, 230n100, 243n61
Esquina, Gaspar de la, 142, 256–257n65
Esquivel, María de, 142
Estenssoro, Juan Carlos, 14–15
estofa (quality, class), 152
ethnic identities, 110, 201–202, 206n27
ethnogenesis, 16, 90, 91–92, 198, 208–209n50, 237n6, 245n83. *See also* identities; Indianness

Falcón, Francisco, 215n49, 219n86
falconry, 89, 236n1
family: and bicultural networks, 223n10; and *cacique* status, 264n19; and fictive kinship, 239n25; and social hierarchy, 114–115; and transatlantic journeys, 94; and transatlantic networks, 95, 97, 235–236n153; and travel licenses, 96

Farrochumbis, 187
Ferdinand (king of Aragón), 127
Ferdinand VI, 136, 244n71
Fernández, Martín, 86–87, 255n51
Fernández Coronel, Ana María, 217n72
Fernández de Mesa, Alonso, 234n133
fictive kinship, 169, 239n25, 266n38
Figueroa, Diego de, 242–243n58
Figueroa Cajamarca, Diego de, 121, 207n35, 239n26, 249n139
First Evangelization of the Andes (1532–1583), 102
First General Land Inspection (1594–1596), 75, 80–81, 233n124. *See also* land titles
fiscales (Crown prosecuting attorneys), 63, 74–75, 134
Flores, Nicolás, 148, 236n160, 267n47
Flores Caxamalqui, Rodrigo, 234n131
forasteros (outsiders), 202, 228n64, 247–248n117
forced labor. See *mitas*
forgery, 163–167, 169, 267nn40–42
Franciscans, 100, 269n64
free black militia, 113, 116
frivolous lawsuits, 56, 60, 224n18
fueros (customary laws), 59, 68, 125, 163

Gama, Antonio de la, 21
Gante, Pedro de, 62
García de Castro, Lope (governor 1564–1569): and Pedro de Balboa, 221n115; and Cuenca's ordinances, 226–227n54; on indigenous notions of *rich* and *poor*, 215n49; and judicial reform, 57, 60–62, 64; and provincial governors' appointment, 63; as Titu Cusi's legal agent at court, 84–85; and Toledo's 1572 Inca trial, 140
García Maldonado, Diego, 97, 257n69
Gasca, Pedro de la, 51, 238n22
genealogy, 23, 164, 169
General Indian Court (Lima), 119

242n55; and humble petitioners, 8; and indigenous officials, 118; and *indios criollos*, 245n87; and king's image, 126; and legal activism, 48; and *mandones*, 187; and migrants to Lima, 107; and salaries of *corregidores* and *protectores*, 69; and *sapci*, 42; use of, 219n92

Trujillo (Peru): and Andean cosmopolitans, 193, 196; and Carlos Chimo, 157–158, 191, 263n11; and Gregorio González de Cuenca, 60; and first native municipal councils, 225n30; and indigenous travelers, 96; legal experiments in, 65; and migrants to Lima, 104, 112; and *Nación Índica*, 15; and public attorneys' corruption, 229n85; and Toledan reforms, 226–227n54; and transculturation, 245n82; and tributary dues, 242n55

Trujillo, Diego, 234n133

Tupac Amaru, Felipe, 267n46

Tupac Amaru, José Gabriel, 15, 176, 210n2. *See also* Great Andean Rebellion

Tupac Inca, Calixto de San José, 136, 197, 238n22

Tupac Inca Yupanqui (Inca emperor), 210n5, 215n52

Tupac Inca Yupanqui, Felipe, 21, 22f

Tupicocha, 31–32

Turmequé, 146–147, 236n156

Uchu Hualpa, Gonzalo, 22f

Uchu Inca lineage, 21

Ulpo, Francisco, 97

urban elite: and church service, 243n60; criticisms of, 108–109; and education, 105; and Indian aristocracy, 111; and military posts, 112; as segment of Andean travelers, 197; and status markers, 116. See also *indios criollos*; *indios ladinos*; Lima

urban settings: and Inca nobles, 209n53; and indigenous networks, 244–

245n80; and indigenous travelers, 96, 195; and native ethnogenesis, 92

Vaca de Castro, Cristóbal, 210n3

Valenzuela, Francisco de, 70

Valera, Blas, 216n59

Valladolid, 144, 145, 204n15

Van Deusen, Nancy, 251n5, 251n14, 253n27

vara de justicia (staff carried by magistrates), 61, 121

vecinos (permanent residents of a Spanish or Spanish American city or town): dress of, 153; and early modern identities, 151; and *indios*, 152; and power of attorney, 83; protections afforded, 11; social and legal condition of, 268n58; status of, 174, 207n35; and travel licenses, 96; as witnesses, 149; and Zamudio papers, 170

Vega Inca, Garcilaso de la, 87, 234n133, 238n22, 241n43

Velasco, Luis de (Jacán *cacique* named after viceroy). *See* Paquiquineo

Velasco, Luis de (viceroy 1596–1604), 119, 120–121, 238–239n23; and Melchor Carlos Inca, 141, 143–144, 152; and Ana María Lorenza de Loyola Coya, 258n78

Vélez, Juan: Christian education of, 101, 102; as Huancas' informal attorney, 218n77; on *indios criollos*, 108–109, 245n87. *See also* interpreters

venue-shopping, 75–76

Vespucci, Amerigo, 127

viceregal court: and collective representation of Indians, 191; and early modern identities, 172; and elite urban Indians, 200; indigenous travelers to, 19; and Lima political capital, 120–121; and New Laws of 1542, 22; and *pleitos particulares*, 28; as power center, 202; and *sapci*, 43

viceregal decrees, 133